The Cultural Definition
of Political Response

LANGUAGE, THOUGHT, AND CULTURE: *Advances in the Study of Cognition*

Under the Editorship of: E. A. HAMMEL

DEPARTMENT OF ANTHROPOLOGY
UNIVERSITY OF CALIFORNIA
BERKELEY

Michael Agar, Ripping and Running: A Formal Ethnography of Urban Heroin Addicts

Brent Berlin, Dennis E. Breedlove, and Peter H. Raven, Principles of Tzeltal Plant Classification: An Introduction to the Botanical Ethnography of a Mayan-Speaking People of Highland Chiapas

Mary Sanches and Ben Blount, Sociocultural Dimensions of Language Use

Daniel G. Bobrow and Allan Collins, Representation and Understanding: Studies in Cognitive Science

Domenico Parisi and Francesco Antinucci, Essentials of Grammar

Elizabeth Bates, Language and Context: The Acquisition of Pragmatics

Ben G. Blount and Mary Sanches, Sociocultural Dimensions of Language Change

Susan Ervin-Tripp and Claudia Mitchell-Kernan (Eds), Child Discourse

Lynn A. Friedman (Ed.), On the Other Hand: New Perspectives on American Sign Language

Eugene S. Hunn, Tzeltal Folk Zoology: The Classification of Discontinuities in Nature

Jim Schenkein (Ed.), Studies in the Organization of Conversational Interaction

David Parkin, The Cultural Definition of Political Response: Lineal Destiny Among the Luo

In preparation

Stephen A. Tyler, The Said and the Unsaid: Language, Thought, and Culture

Susan Gal, Language Shift: Social Determinants of Linguistic Change in Bilingual Austria

Ker addressing a Luo Union meeting in Kaloleni Hall, Nairobi, to discuss the Luo response to Mboya's assassination.

The Cultural Definition of Political Response

Lineal Destiny Among the Luo

DAVID PARKIN

School of Oriental and African Studies
University of London

1978

ACADEMIC PRESS
LONDON   NEW YORK   SAN FRANCISCO
A Subsidiary of Harcourt Brace Jovanovich, Publishers

Academic Press Inc. (London) Ltd.
24–28 Oval Road
London NW1

US edition published by
Academic Press Inc.
111 Fifth Avenue,
New York, New York 10003

Library of Congress Catalog Card Number: 77–93213
ISBN: 0–12–545650–6

Printed in Great Britain by
W. & G. Baird Ltd,
Antrim, Northern Ireland

To my father and the memory of my mother,
and to Zablon Onguto.

Preface

The fieldwork for this study was carried out in Nairobi, Kenya, with periodic trips to Nyanza province, from August 1968 through September 1969. The forces for cultural transformation depicted here, namely population growth, educational expansion, increasing wage dependency, and, paradoxically, urban unemployment, have clearly not abated, and this study will shortly enable us to look back at how far significant "changes" in Luo culture are in fact turning on new definitions of marriage, filiation rights, and relations between men and women, as was hypothesized would eventually be the case. From recent impression, the changes are still not extensive, a fact which may testify to the resilience of cultural systems and justify the intensive study of them in terms of the dialect not just between infrastructure and superstructure, critical though this is, but also of one within superstructure itself. This focus on the dynamics of cultural systems goes beyond any facile descriptions of cultural differences as being examples only of "false consciousness" and therefore hardly worth investigation. By ignoring or cursorily dismissing the meaning and potency for people themselves of their own belief systems, such views curiously exhibit a reactionary intellectual ethnocentrism. To add to what I have written elsewhere (1975, p. 10), ethnicity, like religion, may well be regarded at a particular point in time as a form of "false consciousness" or "mystification" which deflects migrants' and urban workers' attention from the fundamental cleavage arising from their displacement from a peasant to an industrial mode of production. But it can also be argued that ethnicity and religion, as powerful and autonomous systems of ideas, also play a part in shaping people's responses to such displacement. Either way, whether they simply divert attention or shape different responses, then there is all the more reason to recognize the power of and so focus analysis on the

cultural contrasts and oppositions which we conventionally charac-
terise as ethnic and religious.

The study was done while I was a research fellow in the Language
Survey Unit of the University of Nairobi, on secondment from the
School of Oriental and African Studies, University of London. That
Unit's task was to contribute towards and coordinate the work of the
Language Survey of Kenya and resulted in the volume "Language
in Kenya", edited by the late W. H. Whiteley and sponsored, like the
Unit itself, by the Institute for African Studies and the Ford Foundation. As a speaker of Swahili and, to a much lesser extent, Luo, and
with previous research experience in both languages, my job was to
analyse social anthropologically some significant contexts of language
use in Nairobi, the multilingual capital of Kenya, some results of
which have appeared in the above volume. None of those results are
repeated in this present book, which is intentionally more social anthropological than linguistic but which places critical importance on
the use among Luo speakers in Nairobi of certain key semantic constructs as revealing the dominant paradigm of their culture and its
emergent counterpart. In fact I have tried not to overload the book
with such concepts and I use them sparingly in the narrative of the
text itself, and never without explanation. A glossary is not therefore
necessary and all vernacular terms are included in the index.

After a total though interrupted period of some three years' fieldwork mainly or partly among the Luo (two years in Kampala, Uganda,
in 1962–4), I still could not easily follow other people's conversations
in Luo, though I might get the gist and, in this, pick out what later
seemed, on questioning friends, to be key verbal concepts. In partial
justification of a non-Luo with a limited competence in the vernacular analysing such phenomena, I might remark that, often, Luo themselves would express surprise at what they later agreed was a semantically central word or phrase in a conversation in which they had
just engaged. I have certainly had non-native speakers of English
similarly surprise me. Those from outside who hear and see the flow
of a culture, including its language, through a filter, may yet be able
to pick out its most salient features. That said, the distance was still
too great for my liking and I offer this account humbly as a small contribution to the modern ethnography of a people whose language and
culture will continue to fascinate the non-Luo as well as the growing
number of Luo scholars themselves.

Some of these Luo scholars whose work I have read are listed in the bibliography, together with many non-Luo who have studied Luo culture and language. In this preface I can also at least mention those scholars who have recently completed work which has come to my attention too late for inclusion in my analysis or bibliography: A. Ocholla-Oyaya, whose work on Luo philosophy has been published as "Traditional Ideology and Ethics among the Southern Luo" (1976, The Scandinavian Institute of African Studies, Uppsala); Achola Pala, who has studied Luo women, and Atieno Odhiambo and William Ochieng, whose historical research focuses on Nyanza.

I would here like to thank those many Luo among whom I worked who, though they do not write books about themselves, are no less interested in their culture. For the record which anthropologists seem to like to make, I am nominally regarded as a *jakabar*, i.e. a member of the Kabar Kogola maximal exogamous lineage (or "clan" as it is known in English), one of whose most eminent living representatives is the Honourable Onyango Midika, M.P., who I first knew at Makerere University College (as it was then), and who continued to offer friendship for which I am most grateful. I cannot express enough thanks to another *jakabar*, thereby repeating a sentiment expressed in the preface to an earlier volume on Kampala (1969), namely Zablon Hezron Onguto, to whom this book is dedicated as well as to my own parents. My wife and I have known Zablon Onguto and his family intimately since 1962 when he first introduced me to fellow-Luo in Kampala and in Ombeyi "village" near Ahero in East Kano. Out of his network, based first in Kampala and later in Nairobi, grew my own. Because it is a network comprising ties of kinship, affinity, and friendship, it includes many Luo from "clans" other than Kabar and from areas other than East Kano, and the data used in this book reflect that diversity.

Apart from formal surveys, my fieldwork involved going to soccer matches, accepting invitations to visit and dine at people's homes, both in town and country, attending association meetings when permitted, and simply talking, walking, and drinking. Unlike extensive rural fieldwork which, I learned from my work among the Giriama, invariably requires one to wield a hoe or pull a bull, I cannot pretend that my fieldwork in Nairobi was physically difficult nor rarely any other than one long round of conviviality punctuated by the occasional quarrel. Had I worked on the factory floor, in the office, or at the market stall, as did those with whom I shared my recreation, the situation would have been quite different. Nevertheless, fieldwork in a town does have its difficulties of at least a technical nature, principal among which is the problem of the "representativeness" of one's impressions, cases, life histories, or survey figures in such a large and diverse urban population. Here I must especially thank Joseph Onyango of Asembo, who I first paid to help me with my formal surveys but who was originally "recommended" to me through the network and so who soon covered the contract with comradeship to the extent of letting me share house No Y8 in Kaloleni estate, while my and my family's formal address continued to be at the other end of town. I also thank his sister Catherine, and her husband, Charles Omeno, together with the late Ohanga and his son Luke, Barack Oduor-Otieno, Hammon Otieno and his wife Julia, and the many others who gave of their time, frankness, and wisdom. Rufus Ndungu helped me understand the wide variations in Kikuyu custom which I encountered in Nairobi and I am much indebted to him. I hope all these regard this as a reasonably accurate account.

I am also heavily indebted to those who were able to read parts or the whole of a draft of this book and offered comments: Lionel Caplan, John Gumperz, Mark Hobart, Scott MacWilliam, Nici Nelson, and James (Woody) Watson. At different times, and in some cases years ago, I have benefited from conversations about the Kenya Luo with others who have worked among them such as David Goldenberger, Ralph Grillo, Christine Obbo, Betty Potash, Bill Sytek, and, especially, Aidan Southall, whose knowledge of Nilotic cultures generally is formidable. I was fortunate also in getting to know Tom Weisner in the field, whose detailed study of a Luyia rural–urban network provided a constant, stimulating source of comparison. I am grateful to Marc Swartz for first giving me the idea of studying Luo attitudes to family size, which led to other important findings, to Scarlett Epstein for inviting me to participate informally in her project on population growth and rural poverty, located at the Institute of Development Studies, University of Sussex, and to George Mkangi and Joseph Ssennyonga, members of that project working on Kenya, for sharing their interests.

Theoretically, I regard this study as a development out of the work of my departmental colleague, Abner Cohen. I have benefited over the years from his approach much more than I have repaid, and am happy to acknowledge the influence of his ideas. Indeed, it is appropriate here to pay tribute to the SOAS Department of Anthropology as a whole, headed by Adrian Mayer, for providing a happy mix of intellectual challenge and personal compatibility. Finally, I thank Eugene Hammel, the editor of the series in which this book appears, and my wife, Monica Parkin, for advice and help in its preparation. Full responsibility for any errors of fact or interpretation is mine.

July 1977   DAVID PARKIN

Contents

List of Maps and Plates

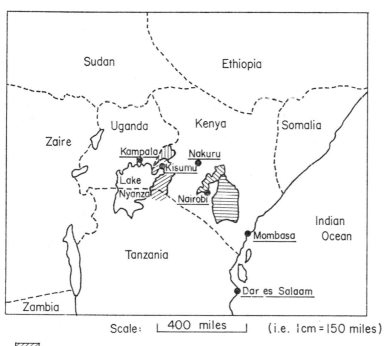

Scale: |⎿ 400 miles ⏋| (i.e. 1cm = 150 miles)

▨ Area occupied by Kenya Luo speakers

▧ Area occupied by Kikuyu speakers (including Embu, Meru and Mbere).

▤ Area occupied by Kamba speakers

▥ Area occupied by Luyia speakers

Nairobi = Principal urban areas in Luo migration and settlement

Map 1. East Africa.

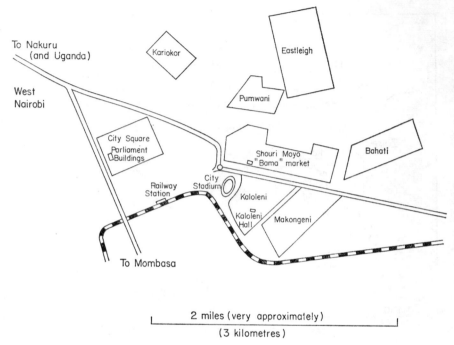

Map 2. Eastlands, Nairobi, showing Kaloleni and some nearby city council housing estates.

Introduction

The problem: cultural definitions of environmental change

In 1963 an American anthropologist was able to say with complete justification to a select body of British anthropologists gathered at Cambridge, England, that "the term 'culture' has by now acquired a certain aura of ill-repute in social anthropological circles because of the multiplicity of its referents and the studied vagueness with which it has all too often been invoked" (Geertz, 1966, p. 3). At that time many social anthropologists still held to a firm distinction between culture and social organization of the kind made by Fortes and Evans-Pritchard (1940, p. 3), deriving from Radcliffe-Brown, and approvingly cited by Gluckman as the basis of his own work and that of a generation of anthropologists (1958, p. 56). The same citation from Fortes and Evans-Pritchard tells of "social processes" being "stripped of their cultural idiom". The authors advocate comparative study so that "the structural similarities which disparity of culture conceals are then laid bare and structural dissimilarities are revealed behind a screen of cultural uniformity" (ibid.).

Poor culture. To be little more than an "idiom" or "screen" mischievously "concealing" more important essentials. In so far as culture includes ideology, religion, and ritual, we can hardly deny it this role of sometimes "masking", for example, the existing or changing social inequalities on which, in different ways, every society is based and which is implicit in the concept of social organization. But if the outside analyst can, usually with hindsight, see behind the mask, this is not easy for members of the society. To question what your culture "hides" is to question the very premises on which it is based and, as we well know, the radical logical switch required by such questioning disrupts the normal channels of communication on which the day-to-day living of most people depends. It is therefore not surprising that normally so many of the old channels are carried over into the creation of a new cultural mask, that it begins, often imperceptibly, to assume much of the shape of its predecessor. A distinction between rebellion or revolution is, then, a difference not of kind but in the degree to which old communication channels are retained in what is a culturally explicit "new" social order.

Culture, then, consists of the channels of communication used by people in regular interaction and the messages conveyed in them. The messages range from commands of a manifestly unquestionable nature, questionable exhortations, and new inspirations yet to be articulated as propositions. Culture is here no inert "screen" but a potent system of ideas which imply responses of word and/or deed. This is similar to that broader and more positive view of culture as the media of all intelligible communication between humans, as something which orders men in groups, resolves their most painful intellectual puzzles, and directs and even inspires them to follow rationalities different from each other. Of course, the above British scholars have subscribed to this view too, but this emphasis on the power, dynamism, and autonomy of culture has grown as the years have passed and as social anthropologists have become increasingly loathe to see their subject as simply a branch of "comparative sociology". While Levi-Strauss, influenced by the linguistically minded Boas and the linguist Jakobson in America and Saussure in France, has come to dominate much European thinking on the autonomy of the culture of *all* groups, i.e. of mankind as a whole, Boas and Kroeber have given rise through their successors to the present American interest in linguistic anthropology, much of which stresses the autonomy of the cultures of *particular* groups. Culture and language may indeed screen our perceptions of some kinds of reality but it is a screening process which is also the very essence of our reality. Culture here includes social organization. There is nothing from which to "strip it off", apart perhaps from an unsocialized human psyche. Generally, then, I agree with Harris's standard definition of society as a group whose boundaries vary according to the analyst's research interest, and of culture as "their behaviour stream" (1964, pp. 182–3), which I regard as their system of communications and responses.

The relevance of language in this shift away from the study of the cultural as separate from and opposed to the social, is two-fold. First, culture is studied as if it operates like language. This is the position adopted by Levi-Strauss and those strongly influenced by him (see Ardener, 1971; Leach, 1976a). Second, culture is studied as including an autonomous component, language itself, which can be studied much like religion or kinship as a system of autonomous ideas and practices. The two points of view are not in fact incompatible: the former requires one to see language use as one of a number of meta-levels of communication including the exchange of wives, goods, and services; the second viewpoint isolates the differential impact which the use of language has on people who interact with each other and they on it.

This book analyses the interrelationship between the conventiona-lized activities, cultural ideas, and key verbal concepts among a sec-tion of a large ethnic group, the Luo of Kenya in East Africa, and seeks the "grammar" or logic underlying them. But the analysis also follows the tradition of pre-structuralist socio-cultural anthropology in beginning with an empirical problem which includes the prag-matics of language use.

Ethnicity is a topic which has engaged considerable anthropological attention in recent years, to the extent indeed of having become fashionable. Two main points of view have been taken. One regards ethnicity as essentially a political phenomenon in which a group's culture provides an informal system of communication enabling its leaders to take decisions about the group's strategy in the face of poli-tical pressure or opportunity, or economic deprivation or advance (e.g. Cohen, 1969, 1974a; Parkin, 1969; Caplan, 1970; Dahya *et al.* in Cohen, 1974b). Another view is of ethnicity as essentially a classifi-catory system for defining the membership of groups which need not be politically opposed (Barth, 1969, p. 10; Vincent, 1971; Arens, 1973; Boswell *et al.* in Cohen, 1974b). In fact both views can be accommo-dated if we analyse their interrelationship over time. The main point is to recognize that any classificatory system, in trying to explain even new events occurring in the contexts in which it is used, retains considerable autonomy as a system of putative or stereotyped rela-tions between groups, often exaggerating grossly the real distribu-tion of resources and power between the two groups. At one point in time, the classification into distinct groups may indeed quite ac-curately reflect marked discontinuities in the flow of resources and privilege. At another point, the classification persists or becomes in-ternally transposed, but does not mirror the "reality" of power and privilege. Such classificatory systems are the emics of ethnicity, while the "actual" flow and distribution of resources as analysed by the "outsider" represent the etics (Pike, 1964; Harris, 1968, pp. 601–2). It would be surprising if a people were ever, at any time, able very accurately to discern and then classify precisely which groups dominated which and possessed what. We may assume that the classifica-cation and "reality" are always likely to be out of fit with each other, sometimes greatly but sometimes less so. This draws attention to the dual perspective in which ethnic political and power relations are held: we, the outside analysts, make our abstractions from the flow of political and economic events, while the people we study make their own abstractions. In so far as this latter constitutes a people's "world view" of their political and economic environment, it is part of *their* cultural construction of the "reality" which *we* perceive and construct.

These are simple points and need not be laboured. But few studies to date have concentrated on how an ethnic group's culture shapes its members' definition of their political and economic environment and their response to changes in this environment (cf. Lloyd, 1974). In this book I suggest that the rural segmentary patrilineage culture of the Luo moulds a particular kind of response in the polyethnic town of Nairobi. This response may be glossed as a concern for cultural self-perpetuation through an expanded notion and traditional lexicon of family and kinship relations. This concern for cultural self-perpetuation both encourages and is encouraged by Luo men's increasing dependency on urban wages: surplus incomes are still heavily invested in additional wives and thereby many children. This is not a case of culture tamely adapting to new economic conditions. Rather it is culture which plays a major part in shaping the political consequences of these new economic conditions.

Population growth and educational expansion

Many countries in the world follow two major policies in their attempts at economic development. They try to stem a high national population growth rate of about three per cent for poor countries, including the imbalance of an urban increase of six per cent and a rural one of two per cent. They are often also committed both ideologically and for practical reasons to expand educational opportunities. The expansion of education in the face of largely uncontrolled population expansion produces a conflict of forces resulting in many examples of socio-cultural change.

While some educated young job-seekers continue to move from country to town, many others were themselves born and reared in cities as a result of increased urban family settlement. Cohen's pioneering work (1969) showed that in Africa a process of "urbanization" need not, by itself, reduce an ethnic group's cultural distinctiveness. His study of a localized, face-to-face Hausa trading community in Ibadan, Nigeria, which is occupationally self-sufficient through its control over certain kinds of trade, depicts a situation which contrasts with the position of many other ethnic groups in Africa. These are the groups which, while retaining their cultural distinctiveness, are residentially dispersed within and between towns, are occupationally differentiated, and compete among themselves and with other ethnic groups for jobs, housing, and the education that is believed ultimately to provide access to these and other scarce resources.

An ethnic "melting pot" hypothesis would characterize these dispersed ethnic groups as eventually likely to merge with others and to lose their cultural distinctiveness and autonomy. This was the suggestion made by Cohen (1969, pp. 187–8, 1974, pp. 92–3) with regard to the Ibo in Ibadan who, though originally an immigrant localized grouping in the city like the Hausa, had become residentially scattered and occupationally and educationally differentiated, while their children had become bilingual in Ibo and Yoruba, the vernacular of the Host group. Later, the civil war of Nigeria apparently re-emphasized Ibo ethnicity and so halted the process of "detribalization" which might otherwise have occurred.

This example raises the question of the durability of ethnicity as an internally changing and yet externally constant cultural system denoting group boundaries. A civil war is a momentous crisis of the kind, hopefully, rarely repeated. But there are the less momentous crises which punctuate the course of everyday and world events and which, in some respects, almost constitute the norm. The conflicting forces set up by an as yet uncontrolled population growth and the commitment to educational expansion are part of this "normal" flow of crises. Population growth may one day be stabilized; educational facilities may one day match the needs and aspirations of this stabilized population; and urban and rural employment opportunities may one day equal those seeking them. But these are clearly very long-term aims, if not Utopian. Indeed, it can be argued that parts of the industrialized world, in their unintended gropings towards a possible and partial de-industrialization, are moving closer in essence if not in severity to some of the problems experienced in "third world" countries.

Under these conditions, a socio-economically and residentially or geographically dispersed ethnic group like the Ibo in Ibadan before the Nigerian civil war, and the many other similarly dispersed ethnic groups in Africa, are unlikely for a long time, if at all, to lose their cultural distinctiveness in the competition for unevenly flowing and frequently scarce resources. This kind of dispersed ethnic group, as well as being probably more typical of African towns than localized, educationally undifferentiated, and occupationally specialized ones, presents a special test case of the capacity of a culture to retain its autonomy and distinctiveness in the face of continuing lines of internal socio-economic and geographical differentiation.

The most obvious general problem confronting the cultural self-perpetuation of these dispersed groups is posed by the conflict of their expanding populations keeping in cultural contact with each other as against the attempts by individual members to make use of scarce educational facilities as the key to personal and family occupational and economic success. This is to emphasize, then, the threats *within* the socio-cultural group posed by emerging lines of socio-economic stratification as well as the threats perceived to exist between groups.

There is considerable discussion of the conceptual applicability and extent of "class" formation in Africa. Whatever the long-term developments, there is much agreement that the differences of already existing language, custom, life-style, and region, each coinciding with one another, and conventionally called ethnic, constitute more immediately communicable idioms of competition and conflict than those of "class" or socio-economic status. The latter are no more than emergent. That is to say, though fundamental national and international political and economic forces are currently transforming new peasantries into large urban proletariats and small urban-rural ruling elites, the visible signs of such "class" differentiation are at present inconstant, changing, and subservient in affective appeal to those of ethnic group. It is the ethnic framework of competition and struggle which most people use to assess political and economic opportunities and as their ideological rallying-points.

We call this "subjective" primacy of ethnic group membership a kind of "false consciousness" or an example of the mystification of emerging social inequality by class. But, except in a programmatic sense, the details of any subsequent process of "demystification" are a matter for history to decide. The most we can do is either speculate on the range of possible forms this will take, drawing comparatively on supposed "progressions" in the paradigm, or concentrate within the limited time-span that our fieldwork and recent documentation allow us on the current socio-cultural effects of forces in conflict and contradiction with each other (A. Turton, 1976, p. 268).

The social anthropologist, with his knowledge of a vernacular, his intensive observation of the cultural and social details of face-to-face, small group behaviour is surely best fitted to this latter task. It is not that the social anthropologist is thereby best suited to the study of an ethnic group *per se*. It is rather that he excels in the "objective" study of the way in which groups organize themselves externally and internally by "subjective" reference to their languages and cultures. These may be socio-cultural groupings of any kind, including emergent or established ruling elites, petty bourgeoisie, and proletariats, and need not be ethnic ones, but, in urban Africa, these latter currently provide the most consistent emic frameworks.

The perpetuation of cultural definitions: Luo segmentary lineages

The most general interest in social anthropology, then, is the way in which groups perpetuate themselves culturally under different external conditions. One such group, I have suggested, which is widely found in African towns, is the residentially and socio-economically dispersed ethnic group.

The Luo of Nairobi, Kenya, are one such group. In addition, the Luo fall into that wide category of societies which have traditionally been labelled segmentary lineage-based. Evidence is mounting both within Africa and from outside that the segmentary lineage structure of some societies may not only "survive" dispersed incorporation in urban wage economies but may actually thrive in modified form. Southall (1975) has surveyed this tenacious adaptability in urban Africa by comparing the Luo and Luyia of Kenya, and the Tiv and Ibo of Nigeria, hypothesizing that it is the rural *localization* of poly-segmentary lineages that is the main factor facilitating their modified but recognizable cultural continuity under urban conditions. We may here suggest that "random" urban population dispersal beyond a people's control is thus checked by their culturally ordered rural localization. Watson analyses in detail how a large rural localized Chinese lineage in Hong Kong is not only "ideally suited to the needs of large-scale *chain* migration" (1975, p. 101), but also mobilizes a commercial network of its members within and between the cities of Britain as restaurant owners and workers. The internal segments are *possibly* becoming less significant (p. 209) but the localized lineage comprising them remains strong. Moreover, he points out that many overseas Chinese commercial networks of this kind are similarly arti-culated through persisting lineage structures. The transformation of huge, exogamous, localized lineages effectively into commercial net-works of the kind discussed by Watson for the Chinese may represent a stage which the remarkably persisting polysegmentary lineage sys-tems of Africa may or may not reach. Hart's study of modern Tallensi patrilineages (1972) and Okali's of Akan (including Ashanti) matri-lineages (forthcoming) show something of this resilience and further development into commercial networks.

Luo lineages have not achieved significance as commercial net-works or corporations and may never do so. But their persistence with-in a polysegmentary structure in Nairobi is impressive compared with other ethnic groups in the city, and is not without economic and poli-tical significance. For these Luo it is by no means a foregone con-clusion that "as a result of migration even those migrants who come from tribal societies which have traditions of extensive kinship organization [here specifically referring to the polysegmentary patri-lineage system of urban Luo] tend to become bilateral as they settle in town" (Cohen 1969, p. 209, my bracketed inclusion). Through poly-gyny, as described in this book, and through the circulatory move-ment of family members between town and country, Luo urban family settlement occurs in conjunction with and not to the exclusion of strong rural lineage involvement. Polygyny here presupposes the

Luo segmentary structure in both town and country. This is because the Luo speak and think of a man's family of co-wives and respective sons as the prototype of future lineage expansion and segmentation. The persistence of Luo polygyny and therefore of the segmentary lineage system, depend on a relatively unambiguous distinction between women as producers of children for men and their lineages, and men as producers of urban labour. A shift to "bilateral" kinship organization necessarily involves changes in such descent rules and so depends on changes in status relations and filiation rights between women and men rather than on urban settlement *per se*.

Cohen's equation, cited above, of a segmentary lineage system with "extensive kinship organization" is unfortunate, for it misses the critical point that segmentary patrilineage systems (or matrilineage ones for that matter) have abundant potential for defining quite unambiguously a person's descent group membership, whereas kinship, as the web of "optative" consanguineal relations transcending lines of descent, clearly does not. Its very optativity weakens its potential for specificity.

It may be difficult, as many scholars have argued, to construct an empirically based typology neatly distinguishing unilineal from cognatic descent group systems, for there is in fact much overlap. But this should not deter us from recognizing the usefulness of applying a logical contrast between that kind of folk system of classification which itself stresses unambiguity of membership, as in a "nesting" segmentary lineage system, and that which stresses or concedes fluidity of membership. The relative unambiguity of unilineal descent group membership, taken together with further unambiguous identification at different levels of lineage segmentation, can constitute a remarkably specific system of classifying persons. When we find this same classificatory system operating in a polyethnic town like Nairobi among a dispersed and socio-economically differentiated people like the Luo, directing their marriage choices and continuing to circumscribe locally the rural ends of their urban relationships, then we must recognize its considerable autonomy as a system of ideas in consistent relationship to each other.

It is important here to recognize that the unambiguous classificatory nature of a segmentary lineage system precedes any later development of lineages into commercial networks or corporations. That is to say, the classificatory system precedes and accommodates new economic and political forces, however much it may in turn later be modified by them. To that degree, the classificatory system or "ideological" components are not only autonomous of but actually play a major role in shaping a people's response to a changing economic and political environment, which may include such recent developments as rapidly increasing population growth, urban wage dependency, and the quest for education.

Southall (1952, pp. 6–8) stresses that Luo see the compound polygynous family of a man, his co-wives, and their sons, as the prototype of future lineage formation and segmentation. This emic forward-looking conceptualization is reinforced by the use of female eponyms to denote existing lineage segments originally founded by the sons of the different co-wives of a man, whose own name remains the eponym of the large lineage of which he is founder. We see from this that the conceptual and verbal autonomy which characterizes the system of segmentary lineage classification among Luo in Nairobi extends to the polygynous family, which is also represented in the city.

This study shows that urban family settlement and increasing wage dependency among Luo have modified the meaning and functions of polygyny among the Luo but have not eliminated it as a viable institution nor reduced its metaphorical significance in political discourse among Luo: to talk politics with fellow-Luo in the new nation of Kenya is still to talk in terms of the expanding polygynous family and lineage, and of kinship and affinity. Indeed, whereas the practice of polygyny has adapted to new economic and political conditions, it is the key words used to describe polygyny and the linked relationships of lineage and kinship which have remained almost unaltered through these changes.

The Luo emphasize that polygyny and large families continue to be politically and economically important under urban conditions. But this emphasis, verbally expressed in traditional terms, conflicts with an increasingly held view that monogamy and few children facilitate a heavier financial investment in their education than is possible with a larger number. The "customary" view of population expansion as the means of cultural self-perpetuation and political and economic survival is expressed in speeches at public meetings of

Luo, and in the formal speeches characterizing family and lineage events and crises. The Luo, like most peoples, place great cultural value on the appropriate qualities of speech-making (Parkin, 1971; cf. also Robertson, 1971, pp. 158–61; Bloch, 1971, pp. 49–52; Bailey, 1973, pp. 172–3; and contributions to Bloch, 1975a, for some recent studies).

The contrary view, that personal and family success depends on monogamy, few children and their full education, is confined to the private and informal speech of friends and confidants. There is here a dilemma. For the movement from polygyny to monogamy is seen to involve radical changes in the status of Luo women, a subject alluded to but rarely discussed openly by either sex. The conditions for open debate of this dilemma among Luo do exist, but the formalized use of key terms contains it. This, in a nutshell, is what this book is about.

It raises three main theoretical questions. First, is it legitimate to speak of intrinsic variations in cultural autonomy? Second, what is meant by the notion of "continuity of custom" expressed in many studies of political and economic change? And third, how significant are a people's cultural ideas and taxonomies for defining and influencing their political response?

Cultural autonomy

Levi-Strauss's comprehensive view of culture as being the totality of man's created expressions of his psychic unity includes what we conventionally distinguish as religion, kinship, marriage, economics, and politics. It leaves nothing except that part of nature which has yet to be intellectually classified. There is so little left, indeed, that we may wonder what something so totally cosmic can be autonomous of. Perhaps culture becomes autonomous of mind, for once constituted the elements of culture can constantly transpose their order in relation to each other, as, for instance, in the transformation of a hierarchical caste system into a segmentary totemic one (Levi-Strauss, 1963). Perhaps also culture becomes autonomous of nature which, once classified as culture, can either become cyclically re-ordered as mythological bricolage or can be used to structure the "new" events and inventions of the scientist which have no immediate dependence

B

on nature and may often be turned against it (Levi-Strauss, 1966, pp. 19–22).

Numerous anthropologists have rejected the comprehensiveness of this view but have embraced the idea that culture, as a system of ideas and conventionalized ("ritual") practices, is kept together by an underlying logic. For Mary Douglas (1970) and sometimes for Leach (1961a) this is the view of an autonomous culture or symbolic system which tends to become consonant with the everyday realities, demands, and divisions of social organization, not because it is dependent on "society", but rather because the common messages denoting a group's boundaries ("society") and its members' behaviour ("culture") are best communicated through the redundancy of congruence. The influence of Durkheim, mediated by Levi-Strauss, is undeniable and, if this influence were stronger, the viewpoint would surely not be so very different from that of Abner Cohen. Distinguishing symbolism and power relations as autonomous variables in dialectic relationship with each other, Cohen says that they are "not reducible one to the other . . . symbols are not mechanical reflections, or representations of political realities. They have an existence of their own, in their own right, and can effect power relations in a variety of ways. Similarly, power relations have a reality of their own and can in no way be said to be determined by symbolic categories." (1969b, p. 222, and see 1974a, p. 36.) Cohen is clearly much closer to the Durkheimian position as he himself states. Indeed, it can be argued that he does not give the two variables equal autonomy. He portrays a new distribution of power between groups as, after some time, more likely to change their respective symbolic configurations than vice versa (1974a, pp. 6, 14, 91–118).

A problem here is the definition of "culture". "Customs" and "symbols" are treated as synonymous (1974a, p. 93), but so also are "customs" and "culture" (p. 94). So, while symbolism is described as an "autonomous" (sic, p. 64) variable throughout the study, we also encounter statements like ". . . culture is not an independent system, but is a collection of diverse types of norms, values, beliefs, practices and symbols which, though affecting one another, are largely systematized, or structured in social situations" (i.e. by power relations?). The impression given is that constituent features of culture have a loose almost arbitrary relationship to each other, and that their interrelationship is secondary in importance to the individual social situations structuring isolable cultural items. In the end, neither "culture", "customs", nor "symbolism" are really distinguished from each other, often being used interchangeably or with different meanings.

Definitions of phenomena are certainly boring, but I think that we need to ask what is meant by the autonomy of culture, or customs, or symbolism, and then to ask to what extent it (they) can be said to be in dialectical relations with an autonomous variable of power relations.

Hanson has introduced the concept of "implicational meaning" to explain the view that culture is a logical system "with internal contradictions and tensions as well as reinforcements" (1975, p. 10). His view of culture is broad and, like Cohen's, actually includes social institutions as well as norms, customs, beliefs and, we may suppose, symbols. The concept of "implicational meaning" helps us understand the rationality of alien beliefs in other cultures by seeing how they, and the customs and institutions to which they refer, presuppose each other in a logical system. Logical presuppositions are not intended by actors or "speakers"; they are part of the actor's culture or the "speaker's grammar". Not surprisingly, Hanson notes that "the concepts of unintended consequences and implicational meaning emerge as remarkably similar" (p. 72).

This view (a) that institutions and customs can be regarded as logically connected to form a whole culture, and (b) that the implicational meaning of an institution or custom is really its unintended consequence, keeps us well in the mainstream of "holistic" (i.e. group) anthropology. Cohen, a holist, rejects the emphasis in much "thought-structuralist" anthropology on studying the underlying logic behind customary practices and beliefs. He believes that it diverts attention from the political realities facing a cultural group. And it is certainly true that those scholars who have been influenced by Levi-Strauss and French structuralism do not isolate political factors as an autonomous variable. Rather, they prefer to see politics as being as much a manifestation of intellectual problems originating in the human psyche as such other institutions as marriage, kinship, religion, and economics. (In this sense, the structuralists are the most holistic of all.) A political institution, in other words, exhibits for structuralists no special features that justify its being treated as analytically separable from other institutions, and certainly not as an autonomous variable.

Hanson's view of culture as a logical system is quite different from that of Levi-Strauss. Levi-Strauss sees culture as based on the logic of the human mind, at any time in any "society". Hanson sees a culture as based on the logical presuppositions of its constitutent customs and institutions. Levi-Strauss aims, ultimately, to understand the grammar of all cultures, while Hanson's concept of implicational meaning gives us the logic of one.

Hanson and Cohen are in fact closer to each other than they are to Levi-Strauss and other "thought-structuralists". Yet Hanson, unlike Cohen, does not pick out politics or power relations as a separate variable. For him, politics are included under the institutions of culture. Hanson does, however, equate some part of what Cohen would call power relations with the "environment" of a culture (pp. 14–15). He repeats this view when, in discussing Rappaport's ecological work (1967, 1968, 1971), he distinguishes (a) "the intrinsic, implicational meaning of institutions which make up culture" from (b) the ecosystem as something external to culture in its changing effects yet ultimately comprehensible in terms of the culture (pp. 104–6).

It would seem from all this that it may be useful to see the concept of power relations as divided into two. First, the way in which a people's institutions and customs (their culture) are logically interconnected shapes their views on the distribution of power among themselves and between themselves and other groups. Second, this emic view of the distribution of power may or may not correspond with the "real" distribution of power or with our own, the outside analysts' view. This "real" distribution of power, e.g. whether one group really is amassing territory or jobs at the expense of or at a rate exceeding the other, is part of a group's environment of opportunity (cf. Hart, 1972), which "we" analyse etically as external to its culture but which members of the group interpret emically through their culture. These emic and etic views of power do not always coincide, which is precisely the idea behind such concepts as "false consciousness", "ideology", and "the mystification of social inequality". By this approach we still have two main variables, that of culture, and that of an environment of opportunity, which may contract or expand. But we now have the possibility of understanding why cultural groups sometimes vary in their political responses to similar environments, because we have placed emphasis on the view that a culture consists of institutions and customs logically presupposing and implying each other and so constituting an interpretative framework.

The relevance of this approach in the present study is to suggest that the way in which the Luo have defined their political relations with other ethnic groups is very much shaped by their segmentary lineage culture, and that this culture can be broken down into key customs and institutions which have mutually implied consequences and meanings. I shall show that, among the Luo, the polygynous family implies the relatively rapid circulation of valuable cash bridewealth, which has increased rather than dropped in value as Luo have become more and more dependent on urban wages; that this bridewealth and a high polygyny rate implicates agnates of different segmentary levels, either as elders advising on marriage "choices" or as fathers or brothers wishing to secure financially reliable husbands for their daughters and sisters; that this involvement of agnates as advisers and as transactors of cash or brides, is given further meaning through the complex segmentary pyramid of Luo urban lineage associations; and that all these activities and beliefs imply roles for women defined by men.

I also show that this cycle of institutional presuppositions may be questioned by individuals. Individual men and women sometimes express a preference for monogamy, for bridewealth of low value, and for few children who may thereby be educated with the cash saved from otherwise expensive bridewealth. But these same people may themselves enter into polygynous marriages and aim for many rather than few children. It is reasonable to assume that this continual stress on an adherence to customary family expectations may be a solidary response to external ethnic pressure exerted by competing ethnic groups in a contracting environment of opportunity. But it is also clear that the Luo cultural cycle of institutional presuppositions has a powerful autonomous effect on maintaining conformity to custom. In this study I document the changing and generally contracting Luo environment of politico-economic opportunity. But I emphasize the internal dynamics of their culture in an attempt to isolate the critical variables which define the Luo view of and response to the external political and economic constraints on them. To describe how group X becomes more powerful than and threatens group Y and, how, as it does so, each group emphasizes its own endo-culture, is very important in showing how power can be retained by a group even though some of its institutions, customs, and symbols alter while others do not.

The other half of the equation is to conduct intensive studies with a view to understanding *how* such customs change in relation to each other: to what extent do they change in constant relationship to each other, and to what extent does the change involve inconsistencies and contradictions? In other words, how do cultures each differ as a logical system of institutions, customs, and symbols? In so far as this takes a relativist view it is no more than that, under comparable environments, a group with, for example, a segmentary patrilineage culture may respond differently from one with contrasting and therefore inverse cultural features. There is a possible analogy. While all languages may ultimately be governed by a common underlying logic, quite unrelated languages may also each be said to have its own logic of grammar, syntax, phonology, morphology, and semantic disclosure, and therefore to respond differently to a common situation of linguistic change. Our level of analytical abstraction determines the relevant features of contrast, which are seen ultimately as inversions of common features at a higher level. Though more comparative data are needed, and, contrary to other predictions, I suggest that: (a) polysegmentary lineage cultures become modified but show a remarkable resilience and relative autonomy under the rapidly changing conditions of urbanization and wage dependency which characterize Africa and much of the third world and which encourage ethnic residential dispersal and socio-economic differentiation within the lifetime of single generations; and that (b) for possible alterations to this cultural consistency we must look to changes in the relations of women to men, such as new filiation rights and a wider range of modes of cohabitation. But what are the dynamics of this cultural "continuity" and what, exactly, is being "continued"?

The continuity of custom

It is no exaggeration to claim that "continuity through change; and change through continuity" was the dominant theme of studies by social anthropologists of the so-called "Manchester University/

Rhodes-Livingstone Institute school" under Gluckman from immediately after the second world war through the nineteen sixties. Gluckman's "Analysis of a Social Situation in Modern Zululand", originally published in the early forties, was the master exemplar of the idea that "actual changes within a repetitive pattern may accumulate gradually to produce changes in the pattern; in a changing system there are many repetitive changes and a whole section of a changing system may appear to be repetitive" (1958, p. 55). In other words, some parts (i.e. customs, p. 58) of a culture change while others continue; and this happens as groups carrying these cultures cooperate or compete with each other. Gluckman comes close to seeing a culture as having its own internal logic. He says: ". . . every change in the items of culture is both the product of many previous causes and the cause of many further effects . . . and when we come to discuss how culture dies out for sociological causes, and may later be revived with different values in a different system for other sociological causes, how culture of one group is adapted by another group, etc., we must recognize that there is a core of behaviour and belief which, both for its bearers and the sociologist, has a measure of historical continuity." (p. 58.)

This and other statements by Gluckman certainly come close to Hanson's view of culture as a logical system of institutional practices and beliefs with internal contradictions and tensions as well as reinforcements. Whereas Gluckman places emphasis on cleavage or cooperation between groups as prompting alterations to a culture's internal pattern, Hanson looks internally at the dynamics of this pattern as an autonomous system of beliefs and customs based on its own logic, just like a language. If changes in the logic occur, then they are analysed in terms of logical incompatibilities arising as a result of changes in the culture's environment. For Gluckman the groups carrying their respective cultures are primary. For Hanson, as I interpret him, membership of a culture, which is a system of logically interconnected ideas and practices, presupposes but to a large extent overrides group membership.

Nadel represents an intermediary view. While proposing the now conventional definition of an institution as a standardized mode of coactivity (1951, p. 108), i.e. as based on "custom", he talks of the "logical consistency" of institutions and culture. By logical consistency he understands "a cognitive operation" imputed to actors which "consists in some (underlying) judgement on their part that, acting in a certain manner in one context, they should act in a consistent sense in another . . ." (pp. 258–9). Nadel brings in the role of semantics (pp. 43–5) and non-verbal symbolism (pp. 261–5) in this process and stresses that logical consistency is what we would nowadays call an emic process specific to a particular culture. By contrast logical *necessity* "characterizes certain relations between facts" presupposing "inevitable entailment" as etically perceived by the observer (pp. 258–9).

In other words, logical necessity is to do with "our", the analysts' logic. Logical consistency is the logic of particular cultures. Except as a figure of speech, these do not imply different "kinds" of logic, but rather different levels of logical abstraction. Thus, the actor's own cultural logic or eidos may seem to him to involve activities which inevitably entail each other. That is to say, the cultural actor turned analyst sees his institutions as logically necessary for each other. A particular Luo may say that polygyny is necessary for many children; that large families are necessary for powerful lineages and political survival; and that the value of women's reproductive powers lies in these entailments and so necessitates that they be secured unambiguously; and that a valuable bridewealth transacted for a Luo girl married according to customary exogamic and relationship rules is what secures these powers. Stated thus, this emic formulation stresses agreement between the meanings of institutions and does not admit of the possible development of inconsistencies as a result of environmental change, such as an emerging redefinition of women's roles as wives and mothers, and does not compare alternative cultural formulations which may arise. The difference between the "inside" and the "outside" analyst (who could be, say, a non-Luo or Luo "sociologist", or "revolutionary" trying to raise and transform cultural consciousness) is that the etic analyst does strive for logical operations of a higher level of abstraction by comparing Luo culture with that of, say, the Tallensi and grouping them together as, for example, both based on segmentary lineage system and so logically contrastable with non-segmentary lineage systems, and so on. All this is implied in Nadel's rules of method. In this sense Hanson is like Nadel.

As well as seeing culture emically as comprising logically consistent institutions, Nadel also sees the process of institutionalization etically as dependent on group formation, i.e. on that "summation of persons" through time that he calls "society" (pp. 78–95). Here he is like Gluckman rather than Hanson. Nadel's "two-dimensional" view of "socio-cultural" anthropology, to use his terms, has influenced the position taken by Cohen (1974a). For Nadel's etic concept of "society" Cohen substitutes the concept of power relations and for Nadel's emic concept of "culture" that of symbolism. The great virtue of Cohen's approach is that he has been able to apply his ideas solidly to empirical problems. The big methodological difference between Nadel and Cohen is that the latter does not see usefulness in pursuing the idea of a logical consistency of the institutions of culture as expressed in the semantic formulations as well as behaviour of its actors.

Here it must be remarked that, arrived at by different routes but from common philosophical sources, the distinction between emic logical consistency and etic logical necessity parallels the distinction implicitly or explicitly made by generative semanticists in their analyses of communicative competence between (a) the speaker's presuppositions derived from his and his hearer's culture and (b) the "standard" logical presuppositions based on truth conditions of sentences, both occurring within the same speech act (Grice, 1969; Lakoff, 1971; Kempson, 1975, p. 51; Gumperz (a) and (b) unpublished, and others). Since this distinction further roughly parallels that between illocutionary and propositional force in speech (Searle, 1968, 1969), we see how remarkably convergent at a general level are some of the key ideas in socio-cultural anthropology and in recent studies of semantics. This appears to justify further the view of culture as being essentially and not merely analogously a system of communication, with all that this implies with regard to its constituent features of logic and semantics.

It should be emphasized that Nadel's notion of logical consistency does not rule out the possibility of inconsistencies developing and so leading to "social change" (1951, pp. 263–5). However, he certainly emphasizes logical harmony as his primary focus, whereas Gluckman's analytical starting point was conflict, either between groups or institutional rules, and sometimes but not always leading to cohesion. The antinomy of conflict to cohesion has spawned interesting conceptual parallels, and it is relevant to this discussion to ask what they offer to the view that culture may be regarded as understandable in logical terms. Moore (1975, pp. 210–38), much influenced by the

"Manchester school", has recently extended Turner's distinction between "structure", the essentially perduring order of values and relations, and "communitas", the interim moments of new structural creativity. She accepts the views of Turner and others that the socio-cultural process is full of indeterminacies, inconsistencies, and contradictions, but that the two processes, of regularization, i.e. of putting order back into disorder, and of situational adjustment, act as counterbalancing forces which both limit chaos and yet provide outlets for individual creativity. After a decade or so of studies which have increasingly characterized socio-cultural processes as a flow of inconsistent situations requiring individual adjustment through manipulation, Moore's approach re-emphasizes the apparently not so obvious assumption that order and continuity and not flux most characterize the process of culture. I agree and would add that this stress on cultural order presupposes a high degree of logical consistency.

The differential concern with continuity and change is admittedly a matter of emphasis and illustrates the reactive and counter-reactive nature of the history of unfolding ideas. It is again relevant here to note two of the citations used by Moore to illustrate the reaction against allegedly "static" views of society and culture (1975, pp. 215–16). The first is the famous one by Leach which argues that "inconsistencies in the logic of ritual expression" (1954, p. 4) do not impede but are essential for society's continuity, because the inconsistencies offer choices and therefore the possibility of adjustment to new situations. The second citation is from Turner and contains the view that "a social system is not a harmonious configuration governed by mutually compatible and logically interrelated principles. It is rather a set of loosely integrated processes, with some patterned aspects, some persistencies of form, but controlled by discrepant principles of action expressed in rules of custom that are often situationally incompatible with one another." (1967, p. 196.)

Leaving aside the question as to whether the existence of "patterned aspects" and "persistencies of form", whatever they may be, does not already presuppose some logical consistency, this and the previous citation gloss over the possibility that cultures may differ in the extent to which their constituent institutions are logically inter-related in a mutually compatible way. It is nowadays such a truism that action and norm, and some of the norms themselves, are discrepant in any society that it may well be instructive to reconsider the logical bases of the interrelated customs making up culture, recognizing that no cultural logic is without its inconsistencies and contradictions but that one may have less than another in "explaining" a particular kind of environmental change (Kaplan and Manners, 1972, pp. 121–7). My own approach turns on the idea of a culture as a system of communication and responses, and asks to what extent inconsistencies in the logic of communication develop under externally changing conditions and become reformulated within a new paradigm of institutional assumptions. The "repetitive equilibria" identified by Gluckman as characterizing socio-cultural change may be regarded as cultural reformulations of this kind.

How do we understand when such reformulations are occurring? A culture may indeed be regarded as made up of those units which Gluckman called customs, but these customs can be seen as possessing three attributes: conventionalized activity, concepts, and lexicons. We may compare here Nadel's three "co-ordinates" of culture: physical action, idea systems, and language (1951, p. 85). The three attributes do not necessarily mirror each other. Thus, a conventionalized activity, like a funeral ceremony or the rite attending marriage, may have only one or a few meanings for a large group of people; or it may have a wide range of different meanings for a much smaller group. Similarly, it may consistently be referred to by the group through the use of regularly recurring words or the members of the group may vary considerably in the verbal labels they attach to the activity, sometimes to the extent of not verbally identifying the convention at all, yet evidently conceptualizing it. Because these three attributes making up custom, i.e. conventionalized activity, concept, and lexicon, do not necessarily reflect each other consistently, they can be said to enjoy some degree of autonomy of each other. Up to a point, then, these three are independent variables making up that whole which we call culture.

The point of this breakdown is to draw attention to ambiguities and inclarities in the notion of "continuity" of custom. Is it the practice of the custom which has persisted through changing conditions? Or has the practice itself altered (e.g. among the Giriama of Kenya young men now bury corpses whereas in the past old men did), with the emic meaning of the custom persisting (e.g. that proper burials secure proper relations with the dead)? Or have the ideas as well as the practices been altered (e.g. proper, i.e. lavish, funerals among the Giriama are seen more as a statement of the honour, or lack of it, of the closest senior male agnate of the deceased than of possible future bad relations between these two)? What, then, may have most persisted of the custom are the words used to describe it. Giriama continue to use the terms *mahanga* and *nyere za mwezi* to refer respectively to first and second funerals, but the practice and ideas associated with these have altered. For other customs, and in other cultures, the words used to describe conventions may have changed considerably, while the conventions themselves and the ideas connoted by them, remain by comparison much as before.

Among the Luo described in this book the traditional key terms denoting polygynous family, and lineage and kinship relations, continue to be used in a mutually consistent way. The lexicon is closely tied up with traditional ideas: the term for a polygynist connotes the ability of a man to perpetuate himself and his name through many wives and many children in a culturally approved way; the taxonomy of lineage and kinship terms connotes traditional ideas of Luo political expansion and independence. These are invariable terms and the ideas associated with them are relatively constant. But the practice of polygyny, and the uses to which ties of kinship and lineage are put have changed. What, then, is "continuous" about polygyny and lineages among Luo is not so much how they operate and what practical consequences they have for the Luo people, but more how they are spoken and thought about. Under the compelling cover of unchanging word and thought, significant changes of action are taking place.

This is all a matter of relativity and emphasis. Words, ideas, and action are never wholly constant. Phonologists say that we never repeat the same word in exactly the same way, any more than our images or actions can ever be perfectly repeated. But this is where the cross-cultural contrast of interacting groups steadies the otherwise certain drive to an ever-more microscopic concern with differences of detail. For, through abstracting cross-cultural contrasts, we can depict trends. Thus, in this book I make some comparison with the Kikuyu in Nairobi who contrast with Luo in their far wider range of lexical reference to domestic and related activities and in expressing a wider range of meanings connoted by these activities. Moreover, they are more likely, when confronted by a common lexicon intended by the speaker to identify a custom, to understand by it a wider variety of practices. In other words, the key customary words, deeds, and concepts making up these domains of Kikuyu culture pre-suppose each other to a much lesser extent than among Luo, almost to the point at which, if my impressions are correct, we must wonder whether it is still permissible to speak of *the* culture of the Kikuyu, among whom alternative life-styles based on socio-economic status have each begun to assume separate autonomy.

It is obvious that *within* a culture, one can always find individual customs which differ from each other in the extent to which words and ideas are consistently applied to the same conventionalized activity. This is part of the understanding of the dynamics of culture. But the ultimate aim is to formulate cross-cultural generalization based on contrasting features of the kind that may be said to distinguish Luo from Kikuyu. This is not just a distinction based on groups. It is also one based on people's perceptions of where the diacritical boun-daries defining their membership are, and these, we well know, may operate at different levels. Obbo has pointed out how, in Kampala, being a "Luo" could extend to membership of the distantly related Nilotic-speaking ethnic groups of Northern Uganda but in other con-texts clearly meant only those Luo from Kenya (Obbo, unpublished paper). Similarly, "Kikuyu" in Nairobi can include the "Meru" and "Embu" but in other situations excludes them. On the other hand, linguistically and, on the surface, culturally quite unrelated but neighbouring peoples may yet share underlying assumptions and be-liefs (Southall, 1971, 1972). The distinctiveness of interacting cultures occurs as a result of a constant emic polarization of their respective attributes. This is best seen as the operation of a kind of "phonemic" principle of distinctiveness through opposition, by which, over time, complementary customs in each of two cultures are seen to be not simply different but more and more the total inverse of each other. In Kampala, the Luo and fellow non-Bantu, and the Ganda and fellow Interlacustrine Bantu, would often specify these points of cultural contrast in conversation among themselves or with each other (Parkin, 1969, pp. 95, 127–47). The Kikuyu and Luo do likewise in Nairobi, and, I have witnessed, the non-Muslim Mijikenda and Swahili do so in coastal Kenya. In all cases, cultural contrasts are cited which often exaggerate the observed differences of practice between peoples.

I emphasize that these are in the first place conceptual contrasts made in conversation, and sometimes constituting lexical and even taxonomic contrasts. They do not, by themselves, imply contrasts of practice. Within otherwise conceptually opposed cultures, there is the variation of customary "fit", to which I have referred, of word, idea, and deed.

To repeat, for the Luo, their traditional lexicon of family and lineage relations has persisted relatively unaltered as have the ideas which the terms connote. But the actual conduct of family, kinship and lineage relations has altered, in some cases considerably. In other words, the Luo consistently use "traditional" key verbal concepts (what some might call verbal "symbols") to refer to activities which have adapted to Luo men's increasing dependency on urban wages in, paradoxically, a diminishing environment of opportunity, and which contain within themselves the potential for far more radical changes of a kind likely to disrupt the current autonomy of Luo culture.

By contrast, the Kikuyu do not appear to make formalized use of "traditional" key verbal concepts of family and kinships to anywhere near the same extent. Rather, their verbal rallying-points are those of the Kenya state, of the ruling political party, the Kenya African National Union, whose slogan is the non-vernacular coined term *Harambee* ("Let us pull together"), and the person of the President, who is known in Swahili as *Mzee Mheshimiwa Baba Taifa Rais Kenyatta* (the Elder, the Respected, the Father of the State, the President *Kenyatta*). Prominent Kikuyu often point out that they see themselves and their people as rightful custodians of the state: the symbols of statehood are their symbols, and others are invited to share them.

The lexical definition of political response

The view that it is key verbal concepts that show the greatest continuity of custom among Luo is another way of saying that it is partly the formalized use of the Luo language which provides this continuity. Bloch has emphasized how the formalization of speech can restrict the content of what is being communicated to a limited range of assumptions, expectations and responses (1975a, pp. 1–28). It is an ideal way in which traditional authorities can exercise their power, for it tends to stifle the linguistic expression and exchange of new ideas and so maintains the *status quo*. Thus, when Luo co-wives in Nairobi dispute, senior agnates of the husband (and sometimes the husband himself) can lecture them on the need to preserve traditional co-wife seniority rules, turning constantly on the unquestionable hierarchy implicit in the key terms distinguishing first, second, and third or subsequent wives. When young Luo monogamists equivocate about the advantages of taking a second wife, elders place repeated stress on the word for polygynist, which has the additional connotation of arbiter and man of eminence and authority. When politicians appear to forget their fellow Luo, parable-like allusions are made to sons leaving the home and lineage of their fathers, with constant repetition of key terms denoting these roles and relations. And so on. Formalized speech is, of course, based on more than the constant repetition of key verbal concepts (Bloch, 1975a, p. 13). But key verbal concepts appear to be central, having their "illocutionary" and persuasive effect even when embedded in some degree of stylistic and syntactic variation and creativity.[1]

I have said above that the repeated use of such terms can act as a compelling, even "mystifying" cover under which changes of customary practice may occur. That is so. But, since people are unlikely to be deluded all the time by all that they see of customary practice, some activities must appear to reflect the implications of the statement. Thus, elders *do* monopolize positions in the Luo segmentary pyramid of lineage associations which are important in politics and marriage; polygynists *do* tend to be well above the socio-economic average and so appear to confirm their reputation for eminence and authority; Luo politicians who preach policies which are interpreted as directing resources away from the Luo community *are* subject to harsh reprimand in public speeches.

This is precisely why I want to see key verbal concepts, unverbalized ideas, and conventional activities as each autonomously based on their own internal systems of logical presuppositions, and yet, as autonomous systems, in constant interaction with each other and so

---

[1] I view the illocutionary aspect of speech as having its greatest effect not just through verbs of warning, ordering, commanding, requesting, urging, advising, and even telling (see Searle, 1968, on Austin, 1962), but also through the use of culturally key noun phrases, including role terms and abstract concepts, which, used together with such verbs, reinforce assumptions about the speaker's "unquestionable" authority. I agree with Searle (*ibid.*) that all speech acts have an illocutionary framework of some degree, within which propositions, however limited, are articulable. The use of key verbal concepts, which I define as recurrent "words" of central cultural and semantic significance in a speech act, would seem particularly to increase the illocutionary force of utterances.

making up the more comprehensive autonomy of a particular culture. In one instance or at one time people generally agree on the ideas and actions denoted by particular key terms; in another instance or at another time, they disagree profoundly; but at all times, lexicons must retain "shadows" of at least some of their former representations or significations, which are abandoned for the moment but which are potentially retrievable. The link between them is not, after all, so arbitrary as Saussure suggested. In other words, the lexicons and taxonomies of cultural ideas and actions are in dialectic relationship with each other. Key verbal concepts shape people's perceptions of changes in the group's environment of opportunity, which may in turn redefine the lexicons and taxonomies. The Luo see their apparent political and economic demise as proof of the need to strengthen the family and polygyny, and the relations of kinship, and lineage. They speak and act accordingly, sometimes drawing on past and allegedly traditional experiences and images. And yet it is precisely the environmental changes, especially those to do with the possibility of investing surplus wage incomes in education, which threatens to redefine such perceptions by offering new ways of talking about them.

In his forward to the recent volume edited by Sanches and Blount (1975), Gumperz summarizes its findings and draws attention to the work of ethnographic semanticists which does indeed demonstrate how culturally specific lexicons or terminological systems shape perceptions of reality. "Verbal categories become conventionalized ways of communicating environmental cues, but they are only imperfect representations of reality. They tend to maintain themselves because of the need for communication with others, unless new circumstances arise to force re-categorizations." (Gumperz, 1975, p. xviii.) This is not the same as the "Whorfian" theory that a people's grammatical categories shape their world-views. Rather it suggests that lexical rather than grammatical categories can significantly affect their perceptions. Thus, the Luo are perfectly aware that their political representation in Nairobi has diminished since just before Kenya's independence. But the way they attempt to deal with this situation is significantly shaped not just by the existence of the segmentary lineage system which underlies their culture. They are also *persuaded* that to respond within this facet of their culture is the best mode of response. And the "illocutionary force" of such persuasion stems in large part from the repeated use in public and private formalized speech of key role terms and verbal concepts. These often presuppose each other in taxonomies or as contrast sets, and together constitute a continuing element of the traditional family and lineage system.

The quotation from Gumperz notes that words exchanged are "imperfect representations of reality" which, to repeat my earlier point, is to emphasize that they do have some conceptual leeway, some partial autonomy, over and above their sometimes loose anchorage in activities.

The work by ethnographic semanticists is necessarily detailed. It has expanded from the analysis of semantic domains of *concepts*, e.g. the colour spectrum, kinship terminologies, numerical systems, botanical classification, zoology, etc. to the analysis of *activities*, including speech events, ceremonial or status-marking events, as well as events of a day-to-day kind (see the contributions to Hymes, 1964, pp. 167–211; Hammel, 1965; Tylor, 1969; Gumperz and Hymes, 1972; Baumann and Scherzer, 1974; Sanches and Blount, 1975). This is a significant progression and is clearly consistent with my breakdown of custom into the three relatively autonomous spheres of lexicon, concept, and conventionalized activity. In this study I deliberately refrain from analysing to the level of detail undertaken by the ethnographic semanticists of particular conversations, not because I ignore the value of such studies but because I am here concerned to show in broad cultural terms, and over time, how during one large ethnic group's geographical dispersal and socio-economic differentiation the greatest expression of its cultural continuity has been the constant use of key verbal concepts to depict its changing customs. This is, then, an institutionally holistic study with a diachronic rather than synchronic perspective, and while an outgrowth of traditional "socio-cultural" anthropology, draws fresh inspiration from linguistic anthropology and ethnographic semantics. The latter enable us to include the analysis of lexicons within the systematic study of custom.

Outline of the argument

It may help the reader to follow the argument by seeing each chapter as concerned with two opposed forces, which are indicated in the chapter's sub-title. These sets of opposed forces run parallel with each other through successive chapters. The essence of the book's argument can be glossed by reading the content's list.

Thus, the first chapter shows how urban polygyny among the Luo paradoxically enables a man to set up an urban nuclear family household: his two or more wives take it in turns to stay with the husband in town with their children while the other looks after the rural land at home. This establishes an initial basic opposition between women's mobility and men's stability: by their recurrent movements between town and country wives enable men to remain in town and earn cash wages while retaining rural land rights. In Chapter 2 we see how this practical usefulness of polygyny conflicts with the value placed on education for children: for polygyny produces many children within a family while education, which can be expensive beyond an elementary level, can only be provided for a few. Though this conflict is occasionally referred to in casual conversation by both men and women, full discussion of it tends to be smothered, so to speak, by a greater value placed on polygyny and many children as prestigeful prerequisites of political credibility and as a cornerstone of Luo cultural autonomy. A description of household composition in Nairobi in Chapter 3 reveals the ideological strength of Luo agnatic obligations compared with other ethnic groups. Agnation and kinship generally are shown to be important ideological factors directing men and women into polygynous unions. Friends are conceptualized as opposed to agnates and close relatives. Friends are said to offer "escape" from such constraining relationships. But, in the end, it is through friends that customary marriage "choices" are made and the institutions of polygyny and of expensive bridewealth are perpetuated. Friends turn out to be, quite unconsciously and unintendedly, false allies in the attempt to escape kin.

Chapter 4 gives the economic background to the ideological persistence of polygyny. Men who came to work for wages in Nairobi a generation or so ago are now the fathers whose sons and daughters are of marriageable age. For various reasons, these middle-aged men invested in the past in polygyny more than in, say, trade or business or the purchase of land. They became more and more dependent on skilled and white-collar urban occupations. Paradoxically, their older wives have been left with greater freedom themselves to engage in self-employment in Nairobi. But this is a restricted freedom, for their husbands retain some control over the money earned from such trading and over trading licences. These women therefore provide a glimpse, but no more, of their potential for economic independence. Their situation is in this limited sense ambivalent. The economic ambivalence of some Luo women, and the potential threat to male control that they are seen by some men to pose, is paralleled by mystical ideas concerning their status as wives and mothers, as discussed in Chapter 5. While in the rural areas of Luoland, witchcraft accusations are the primary means of explaining domestic misfortune, in urban households sterility, and sickness and death especially affecting children and wives, are believed to be caused by a mystical affliction called *chira*. In a general statement of belief by both Luo men and women, *chira* is said to be caused by adultery and incest, but in actual cases of diagnosis by a diviner, it is men's rather than women's mismanagement of seniority relations within the family and lineage which are blamed. Thus, while women are held as much as men to have the mystical power to destroy their family and lineage, it is only men who are actually shown, in particular cases, to have this power of family self-destruction. Once again, women's status shows glimpses of a power to threaten male dominance, but verbal diagnoses sanctioned by mystical authority contain it.

This opposition between, from a male viewpoint, threats of disorder and reassertions of order is most vividly expressed in Luo public political life and speeches, which are almost exclusively the domain of men. The most enduring elements of modern Luo politics are expressed in their pyramidal structure of urban lineage associations which are headed by the Luo Union. A modified version of the "traditional" Luo segmentary patrilineage structure constantly reshapes and reorders the endemic factionalism which pervades internal Luo politics. This is the theme of Chapter 6, and in Chapter 7 it is further examined by way of a comparison of the leaders, Odinga and Mboya. These two represent an opposition between two paradigms in Luo culture. The "traditional" paradigm summarily links together gerontocratic and genealogical authority as logically presupposing and presupposed by polygyny, valuable bridewealth in exchange for a wife's reproductive powers, and the preservation of the exogamic segmentary lineage structure. A contrary paradigm denies the interconnected relevance of these institutions and posits instead individual achievement, if necessary to the neglect of family, lineage and relatives, through educational and occupational success for oneself or for one's intentionally limited number of children by one wife. This latter paradigm would necessarily have radical implications for the status of Luo women, a point alluded to by Luo men which I discuss in Chapter 8. For it is only through their attempts to render unambiguous the status of Luo unmarried daughters and sisters as future co-wives and child-bearers for other men, that fathers and brothers can maintain their jurisdiction over them and convert this into control by husbands over their women and children.

Verbalized evaluations opposing polygyny to monogamy, many children to few, relatives to friends, and "collectivism" to "individualism", therefore turn on an idealised opposition between men as "producers" of urban wage labour, and women as co-wives and producers only of men's children. But wives already provide essential rural labour and have moved into trade, and so are seen by Luo men to be on the threshhold of departing from the idealized, unambiguously defined roles, and so of unhinging the segmentary lineage culture.

At present men successfully contain this ambivalence within the status of women through controls which draw much of their efficacy from the use of customary verbal concepts in domestic and political speeches. But men's growing dependence on urban wage incomes and their conversion of these cash incomes into inflated bridewealth payments produces a logical inconsistency in the main premises on which Luo culture is based. For cash can also be invested in education for one's children, including one's daughters. Elite Luo, at least, earn enough to invest in both valuable bridewealth and a high standard of education for their children. Yet highly educated Luo women seem, from the few cases we have of them, much less likely to accept the formalized arguments posed by men in favour of polygyny.

Women's rejection of polygyny would in time have many implications: senior men could no longer retain control over rural interests through a co-wife while remaining in town with another co-wife and children; a larger number of marriageable women would be available to young men who would not then need to compete for them to the same extent; this would lessen the authority of em-

ployed "fathers" over unemployed sons which is at present based on
the control by these fathers of high bridewealth payments for scarce
brides, and on strict exogamic rules facilitating control of son's marriage choices; sons and daughters would then be less obliged to heed
parental demands for valuable bridewealth and the observance of
exogamic rules, or at least could interpret them more widely; a wider
range than at present of modes of cohabitation might then develop,
some accompanied by a transfer of valuable bridewealth and others
by low or absent bridewealth, together with varying arrangements
regarding the paternity of children and their custody in the event of
divorce and separation; these varying modes of cohabitation affecting
the disposition and exchange value of bridewealth and children
might be expected to correspond with clearly expressed differences of
socio-economic status, which are at present constantly played down
or "tamed" in speech events.

These consequences would surely remove the main premises on
which Luo segmentary lineage culture is based and would constitute
part of an entirely new paradigm of institutional meanings and assumptions. But of course such consequences could only follow a significant decrease in the rate of polygyny. For this to occur, the few
highly educated women who do reject polygyny would have to be
joined by others, probably first by those Luo women who currently
engage in trade under the control of husbands but who might use
the articulate minority of educated women as a reference model in
securing for themselves full rights over their enterprises.

For a variety of historical and political, but also cultural reasons,
a marked change in the status of many Kikuyu women has occurred
independently of higher education among some of them. An increasing number of Kikuyu women in Nairobi set up matrifocal family
units and move into various kinds of self-employment. What Kikuyu
women have been able to do economically, Luo women may need to
do firstly by power of verbal argument. That is to say, many Kikuyu
women have drawn on traditionally acceptable ambiguities in their
roles as mother, wife, and daughter, and have negotiated and so redefined these roles in the modern economic idiom which has become
available to them. By contrast the absence of such openly recognized
ambiguity in these roles among Luo women precludes their negotiation in an economic idiom, at least initially, but requires instead

that tactit role ambiguities first be made semantically distinguishable and thereby negotiable.

In the conclusion I follow on from this by suggesting that a taxonomic and logical contrast between descent group systems as either "unambiguously pyramidal", like that of the Luo, or "overlapping and parallel", like that of the Kikuyu, provides an initial basis for cross-cultural comparison of changes in the status of women and, by implication, for those paradigmatic shifts underlying socio-cultural processes which we conventionally call "social change" and which includes a group's political responses to altering environments of opportunity.

1

Polygyny and Family Settlement

Two Wives Equal one Nuclear Family Household

In this opening chapter, I describe the ecology of urban family settlement. That is to say, I show how such external restraints as the changing availability of urban housing, jobs, and education, and access to rural land, affect the pattern of family relations that has emerged among a group of Luo in Nairobi who have lived there longest. At one analytical level, this environment of varying opportunities can be viewed as governed by the national and international relationship of capital to labour in the context of a burgeoning population (Parkin, 1975b, pp. 3-44). At an emic level, however, it may be understood by looking at the way in which members of different ethnic groups see themselves as opposed to or in competition with each other. Government policies concerned with the allocation of houses, jobs, and education do not officially recognize competition between ethnic groups. But most people see them as interrelated and, in the manner of a self-fulfilling prophecy, the ethnic framework does seem in recent years to have become for individual "patrons" within the bureaucracy the most immediately significant ideological criterion of entitlement to such resources.

The Luo I studied in Nairobi, the area in which they live and interact with each other, and their long urban residence and above average socio-economic status, are not necessarily "typical" of other Luo in Nairobi. That is not the point. They do, however, represent a possible direction which other Luo may follow under similar circumstances, or have already followed. Their significance is that, while being among the most dependent on urban wage incomes, they subscribe to what they perceive to be customary family ideals.

Here it must be emphasized that Luo migrate and work in towns throughout East Africa. Most of the Luo I studied have at some time lived or worked in other towns. Luo are well represented as workers in the (former) East African Railways and, as Grillo (1973, 1974) has carefully documented, are dispersed along the line of rail from Uganda, through Kenya, to Tanzania. Railway workers are also subject to sudden transfer: a man may be working in Kampala one month and in Nairobi, nearly five hundred miles away, the next month, and a few months later in Dar es Salaam, another few hundred miles away.[1] Few of the household heads of the families I studied were railway workers and so, comparatively, were more settled in the one town of Nairobi. But most had lived and sometimes worked elsewhere and, what is particularly important, most had relatives working in the railways to whom men might go and younger wards be sent in an attempt to have jobs found for them. The wide geographical dispersal and mobility of the Luo, then, is based on (a) their strong association with railway working, and (b) a preparedness by relatives unconnected with the railways to use these far-flung workers as hosts for job-seekers. The relatives and affines geographically and socially connected in this way thus fall into a wide range of occupations and incomes. They are also of widely varying educational levels. It is through largely unquestioned appeals to kinship and affinity and sometimes through close friendships, verbalized as having broad kinship qualities, that these ties are used. Their obligatory nature puts them into the category of relationships based on "generalized reciprocity" (Sahlins, 1965, p. 147), in which, among the Luo, kinship between two persons is sufficient grounds for the less privileged to expect or at least request help which need not be reciprocated precisely nor immediately, nor even at all. The "generosity" of the donor is seen to be an implicit feature of the relationship and does not necessarily have to be acknowledged in this way nor by deferential behaviour on the part of the recipient.

As a general proposition, we can say of a segmentary lineage

---

[1] This was written before the recent virtual collapse of the East African Common Services Organization, a development likely to have radical consequences for Luo.

society that the longer the genealogical depth of its exogamous lineages and the higher its polygyny rate, the greater will be the number
of kinship and affinal ties centred on a middle-aged man (i.e. who is
himself likely to have more than one wife, married children of his
own, and a correspondingly large number of known affines). The individual Luo's extensive network of kin and affines can, as we shall
see, be understood as resting ultimately on a continuing rural localization of many exogamous lineages and lineage segments. But, as
more and more Luo have moved between and settled in distantly
located towns and other employment centres, they have transformed
this extensive network into one of added socio-geographical significance.

In studying only one housing area in one city, that of Nairobi, I
can hardly claim to know all parts of this ethnic network, which comprises a significant proportion of the one and a half million Kenya
Luo. But the intensive analysis of one localized section of Luo does
give a base from which I can see how people are connected to each
other both in different areas of Nairobi and in other towns, as well
as between towns generally and the home rural areas with which almost all Luo keep in regular contact and where they have valued
land rights (see Map 1).

This wide-flung movement and connectedness of Luo provides
channels along which customary practices are carried to and fro and
modified in similar ways in response to a common largely urban,
wage environment. Leach (1976b, p. 25) has recently criticized Radcliffe-Brown's formula that "language usually constitutes the line of
[territorial and social] demarcation" (my bracketed inclusion), as
empirically often inaccurate and as theoretically falling short of the
structuralist view that a natural science of society may well turn out
to be based on a general linguistics of all culture. This is certainly
the prevailing theoretical direction to which I also subscribe (Parkin,
1976). But, at the more empirical level of analysis attempted in this
book, which is by no means incompatible and is indeed the *sine qua
non* of such high-level theoretical abstraction, there is a sense in
which the *dispersed* territorality of modern Luo *is* culturally demarcated for them by their common language. That is to say, while customary practices must, however slightly, take account of immediately
local urban constraints of space, time, and money, the Luo vernacular is for them one medium of communication which can remain

relatively unaffected by such local variations. They can transact the same key verbal concepts, and it can be argued that these constitute the last line of resistance to cultural change should the socio-geographic dispersal of Luo ever presage significant socio-cultural divisions among them.

Introducing Kaloleni

In the eastern part of Nairobi, in an area known as Eastlands, there is a municipal housing estate called Kaloleni (see Map 2). Of all such estates, it has by far the largest proportion of Luo. It is often called a Luo estate by members of all ethnic groups in the city. Luo hold almost all of their numerous ethnic association meetings there. A trusted visitor may be shown the houses used by prominent Luo politicians. Adjacent to the estate is the national sports stadium, which is mostly used for soccer matches between Luo teams and teams drawn from another ethnic group, the Luyia.

There are two municipal beer bars in Kaloleni. One is small and run by a Luo, and the other is larger and run by a Kikuyu. The Luo's bar is patronized exclusively by Luo and, very occasionally, Luyia. The Kikuyu's bar is patronized by members of all ethnic groupings, including Luo. But the kind of Luo who frequent their own "ethnic" bar do not normally go to the ethnically mixed one. They are almost exclusively married men, many of them in their forties and fifties and referred to by the vernacular term for elder, *jaduong* (pl. *jodongo*). In their bar their talk centres on two topics: politics and young people. Bottled beer is available but most men drink traditionally prepared beer. The Luo proprietor serves his customers with the help of a couple of Luo women who are probably past child-bearing age. Entertainment is provided by a Luo minstrel (*jathum*), who may be of any age, and who plays the *nyatiti*, a traditional kind of lyre, and who sings up-to-date songs about contemporary politics, mixed with praise songs in honour of Luo leaders.

Forty yards away in the ethnically mixed bar, the juke-box plays incessantly. Its repertoire ranges from American soul music to the songs of Nairobi pop groups. The bar girls are young and are from all ethnic groups. They serve only bottled beer. Groups of men speaking their respective vernaculars are interspersed with a much

smaller number of ethnically mixed groups speaking Swahili, sometimes mixed with English words and phrases. There is relatively
little talk about politics as such, but a lot about the scarcity of jobs
and housing, and to a lesser extent about women and young wives.
A few of the men are accompanied by wives or girl friends. It is
normal, however, for men without female partners to dance alone, in
a tacit tussle with each other to display their own extraordinary
brands of inventiveness. There are very few Luo over thirty years of
age in this bar, and not many more from other groups who are above
this age. The genuine enjoyment of these facilities is greatest at the
end of the month when salaries are paid.

Although I was very struck by the marked contrast in social composition, general ambience, and conversational topic between the
two bars, it was not until I had finished my fieldwork that I realized
that together they aptly represented many of the socio-cultural
themes which I had been encountering in a range of other contexts
in Nairobi. It would be an injustice to Levi-Strauss (1963, p. 291) to
read much into this interesting spatial opposition of social categories
and cultural interests. It is sufficient to take a simple Durkheimian
view of it as manifesting socio-cultural distinctions which characterize relationships in Kaloleni as a whole and, beyond the estate,
the Luo collectivity itself both internally and in relation to other
ethnic groups.

The contrast between the two bars is a conveniently graphic starting point for a discussion running throughout the book of three
types of social divisions: ethnic, generational, and sexual. We begin
where the bars are situated, in Kaloleni housing estate.

Kaloleni: a spatial commentary on changing ethnic and generational relations

How does Kaloleni and the changes to which it has been subject fit
into the recent demographic picture of Nairobi as a whole?

The official population of Nairobi at the 1969 Census reached
509,286. Even allowing for the recent extension of the city's boundaries which partly explain the much smaller population of 266,795
recorded at the 1962 Census, there is general agreement that Nairobi's overall population has been expanding at seven per cent per

annum at least. The proportion of Africans in the city has increased during the same period from nearly 60 per cent to some 80 per cent. This is partly explained by the inclusion of densely populated areas of African residents within the recent boundaries and partly by the reduction in the number of Asian residents, many of whom have left Kenya. But probably the most significant factor behind the increase is the high immigration rate of African job-seekers. A comparison of the four main ethnic groups in Nairobi between the two censuses reveals that in this short period of seven years the proportion of Kikuyu in the city's African population has increased slightly more than the other three groups (Table 1).

TABLE 1

| | 1962 | | | 1969 | |
	Number	%		Number	%
Kikuyu	65,560	42.0		191,367	45.5
Luyia	26,332	16.9		65,056	15.5
Luo	24,870	15.9		62,865	14.8
Kamba	23,864	15.3		60,716	14.4
Others	17,239	9.9		41,075	9.8
Total	158,865	100.0		421,079	100.0

This slight difference in proportional increase is at variance with the frequent claims made by members of the other three groups that the city is becoming inundated with Kikuyu. But looked at from the viewpoint of any one of these groups it means that for every ten members of their own group who have arrived in Nairobi over the period, there have been 12 Kikuyu. Given the very high proportion of Kikuyu in Nairobi anyway, a difference of this kind can assume far greater significance than it really has, especially when talked and gossiped about in triple by three groupings who perceive a common numerical subordination to the dominant one. For all that, the tendency for Kikuyu to assume even greater numerical preponderance does seem to be a continuing one, and at the current growth rate over a generation of, say, 28 years from the census of 1962, would make Kikuyu about 58 per cent of the city's African population.

These census figures do not reveal that it is since the ending of the Kenya Emergency, which lasted from 1952 to 1959 and which was principally aimed at containing the movement of Kikuyu, that the increase in the Kikuyu proportion really began. At the ending of the Emergency the remaining restrictions placed on Kikuyu were lifted and they were again able to move freely to and within Nairobi. Their proximity to Nairobi has always been a factor in their numerical preponderance there and it can fairly be argued that recent years following the ending of the Emergency have merely seen a return to the Kikuyu proportion as it was before the restrictions imposed in 1952. This is so, but it is surely only a matter of time before that proportion is far exceeded. And in any event, since we are dealing with the situation as Nairobi people themselves perceive it, the increase in the Kikuyu proportion is taken by them at its face value, as indicating a kind of city "take over", and not in part as an inevitable consequence of their proximity to the city and a return to their previous numbers.

Apart from the real but not dramatic change in ethnic composition and people's exaggerated view of it, there is the phenomenal increase in the total African population affecting everyone. No city government in the world could possibly have provided sufficient jobs and housing for this number of newcomers, and it is the scarcity of these two resources which underlies the nature of many day-to-day relations between ethnic groups, generations, and men and women.

When we turn to Kaloleni estate itself, we are struck by a virtual reversal of ethnic distribution compared with Nairobi as a whole. Table I above indicates that the Luo proportion in Nairobi has declined more than any other group in the period from 1962 to 1969, falling to under 15 per cent. And in Kaloleni estate also, the Luo proportion has dropped in recent years. But Luo are still by far the largest group there with 39 per cent of all household heads in 1969. Interestingly, their fellow Western Kenyans, the Luyia, are also well over-represented in the estate at 26 per cent. Kamba, at under 16 per cent, most nearly approximate their proportion in Nairobi as a whole. But the Kikuyu who number only 14 per cent are greatly under-represented, having moved into Kaloleni since the ending of the Emergency. Some thirty-odd ethnic groups making up the rest of the estate's household heads are also under-represented at five per cent.

Kaloleni has a population of nearly 5,000 men, women and child-

TABLE 2

Numerical profile of the household heads of Kaloleni estate (late 1968)

	Luo (333)	Luyia (222)	Kikuyu (122)	Kamba (133)	Others (42)
Per cent of household head population	39.0	26.0	14.3	15.6	4.9
Median age	37.3	36.4	37.1	37.0	38.7
Median education (in years)	8.2	6.6	7.1	6.2	6.0
Median formal instruction in Swahili (years)	1.4	1.1	1.3	1.2	—
Median income (Shs.)	539/-	475/-	549/-	450/-	542/-
Median length of residence in Nairobi (years)	17.6	15.2	16.7	14.2	16.9
Median length of residence in Kaloleni (years)	11.3	9.1	6.7	8.3	7.6
Per cent proportions in:					
a. white-collar employment	36.3	30.2	39.3	27.1	30.9
b. blue-collar/manual	38.1	39.2	23.8	43.6	40.5
c. unskilled employment	10.2	24.3	21.3	23.3	19.0
d. self-employed	13.2	4.5	15.6	5.3	4.8
e. unemployed	2.1	1.8	—	0.7	4.8

ren, and is one of about a dozen city council housing areas accommodating between a quarter and a third of the Nairobi African population. Though exclusive ethnic enclaves do exist throughout Nairobi, it is rare to find them in areas of city council housing. Enclaves with a very high degree of ethnic exclusivity are more commonly found as pockets in the spreading areas of privately built semi-permanent housing. Certainly council estates vary in their ethnic composition, with some showing a definite tendency to attract an disproportionately high number of members of particular ethnic groups. This fact is of significance in providing ordinary townspeople with some way of geographically placing people from their own and other ethnic groups. But no estate has as high a proportion of Luo as Kaloleni and it is not only referred to as a "Luo area" but also as "the Luo headquarters".

How can we explain this inordinately high proportion of Luo and the correspondingly low proportion of Kikuyu? The grounds given by the British for singling out Kikuyu for detention, restriction and imprisonment throughout Central Province was that the Mau Mau nationalist movement was led by them. In Operation Anvil of 1952–53 Kikuyu in Nairobi were removed from ethnically mixed housing estates and concentrated in guarded areas of their own. Kaloleni estate had been built in about 1945. By the time of their removal in Operation Anvil, Kikuyu seem to have been easily the largest grouping on the estate. But thereafter it was mainly Luo who took their place.

Kaloleni was one of only a few housing estates specifically catering at that time for family accommodation. The Luo who moved into Kaloleni included a large proportion of married men with their wives and children. The Kamba, who were left undisturbed in Operation Anvil, tended by contrast to occupy the minority of bachelor quarters on the estate. This pattern has continued until present time. Like the Luo, the Luyia household heads tend to have their families with them, while Kamba, though married and with children, mostly leave theirs in their rural home areas. The Kikuyu "newcomers" to the estate tend also, like the Luo and Luyia, to bring their wives and children to live with them.

There has certainly been some residential turnover in Kaloleni among household heads of all four ethnic groups. But some are very much more settled than others as we can see by comparing their median lengths of residence in both Kaloleni and Nairobi as a whole. Thus, though the Luo have not lived much longer in Nairobi than the Kikuyu, they have been in Kaloleni for two-thirds more of the time spent there by Kikuyu. The Luyia similarly have been in the estate significantly longer than the Kikuyu, though not as long as the Luo (see Table 2 above). In other words, not only are the Luo the largest group in the estate, they are also its longest residents. They constitute a numerically dominant and long-settled ethnic core. This is particularly interesting in view of the fact that since the ending of the Emergency in 1959 many more family housing estates have been built in Nairobi, all with far better facilities and amenities. The rents at Kaloleni are correspondingly lower[1] and this may well be the primary reason disinclining many from moving on to those newer

---

[1] Being no more than Shs.160/– (in 1969) for the largest (3 rooms) and best equipped house (with lavatory and shower), including water rate and electricity, and much less for one-roomed "houses". Ross (1975, p. 28) gives the general range as 45/– to 90/– for rent without the amenities, compared with 100/– to 240/– for other more recently built estates, though again excluding water rates and electricity. Illicit sub-letting results in even higher rents.

areas. The consequence, however, is that Luo can regard Kaloleni as an area which is not only their "own" but also one in which some of their most settled members live. The older household heads among them have come to act as key figures in the organization of the Luo collectivity throughout Nairobi. To return to our contrast between the two Kaloleni beer bars, it is these Luo male elders who patronize their own rather puritanical bar where they talk, as I have noted, about politics or about the younger generation. A combination of historical and demographic factors has thus fitted them into the role by which they are now characterized. They are focal points in the definition of ethnic boundaries, of generational distance, and, as senior family men who are long settled in town with their wives and daughters, of relations between the sexes.

Luyia elders, though characterized by the same general role, do not have a particular bar which is exclusively used by them. This is related to the more fragmentary way in which Luyia conceptualize their collectivity. Indeed the term Luyia (or Luhya) only came into use in the 1940s, before when the constituent dialect groups distinguished themselves as separate but related "peoples", with no clear notion of common ancestry. This difference from the Luo remains marked today. But both Luo and Luyia elders are much concerned with the discussion of ethnic and generational relations. The one large institutional sphere which brings together both these ethnic groups, including their younger as well as older members, is that of their respective ethnic associations, nearly all of which hold their meetings in Kaloleni. The structure and viability of urban ethnic associations may not only accentuate ethnic distinctiveness but may also direct and indicate the nature of relations between ethnic groups. Among Luo and Luyia there are many such associations and many different activities connected with them, not all of which involve the elders closely. The one activity which does engage the attention of certainly the majority of Luo and Luyia males of all age categories and also of many unmarried women is the formalized soccer competition involving frequent matches between Luo and Luyia teams, as well as others, in the Nairobi city stadium immediately adjacent to Kaloleni.

It is impossible to analyse the Luo and Luyia ethnic associations without also analysing the social significance for them of soccer. We must note the often crucial part played by sport in the organization of many societies. The intense interest shown and emotional pitch reached in spectator sports in so many countries sometimes exceeds that of the world religions. And like the world religions, organized soccer, with its hierarchy of leagues, its international, national and regional distribution of fixtures spread over set seasons, and its sometimes considerable financial implications, provides foci for the expression of local distinctiveness and of wider incorporation, particularly through the mass media.

An interesting feature of the soccer fixtures in Nairobi (in 1969) is that the key matches in the Kenya championship are between Luo and Luyia teams. Though at this level Luo and Luyia are intense rivals in sport, political developments in Kenya since independence in 1963 have drawn these two peoples closer together, almost to the extent of their forming an informal alliance. This is a complete reversal of the situation before independence. Then Luo were "allied" with Kikuyu and Kamba in opposition to the Luyia and most other less numerous Kenya peoples. Now, in spite of the fact that they speak quite unrelated languages, the Luo and Luyia acknowledge their broadly similar customs and common home area of western Kenya. They still do not intermarry to any great extent, however, and in other respects maintain their distinctiveness. Rather, they stand on the threshhold of a closer association. For some time yet it will continue to be legitimate to view the Luo as an endogamous socio-cultural grouping with a remarkably high degree of agreement among its members as to what constitutes the boundaries and content of Luo customs or culture. This study is, then, focused on the Luo. Where appropriate, I compare the Luo with those other groups with whom they interact.

The ethnic framework of political activity, the powerful Luo sense of socio-cultural distinctiveness, and their almost total endogamy, are the factors which, over and above their occupational and residential dispersal, induce me to take them as my starting-point of analysis. This of course methodologically turns on its head Mitchell's (1966, p. 248) famous dictum (after Gluckman, 1961, p. 80) that "tribe" should never be an analytical starting-point in a study of an ethnically mixed town. As a warning against a priori assumptions about the relevance of apparent linguistic and cultural differences in a

c

population, this remains sound advice. But emic distinctiveness translated into an observably high degree of interaction and self-perpetuation through endogamy, as among the Luo, justify this alternative starting-point.

Luo family settlement

Having established that Kaloleni is a predominantly Luo area with a long-settled core of older household heads, we may now ask what special consequences family settlement has had for the Luo in this estate.

Luo stand apart from other ethnic groups in having (a) the largest households, (b) the largest proportion of wives resident in Nairobi at any given time, and (c) the largest proportion of children located in Nairobi.

All households in Kaloleni are large in relation to the limited room available in dwellings, as is the case in most other areas of Nairobi. The 852 houses of only one or two rooms accommodate 4,602 persons including 1,487 men (32 per cent), 852 women (19 per cent) and 2,263 children (i.e. under 16 years of age) (49 per cent) at an average of 5.4 adults and children per dwelling.[1] Luo households ex-

TABLE 3

Household size by ethnic group

	Average size of household (persons)	Average number of men per household	Average number of women per household	Average number of children per household
Luo (333 households)	6.33	1.81	1.2	3.32
Luyia (222)	5.28	1.68	0.95	2.65
Kikuyu (122)	5.02	1.69	1.04	2.29
Kamba (133)	3.85	1.83	0.59	1.43
Others (42)	4.69	1.45	0.88	2.36

[1] This is based on my own survey of late 1968. The Kenya Population Census conducted a few months later in 1969 had the following figures: a total population of 4,787, with men 1,763 (36.8 per cent), women 894 (18. per cent) and children 2,130 (44.5 per cent). The overall population total is similar considering the time between the two surveys. Men are slightly more and children slightly less numerous in the government Census, a difference which may possibly be explained by more of the older male children being counted as "adult". In any event, the difference is not great.

ceed this average not so much by having a higher proportion of men as by a higher proportion of women and children, as we can see from Table 3 (above).

Many of the Luo women in Kaloleni are wives of the heads of households or of relatives, or are themselves relatives of the heads. Nearly all household heads are men, the only exceptions being a few widows past child-bearing age. For consistency I omit them from my figures. The Luo have a much higher polygyny rate than other ethnic groups in the estate and this partly accounts for their high ratio of wives to male household heads, which is summarized in Table 4.

TABLE 4

Polygyny rate of household heads by ethnic group

	Total number of household heads	Number married	Proportion with two or more wives	Total number of wives	Ratio of wives to married heads
Luo	333	309	33.3 (103)	435	148%
Luyia	222	210	17.1 (36)	249	118%
Kikuyu	122	102	6.9 (7)	109	107%
Kamba	133	123	16.3 (20)	144	117%
Others	42	39	10.3 (4)	46	118%

The sheer fact of there being a larger "pool" of wives among Luo household heads partly explains why so many are in Nairobi: thus, among Luo polygynists senior and junior co-wives customarily alternate in residence between Nairobi and the rural home so that polygynous husbands are rarely without at least one wife with them in the city. But this is not the only reason, for when we compare monogamists alone with those of other ethnic groups, we find that the median length of residence of wives in Nairobi during the previous 12 months is still longer among Luo: for the 206 wives of monogamous Luo household heads, the median is just over six months, while for the 174 Luyia and 95 Kikuyu wives it is little more than four months and is only three months for the 103 wives of Kamba monogamists. It is true that Kikuyu, by virtue of the general proximity of their rural homes to Nairobi, can in some cases commute on a monthly or even weekly basis between their rural and urban households and so can maintain close family ties without having to base their wives and children for so much time in Kaloleni. Nevertheless, recognizing the distance of the Luo rural homeland from Nairobi, some 250 miles, the Luo in Kaloleni clearly place great stress on as much conjugal settlement in Nairobi as possible. They also wish to maintain a foothold in their rural homes, sometimes with a stated view to developing land there or, eventually, setting up a small retail business or workshop. And so, a wife is required to see to her husband's rural interests while he works full time in Nairobi. It is often remarked by Luo that a man with two wives can solve this problem of maintaing rural and urban interests simultaneously by having one with him in town and the other in the rural area. It should be noted that only 21 (20.4 per cent) of the 103 polygynists have more than two wives, which may indicate an optimal number.

It is, then, Luo co-wives of child-bearing age who normally alternate in residence between Nairobi and the rural home. Most women in fact state a preference for living in the city. Taking it in turns under the husband's supervision is the compromise to which they agree. This alternation of residence by co-wives, taken together with the movement to and from the rural home by wives of monogamists, results in there being a constant, overall circulation of Luo wives between town and country, with husbands who are household heads remaining relatively fixed points of reference in Nairobi.

Children under school age accompany their mothers between town and country. But from the age of six or seven, a large proportion of the children of Luo household heads are sent to schools in and around Nairobi. The older the child, the more likely is he or she to

TABLE 5

Ratios of children currently in Nairobi or the rural home by ethnic group

	Household heads with children	Their total number of children	Children currently at the rural home (per household)	Children currently in Nairobi (per household)
Luo	307	1,586	1.87	3.27
Luyia	201	1,016	2.41	2.64
Kikuyu	109	523	2.29	2.56
Kamba	120	591	3.34	1.58
Others	40	197	2.35	2.58

be undergoing schooling or, at a later date, formal training for a trade in Nairobi.

When we compare the families of other ethnic groups in Kaloleni, we see how pronounced is the Luo propensity to locate their children in Nairobi, primarily to give them education or training, but also to find the older ones jobs (see Table 5 above).

A Luo household head, then, has many more of his children with him in Kaloleni. Finally, as Table 6 shows, he sends significantly more of his children to school or for training in Nairobi, rather than in his rural home area.

TABLE 6

Ratios of children at school in town or country by ethnic group

	Number of children at school in the rural home area	Number of children at school or college in Nairobi
Luo (307 household heads)	316 (1.03 per household)	596 (1.94 per household)
Luyia (201)	252 (1.25)	294 (1.46)
Kikuyu (109)	142 (1.30)	153 (1.40)
Kamba (120)	197 (1.64)	98 (0.82)
Others (40)	42 (1.05)	55 (1.38)

This propensity among Luo to locate wives and children in Nairobi has been evident for some years and has been noted by observers in other towns (Halpenny, 1975, p. 278; Mushanga, 1975, pp. 160–1). It is particularly misleading in the case of Luo children and adolescents to ask whether they were actually born in Nairobi and to use this is an index of their "exposure" to the town or their "urbanization rate". For it has been and still is far more common for Luo women "normally" living in Nairobi to deliver their children at their husband's rural homes rather than in Nairobi itself. But a Luo mother will be expected to return to her husband in Nairobi with her child a few months after its birth and thereafter to alternate every six months or so between town and country as she had been doing previously. It follows that Luo children and adolescents who have been brought up in this way are numerous. In Kaloleni practically all the children and adolescents of Luo household heads are having this kind of upbringing, and it is calculated that even including the youngest children, nearly three quarters of them have spent as much or significantly more time in Nairobi than at their rural homes, with most of the older ones at school or undergoing training for a job. Indeed, the older the child and the closer he or she is to adolescence, the more time he will have lived in Nairobi, eventually living there on what he and others regard as a virtually permanent basis and only visiting his rural home for no more than a few weeks at a time. As Table 7 shows, the proportion of children and adolescents who have spent at least two-thirds of their lives in Nairobi, in some cases having been born there, is much higher among the Luo of Kaloleni. It exceeds even that of the Kikuyu, though, again, the proximity of Kikuyu country to Nairobi does mean that many of their children can still be involved in the city while actually resident for most of their time in their rural homes.

TABLE 7

Proportions of all children and adolescents (of Kaloleni household heads) predominantly reared in Nairobi

	Total number of household heads with children	Total number of children of household heads	Proportion predominantly reared in Nairobi
Luo	307	1,586	58.7% (931)
Luyia	201	1,016	48.9% (497)
Kikuyu	109	523	49.1% (257)
Kamba	120	591	26.6% (157)
Others	40	197	47.2% (93)

As they approach adolescence, girls are only about half as likely as boys to remain in Nairobi and less likely also to continue at school. It is recognized that an educated daughter is an asset to a family. This is partly because the bridewealth received for her is greater than if she is uneducated and partly because, as Luo parents almost invariably claim, "daughters are more likely than sons to care for you when you are old", and that an educated daughter who may be earning independently of her husband is more easily able to do this effectively. In spite of this, boys generally do get a larger share of the domestic budget spent on their school fees than girls, especially in polygynous families in which co-wives strive to strengthen their own sons's positions against those of their half-brothers. Nevertheless, a substantial number of Luo adolescent girls do receive education or training in Nairobi. Though very few of them achieve a genuinely superior level of education sufficient to equip them for a salaried occupation, they advertize the possibilities at least of a radical change in Luo women's status and so, indirectly, influence ideas and, in the case of many men, fears regarding the future pattern of family life.

The bridging of rural and urban relationships

Weisner (1969) has aptly characterized the general kind of situation described here in the title of a paper "One family—two households" (i.e. rural and urban), about a Luyia group in Nairobi. There may be a number of variations on this model. The Luo family in Kaloleni has a father/husband almost permanently tied to a job in Nairobi and so resident there. Such men have shown very little job turnover, especially since employment opportunities have slackened in recent years, and so do not engage in circulatory migration backwards and forwards between town and country every few years, of the kind described by Mitchell (1959) for an earlier period. Constantly moving between the father/husband and his rural home is his wife and her younger children, with older children, increasingly boys, staying on in Nairobi for longer periods with their father until, and very much if, they get a job, marry and live independently.

This particular family straddling of an urban and a distant rural homeland is probably quite widespread in Africa. Cohen (1969, pp. 51–70) described a migratory cycle of traders combined with their family settlement in a Hausa ethnic enclave in Ibadan. This example, that of the Luo and others from outside Africa (e.g. Hammel and Yarborough, 1973, on Belgrade), suggest that we view a migratory process not necessarily as somehow transitional between a wholly rural or urban state of existence, but as enabling some degree of urban family settlement to be combined with the maintenance of the family's rural interests. Luo men stay in Nairobi to earn, while wives and younger children move between town and country, with older children increasingly adopting a rough pattern set by their parents: boys and some girls stay in Nairobi and some girls eventually move back to the rural home to be married. While town represents for Luo more the forces of economic production, country represents those of biological reproduction in the idiom of self- and cultural perpetuation through descent.

The mobility of wives and daughters is crucial to the system in two main ways. First, the marriages of urban-dwelling men largely take place in the rural area, but are preceded by extended and complicated arrangements initiated by a "go-between" (*jagam*), usually characterized as an urban "friend". This ensures continuity of rural and urban relationships among a wide range of fellow Luo. Second, the systematic movement of their wives between town and country enables townsmen to retain and work their rural land.

The rural marriages of townsmen

Luo men in Nairobi continue to arrange customary marriages in the rural areas by handing over bridewealth to the bride's parents, whether or not they also undergo civil or church weddings in the city. Bridewealth now mainly takes the form of cash, with a value of at least K.Shs. 3,500/– (about £175 or U.S. $490) in 1969. The contacts leading to the eventual choice of bride are frequently, and increasingly, urban: a wife-seeker in Nairobi has a girl recommended to him by a trusted friend who may become the go-between, and who is also living in the city (see Parkin, 1969, p. 109; and Grillo, 1973, pp. 52–5). She may be the friend's full or classificatory sister, but is often the sister of his own friend, not necessarily known to the prospective groom (see Chapter 3). Whether or not the girl may have previously lived in Nairobi or some other town for a long time, she is likely to be living in her rural home when recommended, sometimes having just been strategically sent back there from town at a prospective go-between's discreet suggestion. Of all the 435 wives of the 309 married Luo household heads in Kaloleni, only 45 first met their husbands in Nairobi or in some other town, while the rest were first introduced to their husbands in rural Luoland via go-betweens.

Most marriages of Luo men in Kaloleni are with Luo women with due account taken of rules of maximal lineage (i.e. the "clan" of Evans-Pritchard, 1965, p. 213) exogamy about which Luo elders are regarded as the best informed. In so far as marriage among Luo, whether initiated in town or country, continues to observe exogamous boundaries, it involves an exchange of men and women between units usually called "clans" in English, and in Luo *dhoudi* (sing. *dhoot*). Marriage is prohibited with a girl of one's mother's and mother's mother's maximal exogamous lineages (and in theory beyond this if traceable), but is normally "resumed" with these lineages after these two generations have passed. Sororal polygyny occurs, and brothers may marry into the same lineage as each other. This delayed or direct exchange between lineages is also along a rural–urban dimension: women are constantly being married to men earning in Nairobi, who then periodically direct their wives back into the rural area to manage their land. There, a wife gradually becomes incorporated in the husband's homestead, becomes familiar with the internal lines of segmentation of the maximal exogamous lineage into which she has married, and so eventually comes to see her own sons' and daughters' prospective marriages as regulated by the rules of exogamy.

The rural role of wives

Nearly all Luo claim to "have" land worth cultivating for subsistence and to a lesser extent for cash crops, though as the small acreages given below suggest, money earned from cash cropping can rarely do more than supplement the higher incomes earned from urban wage employment. Only 34 household heads (i.e. 10 per cent) say that they have no land at all, and 22 (i.e. 7 per cent) have more than one plot. There are two main categories of land. First, most Luo land is "family" land which has been, or in a few cases will be, inherited from a father or father's brother and in many cases was or is part of his compound polygynous family property. Second, a small but not insignificant proportion of land has been "purchased", either informally from a neighbour or relative, or on a government settlement scheme.[1] Purchased land is 15 per cent of the total acreage farmed by these Luo and is held by 15 per cent of those who have land of either kind. The median size of all plots is just over eight acres.[2] Only 17.5 per cent of the family and informally purchased

---

[1] These are mainly the Muhuroni, Lambwe and Kitale schemes.
[2] Assessing farming plots by acreage is fraught with uncertainties and it is difficult to know how inaccurate assessments are. As a median, over eight acres seems high and may well be land shared with brothers, though attempts were made in questioning to obtain assessments of individual entitlements and "ownership". It is to be hoped that any errors are at least consistent throughout the sample, and so provide some comparative impressions, which is all that this analysis requires.

plots have been registered by the owner with the government district office. The conclusion to be drawn, then, is that not only are the overwhelming number of plots held by Luo household heads in Kaloleni family land, but also that, in default of their ownership being registered, members of the family must continue to be relied upon to guard and supervise the use of the land during the plot-holder's virtually permanent residence in Nairobi.

In all there are 321 rural plots at least nominally owned or held by 299 Luo household heads. When we compare the range of relatives who are cited as currently responsible for the maintenance of these plots, we see the importance placed on wives in this role of guardian (see Table 8).

TABLE 8

Persons currently regarded by the owner as looking after his land

	Grand-father	Father	Father's brother	Full brother	Half-brother	Paternal cousin	Maternal cousin	Wife	Any other
321 rural plots	2	115	15	54	7	1	0	108	19
100%	0.6%	35.8	4.7	16.8	2.2	0.3	—	33.6	5.9

For men under forty, fathers and brothers tend to perform the role of land-guardian. But as they get older and as their fathers die and their brothers themselves migrate away from the rural area, wives are much more likely to be given the role. Given that wives spend on average only six months in the rural area, men with only one wife have to find a replacement during the wife's period in Nairobi. Men with two or more wives, who are generally older than monogamists, alternate the residence of their wives between town and rural home and so are less affected by the deaths of agnates of the parental generation and by their brothers' migration away from the rural area.

This special Luo use of wives to supervise rural farms at an advanced stage of a townsman's life suggests an extension of Watson's familiar thesis drawn from his data on the central African Mambwe. Watson demonstrated that the rural patrilineal extended family of the Mambwe provided a sufficiently large pool of agnates for some of them to migrate to town and for others to remain behind and look after the family land. Luo brothers and other agnates do perform

Plate 1a. A wife in Kaloleni.

Plate 1b. A wife at the rural home.

[*Facing* p.53

this role, but so, too, can men's wives as a result of their systematic movement between town and country. The high rate of Luo polygyny means that many urban-dwelling men can reduce their dependence on brothers and agnates for this role. Polygyny among the Mambwe, by contrast, characterized men who had already retired from urban wage labour, usually by the age of thirty (1958, p. 225).

Polygyny and family settlement

A high degree of urban family settlement among Luo in Nairobi, then, is counterbalanced by a marked "ruralization" of marriage choices and arrangements and by the use of wives and close agnates to look after rural land. To repeat, this straddling of urban and rural interests is made possible by the circulation of women and children between the two households. All married Luo household heads shift their families in this way, but it is recognized by Luo themselves that polygynists simply have the extra wives and, usually, also children to do it more frequently and with different consequences. One consequence is that a polygynist tends at any one time to have at least one of his wives and some of her children living with him in his Nairobi home, justified, Luo say, by the custom that co-wives should not live in the same house (in this case urban). A polygynist's household in Kaloleni, therefore, nearly always has a basic nuclear family in it, which consists of himself, and a wife and younger children who are periodically replaced by a co-wife and other younger children coming from the rural home: adolescent children may also be members of the urban household. Unlike the monogamists, most of whom are young and without adolescent offspring, the polygynists in Nairobi are unlikely to spend periods amounting to about half a year without either their wives or children with them in Nairobi.

In sum, then, urban polygyny among these Luo provides the greatest possibility of nuclear family settlement in Nairobi but also enables a man to retain a foothold in his rural home. Far from diminishing as a result of increased family settlement in Nairobi by Luo, polygyny has thrived as an institution partly because it has enabled men to build and maintain a viable bridge between a full-time career in urban employment and their interests in agricultural land at home.

The term for a polygynist, *jadoho*, enables the conceptualization of the advantages to be bracketed together with associated ideas of "traditional" respect and authority. The root of the term *doho*[1] refers to a customary moot or court, with the implication that a polygynist is *ipso facto* an elder worthy enough to arbitrate. *Jadoho*, a polygynist, now comes to mean someone who both satisfies traditional ideas of status achievement and, by successfully straddling rural and urban economic and political interests, modern ones as well.

Polygyny and the forces of disorder

While the Luo themselves see the circulation of co-wives between town and country as persisting because it provides these practical advantages, there are customary rules to do with co-wives' seniority which also perpetuate the system. Indeed, since the seniority rules existed before the Luo migrated and settled their families in Nairobi, we can argue that these ideological factors actually preceded the utilitarian ones. Both then come together as mutually self-justifying.

The rules are that the first wife, *mikayi*, should always take up residence before the second (*nyachira*) or subsequent wives (*rero*) in any movement from one household to another. Thus, if the second wife is currently in the urban home, and the first in the rural, then the second wife must join the first wife in the rural home before the first wife moves to the urban home. The first wife must always "lead" as the Luo say. The same precedence applies in the relationship between a second and third wife, and so on. A mystical affliction called *chira* bringing sickness and death to the family may result from breaking this rule. The belief has assumed considerable importance in Nairobi as I show in Chapter 5.

But it is often only after a diviner has diagnosed the causes of a crisis that the mystical beliefs take on significance. In every culture there are some men and women who happily ignore the "superstitious" in the course of their everyday lives, attributing belief in it to the "ignorance" of others and claiming that a break of the taboo would

---

[1] Like some other Luo terms long credited with "traditional" significance, this is probably of Bantu origin.

not affect themselves. But a catastrophe occurs and the doubter re-examines and widens his explanations of misfortunes.

On the whole, men and their co-wives in Nairobi do observe the rules of co-wife seniority. But the rules are sometimes ignored. A senior co-wife may feel that she has been left too long at the rural home by her husband and, resentful at the apparent favour enjoyed by the second wife in town with her husband, may insist on joining them before the second wife has joined her. Or it may be that the junior co-wife herself refuses to leave the urban home. The inevitable quarrels and resentment between co-wives are said by Luo to result from *nyiego* (jealousy), which is linked to the term for co-wife, *nyieka*,[1] and both of which derive from the verb *nyiego*, to snatch suddenly and by surprise (Southall, 1952, p. 20).

Luo use the term *nyiego* to refer to jealousy generally, between men as well as between women. Indeed, it occurs frequently in their conversations. As in the occasional cases in which co-wives struggle against each other and ignore, or induce their husbands to ignore, the prohibitions surrounding the rules of co-wife seniority, so, generally, the Luo see *nyiego* as a random, potentially uncontrollable element in their lives. It is cited as a major reason that Luo, as they themselves allege, have not cooperated in business ventures, politically, or in welfare development schemes. A different word, *libamba*, clearly connotes rivalry between complementarily opposed lineage segments which is ultimately reconcilable through subordination to a higher lineage (cf. Southall, 1952, pp. 6, 28). But *nyiego*, whatever its original referent, is nowadays the nearest word to translate what we normally understand by the term "fission" or the "general" segmentation inherent in all politics and social organization (Southall, 1965, pp. 126–7; Smith, 1974, p. 27, 1965, p. 64). It approaches anarchy without order. When *nyiego* disrupts relationships between urban-dwelling co-wives, order can be restored by pointing to the status-names of *mikayi*, *nyachira*, and *rero* as indicating the boundaries of obligations which must be observed, the breach of which incurs or is diagnosed as having incurred the mystical affliction *chira*. When the Luo community itself is seen to be split apart by the same force of *nyiego*, in the way I describe in Chapter 7, order is then

[1] Though other cultures have a similar linking of term and concept, e.g. the Hausa for co-wife is *kishiya* and jealousy is *kishi*, its full significance among Luo draws on the wider segmentary lineage structure.

restored by appeal to the ideal polygynous family nature of the relations of Luo groups with each other. We shall in due course see
how the alternating interpersonal struggles and order in urban polygynous households are seen to mirror the way in which Luo leaders
define the political constitution and responses of the Luo people as
a whole.

Let me briefly illustrate this idea that the strict observance of co-
wife seniority is helped by each wife having distinct status-names.

1. Onyango brought his newly married wife (*miaha*) to Nairobi. His first wife
(*mikayi*) had gone on ahead of them and she was able to welcome them when
they arrived. She herself had seven children (four sons and three girls) and was
still fertile. Here it may be noted that relatively few polygynous marriages
occur simply as a result of a first wife's apparent barrenness. Barrenness is more
likely to result in divorce, following a succession of quarrels and separation. A
first wife's apparent inability to produce sons does seem likely to induce a
husband to marry a second wife, but there are many cases like that of
Onyango where other motives and pressures operate.

The first wife left Nairobi and returned to their rural home as is the custom.
Onyango's bride was then welcomed and entertained by his friends in Nairobi.
This is the custom of *budho miaha* (conversing with/entertaining the new
wife). It is normally a difficult time both for the new wife and the husband. She
is expected to present herself as a dutiful and hospitable future wife, and able
to accept the banter and teasing, and to parry the sexual innuendos. The husband has to provide a lavish supply of beer for his friends and appear the ideal
host while at the same time watch out for any liaisons his friends may be attempting to make with his new wife.

Onyango seemed particularly anxious regarding the latter, especially since
his new wife soon overcame the shyness normally characteristic of the event. She
proved to be as confident in the months following as that first welcoming suggested, and expressed a very strong preference for city living. She persuaded
her husband to keep her in town with him for over a year by which time she
became pregnant. Friends and relatives observed that she was now really
nyachira (second wife, i.e. no longer just *miaha*).

The first wife (*mikayi*) had, through her sisters in Nairobi, been expressing
resentment that her husband had not sent the second wife to join her at the
rural home now that she was pregnant, to enable the first to take her "turn"
in town. The sisters told the husband who did nothing.

Finally, defying the custom that a second wife should never "receive" a first
wife in the home, the first wife came to Nairobi, accusing the husband of
favouritism and of sending more of his salary to help the second wife's parents
than to her own. Quarrels developed and neither co-wife would return home.
A brother, a half-brother and two lineage elders living in Nairobi were
brought into the affair and, at a characteristically formal Luo domestic meet-

ing, presided over by one of the elders in his late fifties, warned the husband and co-wives of the possibility of *chira* coming to the family and lineage if this matter were not settled and reversed. They reiterated the point, with a style and emphasis that indicated that it was beyond question that a *mikayi* must always be respected above a *nyachira*, whatever the husband's personal preference for the latter, just as *nyachira* must always take precedence over *rero* (third wife). They blamed the husband for his foolishness and wondered whether he was really worthy of being a *jadoho* (polygynist) and also scolded the second wife for her "modern ways". *Manyasi* (medicine) was brought into the house for purification of the "sin" (*rochruok*) committed, which might otherwise have caused *chira*. The husband apologized to the meeting, and the second wife went back to the husband's rural home with the first wife and one of her sisters. The first wife returned to the husband in Nairobi immediately, having exerted her power through the power of the belief in *chira*.

A *jadoho* clearly has a reputation to make and live up to and may, in extreme cases, react desperately.

2. A policeman in his mid-thirties brought his new wife, whom he had married against his first wife's wishes, to stay with him in Nairobi. The first wife, who had three young children, persistently refused to return to the rural home (in Asembo location), and demanded more time in town. The husband, by way of a possible compromise, told the second wife, still termed a *miaha*, to return instead. She replied: "I have never been to your home without you, always the first wife has been there before me. How can you expect me to return there without you and ahead of her? You know that is strictly against Luo customs. Do you want me to fail to produce children (i.e. reference to *chira*)? I have only just been married and I should be here with you. I cannot go home."

The two co-wives refused to speak to each other and eat together, the latter a powerful symbol of enmity, each cooking her own food separately in the same one-roomed house. The husband angrily demanded that they both return home because they were "shaming" him in the town. They refused. One day, in January 1969, after returning from work in the evening, he covered himself in a blanket, poured petrol over it, and set fire to himself. The co-wives screamed, and neighbours (who were fellow police employees living in the Police Quarters of Shaurimoyo) stifled the fire. The husband was taken to hospital where he spent some weeks. Elders called a formal meeting and severely reprimanded the two co-wives who, very shocked by the affair, dutifully obeyed their commands to return to the rural home, treat each other "like sisters", and in future follow Luo rules.

We see that co-wife rivalries implicitly challenge a polygynist's ability to exercise domestic authority. When co-wives manage to reconcile their jealousies, they may become a formidable force in redefining a marriage. A husband then really has to work hard for the title of *jadoho*. Most succeed even if sometimes they need support from other senior men as in the above cases. Occasionally they fail, and news of their failure and the implication of female power behind it spreads throughout the Luo community in Nairobi and sometimes beyond. This, for men, is the threat of anarchy without order. I cite the following case at length, including verbatim a husband's rare acknowledgement of his inadequacy as a polygynist.

3. A clerk from Sakwa location had three wives. The first was at home with her young children who were at school there. The second and third, both from Kano and originally friends, were with the husband in Nairobi, in Kaloleni. Both were in their early twenties but had not yet produced children, after three and two years' marriage respectively. These two co-wives argued with each other that their husband should sleep with them every night, not on alternate nights, having (ostensibly) become anxious about their ability to become pregnant. The husband was unable to meet this demand and, after weeks of quarrelling with each other while he was at work during the day, the co-wives turned upon him with a knife and drove him from the house. Much distressed, he later returned, when matters had cooled, collected his mattress and personal belongings and left to stay with a friend in Jericho, a nearby housing estate. He let the two co-wives keep the rest of the furniture. They eventually turned to brewing *buzaa*, a Luo beer popular in Nairobi, and brought two younger sisters to help them.

The husband's friends and relatives including elders were amazed at this, pointing out that disagreements were a normal problem when wives were slow to produce children. They urged him to return to them but he refused. They said, "You know we shall help you and take them home [i.e. the husband's rural home]". He replied: "I have had nothing but quarrelling from them and have complained to their separate parents who blame me for everything, for not controlling them properly. What more can I do?" An example of the reply by his friends and relatives was: "According to Luo traditions, it is very shameful indeed for a man to be sacked from his house by his own wife. Do you know that they are able to pay the house rent only by having become prostitutes? [Beer brewing by 'independent' women is associated with prostitution, though in this case there was no apparent evidence.] You paid enough bridewealth (*ninyombo maber*) and so you had better get it back, or go back with them."

The husband answered: "Look, I have tried and I cannot control them. Some of my family in Nairobi have helped and we have also failed. I am content now to stay with my first wife and our children until I die. I don't want anyone commenting or interfering in my affairs. It is because they must have been prostitutes before that they did not produce children. I know them."

The friends asked: "Are you going to leave all that bridewealth to their parents, then? As they have not produced and were the cause of the separation, then according to Luo customs, the bridewealth must be returned."

The husband answered: "I am still alive and I am not a poor man. Trying to get the bridewealth back will cost me a lot in expenses and time. I paid for the bridewealth from my own cash earnings. No one helped me. I shall not even ask for my furniture back. I have plenty at home. Anyway, their parents will co-operate in getting some other wives instead, because they are annoyed at how these two have turned out. So don't worry on my account, my friends. I know what I am doing. I am leading a happy life now."

We should note the husband's ambivalence, later interpreted by his friends as unmanly equivocation. On the one hand, the husband seems not to want his failure as a polygynist to be further publicized in an attempt to regain his bridewealth, which, as in other comparable cases, could certainly have been done through his lineage and location association in collaboration with the Chief (a Luo) of the nearby Makadara Court. He claims that he will content himself with his one wife and children. On the other hand, he points out that the co-wives' parents are themselves disappointed in the women and will find replacements. He had, incidentally, earlier mentioned their criticism of him. By the time I had left the field a few months later, nothing had been settled, though the husband's relatives had successfully obtained the co-wives' respective parents' agreement that they find substitute wives.

His friends' comments afterwards showed concern less for the "broken Luo customs" but more for his feeble and unmanly withdrawal, and observed that if more Luo men took such a weak line then they would all be dominated by their womenfolk. For men, "order" in Luo customs here means continuing male control over the domestic sphere, while "disorder" means women's threats to it.

It is relevant here to note some other terms making up the semantic domain of "womanhood": *nyako* (pl. *nyiri*) means unmarried girl and is the "respectable" term, as distinct from *gigo* (literally "those things" and also used for "money") as used by young men for unmarried and therefore accessible girls; *dhako* (*mon*) means "mature" woman with the implication that she must also be, or previously have been, married; *miaha*, as already described, connotes the liminal status of the woman who is not yet a "full" wife and is entitled to the light-hearted conversational attention of other men notionally until she becomes pregnant by her husband; the root term *chi-* means "wife" as in the possessive form *chi-ega*, my wife, and is also used as a prefix for certain other kinship relationships through a wife; finally, the term *wuon ot* (literally owner of the hut or "house" from which, ideally, emerges the patrilineage of uterine brothers) may refer to a monogamously married wife as the senior woman of a household, or to his mother (*min-*) by a son without distinction as to whether she is his father's first or subsequent co-wife. Here it may be noted that, at the overlapping boundaries of the semantic domains of "womanhood" and "manhood", the term *ja-ot* (the man/person of the hut) is a term that may be used of a man who is a monogamist but may also be used to refer to a man's wife or mother in the same way as the "feminine" *wuon ot*. *Wuon dala/pacho* means owner of the homestead, which by definition comprises more than one *ot* or hut including that of the husband and one for each of his wives. The term nearly always refers to a man but may be used of either a monogamist or polygynist, provided that he is the senior male.

These terms connote varying degrees of status ambiguity. For example: At what age does an unmarried girl (*nyako*) have to be reclassified as *dhako*, even though she has never, for whatever reason, been married? When does a "new wife" cease being referred to as *miaha* if, after some time, she is still not pregnant? What are the full semantic implications of calling a man *ja-ot*, as distinct from *wuon dala*, in view of its semantic near-equivalence to *wuon ot*, the senior female? Does *ja-ot* refer simply and innocently in a particular situation to his monogamous status or, as was sometimes pointed out to me, to the innuendo that he only has "one house", and is therefore like a wife/woman?

By contrast the status names for polygynist, *jadoho*, and for first, second, and subsequent wife, *mikayi*, *nyachira*, and *rero*, are quite unambiguous. Use of the one term presupposes the others. It is precisely this semantic order that is imposed by elders in their formalized and rhetorical speeches admonishing conformity to the customary hierarchy of family relations. In this context the potential of these terms for illocutionary effect derives from their unquestionable assumptions of unambiguous status hierarchy. They can be used to smother the implicit threat of the *nyiego* or jealousy inherent in polygyny. I do not claim that such unambiguously defined status terms by themselves necessarily determine hierarchy, but rather that, in conjunction with its practical and ideological underpinnings, they may play a significant role in stifling discussion about the hierarchy.

Later in the book I shall show that though discussion about polygyny may be stifled in this way, underlying if tacit changes in the status of women may still occur.

Summary and conclusion

One result of the Kenya Emergency in Nairobi in the early fifties was the creation of a large core of Luo residents in Kaloleni, one of the city's few public housing estates. This was achieved by the removal and concentration elsewhere of Kikuyu residents. Numerous Luo families were thereafter able to settle in Kaloleni and were the first large, local grouping of Luo to do so. Kaloleni attracted prominent Luo to the estate, which also became the locus for meetings of its sectional ethnic associations and the more widely representative Luo Union. Since the ending of the Emergency in 1959, the proportion of Luo residents has dropped and that of Kikuyu increased, reflecting a general trend in Nairobi as a whole, but the Luo still preponderate at Kaloleni.

In spite of their increasing dependency on urban wage employment, most Luo in Nairobi still marry a girl "chosen" from a rural area. The girl may previously have lived, or may still be living, in Nairobi under the care or supervision of her parents, but Luo conceive of this as a "rural" marriage, provided she is returned to her rural home once the possibility of marriage has been broached. An "urban" marriage is with a girl who was chosen while she was actually living in Nairobi and may imply that her parents were unable to control her behaviour, including premarital relations with other men. Given the considerable circulatory movement of children, including adolescent girls, between rural Luoland and Nairobi, this distinction is essentially conceptual and more a moral judgement on a girl and her family than a statement about her actual physical location.

As we shall see in Chapter 3, the role of the urban "go-between" (jagam) in arranging a rural marriage for a fellow townsman friend has assumed great importance. On the one hand, he harmonizes marriage relations between town and country. On the other hand, his mediatory role highlights the conflict expressed by men between the demanding obligations of kinship and the promised freedom of friendship: the urban go-between is normally an unrelated male friend and so is part of a set of alternative urban relationships to those of kin, yet he is also the instrument by which customary rural marriages for townsmen involving kin are perpetuated.

Luo family "settlement" in Nairobi has taken an unusual form. Luo have the highest proportion of wives and children in Kaloleni at any one time; but these wives and their younger children move periodically every six months or so between Kaloleni and the family's rural home; husband/fathers work and live permanently in Nairobi together with older and adolescent children, who are being educated or are employed, or who seek education or employment in Nairobi.

In the rural area, fathers eventually die, and brothers may eventually migrate away from the rural home. In the absence of these men, wives assume even more the role of guardian and supervisor of a townsman's rural land, while freeing him to continue in full-time employment in Nairobi.

This straddling of urban and rural homes and interests operates most efficiently in polygynous families, for co-wives and their children are able to alternate with each other every few months between living in town with the husband/father and living at the rural home without him. The result is that polygynists in Kaloleni are rarely without a wife and children: in other words, polygyny enables a man to head a nuclear family in Nairobi all the year round.

The polygyny rate among Luo is much higher than that of other groups, and one in every three Luo household heads in Kaloleni is polygynous. Though it is quite possible that an increasing growing proportion of young and highly educated Luo men and women will in future reject formal polygyny, the persistence of this modified institution among a people who have been migrating to and living in urban areas throughout East Africa for generations is significant. "Modernization" theories suggest that nuclear families will replace extended ones in the development of urban communities and industrialization. While it is perfectly true that the compound polygynous family does not exist among Luo in Nairobi, polygyny has actually made it possible for a nuclear family "form" to operate there but with regular circulation of the constituent wife and younger children. This is an ingenious adaptation of a customary "form" among a people for whom rural and urban interests are complementary rather than conflicting.

Some of the ideas and practices traditionally associated with polygyny have clearly had to "change" in order to adapt to the new ecology of rural–urban living. The strongest element of continuity of this customary "form", then, are the status-names and role-terms for co-wives, *mikayi*, *nyachira*, and *rero*; for polygynist, *jadoho*; and the associated terms, *nyieka*, and *nyiego*, for co-wife and jealousy; and *chira* for the mystical affliction which may arise from such jealousy or for other reasons. Through the situational use of such terms in formal domestic meetings involving elders and younger people, the otherwise shifting concepts and practices covered by what we term polygyny, are kept in some ordered relationship with each other. In this way, polygyny persists. However, polygyny is also seen as incompatible with other developments occurring within the Luo community, to which I now turn.

2

Conflicting Commitments

Polygyny and Education

Many children for little education

Luo recognize the advantage of polygyny in bridging rural and urban family interests, but paradoxically they may also claim that an extra wife and children waste family money and resources that could be invested in advanced education for a few rather than elementary education for many children, or even in the purchase of a business or land. It is indeed a fact that Luo polygynists do have more children than monogamists. Individual Luo, both men and women, express ambivalence about this as a possible advantage. The same person will make contrasting judgements at different times, i.e. in the impromptu conversations of everyday life, at family crises, or in response to questions posed in formal surveys.

Regarding the latter, I interviewed a quasi-random sample of every fifth Luo household in Kaloleni, which comprised 64 male household heads (most married), 65 of their wives, interviewed separately, and asked what family sizes they regarded as ideal. Ideals vary according to the respondent's sex, own family size, age, and education, though not always as widely as might be expected. Thus, women's ideal number of children is only slightly fewer than their husband's, with an average of 7.1 (median 6.5) as against 8.1 (median 7.0), with both men and wives preferring roughly equal proportions of boys and girls. Fourteen men in managerial, highly technical and professional (i.e. teachers) occupations report a very low average ideal of only 3.9 children, but 24 male clerical workers have an average ideal of 7.9 as against the average of 9.0 among 26 blue-collar, skilled and unskilled workers. Eighteen men educated to Ordinary School Certificate level (twelve years and more) claim as ideal an average of 6.7 children as against 46 men with less than this educational level who prefer 8.6.

If we compare the 29 men who have had secondary education of any level with the 35 who have only primary or no education, the difference is much the same: 7.0 as against 8.9. Finally, while 24 men with incomes over Shs.1,000/– see 6.7 children as ideal compared with the average of 8.8 of 40 men earning less than this, the average ideal among eleven earning more than Shs.1,500/– is 7.3. This suggests a U-curve in the relationship between income and ideal family size.

The occupational and educational spread of the wives is too limited to enable inferences to be drawn, though it may be noted that the very few young wives with secondary education do prefer fewer children than others.

With regard to the men, there is a polarized clustering of these factors, except for that of income. Thus, young, relatively well-educated monogamists in well-paid managerial, highly technical and professional jobs state a preference for fewer children than the ideal given by older, less educated polygynists in well-paid blue- and white-collar jobs. But whereas the former are very few in the Luo community as a whole, the latter are more numerous. Between them are the men of average socio-economic status who are, in a sense, caught between the conflicting ideals of large as against small families, and polygyny as against monogamy.

How will these ideals match up to future family sizes? We cannot answer this yet, but it is worth noting that the ideal average of 7.0 children (median 6.5) given by both men and women in the sample as a whole is only slightly lower than the actual average number of 7.5 in families headed by the oldest husbands (50 years of age and more), which most closely approximate "final" size. Monogamists over 50 years of age, most of whose wives are no longer fertile, have an average 6.4 children, which is smaller than the ideal of men and women of all ages in the sample. Polygynists of this age, most of whom have at least one wife still fertile, have an average 8.3 children, suggesting that the individual preferences of some co-wives, if they are to be taken literally, have yet to be met or, if these women are now past child-bearing, remain unfulfilled.

Complementing these attitudes acquired by formal questioning are those which are expressed spontaneously during the normal flow of daily life or during periods of sickness and death in one's own family or in that of a relative, friend or neighbour. Here we notice often striking differences of opinion expressed at different times by the same person. As an example, a Luo clerk in his late twenties and with Ordinary School Certificate education, whom I know well and who genuinely appeared to value education for few children as more suited to his aspirations than polygyny producing many children, later yielded to pressure from his own family to marry a second wife. His only younger brother had now married and his parents were worried that the small number of grandchildren would be unable to "defend" their unregistered family land from encroachment by agnatic neighbours. The man earned nearly Shs.1,000/- a month and had the "surplus" cash, in their eyes, to marry again. But the "surplus" was clearly not going to be sufficient to keep more than two or three children at school beyond the primary level.

As another example, a relatively well-educated man and his wife told how they had once expressed interest in controlling the size of their family by going to the family planning clinic. But two of their four children became seriously ill after having measles with complications, and they vowed never to consider such measures again and to continue to produce "as God wishes". In yet another, tragic example, a couple are both carriers of sickle-cell anaemia which has afflicted three of their four children. The hospital prognosis is bad. They have also spent a small fortune on traditional diagnosis and medicines but to no avail. The husband is under pressure to marry a second wife and is now willing to do so, but was once against this as a "waste of money". The wife confided her suspicion that her husband has been "roaming" with other women and may have inflicted the children with *chira*, a wasting disease (see Chapter 6), and, though the diviners have never even hinted at this as a cause, she is encouraging him to take a second wife as a way of curbing his alleged outside relationships.

One could go on. These are cases involving couples with average or above average education and income. The uncertainties are certainly as great among other couples. The cases explain the ambivalence and inconsistencies in attitudes to an ideal family size which centre on the fear of losing children through sickness and question whether it is therefore wise to educate a few children to a high standdard or to have many and hope that, from among them, some will succeed. The latter is often given as a reason for large families.

In short, men and women of all ages and educational levels recognize the modern financial problems of a large family and sometimes state a preference for few children. But they continue to have more, sometimes taking a second wife, rather than taking positive steps to limit or retard the family's size. This is not just a matter of apathy or of lack of access to birth control facilities. Imposed, so to speak, on this underlying commitment to family growth is the observable and oft-mentioned fact that a man or his wife with many children does receive commensurate respect as one who has gone some way to perpetuating his or her own name in successive generations: the husband is a potential lineage founder, and each of his co-wives may be eponymously remembered as the founder of a lineage segment produced by her sons (Southall, 1952, p. 6). Indeed, if a woman does have an interest in being remembered in lineage perpetuity, she can only do so by producing sons as a man's co-wife. For this reason she may conceivably encourage her husband to take a second wife, whose own sons will produce a lineage segment eponymously distinct from and junior to that of the first wife's.

In addition to these long-term benefits, prolific parents are regarded as "secure" in their old age. None of these benefits, nor the fears of child mortality, need by themselves push doubting men and women from monogamy to polygyny. But their combined effect, backed up by pressure from their own parents and close agnates, seems likely to do so if the cash for bridewealth becomes available.

Luo are quite unambivalent as to the potential benefits of education. In so far as the quest is for as much education for one's children as possible, this represents another, but conflicting commitment to growth: education beyond an elementary level can only be provided for a few children; but polygyny provides many.

This conflict between two kinds of commitment to growth is an interesting variation on a model proposed by Spencer (1974, pp. 419–27). He notes that "the notion of growth as a traditional propitious ideal is widely shared by most African societies. This is echoed within the family by a general concern for fertility and establishing a large lineage; within the local community in many traditionally stateless societies by a popular ambition to build a personal faction and found a new village; and within the traditional states by a pervasive ambition of expansion and absorption" (p. 425). Spencer sees this ideal of population growth as incompatible with the new notion of growth expounded by modern economic planners. These take their ideological assumptions from industrialized countries and aim for higher material living standards, to be measured by an increase in individuals' (i.e. *per capita*) production and consumption. This attempt to provide the conditions for individual material aggrandizement is ultimately at odds with traditional ideals of population growth and diminishes common but finite material resources, including land.

Unlike material resources, education need not be finite and, indeed, access to it is supposed to be a fundamental human right. Nevertheless, from the viewpoint of parents with many children, education is like a finite material resource. There are limits to how much money can be spent on school fees for each child, while the increasing competitive educational hierarchy highlights the diminishing job opportunities available to a child obliged to leave school early. Formal education is inextricably tied to the employment structure by the expectations it generates, and these are themselves a product of the modern economic planner's commitment to growth, to which Spencer refers. The conflict is not, then, really between education as a finite resource and population growth, but lies more in the nature of and expectations surrounding the uses to which education is to be put. Spencer's point is precisely this, that the conflict is essentially an ideological one: between the economic planners who emphasize material growth to the benefit of individuals, preferably few of them; and those pastoralists and agriculturalists who emphasize population growth itself as a means of personal aggrandizement. Both have in common ideological commitments to growth which in their different ways deplete material resources.

Generalizing out in this way enables us to see the wider perspective in which the problem of this chapter can be placed: polygyny among Luo in Nairobi is the ideal way to bridge rural and urban interests and fulfils men's and women's hopes of self-preservation and perpetuation, but it produces many children; education beyond an elementary level can only be provided for a few.

Here, we should note that polygyny actually produces a lower overall fertility rate in a society than monogamy (Goody, 1973, p. 129). This is because men tend to marry late and, especially, because co-wives' fertility is not, so to speak, used to capacity by their husband. We may assume, then, that the increasingly monogamous Kikuyu are reproducing themselves faster than Luo. Nevertheless, a polygynist *is* likely to have more children than a man with one wife, as we can see if we compare Luo polygynists and monogamists in Kaloleni within age categories (see Table 9). A polygynist begets a large proportion of his children during the relatively short period of 10 or 15 years when his two or more senior and junior co-wives are all still fertile. Hence the appearance of a numerical explosion of children in Luo polygynous families in Kaloleni headed by husbands in their forties, as indicated in Table 9.

TABLE 9

Average numbers of children of Luo monogamists and polygynists within age categories

| | Age of household heads | | | |
	20–29	30–39	40–49	50+
Average number of children of monogamists	2.2	4.2	5.7	6.4
(Total number of monogamists = 205)	(41 monogamists)	(92 monogamists)	(54 monogamists)	(18 monogamists)
Average number of children of polygynists	3.3	4.9	8.3	8.3
(Total number of polygynists = 103)	(7 polygynists)	(26 polygynists)	(47 polygynists)	(23 polygynists)

From appearances then, the Luo ideal that polygyny creates many children seems to them reasonable, and they can always substantiate it by referring to particular cases. Similarly, and by contrast, they can always point to large families in which the advanced education of one or two children appears to have been impeded by the demands of competing brothers and sisters.

The inherent contradiction: the pattern of socialization in Kaloleni

It might at first be thought that young, unmarried men and women must surely be rejecting polygyny and the ideal of many children as a result of their long residence in Nairobi as children and adolescents themselves. But the wider system of ethnic relations impinges itself subtly upon them in Nairobi, and they increasingly concentrate their relationships within their own ethnic group and thereby retain, first, ethnocentric marriage preferences and, second, a largely tacit acceptance of polygyny. Yet, at the same time, this ethnocentric channelling of preferences does not free them from the belief that the *sine qua non* of employment or advancement in a job-starved world is adequate education. Indeed, it is precisely in the leisure activities of the very young that we see how ethnocentric preferences originate alongside a growing realization of the value of education. It is the social situation in which their leisure activities are carried out and not simply parental admonition that induces Luo adolescents to accept ethnocentrism on the one hand and a somewhat contrasting view of education as an "open market" key to employment on the other. Let us look at how young Luo are socialized into this ambivalent pattern of expectations and aspirations which both reflects and perpetuates the dilemma resulting from the coexistence of ethnicity and an ostensibly meritocratic system of education.

Any discussion of the activities of children and adolescents must take into account the nature of neighbourhood and local relations in Kaloleni. For their leisure pursuits tend to be locally restricted. Some preliminary description is necessary.

It is obviously true that different kinds of town have different kinds of residential areas, which encourage or permit a variety of types of relationship between neighbours. The physical lay out of a housing area, the administrative policy governing its residents, whether or not they need pass laws to work in town, its socioeconomic composition, level of congestion, rate of internal mobility are a few of the many variables affecting the shape of these relationships. Much relevant work on this "plant" aspect of social relations in towns has been done by sociologists and geographers and here I do no more than indicate the salient features of Kaloleni.

Unlike two other public housing estates which I studied in Kam-

pala, Uganda, in the early sixties, the houses in Kaloleni are not arranged into small on-facing groups. In Kampala these small groups
developed their own distinctive neighbourhood identities, with the
wives, men and children of the houses of each group cooperating,
competing, protecting, quarrelling and gossiping with each other
and sometimes giving their own areas special names. And, at a wider
level, parts of an estate, and beyond that, a whole estate, would display similar distinctiveness in particular contexts. The number of
public estates in Kampala at that time was small and it was possible
for these characteristics of a face-to-face local "community" to develop, especially since most of the residents were also politically and
economically set apart from other people in Kampala (Parkin, 1969,
pp. 52–91).

In Kaloleni there are two main differences. First there is the difference of sheer scale. This affects men's relationships more than
women's and children's. The estate was one of the earliest to be
built, in 1945, specifically for family accommodation but is now one
of the very many spread all over the eastern part of Nairobi. Individuals' relationships are correspondingly dispersed throughout the
many different housing areas: Luo are particularly numerous in
Pumwani-Majengo, Shauri Moyo, and Jericho-Lumumba, but are
also found in large numbers elsewhere in Nairobi. Second, the physical lay out of the houses in Kaloleni does not encourage the development of small neighbourhood units, for houses are arranged more in
lines than in small on-facing groups. Women with very young children who cannot often visit friends and relatives located elsewhere in
eastern Nairobi may interact closely with their immediate neighbours, but the absence of clear physical boundaries marking off small
groups of houses puts these relations on an individual rather than
collective basis much more than was the case in Kampala East,
where, for example, a communal water tap was a regular meeting
place for the women of a neighbourhood. Houses in Kaloleni have
their own tap water and most also have lavatories, and these are additional factors limiting the development of collective neighbourhood
relations. Luo men and women do refer to Kaloleni as a predominantly Luo area and even as their "headquarters" in Nairobi, for it
is the locale for the meetings of their many associations and is adjacent to the city stadium where the famous Luo soccer teams play.
But though the estate is a base for Luo activities it does not generate

a large number of relationships specifically based on neighbourhood ties among adults.

The big exception to all this is among children and adolescents, and by seeing how the latter develop out of the former, we get a remarkably clear view of the way in which the pressures to ethnic conformity operate on the growing child and seemingly fit him into ready-made adult roles and expectations.

The languages used by these children and adolescents are a crucial index of their familiarity with Kaloleni and Nairobi and also show whether the peers they interact with are from their own ethnic group or are ethnically mixed.

Children and adolescents who have spent some time in Nairobi speak Swahili in addition to their respective vernaculars. Most adolescents can also speak some English. Swahili is the main lingua franca for all residents.

A remarkable feature of young children in Kaloleni is their wide use of Swahili. It is characteristic that a group of brothers and sisters will speak their vernacular to their parents and to each other in the urban household. But, literally on leaving the threshhold, they switch to Swahili both in talking to each other and to friends of other ethnic groups. Their play groups tends to be ethnically mixed and Swahili is used. From an early age boys become avid and skilful soccer players and form teams which are organized in part imitation of the Kenya League teams. It is interesting to note that, whether or not the group of children playing soccer on a piece of spare land in Kaloleni is ethnically mixed, Swahili is the medium of communication, with English loan words used only to refer to specific rules or properties of the game: e.g. goal, penalty, handball, corner, dodge, win, etc.[1] In other play contexts, Swahili is also frequently used between children of the same ethnic group, but with interference from the vernacular as well as from English.

A noticeable change occurs in the composition of play groups as children approach puberty. Whereas the play groups of young children comprise the four main ethnic groups of Luo, Luyia, Kikuyu and Kamba, the peer groups of older children gradually polarize into two types: Luo with Luyia on the one hand, and Kikuyu with

[1] It may be noted that English verbs incorporated in predominantly Swahili utterances normally (perhaps invariably) take Swahili pronominal and tense prefixes and English pronominal suffixes.

Kamba on the other. Both represent prototypes of the two main adult political and/or cultural "alliances". The use of Swahili diminishes slightly at the expense of Luo in the first case, and of Kikuyu in the second.

As they become adolescent, these groups harden into *societies* and *gangs* of the familiar juvenile type each consisting of between 30 and 50 members, not all of whom are likely to be interacting with each other on any one occasion but among whom is a regular core of 10 to 15. Thus, an adolescent is ethnically identified as belonging to either a Luo-Luyia or a Kikuyu-Kamba group. Within this group he is also identified as belonging either to a gang or a society. (See Fig. 1 and explanation following in text.)

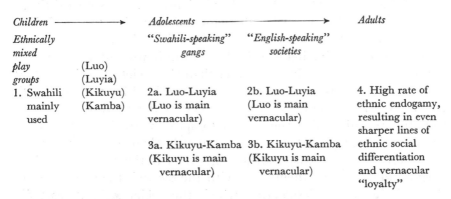

Fig. 1. Socialization in a polyethnic speech community.

First there are those which may actually call themselves student welfare "societies" and, in English, write their own constitutions, elect officers, attempt to collect subscriptions and closely imitate the ethnic and other voluntary associations of their elders, perhaps even becoming registered. They consist of boys and girls still at school but include a minority who, though they may be obliged to drop out, hope to return soon. Though they imitate their parents' ethnic associations, they are only loosely ethnically exclusive: Luo-Luyia on the one hand, and Kikuyu-Kamba on the other but with some overlap and juveniles from other groups attached to either. Two such societies whose members I knew well in 1968–69 in Kaloleni were Benfica and Black Santos, the names of two prominent international soccer teams of the time. Members consciously link their personal

educational status and aspirations to the formal aims of their societies and set up debates, dramatic performances, table tennis matches
and profess themselves to be unconcerned with the ethnic background of their members, though there is the ethnic clustering I
have mentioned. Members claim that they communicate with each
other more in English than in Swahili. The claim holds good for
formal activities of this kind, but is less consistently valid for informal leisure and recreational activities which provide the most important basis for regular interaction.

Second, there are what I call the gangs, who call themselves by
such "revolutionary" names as Black Power, Biafra, Korea, The
Henchmen, etc. They are not formally organized with elected officers
nor do they attempt to collect subscriptions. Members regard themselves as having lost virtually all chance of returning to school, having dropped out early for lack of school fees, incompatible home
conditions, or not having acquired the examination grades required
for continuing. They play less soccer than the societies, claiming that
this is because those still at school can be trained for the game with
proper facilities, whereas they themselves are deprived of such facilities. In Swahili, which they claim to speak more frequently than
English (though in fact no more frequently than members of societies in informal contexts), they jokingly refer to themselves as *wakora*
(rogues) and contrast themselves with the *wazuri* (the good ones) of
the societies, a self-designation which the societies light-heartedly
echo. The gangs also claim to be always on the look-out for "war"
and take pride in this facet of their philosophy in a way that is reminiscent of Anglo-American Hells Angels, or the recent "bovver
boys" of South London, or the Rockers in Britain of the early sixties (themselves contrasted with another category called Mods). Most
importantly, unlike the societies, these gangs are associated with
particular areas of Kaloleni: thus Black Power regards its area of
recruitment as house lines U-Z (150 households), Korea recruits from
the FQ houses (46), The Henchmen from A-G (148), and so on.
There are no clear boundaries marking off neighbourhoods in Kaloleni and this facilitates the arbitrariness of areas and partly accounts
for the fact that one aim in the rivalry between gangs is to enlarge
their claimed territories. Certainly the areas are uneven in size and
constantly changing.

In other respects, the gangs and societies are similar and come to-

Plate 2. Peers at play in Kaloleni.

gether more frequently than they are apart. They almost take it in turns to stage dances every weekend in the Kaloleni social hall, to which all come, and there is little doubt that this is the activity which sustains most interest. As members of the gangs and societies themselves point out, these are the occasions also when each group tries to "raid" girls from the others and when most disputes and fights between them occur. These Kaloleni dances involve more gangs and societies with Luo-Luyia membership than those with Kikuyu-Kamba. Kikuyu and Kamba teenagers tend to go outside Kaloleni for their entertainment. This has the consequence that, although Luo and Luyia "take" each others' girls, it is neither normally practicable nor expected that they will have much to do with Kikuyu and Kamba girls. The geographical separation of some Luo-Luyia and Kikuyu-Kamba leisure activities thus partly dictates the emerging pattern of "courtship" and pre-marital ties.

Two features affecting relationships with parents arise out of this development from childhood to adolescence. First, we see that by the time they are teenagers, boys or girls in Kaloleni have already moved away from childhood leisure activities involving all four main ethnic groups, and are now beginning to fall into the ethnic polarization of activities that characterizes their parents' relations. The connectedness of Luo and Luyia in recreation (Luo and Luyia adult teams compete in the Kenya soccer league) and, to a lesser extent, marriage, is already implicit and contrasts with the separate development of relations among Kikuyu and Kamba. Luo and Luyia boys and girls can mix freely and it is only in the years immediately before marriage that each is likely to be steered by parents firmly into choosing a wife from his or her own ethnic group, with the earlier likelihood of mixed Luo-Luyia marriages much reduced and those with Kikuyu or Kamba virtually eliminated.

Second, as well as depicting the trend to ethnic polarization along these lines, the gangs and societies reveal how much education is valued by teenagers as a summary mark of their general worthwhileness. In fact the actual levels of educational attainment, and English competence and usage, are not very much higher in the societies than the gangs. The significant difference is one of hopes and expectations: between those who are able to continue and those obliged to finish their education below the point at which it is likely to help them get a job or at least one which satisfies earlier aspirations. Mem-

D

bers of the societies associate their aspirations with a claimed continuing high usage of English. The gangs accept their "failure" to
continue education with a claimed rejection of the use of English
and its replacement with Swahili.

The concern, anxiety and bitterness variously expressed by teenagers on the subject of education cannot be over-emphasized. As is
common in much of Africa and the Third World sufficient education
is seen as an important key to minimal opportunities: who you
know may be important, but even more so if you are well educated.
Any conversation with teenagers and young people in Nairobi will
soon turn excitedly on the relationship between education, the use of
English, and employment opportunities. Unlike much of the Western world, there must be few if any voluntary educational drop-outs
in Kenya.[1]

The agonizing importance placed on having sufficient education
is thus reflected in the stated aims of, on the one hand, the societies
as concerned with student welfare, and, on the other hand, the gangs
as alienated trouble makers. How does this affect relations with
parents? The societies advertise, so to speak, the success of some
parents in managing to continue their sons' and daughters' education or in possibly helping them to achieve adequate grades, while
the gangs publicize the failure of other parents either to continue
paying school fees or to provide, say, suitable accommodation, books,
or studying conditions for a schoolchild, so contributing to his examination inadequacies. In the minds of most adolescents in this highly
competitive system, apparent parental responsibility or irresponsi-
bility is a prime reason for success or failure.

Luo children in Kaloleni, then, are subject to a pattern of socialization which increasingly channels them into accepting: (a) only
Luo and Luyia as possible marriage partners and preferably only
Luo; (b) "ample" secondary education as the *sine qua non* of successful employment; and (c) the apparently critical role of parents in all
this as authoritative managers of their children's destinies.

It is precisely over alternative definitions of this parental role and
over different evaluations as to how it has been carried out that
parents and their adolescent and adult offspring come into greatest

---

[1] Nelson says that in Kikuyu matrifocal family units in Nairobi a different tendency
has developed in which sons, but not daughters, rebel against the dictates of mothers,
including their insistence that they attend school. (Personal communications.)

conflict. Let me discuss these relations with parents by focusing on the two cases just raised: courting and marriage partners; and the responsibility for providing "sufficient" education for employment. We shall see that quarrels with parents do not actually lead young men and women consistently or effectively to question ethnic endogamy or polygyny, and that all generations are agreed on the desirability of education. Through the intergenerational conflicts, then, there is a continuity of expectations and aspirations.

Courting and marriage partners

As explained, many Luo parents try to ensure that marriageable daughters are actually resident in the rural home when marriage itself is imminent. But girls undergoing education or training or those with adult brothers in Nairobi may have their stay in the city prolonged and so must be "protected" from men. A girl's brothers are as concerned as their father and mother that her marriage should not only suit her particular preferences and emotions but should also be to someone able to honour all bridewealth obligations. Part or all of the bridewealth received for a sister may go towards helping a brother marry. Sisters are not chattel but they do have obligations to their brothers which may be sustained by the normal affection between siblings.

The familiar Mediterranean and Latin cultural codes of honour and shame turn very much on the status of women before as well as after marriage. Virginity in a girl at marriage is no longer expected among Luo and such cultural concepts have taken a new direction. There is now certainly a concept of relative chastity: a Luo girl is not expected to be a virgin at marriage but nor is she expected to have had many lovers. Luo brothers in Kaloleni take it as a personal affront to be avenged if a sister "roams" with someone unapproved by them. A suitor has to be checked upon. Provided he is "reliable", which almost necessitates his being a Luo in the first place, is acceptable in terms of exogamous lineage requirements, and presents himself to the family, the relationship is then approvingly monitored. The number of suitors for urban-dwelling girls is not many because, as explained, most men prefer to take wives directly from the rural area. Since the women are quite likely already to have spent time in a town, this preference is clearly highly subjective and points up the persistent association in men's minds between "urban" females and premarital promiscuity, as if somehow urban unmarried women must necessarily have exceeded even the relative concept of chastity.

It is often claimed that a girl who has had many lovers or who becomes a mother before marriage has devalued status as a prospective bride and is likely to become an older man's second or subsequent wife. It is of course very difficult to ascertain the validity or otherwise of girls' reputations and of whether second or subsequent wives really have been "devalued" in this way. This claim has significance more as a facet of a contemporary myth-in-the-making about urban women than as a statement of fact.

There were a number of cases, too, in which girls who had previously been living in town had returned to the rural home and there were alleged to have procured abortions (*golo ich*) using the traditional herbal medicine (*oboho*). They are then said by men and older women to produce subsequent children with greater difficulty than other girls and as therefore likely to have no option but to be taken on as a second or subsequent wife by an older but wealthy man who is himself prepared to take the risk. Once a girl is widely tagged in this way, there is no visible way of proving that, for example, her return to the rural home was for other "innocent" reasons.

"Steady" relationships between adolescents of the same age are covert affairs but rarely last beyond a couple of months, before parents, brothers, and even sisters of the girl step in to curtail it, and, if they consider it necessary, send the girl home. Some couples of marriageable age are happy to commit themselves to marriage only after a "steady" relationship in which the girl has become pregnant. If *pesa ayie* (agreement money), ranging from Shs.200/– to, in extreme cases, over Shs.1,000/–, has been handed over to the girl's parents or guardians by way of the *jagam* or marriage mediator, then the boy-friend is unlikely to deny his paternity. But, cases of denied or unknown paternity do occur and the pregnant girl is likely to be rejected as a possible wife by unmarried men of her own generation.

Brothers monitor not only a sister's part in steady relationships but also that of the suitor and may exert considerable pressure on him, even to the extent of taking him to court should he refuse to marry the girl after getting her pregnant. In this they are supported by their own parents. None of this is to imply that strong-willed daughters and sisters do not get their own way nor that less resistant girls are ruthlessly badgered into marriages which they cannot tolerate. From the cases I have recorded most are reluctant in the end to sacrifice family approval for a relationship the long-term security of which cannot be guaranteed.[1] Compromises are usually reached after joint discussions between the girl and her parents and brothers as to the acceptability of suitors: a girl will not normally be forced into a relationship she does not want, but nor will she force a suitor onto her parents if he is unacceptable to them.

It is probably true that, over time, a polygynist is more likely than a monogamist to have a number of adult sons able to help him in settling their younger sisters' (or more likely half-sisters') marriages. Nevertheless, sons are not always available or senior enough to take on this task and most fathers will at some time have to call on adult agnates of their own or a junior generation to help them. The courting relationships of adolescent and adult Luo girls in Nairobi, then, have the potential for mobilizing more than the immediate members of one man's family and may bring together himself, his sons, if any, and those agnates who respond to the plea for assistance. The definition of who can be identified as an agnate in this situation is clear up to a certain point: those of, say, a common great-grandfather and called *jokakwaro* have a strong moral obligation to help; but those simply of the same administrative sub-location, usually identified also as a maximal lineage, are under less obligation. But they hear of a particular issue involving a "recalcitrant" girl or man of the lineage through the formal association representing the sub-location or other similar unit of wide agnatic scale. The association calls a meeting to discuss the "crisis" which, it is agreed, may create a precedent contrary to fathers' or brothers' individual interests in securing bridewealth for their daughters and sisters from "reliable" husbands.

The sense of obligation to a man at this level depends on the particular position occupied by the father in the association and on whether he can be relied on to return the help. A man who is dominant and influential in such associations can reasonably expect swift help from its members in domestic crises of this and other kinds.

[1] Betty Potash has recorded rural cases of genuine wife capture, apparently against the will of the bride (personal communication), and for earlier examples see Margaret J. Hay (1976, p. 94–5).

Older men generally and the polygynists among them in particular are easily the most influential. They are characterized, even by young men, as much more "reliable" than themselves. An example of their reputed reliability in a different context is the tendency for treasurers entrusted with holding and managing associations's funds to be older men. We see, then, that though fathers might not by themselves be able to "control" potentially wayward daughters, most of them can draw on one or more of three fairly close sources of support: their own sons, close agnates, and more distant agnates, usually through a formal association.

Personal influence is important. An uninfluential man is one, by definition, who cannot summon the support to control his daughters and who stands to be harangued by his young sons when they reach a marriageable age for having failed to secure the full bridewealth for a sister. An influential man can command this control though, paradoxically, he also may be harangued by younger sons if, in order to substantiate his influential status, he uses a daughter's bridewealth to take a second wife instead of holding it in trust for the sons. In other words, fathers and sons may be agreed on the desirability of finding suitable partners for their daughters and sisters, but may disagree on the destination of the bridewealth. But whereas agnates of a wide span, including a formal association representing them, are prepared to rally round this first issue of the desirability of appropriate partners for their unmarried women, they consider it much more a private family matter to be decided between a father, his sons, and their respective mothers as to who of them should first benefit from any bridewealth received.

In general, then, fathers can draw on agnates to support their side of the argument in a family dispute with sons and daughters concerning their marriage "choices". The extent to which a daughter can become independent of parents varies (a) according to whether or not she has adult brothers or other close agnates prepared to contest her attempts or (b) according to the influence which her father can exert on more distantly related agnates. Sons can only be independent of fathers if they themselves can provide bridewealth for their own marriages, which in turn depends on whether they have a job, or one of sufficient income. The growing shortage of employment opportunities has in fact strengthened this syndrome of control wielded by those fathers with secure jobs and housing in Nairobi.

Here it may be noted that the "fathers" of today are those young urban migrants of yesterday who were more easily able to find urban jobs and, moreover, were expected by their rural fathers to contribute heavily to the bridewealth for their own marriages with their urban-earned cash. This did not in fact significantly loosen parental control at that time over these "independent" young men, for, as I explain in Chapter 4, men were still dependent on the home people to choose "proper" wives for them. Nowadays, with urban unemployment high, parental control has been further strengthened, as fathers in jobs revert to providing more of an unemployed son's bridewealth. However, the high bridewealth payments, largely converted to cash from cattle, that these fathers indirectly encouraged when they themselves married, have continued. Mothers, too, have an interest in securing high bridewealth payments for their daughters, for they receive a small proportion of it themselves which, especially in a polygynous family, is earmarked for their sons' marriages. Young men without jobs and confronted by a cash bridewealth worth at least Shs.3,500/– (1969), plus or including some livestock, at least two heifers and a goat, are therefore caught, so to speak, in an unintended trap of their fathers' making which has redefined but perpetuated parental control.

Under these circumstances there is little that unmarried men can do to bring down their late age of marriage, which is about 25 or 26 years, as against 17 or 18 for women, and which continues to make it possible for older men, i.e. the "fathers" to have more than one wife. The paradox here is that it is young men themselves who claim that these second wives are young women whom they themselves would reject as wives on account of their past "promiscuity" or premarital motherhood or abortions, while happily accepting them as girl-friends. In other words, young men place selective value on the relative chastity of marriageable females to an extent that perpetuates the institution of polygyny of which they regard themselves in other contexts as victims. And yet, as I explained, an acceptance of polygyny implies the creation of large families which strain the family resources available to satisfy the demand for education. Polygynous fathers are especially open to blame for the reduced education a son may receive in competition with numerous brothers and half-brothers, but young men themselves unwittingly subscribe to polygyny by refusing to marry so-called "town" girls, who may therefore be taken as second wives by older men. Moreover, as I now explain, polygynous families are under the greatest pressure to share resources equitably, as co-wives insist on equal treatment for their respective sons, and sometimes daughters.

The provision of education

Fathers, though rarely mothers, are likely to be accused of negligence by sons and daughters whose education has had to be terminated before it is sufficient to qualify them for what they regard as an acceptable job. There are often marked generational differences of opinion as to what constitutes adequate education, with the younger members of a family rather more realistic in their assessments. It is commonly said, not without some justification, that nowadays even an ordinary School Certificate (twelve years of education) is not necessarily adequate for, say, a clerical job and that education below this level offers no particular advantages in finding jobs in any occupational sphere. Fathers of adolescents, by contrast, will have acquired their jobs at a time when they were more plentiful and did not require such a high level of education.

A dominant factor limiting the likelihood that many children will reach a high educational level is the Luo egalitarian view that as many sons and daughters should be educated as possible. It is sometimes recognized by a few younger Luo that a highly educated elder sibling is more likely, on acquiring a secure and lucrative job, to benefit lower-order siblings than if his education is terminated earlier for the sake of providing middle-order siblings with education as well. But this recognition is not often put into effect among the Luo in Kaloleni as it is in many Kikuyu households. In Luo polygynous families, the respective mothers further substantiate the egalitarian view that no children, whatever their birth-order, should legitimately be given preferential treatment. The rules of the house-property complex cannot, of course, be followed in the allocation of education, as they are in the case of land and of a mother's cattle, which are technically divided among sons on their father's death. Though a co-wife tries to ensure that none of her children, regardless of whether they are more numerous than those of another co-wife, receives less education, complete equality is not possible. But her demands, spoken of by husbands as an expression of co-wife jealousy (*nyiego*), may certainly be strong enough to cause a husband to curb the schooling of a promising child of another co-wife.

A few sons and daughters do reach a high enough level to secure good employment and, in monogamous families, fulfil their obligations to younger siblings. But in polygynous families, it is often a boy's or girl's own mother who has contributed substantially to his education with money earned from trading or from rural cash-cropping on a small scale. He is then much less likely to help half-siblings in spite of his father's pleas for a more egalitarian distribution of his assistance. The father may in this case also be accused of favouritism by those of his co-wives whose children are not being helped.

The Luo view that family resources should be used ideally to educate all the children, and the strain under which these resources are placed in polygynous families results in a high overall investment by Luo in their children's education but does not yield a commensurately high number of jobs.[1] Unlike many Kikuyu households in which sons and daughters are urged to consider entrepreneurial activities as an alternative to adequate education, Luo families have been urged to seek salvation through education, with entrepreneurship increasingly ruled out as a viable possibility in Nairobi, as I explain in Chapter 4.

Most Luo do not seriously question the egalitarian emphasis in the provision of education for sons, daughters and siblings. But many, particularly younger Luo, do believe that having more than one wife and having many children does reduce the chances of educating any of them to a sufficiently high standard. And yet the rate of polygyny has not dropped very much. The cultural process accompanying ageing appears to have turned those who were uncommitted and even opposed to polygyny into defenders of the institution.

Summary and conclusion

Even controlling for age similarities, polygynists do have more children than monogamists, though it is of course true that wives of polygynists tend to have fewer children during their fecund life-span than

---

[1] In 1969 the fees for the cheapest government primary school were Shs.60/– p.a. exclusive of clothing and equipment expenses, and Shs.180/– and Shs.600/– respectively for the ex-Asian and ex-European primary schools, and between Shs.450/– and Shs.600/– p.a. for ordinary government secondary schools, and about Shs.3,000/– for elitist secondary schools.

wives of monogamists. Polygyny is a commitment that many Luo men in Nairobi assume, at least as an ideal to be attained, as they get older and become subject to a general ethnocentric channelling of interests and expectations beginning in childhood and adolescence.

The practice of polygyny has become adapted to the increasing dependency by Luo men on urban wage employment; it enables a man to retain a stake in his rural home through the presence there of one of his co-wives while he remains in his job in town together with a wife and children. Luo see this as a definite advantage in having two wives. While specially adapted in this way, polygyny retains its underlying ideological importance as a traditionally desirable way of securing respect for both men and women through many children. At the same time, some Luo men and women have begun to express ambivalence about the desirability itself of having many children. A preference for large families now conflicts with an increasing emphasis on providing education for one's children and so equipping them for employment in a diminishing job market.

In the families of household heads in Kaloleni, the proportion of Luo children receiving education in Nairobi is higher than that being educated in the rural areas and higher than that of other ethnic groups. And the total Luo investment of family resources is believed by Luo themselves to be higher than that of other groups. While this cannot be substantiated it is certainly the case that an egalitarian Luo premise decrees that as many sons as possible and, to a lesser extent, daughters, receive equal education: an older brother in Junior Secondary school may be expected to leave school in order to enable a younger brother to attend. In polygynous families, co-wives insist particularly strongly on this egalitarian premise and demand that their respective children, who are half-siblings to each other, receive as much education as possible. This is in contrast to many Kikuyu families, few of which are polygynous and among whom a preferential system of education is more evident. Few Luo families have domestic budgets which can stretch to the education of all sons, let alone daughters, beyond an elementary level (i.e. primary or junior secondary) sufficient to secure employment which satisfies inflated aspirations.

To conclude: an egalitarian premise in the organization of domestic life among Luo can be said to curb the possible yield to be derived from a family's investment in education in Nairobi. This premise is even more strongly exaggerated in polygynous families by competing co-wives and sets of half-siblings. As we shall now see, this emphasis on equal shares arises from past and present Luo institutions and is conceptually crystallized in polygynous family relations. It has persisted as Luo families settled in Kaloleni and their men became more dependent on urban wages. Egalitarianism now confronts the "new" premises of an educational meritocracy. On the one hand, egalitarianism is the basis of Luo moral claims for accommodation and general aid from kin and affines. Here, it is seen to be a social leveller. On the other hand, egalitarianism can imply individual freedom of control by others. Here, friends provide alternative relationships of a more negotiable and less obligatory kind which, though they are often between people from common home areas, are seen to be based on individually achieved educational, occupational and financial qualities.

3

Conflicting Involvements

Relatives and friends

The Luo insistence on an egalitarian distribution of educational opportunity for their children is paralleled by other facets of egalitarianism in their culture. First, inherited land and property are ideally divided equally between different sets of half-brothers irrespective of the seniority of their mothers. Second, all sons are ideally entitled to be married with bridewealth received from their sisters' marriages. Third, the localized, polysegmentary lineage system discouraged the fixed ranking of territorial groups and the creation of family dynasties. Even today, there are very few recognizably elite families, as distinct from elite individuals. The rejection of fixed notions of rank has its corollary in competitive displays of prestige and prowess in the use of language, clothes, money, and through the drinking of liquor. Indeed, what comes through as a distinctive Luo view of the world is that of a constantly changing rather than fixed horizon of status.

A concept of egalitarianism must be treated cautiously. We may note the familiar distinction between an ideology enjoining equality of position, entailing the absence of achieved as well as of ascribed rank, and that enjoining equality of opportunity. Egalitarianism of the first kind is that described by Bailey and his associates (1971) for some European villages and aptly summarized on the book's cover as "people competing to remain equal", in which the sanctions against "upperty" behaviour are so strong that people play down status achievements. Egalitarianism of the second kind, that of opportunity, is an approved characteristic of, say, the American capitalist economic system in which the ideal is that everyone has basically the same chance in life to stay poor or become rich by his own merits, and having become so, is under no compulsion to play down the achievement. Marx indirectly refers to the ethos thus: "This circumstance, that a man without wealth, but with energy, strength of character, ability, and business sense, is able to become a capitalist, is greatly admired by the economic apologists of capitalism, since it shows that the commercial value of each individual is more or less accurately estimated under the capitalist mode of production." (Capital III VA III/2, pp. 648–9, as cited in Bottomore and Rubel, 1961, p. 197.) Such folk-concepts can only be deduced by observing social situations and listening to conversation. It is unlikely that any culture falling within a capitalist environment does not have both, even though one may dominate a people's behaviour in most social domains.

Among the Luo of Kaloleni the two combine awkwardly in the quest for education to produce a conflict which is insoluble at the present time. On the one hand, the ideal is that all or as many children as possible within a family should receive education and that no one child is entitled to receive significantly more than another. This is supported by the moral insistence that "educated" brothers (and sisters) with jobs should help pay for the education of younger siblings. On the other hand, outside the family, the educational system is nominally, and generally believed to be, meritocratic, with rewards commensurate with a carefully organized system of grades which are competed for not only by different Luo families in contest with each other but also by families of different ethnic groups. In other words, a restrictive, levelling-down concept of egalitarianism (expressed in speech as *winjruok*, "understanding", and to a lesser extent *romruok*, "equality") emphasizes the unity and solidarity of sibling groups at the price of exceptional individual achievement. But it has the effect of weakening the position of family members in the wider "open market" meritocratic system. Many Luo recognize this conflict. It is nicely instanced in the contrast between two main kinds of lodger who are found in Luo households in Kaloleni. First, there are those whom I loosely call kin, who as well as seeking accommodation of their own, or a job, may include some whose education or training in Nairobi is being sponsored by their host. Second, there are those lodgers whom I call "friends" and whom Luo explicitly distinguish from kin and who are ideally seen by Luo as providing relationships uncontrolled by the moral demands of kinship. Almost as if they were adopting a modified version of Maine's distinction between status and contract, Luo see kin relations as less negotiable than those of friendship, in which the optative element is held to be strong. What happens, as we shall see, is that friendships which lose this optative element then become classified by Luo as relations of a kinship kind. These are constructs abstracted and terminologically identified by Luo themselves and constitute a semantic domain of concepts. But it is also true that household heads do pay more out, including school fees, on kin who lodge with them than on friends, for whom they are much less likely to be out of pocket, and in most cases actually benefit from a contribution to rent and food. In summary, then, lodgers who are regarded as related to the head tend not to pay for their keep, while unrelated ones do.

The distinctiveness of Luo lodgers

A household head is acknowledged by the people who live with him as responsible for organizing the payment of rent and other domestic charges and expenses and as having a major say in how much each household member should contribute to the joint budget, and in such matters as the allocation of domestic chores and sleeping arrangements. The great scarcity of housing in Nairobi is a problem which affects everyone. A household head is therefore subject to a barrage of requests for accommodation, many of them by job-seekers. While this situation produces extremely congested living standards it also substantiates the head's recognition and control over those who wish to lodge with him while searching for accommodation of their "own".

All Luo who have "spare" room in their houses are under some obligations to provide accommodation to a range of kin and affines. These obligations apply generally to household heads whether they are unmarried or have one or more wives. Those with large urban families, such as most polygynists, are under less obligation. Older family heads, many of whom are polygynists, are likely to have adolescent sons and daughters of their own living with them in Nairobi. It is recognized that their presence in the household also reduces the head's obligation to provide accommodation for others. While a combination of these two factors of family size and family seniority may provide some partial exemption, there remains an underlying pattern of obligations among Luo in Nairobi as to who can expect accommodation and other kinds of aid from whom. By looking at this pattern of obligations between household head and lodger in Kaloleni, we get a picture of the contrasting pattern of personal obligations between kin and affines on the one hand and between unrelated fellow Luo on the other, as they are met outside as well as within households and domestic life. Here it may be noted that few lodgers are non-Luo. Similarly, it is rare for non-Luo to figure as "friends". The same is true of other ethnic groups, and mirrors the ethnic channelling of relationships occurring in adolescence which I described in the last chapter (see also Ross, 1975, pp. 67–70).

As well as being the largest in Kaloleni, Luo households also have the highest proportion of adults identified by heads as being related to them by kinship and affinity. Correspondingly, they have the lowest proportion of non-relatives.

TABLE 10

Adult lodgers' relationships to household heads in Kaloleni (lodgers' children excluded)

Household heads	Total number of adult lodgers	(Men/women)	Kin and affines of head	Unrelated by kinship and affinity to head
Luo (333)	393	(248 145)	69.2 (272)	30.8 (121)
Luyia (222)	206	(136 70)	60.6 (125)	39.4 (81)
Kikuyu (122)	135	(75 60)	48.8 (66)	51.2 (69)
Kamba (133)	124	(98 26)	44.3 (55)	55.7 (69)
Others (42)	13	(51 13)	62.5 (40)	47.5 (24)

In my survey I asked for adult lodgers and so missed adolescent relatives. From impression they number about a quarter of related adult lodgers and their proportions between the ethnic groups are the same. The distinction between adult and adolescent is, anyway, difficult to elicit by the criterion of age, and what is important for this analysis are the kinds of relationships between dependent lodgers receiving accommodation, food and financial help, and their household hosts. My numerical data, then, refer to adult lodgers, i.e. over, say, 16 years of age. A lodger is defined as someone other than the household head's own wife and children but may include close relatives, including brothers and sisters.[1]

Adult lodgers number 393 and account for almost 40 per cent of all Luo living in Kaloleni. Their children are some 12 per cent of all Luo children. Nearly a third (122) of these lodgers are married and well over a half (68) of them have their wives and usually some children living with them in their hosts' households. The scarcity of accommodation in Nairobi and the accompanying uncertainty surrounding employment have made the institution of lodging important both for sustaining and modifying certain key Luo ideas regarding the nature of kinship and friendship.

The turnover of lodgers among all Luo households is rapid with only close kin likely to stay longer than six months. This means that the distribution of adult lodgers at the time of my survey works out at only about 1.25 per household among Luo, with lodgers' children an additional quarter of this. This may not seem many. But it must be remembered that most individual households experience periods when the number is much higher than this as a result of the build-up of a succession of lodgers within a short time. About one in nine of the households have three adult lodgers, many of whom also have their young children with them. The overall average size of Luo households in Kaloleni is well over six men, women and children in only one or two rooms. The presence or absence of lodgers and their children may easily tip the balance between what can and cannot be tolerated in the conduct of domestic affairs. Indeed, there is frequently a cycle of household congestion and de-congestion followed by increasing congestion. The house becomes unbearably full, tempers become frayed and finally after quarrels the lodgers leave for other accommodation. After a short breathing space during which the household head attempts to recover in relative solitude, vowing never to admit anyone else to stay with him, the news of available accommodation triggers off the next wave of requests. For reasons I shall shortly

---

[1] In Nairobi no one term is consistently used to refer to lodger. Indeed, the most frequently used is the English term itself. Traditional Luo terms like *jalaw nindo* and *jabuoro*, meaning someone who has been offered free temporary overnight or longer accommodation, are very occasionally heard, as is the term *jadak*, which, though it connotes temporary paid accommodation, also means in the rural area a member of an immigrant lineage "leasing" land. None of these terms would be used in the presence of the urban lodger himself.

explain, the head gives in to at least some requests and the household becomes large again.

The majority of lodgers, then, contribute little or nothing for their keep. And most of these are, or are classified as, relatives of one kind or another. There is no doubt that having to accommodate them does constitute a drain on a household head's budget. Most are unemployed. And even if they get jobs, as kin or affines they are under no definite obligation to repay the past hospitality unless the host himself falls on hard times. Otherwise there is no past indebtedness: the good fortune of one man at a particular point in time is no reason for indebting a less fortunate one, according to the Luo egalitarian philosophy. Lodgers who are unrelated and termed "friends" tend to be employed and to contribute towards the household budget. Even so, quarrels about the size of contributions may eventually develop. Though we may analyse the situation as being intrinsically cyclical in the manner described above, for the head of the household lodgers present unstable sets of relationships fraught with uncertainties.

So, why do hosts take in lodgers at all? Undoubtedly the high moral idiom in which requests are made is a factor: even an unrelated person can appeal by using a generalized kinship idiom, e.g. "Am I not your brother?" (i.e. fellow-Luo). But three main reasons combine to substantiate the moral legitimacy of requests. First, there are those genuinely close kin whose requests are buttressed by the interests and sanctions of home people of the parental generation. Second, homeless "friends" are, as I explained, more likely to contribute to the domestic budget if they are employed and, even if they are not, their presence as lodgers is seen to be less binding an obligation and more likely to yield future dividends (though, as we shall see, this is in fact less the case than with relatives). Third, many houses in Kaloleni are not registered in the household head's name. These are houses which the current head took on from a relative or friend who moved out of Kaloleni, sometimes out of Nairobi altogether. Though illicit, this practice enables a man to jump the long waiting list for houses.[1] The practice sometimes takes the form of subletting. These illegal tenancies are a feature of all ethnic groups and in all public housing estates of more than a few years' standing. In the municipal housing estates of Kampala East, Uganda, which I studied in the early 1960s, a resident

---

[1] This was given as 30,000 for all council housing in Nairobi (Harris, J., 1970, p. 39).

estate manager and his resident assistants were able to detect most illicit transfers and subletting. The Nairobi estates are much more numerous and have no resident estate managers. They are administered centrally from a single office in Eastlands. Housing officers do not have specific estates under their supervision and so do not normally go out of their way to discover illegal tenancies. But individual cases do come to their attention and the illegal tenants are evicted. The Luo in Kaloleni claim that the numerical preponderance of Kikuyu housing officers has made them particularly vulnerable. Paradoxically, they also claim that it is often jealous fellow-Luo (i.e. motivated by the extensive force of *nyiego*) who bring about eviction by reporting an illegal tenancy to a housing officer. Luo point to their diminishing number in Kaloleni over the years as proof that they have suffered most. There is no evidence that they have been singled out by Kikuyu housing officers and, indeed, the contradictory claim that it is jealous fellow-Luo who initiate the process suggests otherwise. Treating their undeniably strong belief in their vulnerability as a social fact, rather than seeking to ascertain whether it is true, enables us to understand why Luo are wary of refusing hospitality to fellow-Luo who know of the illegal tenancy. This third reason for taking in lodgers combines with the demands of kinship and home origins and, alternatively, with the possibility of a contribution to the domestic budget by an employed friend, to produce a general ethos which condemns those whose houses are seen to remain relatively empty. In other parts of Nairobi and in other towns too (e.g. Kampala: Halpenny, 1975, p. 278), Luo have the largest households and the highest proportion of lodgers of all ethnic groups, a difference which is independent of such factors as distance of rural home area from town and of socio-economic span and length of urban residence.

To sum up, the taking in of lodgers arises from a general situation of housing scarcity. But the propensity to do so varies among cultural groups and is most stressed by Luo. The Luo are distinctive also in having the highest proportion of kin and affines (i.e. those identified as such) among their lodgers. The general idiom of kinship legitimates most requests for accommodation, either by specifying a known relationship or referring generally to ethnic identity or common home area. But some lodgers are welcomed in the first place by their urban hosts, who may actually have gone out of their way to invite them. In such cases, the lodger's need for accommodation complements a wish on the part of the urban host for someone to share the household rent and expenses and possibly also to provide a child to help around the house. This tacit contractual arrangement can occur between relatives as well as friends, but is said by Luo as more likely to be initiated by and stand more chance of survival among friends.

In stressing a need for accommodation as the main reason behind lodging, I should point out that this is also the reason given by most Luo themselves to explain the presence of lodgers. The unemployed among them may also be seeking work, or some 13–18 year olds who have been obliged to leave school early may really have come to their host, usually a close relative, to be given some kind of schooling or training in Nairobi. (Under this age, girl "nurses", called *japidi* (sing.), may also mind younger children and help around the home.) There is, however, no institutionalized child-fostering on the scale found in parts of West Africa, mainly among, as far as I can judge, groups which reckon descent cognatically or by a highly variable notion of unilinearity.

The motives and needs behind the coming and going of lodgers in Luo households are mixed. But they all point to a relationship of some dependency with the host, who assumes an informal and necessarily temporary role of patron. When we analyse the range of host–lodger relationships we see the Luo premise of equality at work, especially among agnates, and its polarizing effect in setting up contrasting relationships of friendship rather than agnation between host and lodger.

Agnates and other kin

Not surprisingly agnates of the head account for almost a half of all Luo lodgers. This accords with the strong ideological stress on patriliny. Luyia compare superficially with Luo in this respect, and in their urban households in Kaloleni agnates are only a little less than the Luo proportion. The proportion falls to a third among the Kikuyu and Kamba, among whom unrelated "friends" account for over a half of all lodgers. (In parenthesis, we may note that only in Luo households in Kaloleni are non-agnatic kin and affines numerous enough to be given special comment: see below.)

Table 11 focuses on Luo lodgers alone and shows two interesting

TABLE 11

Adult lodgers of Luo household heads in Kaloleni

	Total number of adult lodgers	Agnates	Non-agnatic kin	Female affines		Male affines		Non-relatives[a]
				Wife's sisters (mostly unmarried)	Wives of brothers and agnates	Wife's brothers	"Sisters" husbands	
(206) Monogamists	256 (98 women)	108 (22)	24 (5)	20	17	1	1	85 (34 women)[b]
(103) Polygynists	108 (40)	45 (5)	8 (2)	9	11	3	2	30 (13)[c]
(24) Currently unmarried	29 (7)	19 (3)	1 (—)	—	2	1	—	6 (2)[d]
	393 (145)	172 (30)	33 (7)	29	30	5	3	121 (49)
	(100%)	(44%)	(8%)	(15%)		(2%)		(31%)

[a]There are also about 150 children of lodgers, mostly of non-relatives, and some child-nurses (*japidi*).

[b]Comprising 25 wives mostly of friends, but also of non-agnatic kin and affines, and female affines of affines; and nine other women, mostly friends of wives.

[c]Comprising 11 wives mostly of friends, but also of non-agnatic kin and affines, and female affines of affines; and two friends of wives.

[d]Both are wives of "town" friends.

differences between monogamists and the generally older polygynists. First, Luo monogamists have more lodgers than polygynists, which is easily explained by the latter's large number of children and limited accommodation. Second, monogamists have a proportionally larger number of non-agnates as lodgers, including a very much larger proportion of non-relatives, i.e. "friends". Polygynists, who are generally older, constantly complain that young Luo neglect agnates for the sake of friends as well as sometimes questioning the advantages of polygyny. These elders interpret this as an attack on the Luo principle of agnation. As we shall see later in this chapter, they see friendships as necessarily opposed to agnatic relations and therefore destructive of Luo culture. Paradoxically, as these figures show, it is in fact the monogamists who accommodate most agnates, partly because they are anyway more numerous in Nairobi and partly because, as I mentioned, they have smaller families, and therefore more house-room to accommodate lodgers. As one monogamist in his late twenties put it: "When the elders see my house half empty they soon make sure it is full. The best I can do is to anticipate them and put in friends, for at least they help you with the household expenses."

This difference between monogamists and polygynists is not simply one of tendencies between opposed generations. For when monogamists become polygynists they make the same judgements. We have to look at the forces behind agnation in Luo society as a whole to understand it.

Most of the 172 agnates among Luo lodgers are in fact full brothers and sisters (51 per cent), male patrilateral parallel cousins (21 per cent), half-brothers (15 per cent), with the rest comprising nephews, nieces and other lineage-mates of different segmental levels. The English term "my clansman" is sometimes used to refer to someone merely of the speaker's maximal exogamous lineage, which may be very large indeed, numbering tens of thousands of people in both the rural and urban areas with a traceable though obviously telescoped depth of between nine and 13 generations. The maximal exogamous lineage (which is not really a clan, for alleged genealogical links can be traced) of Karachuonyo in South Nyanza, studied in 1949 by Southall (1952, pp. 22–32) has a traceable depth of some 12 generations and currently numbers almost 100,000 people, none of whom can nor do marry each other. It is localized and occupies two administrative locations. A smaller localized lineage which is coterminous with a location is that of neighbouring Kanyada, with whom Karachuonyo can intermarry, which has a comparable generational depth but numbers only between 25,000 and 30,000 persons. Kanyada in South Nyanza is the "half-brother" of the large localized lineage of Kakan, in distant Alego location (now Boro district) which numbers about 20,000 people with a similar generational depth. It was constantly asserted by men of these two lineages living in Nairobi, not all of them elders, that marriage between them was prohibited and I certainly came across no cases. Kanyada and Kakan though geographically very distant, must then be regarded as a single large maximal exogamous lineage (or "clan"). (See also Evans-Pritchard, 1965, p. 209.)

In Nairobi a Luo household lodger referred to in English as "my clansman" is likely to be of a lower segmental lineage level than either of these two. I can refer to him and to a more genealogically as well as territorially distant lineage-mate both as *jadhodwa* (from *dhoot*, pl. *dhoudi*, a lineage of any range up to the maximal exogamous level, sometimes called a "clan" in English). This term, however much it may sometimes stretch the facts on the ground, carries the idea that "our" common lineage is a localized and even land-holding one. Where common membership of a smaller localized lineage is indicated, other terms used are *jaanyuolwa* (the *anyuola* is of 3–5 generations deep; see Blount, 1975, p. 119), *jakechwa*, and *jakakwaro* ("someone of one great-grandfather" but extending beyond this in many cases; see also Whisson, 1964b, p. 31. *Jalibambawa* ("my agnate with whom I have a relationship of *libamba*, pl. *libembini*", referring to opposed and possibly rival but coordinate lineage segments of 6–8 generations depth (Southall, 1952, p. 28; Blount, 1975, p. 119)) can also be used in this way as well as connoting some idea of complementary membership of balanced coordinate segments. Of these, the two terms I heard most often in Nairobi were *jadhodwa*, for localized maximal exogamous lineages and for major and minor segments of these, and, as alternatives for these latter and smaller units, *jakakwaro* (from *ka-* at the place of; and *kwaro*, pl. *kwere*, ancestor) and personalized references such as *tiendwa kamgang* (my minimal and minor lineage segments, from *tielo*, pl. *tiende*, root or base, with the full meaning of "my root is at the place of *Mgang*"). Finally, *owadwa* is used for my full- or half-brother and sometimes a first patrilateral parallel cousin, but not usually beyond this range.

The different terms for lineage-mates thus refer to the genealogical depth of the connection, its degree of rural home localization, and whether or not membership of coordinate segments is stressed. We shall see the significance of these factors in the structure of Luo lineage associations in Nairobi, which I discuss in Chapters 6 and 7. For the moment we may note that the relatively specific segmentary character of this taxonomy of terms for agnates contrasts with the ambiguity of terms used for non-agnates, and especially, friends.

Among Luyia in Kaloleni full brothers and sisters and patrilateral parallel cousins make up most of their lodgers who are agnates, while among Kikuyu and Kamba the range of agnates hardly extends beyond full brothers and sisters who easily outnumber other agnates.[1] Again, the wider agnatic range among Luo can be presumed to correspond with the extensive patrilineal organization of their home groupings. What is of particular note is that only among Luo is there a significant proportion of half-brothers (same father, different mothers) among their lodgers. This suggests that the high polygyny rate among Luo household heads in Kaloleni carries on their own parents' tradition and underlines how markedly distinctive is this persisting feature of Luo social organization. As we noted in Chapter 1, the polygyny rates among Luyia and Kamba heads in Kaloleni are by no means low but are considerably less than that of the Luo and, if the low proportion of half-siblings included among Luyia and Kamba lodgers is an index, were not significantly higher among their parents. Even among Luo, half-brothers form a small proportion of all lodgers. But they have a significance which goes beyond their numbers. For Luo speak of them as constant reminders of the competition for family land and cattle which exists between uterine half-brothers and which in its intensity certainly exceeds that between full-brothers. Both full and half-brothers are called *owadwa* ("my brother"). But the relations between half-brothers are traditionally and specifically characterized by the term *nyiego*, jealousy, derived from the term for co-wife, *nyieka*, and with a root meaning of "to seize". *Nyiego* has been extended to cover not only jealousy between half-brothers but also between full brothers, other agnates, other kin and affines, and between unrelated fellow Luo. Following the recent decline of Luo entrepreneurial activities in Nairobi which I describe in the next chapter, *nyiego* has become a general concept for explaining economic failure

[1] Though patrilineal, Kikuyu and Kamba lineages are shallow.

within the Nairobi Luo community while retaining its domestic connotations which are nourished, so to speak, by the occasional inclusion of a half-brother lodging in a household.

None of the Luo lodgers includes half-sisters and only a few patrilateral cousins are females. But a quarter of all 90 adult full siblings lodging with Luo household heads are sisters. Why are they there? Nearly all are unmarried. Some have been sent for education or training for, say, secretarial work or dress-making. Some have persistently rejected parents' attempts in the rural areas at arranging their marriages and have been sent to their brothers in Nairobi for "advice". Since a considerable bridewealth worth at least Shs.3,500/– will be due to their families on the sisters' marriages, brothers and parents are all concerned that prospective grooms can be relied upon to honour any agreement reached and that they come from families which are acceptable in terms of the rules of lineage exogamy. Even those sisters who have been sent to Nairobi for schooling or vocational training and are not there ostensibly to be married off, will nevertheless command a higher bridewealth value should they actually receive education and also retain a "virtuous" reputation. The claim, which is familiar to much of Africa, is that parents should be compensated for the loss through marriage of educated daughters and for those who are earning. Among Luo in Kaloleni it is often brothers who provide the fees for the secondary education or technical training of their sisters and, not surprisingly, they expect a share in the compensation. The most customarily acceptable way in which this can be done is to be helped towards the bridewealth for one's own wife. And since most of the household heads in Kaloleni who have sisters with them are already married, this compensation neatly becomes directed towards the acquisition of another wife, unless there are younger brothers ready to marry for the first time. Among Luo it is customary to earmark the cash and cattle received as bridewealth for marriage rather than divert them as capital into, say, the purchase of a shop or land. And so it is possible to find a man who might not normally aim to increase his number of wives becoming a polygynist simply because the bridewealth for a recently married sister is available and his parents and other elders urge him to do so. The provision of accommodation in Nairobi for sisters, then, has to be seen as playing a part in the perpetuation of polygyny and in building up a nuclear family into a polygynous one.

It is not surprising that men do not normally accommodate nor sponsor their half-sisters in Nairobi. The girls' full brothers will have a primary interest in doing that. For, unlike all other agnatic relationships, which tend to draw on a household head's budget, the obligation to accommodate full sisters tends to have some compensatory material value for him.

Most of the few non-agnatic kin who figure among Luo lodgers in Kaloleni households are matrilateral cousins, usually young men seeking work. They are accepted into the household frankly out of obligation to a mother or mother's brother. The household head, one of his own friends, relatives, or affines, may eventually act as a marriage go-between (*jagam*) for a lodger related by non-agnatic kinship. Matrilateral kin, especially the mother's brother himself, are said to be likely to fix a man up with a reliable *jagam*. Unlike brothers, non-agnatic kin are recognized as having neither a competing interest in the rural patrimony nor as being particularly useful in helping the head defend it. By contrast, the head's relationships with full- and half- brothers, though different in the way I have indicated, share this nakedly instrumental component which inevitably gives the relationship a sometimes bitter edge.

In sum, agnation differs from non-agnatic kinship in possessing a greater potential for classifying relatives unambiguously and specifying precise obligations, but both entitle a person at least to claim accommodation if he or she is linked to a household head in Nairobi through either. Only an unmarried full sister offers the head customarily sanctioned compensation in the form of some of the bridewealth received at her marriage. Whatever compensation the head extracts from other kin is more a matter of negotiation between himself and the lodger. Otherwise custom decrees that most kin are entitled to hospitality and help with little expectation that they should repay their host.

Affines

The word *oche* means "those whom we may marry" and is the general term for actual and potential in-laws. As Southall points out (1952, p. 22) it traditionally carried an attitude of hostility between the marriageable groups and was often used interchangeably with the term for enemies, *wasigu*. Nowadays in Nairobi at least and possibly more generally in Luoland the attitude is generally one of cool reserve based on the contractual awareness that the precise amount of bride-wealth must always be bargained for and that bargains can be broken or their fulfilment delayed after the marriage. *Or* is the singular of *oche*. With the possessive suffix this becomes, for example, *ora*, "my brother-in-law". For "my sister-in-law" this is prefixed to form *yuora*. These are reciprocal terms, so that I call and refer to my wife's brother *ora* just as he calls me, his sister's husband, by the same term. Similarly, I call his sister (my wife's sister) *yuora*, just as he calls my sister (i.e. his brother-in-law's sister) *yuora*. In this agnatically based society, my own full or half-brother (and technically any classificatory brother) is referred to by the same affinal terms as for myself. And so I also call my brother's wife's brother *ora* and the latter's sister *yuora*, with both terms duly reciprocated by our respective brothers and sisters. In this way, patrilineage identities and distinctions are unambiguously maintained, as are the on going marriage "alliance" relationships between particular maximal exogamous lineages.

Affines are 17 per cent of all adult lodgers among Luo in Kaloleni, which is over half the population of non-agnatic kin. It is striking that all but eight of these 67 affines are women, called *yuora*, by the head. Nearly a half are wives of the head's own agnates. But many of these women are unmarried but marriageable sisters of the head's wives, brought into the household at the suggestion of the head's wife herself. Why should a household head provide board and lodging for his wife's unmarried sister when, as I pointed out above, it is profitable for her own brothers to do so? The simple answer is either that the wife has no brothers or that they are too young to be earning, or that they are still unemployed and themselves dependent lodgers elsewhere. Just as senior brothers in employment provide for younger siblings, so married women, in the absence of brothers able to do so, try to ensure that younger sisters are provided for. But whereas brotherly relationships are inevitably hedged around with the underlying rivalry deriving from the competition for common patrimony, sister relationships have none of this in-built competitiveness. Sisters clearly value the relationship. In rural Luoland they are likely to become dispersed and live far apart from each other after marriage. But should both their husbands be living with them in Nairobi, they can visit each other comparatively easily and remain in close contact. Sisters see that one way, therefore, of maintaining a desirable relationship is to bring a younger sister to Nairobi in the hope that the man she eventually marries works there rather than in, say, another town like Mombasa, Nakuru or Kisumu. Rapid urbanization and an increasing rate of rural emigration by job-seeking males has thus made it more possible for sisters to remain close friends after marriage. In a few cases a wife's sister becomes a husband's second wife.

A husband who is asked to provide for his wife's younger sister in Nairobi, does not normally resent this extra drain on his resources. He may at least have the opportunity of proposing to the wife's parents that, in return for providing the girl's food and sometimes fees for schooling or training, he should be compensated either by receiving some of the girl's bridewealth or by getting a reduction in any of his own bridewealth still due to his parents-in-law. A consequence of this arrangement is that the husband is in a position to "offer" a bride to a friend and at the same time act as the marriage go-between, without transforming the friendship into a relationship of affinity. Friends can remain friends without having to become affines, and to the profit of the "donor" friend.

In sum, then, very few male affines are found as lodgers. A significant number of lodging affines are unmarried sisters of a household head's wife. I suggest that their inclusion as "wards" in Nairobi households is important in four ways: it consolidates and perpetuates relationships between sisters; husband and wife have joint conjugal interests in the future of the wife's sister; it creates an opportunity for bargain and agreement between the husband and his wife's parents over the proceeds of any bridewealth eventually received for the girl; it enables a man to "offer" a friend a bride without requiring that the men become affines. All these consequences are of a strictly non-customary nature and yet they are ultimately governed by the overall customary expectation, which is rarely effectively ignored, that all marriages should be accompanied by valuable transactions of bridewealth.

In its critical nature, it parallels that other relationship in which bridewealth is such an important factor, namely that between a household head and his unmarried full sister. It will be remembered that this is the one relationship among those with agnatic lodgers from which a sponsoring brother may expect compensation in the form of some of the bridewealth received for her marriage. The distinctive feature of this lodging relationship is that, in so far as the brother is a member of the girl's own natal agnatic grouping, it is much closer to traditional customary expectations that he should benefit from her marriage in this way. But when a man benefits from his sister-in-law's marriage, custom has literally been turned upside down and represents a radical innovation. The important point, however, is that though one represents change and the other continuity of custom, both relationships sustain the overall institution of bridewealth. Thus, in terms of the cultural rules making up the institution, the relationship between a brother and his lodging full sister (*nyaminwa*) is approximately correct, while that between a man and his wife's sister (*yuora*) is quite incorrect. When, as household head, I agree to accept compensation from her bridewealth, *yuora* is being treated partly as if she were *nyaminwa*. In other words, within the relationships making up the institution of bridewealth, there is, so to speak, some rethinking of customary expectations. And in this process of rethinking it is mainly women, as sisters and wives, who are both active and passive agents of change. As I shall show later, these contradictory or ambivalent consequences stemming from the status of women are not confined to the domestic affairs of households. They reverberate throughout the Luo community in Nairobi and represent potential areas of change in the status of women.

Unrelated lodgers ("friends")

These account for almost a third of all lodgers among Luo in Kaloleni and so are more numerous than either affines or non-agnatic kin. A household head in Nairobi is of course surrounded by an infinitely larger number of non-relatives than relatives, and we might therefore expect to find more of them as lodgers. Indeed, it is an index of the combined strength of kinship and affinal obligations among Luo that non-relatives are not even more highly represented as lodgers, as proportionally they are among the Luyia, Kikuyu and Kamba. Nevertheless, since kin and affines *are* able to exert such strong claims on a household head for accommodation, we must ask how and why unrelated persons are accepted at all as lodgers.

The first point to make is that all but nine of these 121 adult non-relatives in Kaloleni households are fellow Luo. Most are men (72) and three-quarters of the women (38) are their wives. Most of the other women (11) are unrelated friends of the household head's own wife or wives. Altogether, two-thirds (53) of the men lodgers are married and three-quarters of them do have their wives and children with them in Nairobi. Most of them are employed but simply have not yet acquired their own accommodation necessary for stable urban family settlement. They are one rather large step down in the residential pecking order and may have been trying to find their own independent accommodation for many months and even years. Initially, they are likely to have stayed with a relative, usually an agnate, as might be expected from the account already given. Then, after staying with a succession of other relatives, they are likely to have used up their moral credit there, so to speak, and to have turned in default of other kin willing or able to accommodate them to unrelated "friends", as their household hosts are called. Sometimes these unrelated hosts welcome the prospect of a joint contribution to the household budget and either offer accommodation or encourage their friends to ask for it.

This is a caricature but depicts the salient features and shows that unrelated lodgers are not necessarily a "different kind" of people from lodgers who are kin and affines but only that they tend to have reached a more advanced stage in the urban life cycle: they may have been living and earning in town longer and also be married and with children. In many cases they are not even younger than their unrelated household hosts.

It is important to recognize that, as the Nairobi immigration rate continues to exceed the availability of new houses in the city, this category of predominantly family men is probably increasing. The discrepancy in good fortune between themselves and the luckier category of family heads with secure housing is seen by them to be growing all the time. They can see that the opportunity gap is widening as an increasingly smaller proportion of them seem to move up and out of the category of urban homeless.

It is against this background of a perceived imbalance in the distribution of good fortune that requests for accommodation are made by these unrelated men. The justification for the request can be phrased in a number of familiar ways : "I came to Nairobi and got a job and married at about the same time as you did, yet you have your own home here while I have done nothing but lodge with other people." "When you were my age it was easier to find housing that it is at this time, so how can you refuse to help me now?" "If you will not give me accommodation, I shall have to return home and lose my job. What will happen to my wife and children? You would not want this to happen to yourself." And so on. These different arguments of justification are, again, based on the Luo egalitarian philosophy that one man's good fortune does not absolve him from caring for the less fortunate. For anthropologists who have encountered the reasoning behind veiled threats and accusations of witchcraft malpractices in other societies, these appeals for accommodation carry a famliar ring. Indeed, some relationships between host and unrelated lodger may eventually crumble under accusations of witchcraft.

Nevertheless, long before this breaking point is reached, and both before and during the period spent living together in the same house, a household head and his unrelated lodger are regarded as friends. The word for "my friend" is *osiepna*. This is used as a term of reference rather than of address, for which the term *omera* is used. *Omera* is also used as a term of reference. As I shall show, it is a key term.

Omera is a difficult word to translate. It is usually translated as "my brother" by Luo themselves but has a general referent and need not specifically apply to my consanguineal relatives, for which the term of reference is *watna* (which is sometimes extended to refer to known male affines of "my mother's brother", *nera*). *Omera* is recognized as *theoretically* quite distinct from the term of reference and address normally used for my full and half-brother and, sometimes, up to second patrilateral parallel cousin, which is *owadwa*. Here, let me mention an observation spontaneously and independently made by some Luo informants whom I knew in Kampala, Uganda, some years before I worked in Kenya. They recalled that in "foreign" Uganda, *owadwa* would be used up to first or second patrilateral parallel cousin but that, in Nairobi in their "home" country of Kenya, it might be restricted to only full brother, with a half-brother and other agnates called and referred to as *omera*. In fact, in Nairobi I did frequently hear *owadwa* used to refer to agnates beyond full brothers, as in Kampala, but these observations are an interesting indication that Luo themselves recognize a segmentary variability in actual use of these terms according to ideas of *social* distance from "home" (in fact Kampala is as geographically close to Luoland as Nairobi) similar to that reported by Evans-Pritchard's Nuer informants. *Owadwa*, then, usually means "close" agnate and, though there may be situational variability in the definition of "closeness", it is regarded as indicating (a) agnation, and (b) a closer agnatic relationship than that connoted by *omera*, which can also be applied to non-agnatic relatives and unrelated friends, as I shall show. To clarify matters, I have outlined the variability and situational overlap of these and other terms which I have yet to mention, in a simple diagram (Fig. 2).

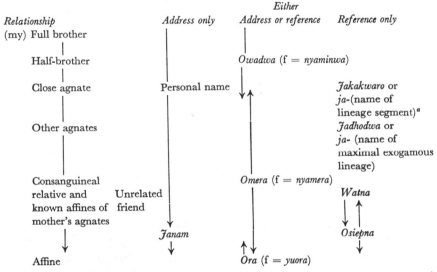

a In differentiating these two levels, I can say *tiendwa kamgang* ("my lineage segment is *kamgang*") as distinct from *dhodwa kabar* ("my maximal exogamous lineage is *kabar*").

Fig. 2. Luo terms of address and reference among generation peers in Nairobi.

As mentioned above, *nyaminwa* means my full or half-sister. There is also a general term for an unrelated female "sister", *nyamera*, which corresponds to the general term *omera*. In practice it is quite common to hear unrelated females addressed as *omera*. As a sexless and general form of address, therefore, *omera* does seem to predicate a numerically preponderant sphere of relationships in the Nairobi Luo community in which camaraderie with the general obligations of kinship are desired but to the exclusion of direct and specific kinship responsibilities. One Luo man summed up the sentiment expressed in the use of the term *omera* in these words: "It is a polite way of addressing somebody if you don't want to use his name. It is a brotherly way of addressing someone. You can call a girl or young woman *omera* and she can call you this in return, though neither of you are real brother and sister. People who use *omera* assume that originally they were from one mother and father." In Nairobi it thus becomes a general term which can be addressed to fellow Luo using their own vernacular, to those Luyia who speak it, and to the very occasional fellow Nilotic speaker from Uganda.

There is a second general term of address and reference. This is *janam*, which literally means "person of the lake". Luoland adjoins the eastern coast of Lake Nyanza and so the term refers to Luo generally. *Janam* is really an ethnic nickname, for Luo often contrast it with their nickname for Kikuyu, *jarabwon* ("potato-man", referring to the Kikuyu diet), or that for European, *odiero* ("a small fierce white bird") but, also, curiously enough, a nickname for their foremost elder, Oginga Odinga. Luo who have lived in Uganda jokingly further note the lexical affinity with the Nilotic people, the *Jonam* (sing. *Janam*), suggesting a wider all-Nilotic connotation.

The main point to make here about the term *janam* is that its use in Nairobi does not ambiguously compound kinship with friendship as does *omera*. It tends to be used selectively between unrelated friends who are not bound to each other by obligations of a domestic kind. It is seen to be devoid of any contractual element and is the most neutral term of endearment or attachment possible. By contrast, the term *omera* connotes the mutual dependence of Luo as a single ethnic group in the face of demands made on them as individuals in a competitive system of education and employment.

The line between who is "real" kin and who is not can be blurred and may vary accordingly to situation. This facilitates the ambivalent expression of group and individual interests connoted by the term *omera*. But Luo can be relatively consistent. Thus, the 2500 or so men of the maximal exogamous lineage of Kabar, which is partly territorially coterminous with the administrative sub-location of Kabar in East Kano, recognize four main lineage segments: Kamlago, Kadieto, Kochieng, and Kamgang. A general term of reference for fellow-members at either segmental level is *Jadhodwa* (which means "man of my lineage"). Sometimes the term for descendants of a common great-grandfather is used here, *jokakwaro*. Further differentia-

tion may require a fellow member to be referred to by the name of
the segments, e.g. *jakamlago*, with outsiders referring to a member of
the maximal lineage as a whole as *jakabar*. At a further, more inclusive level, location membership may be specified, e.g. *jakano ugwe*
("a man of east Kano") as opposed to *jakano imbo* ("a man of west
Kano).

Over and above these precise segmentary appellations, fellow members of the maximal lineage may simply refer to and, especially, call
each other *omera*, with no specific degree of agnation specified. As a
term of address and, to a lesser extent, of reference, *omera* may also
be used for a consanguinal relative, an affine of a mother's brother,
and a quite unrelated friend, as I have mentioned. *Omera* is thus a
convenient term of both address and reference, though heard more as
one of address, which avoids the specificity of particular kin terms
and relationships and yet which carries the connotation of ultimate
ancestral origin and so straddles the conceptual idioms of kinship and
friendship.

Nevertheless, the terminological distinction between *osiepna*, a
term of reference, and *omera*, primarily a term of address, supports
the impression that, in the cognitive categories of Luo culture, there
exists a contrast between two kinds of friendship. One carries few if
any undertones of kinship obligation. The other does carry these
undertones. In conversation, Luo certainly differentiate between
friends who do not make demands like kinsmen and those who do. The
same friends may at different times be classified either way. The
Luo "friend" is another example of a role which has ambivalent connotations and consequences.

Among the unrelated lodgers in Kaloleni we have an interesting
contrast which is pointed out by Luo themselves and which is used to
substantiate the distinction which they hold between those whom I
may call kinly and unkinly friends. Kinly friends are those who come
from your home area and who use this common origin as the main
basis for claiming accommodation and help. They are alleged often to
know the household head's family and may point to some other possible linkages. In the Luo households in Kaloleni twenty-two men
are indicated as being friends of this kind. By contrast, there are fifty
unkinly friends, nine of them non-Luo. These are men with whom
the household head first struck up a friendship in Nairobi and in a
few cases in some other town but not in the rural area. The claim is

E

that they do not come from the same home areas as their household hosts, which on investigation generally proved to be the case. Certainly, immediate home origins were declared to be irrelevant for the relationship.

It is interesting that among these unrelated Luo lodgers in Kaloleni, friends who were first met in town are almost twice as numerous as those previously known in the rural area. And if we include also the nine non-Luo lodgers in the sample, then the incidence of friendship initiated in town is even higher. Luo in Nairobi regard this as reflecting their own preference for friends who are furthest away from behaving like kin. They also say that when urban-initiated friends who are being given accommodation start behaving like kin, then household quarrels begin and the friendship turns to enmity. This may happen when, for example, a friend fails to contribute to the household budget on the grounds of "poverty" or unemployment but expects nevertheless to continue to receive board and lodging. This tendancy suggests that the realms of friendship, of being *osiepna*, and of kinship behaviour should be kept distinct in practice, even though ideologically, through the use of the mediating term *omera*, an element of kinship is approvingly admitted into a relationship of friendship. It is as if, in the concepts and language of Luo, friendship makes up a spectrum: at one end it exists in its purest, most unkinly form, and at the other end it begins to merge almost imperceptibly with "real" kinship; from the household head's viewpoint the ideal is to control the relationship so that it stands in the middle.

This contrast between unkinly and kinly friends is normally expressed in distinct phrases—the paroles of conversation, and not as yet by distinct role-terms (Parkin, 1976, pp. 183–6). We do however see a partial parallel expression of this contrast in the opposed role-terms, *jagam* and *jasem*. *Jagam* is a marriage go-between (cf. Evans-Pritchard, 1965, pp. 230–1 *passim*). He is supposed in Nairobi to be a reliable friend (and sometimes a relative or affine including, though rarely, a female) who introduces a man to a "good" potential bride and amicably mediates between the man's and the girl's kin in arriving at a mutually acceptable bridewealth. He dispels doubts that either set of kin might have about the "character" of their prospective in-law. The term *jagam* comes from the verb -*gamo*, to hand over, and clearly connotes the mediatory role in the exchanges accompanying marriage; the role combines the Anglo-Christian groom's "best man" and the bride's father or guardian who is explicitly asked by a priest if he will "give" the woman. Another Luo "slang" term is *jayo* or *jawang'yo*, literally "the pathway-one", which has the intended double innuendo of connoting someone who not only creates pathways to affines but to the woman herself.

By contrast *jasem* (pl. *josem*) refers to those of a man's or woman's friends who are, for various reasons, opposed to the marriage: it is said that they may have a grudge against either party or may themselves see the woman or man as a spouse. Sometimes, it is said, a *jasem* may pretend to be a *jagam* and then, "secretly", break the prospective marriage. The term *jasem* comes from the verb *-semo*, to dissuade someone from doing something, and has the extra, more sinister connotation of someone who "interferes" destructively, rather like jealous kin. *Josem* are the kind of friends who may so upset a new wife in the urban welcoming party (*budho miaha*, literally, "conversing with the bride"), that she runs away from you. From among one's genuine, what I have called unkinly friends, one is likely to find a good *jagam* (a reliable marriage go-between), but from among one's kinly friends one is more likely to find *josem* (destructive interferers).

In sum, unrelated lodgers in Luo households in Kaloleni are characterized as friends. They form a large proportion of all lodgers. Most of them are also Luo and have lived and worked in town almost as long as their household hosts, and most of them are married and with children. They are not normally much more junior than their hosts in terms of urban experience and involvement, but they do lack housing of their own and have become dependent on a long succession of household heads, ranging from relatives to non-relatives. Most of them first met and became friends with their unrelated household hosts in Nairobi. They are depicted as less likely than friends originally known in the rural area to make inordinate and unreciprocated demands on the host and more likely to provide possible benefits through fair contributions to the budget. Friends originally known in the rural area are said to behave more like kin and therefore as more likely to waste a household head's resources. But it is also recognized that friends first known in town may gradually assume these same undesirable characteristics. The term *omera* means both friend and brother and summarizes aptly the inherent contradiction in Luo expectations of behaviour from persons addressed by this term: on the one hand the relationship is given respectability and warmth by the use of the term rather than by the formal use of the person's name; on the other hand close interaction between two unrelated persons who address each other as *omera* is always likely over time to increase the demands by one for the assistance of the other.

Friendship, then, may be broken by "becoming" kinship. There is a second way in which a friendship may become brittle. I noted above that even in town, close affines may remain cool towards each other, sometimes for years. Much depends on the speed with which bride-wealth (*keny* or *-nyombo*, v.i.) has been transacted. The longer the period of payment the longer affines view the relationship as based on the potential transfer of property than on personal grounds. Even after the bulk of the bridewealth has been paid, perhaps after five or more years,[1] close affines, especially a man and his brothers and his wife's brothers, may visit each other in Nairobi with all the trappings of friendship. But there is always the underlying recognition of the pro-perty basis to the relationship which, if ended by divorce, would en-tail a return of at least some of the bridewealth to the husband and his family, unless the wife had produced as many as four or five child-ren during her marriage.

The increased monetization of bridewealth has, if anything, intro-duced even more uncertainty in affinal relationships. The increased preference for cash among Luo in Nairobi is primarily expressed by those about to receive bridewealth, i.e. the fathers or brothers of brides. One Luo who had spent most of his life in towns said, "It is no good offering me cattle. What can I do with them here (in Nairobi)? They would only go to my rural homestead and can be used by other people there. Let me have cash." And yet, from the viewpoint of the man, perhaps the same man at a different time, transferring a mainly cash bridewealth, this use of money makes its return in the event of divorce less certain than when cattle are used. As another Luo said, "You can see cattle in the (bride's father's) homestead. But cash is a private thing which you cannot see and cannot know if they (the bride's family) have spent it." (cf. Simmel, 1964, p. 335, on this pri-vatizing quality of money.) The view here is that the returnability of the cash component in bridewealth is most in doubt, and with it the credibility of affines.

It follows from this that two unrelated friends, whether they first

---

[1] Betty Potash (1977) has extensive cases from a rural Luo community in South Nyanza in which bridewealth payments are not usually made in less than 10 years.

met in town or in the rural home area, place their friendship in jeopardy if one of them is introduced to and then marries the other's sister or cousin. They convert the relationship from one of friendship to one of affinity. Luo speak of this as a marriage arranged without a go-between, for it is a direct agreement between the man who introduces his sister and his friend. The two friends may reject the possibility of the marriage affecting their friendship, both claiming to be reasonable men who can agree perfectly amicably on the amount of bridewealth and duration of its payment. But once the girl and man agree to the marriage, the two friends cease to be the free agents they had imagined they were: the girl's family put pressure on her brother to extort more bridewealth from his friend and to demand more rapid payment. I know of no case of this kind in which the friendship has been unaffected by these extra demands. The relationship is in all cases inevitably redefined. *Osiepna*, my friend, whom I used to call *omera*, by brother, but without the exactions of kinship, now becomes *ora*, my brother-in-law. Our previously personally controlled relationship now comes under the partial control of our respective families.

The Luo themselves recognize that an ingenious solution to this problem of converting friendship into affinity has arisen in Nairobi. I have in fact already referred to it in my description of affines. There I noted the large proportion of female lodgers in Kaloleni who are unmarried but marriageable sisters of the wives of household heads. I explained that, in the absence of a wife's brothers, her own husband might be given charge of her sister's marriage arrangements. The man then has at his "disposal", so to speak, a woman who is not his own sister and whose marriage to a friend will not convert their friendship into affinity. He acts as the go-between (*jagam*) for his wife's sister's family (i.e. his own affines) and his friend and family. The go-between does, of course, have a material interest in proper and due marriage payments, for he either receives a "commission" or is allowed some remission by his own parents-in-law in paying his own bridewealth. But this is not an obvious benefit and the two friends can see themselves further linked to each other through their wives to the same set of affines and as therefore having a basic common interest in helping each other maintain conjugal harmony as do brothers. *Osiepna*, my friend, whom I may call *omera*, my brother, continues to be called *omera*, and we are free of any kinship or affinal claims on each other.

Apart from these two main possibilities, friends become marriage go-betweens for completely unrelated parties, involving another friend, and the friendship is even less likely to be disrupted. The three marriage possibilities involving friends may be presented as follows:

1. I offer you my sister
2. I offer you my wife's sister
3. I offer you my friend's sister

Whereas the first two possibilities draw on the closed dyadic relationship of the two friends themselves, the third involves a third person who is friend to the go-between but not necessarily to the suitor. Put another way this means that: (a) I have two friends who do not know each other; (b) one wants a wife and the other has a marriageable sister; (c) I act as go-between and arrange for their marriage; (d) I therefore create a relationship of affinity between two of my friends.

Then there is a fourth possibility, which compounds the second and third, namely: 4. I offer you my friend's wife's sister. In this case I help create a relationship of affinity between my friend who wants to marry and my friend's own affines. Here, however, my friend, who is guardian of his wife's sister, is likely to be the go-between and my own role peripheral.

We see, therefore, how friendship is inextricably involved in the delineation of marriage "choices" and patterns, and in the definition of women's status. For, while male agnates and sometimes other male kin consciously apply pressure on their females to marry subject to their "advice" and to maintain conjugal harmony, friends also less consciously perpetuate the involvement of many kin of both the groom and bride in marriage. Friends will point to their relationship as freed from kinship constraint. In practice, and seemingly unbeknown to them, the network of friendships of which they are but a part, draw them into other relations of kinship and affinity and so is limited by them. This is an example of unconscious logical consistency in institutional behaviour to which Nadel referred (1951, pp. 258–65) and which I discussed in the Introduction, and which is seen here to triumph, so to speak, over a potential inconsistency in obligations to agnates and friends.

In summary, the freedom from kin that Luo see as a quality of friendship is grossly exaggerated, if not illusory.

The emic polarization of agnation and friendship

Following conventional anthropological analysis, four categories of lodgers have been distinguished; agnates, non-agnatic kin, affines, and unrelated lodgers who are characterized as friends. Let me summarize their characteristics and then show that they can actually be reduced to two ideal sets of relations: those of agnation which are seen by Luo to survive and thrive only by collective endeavour; and those of friendship which are seen, though falsely, to provide an individual with some control over his destiny.

CONTINUITY: AGNATES AND KIN

Most consanguineally related lodgers in Luo households in Kaloleni are agnates, and most of these are full siblings, half-brothers, and male patrilateral parallel cousins of the household head. Unmarried full sisters are quite numerous but there are no half-sisters and only a couple of female patrilateral cousins. From the household head's point of view this makes sense because he, or a younger full brother, may benefit from the bridewealth received for a full sister's marriage but not from a half-sister's. Some brothers can use a full sister's bridewealth to acquire a second wife. All brothers are potential rivals for land at the rural home but half-brothers much more so, because their respective mothers are taken as the main guides in the division of the property: when a father dies his assets are divided in the first place according to the number of co-wives he has and only then sub-divided between the sons of a particular co-wife.

The number and range of agnatic lodgers in Kaloleni thus reflects very closely the way in which the rural compound polygynous family operates. Common interests in rural property explain why full brothers and sisters, and to a less extent half-brothers, and to an even lesser extent, patrilateral parallel cousins feel justified in asking senior hosts in Kaloleni for accommodation and assistance. The requests are phrased in a moral idiom which indicates that the household head is under a prior obligation to accommodate them. As is characteristic of societies with an all-pervasive patrilineal ideology, the use of this moral idiom to back up requests for help is extended to all persons who can show some agnatic relationship with the host.

On the whole, then, the obligations arising from agnation and the pursuit of the polygynous ideal persist among Luo in Kaloleni even under the urban conditions of residence and employment in Nairobi. One innovation is the greater control which an elder brother with a house in Nairobi may exert over the marriage of his sister and the use of her bridewealth. In a purely traditional rural context, control would rest more firmly in the hands of the girl's father. Even so, the decision to allow an unmarried girl to go to stay with an elder brother in Nairobi will have been taken by her father in consultation with her mother.

Similarly, there are certain persisting features in the pattern of obligations between non-agnatic kin. There are no rural property interests in common and no over-arching patrilineal ideology. A sense of personal obligation to his own mother may prompt a household head in Kaloleni to agree to give board and lodging to a matrilateral relative. The absence of common economic interests and of a supporting ideology explain why so few non-agnatic kin are found as lodgers. What can be said of kinship as opposed to agnatic relationships in Nairobi is that they lose their individual definition and merge to form a loose category of known but normally unspecified ties.

What keeps both agnatic and non-agnatic kinship relations in some sort of ordered relationship with each other are the terms of reference and address. The main terms of address (e.g. *omera/nyamera*, and *janam*) are sufficiently unspecific to "cover" both agnatic and non-agnatic kinship differences. But the terms of reference (e.g. ranging from *jakakwaro* to *jadhodwa*) are still used situationally to define different segmentary levels of agnatic inclusion and exclusion. Potential disorder is checked by order.

CHANGE: AFFINES

The persistence and relatively unaltered nature in Nairobi of agnatic terms, concepts, and relationships, and to a lesser extent those of non-agnatic kinship, contrasts with the change in one affinal relationship. Most lodgers who are affines of the household head are women. Half are the wives of the head's agnates lodging with him and half are unmarried sisters of the head's own wife. The presence of these wife's sisters is a definite source of change. First, the ability of a wife to bring her sister to live with her in the urban household and to have her provided for and her marriage arranged by her husband can represent the wife's greater involvement in his nominal control over the household and its budget and, second, may create an important link in the chain of relationships which women in Nairobi are able to forge with each other. Third, in exchange for providing for a wife's sister and helping her find an acceptable husband, an increasing number of household hosts expect to be compensated by being given part of the bridewealth when the girl marries, or by having their own bridewealth payments reduced or delayed. In some cases they may themselves take her as a second wife. Fourth, this arrangement enables the man to "offer" a friend the girl as a wife without requiring them to become affines. Friendship is more likely to persist if it is not converted into affinity.

It is important to note, here, that these changes involve women, as wives or as full sisters. Even so, their roles are ambivalent and even contradictory. For as women already or about to be involved in bridewealth transactions, from which virtually only men benefit, they perpetuate the institution of bridewealth. Yet, it is through these women that men redefine the flow of benefits.

CONTINUITY THROUGH CHANGE: FRIENDS

The fourth main category of lodger relationships, that of friends, is also one in which customary obligations are rethought and negotiated. "Pure" friends do not make demands like kin but many may eventually do so. Luo think of friendship ideally as a desirable alternative and escape from the incessant demands of kinship and are reluctant to allow it to assume kinship characteristics. But this is always a possibility and is made conceptually easier by the fact that friends are normally addressed by the term, *omera*, which can mean friendship but which strongly connotes also an underlying bond of ultimate kinship. The status of friends, like the status of women, undeniably facilitates innovation in personal relationships among Luo in Nairobi. But, like the status of women, it is also bound up with alternative values which resist change. Just as the changing status of women has done little so far to dislodge the institution of bridewealth, so the alterations to customary behaviour made possible by the inclusion of a larger number of unrelated friends in an urban-dweller's social network do not obliterate the underlying idiom of kinship, nor the terms by which particular relationships of kinship are made cognitively salient.

At this point, we can temporarily dismantle the conventional anthropological distinctions into the four categories of agnates, non-agnatic kin, affines, and friends. Instead we can break them down into two. First, agreed genealogical reckoning ensures that an agnate is always an agnate and can never contract out of this designation. Second, the common characteristic of non-agnatic kin, affines, and friends, is that these are shifting relationships. With friendship at the centre they can shade into each other, both terminologically and conceptually. Though initially contrasted favourably with a relative, a friend may eventually become referred to by general kinship terms of address and reference, and may himself assume commensurate behavioural expectations. Or, he may become an affine to a previous friend through his own or a sister's or daughter's marriage. Where close affines were not previously friends, their initial mutual reservedness may mellow on the basis of relatively frequent urban interaction, but Luo recognize the unlikelihood of it rapidly becoming "true" friendship, for bridewealth payments are heavy and place a utilitarian brake on personal involvement.

As a system of ideas about relationships *consistently* linked to the inheritance of land and the acquisition of bridewealth for marriage, agnation only makes sense to Luo when contrasted with non-agnatic relationships, of which friendship forms the most important component in Nairobi. Abstracted in this way, agnation and friendship represent divergent and potentially conflicting ties.

Conclusion

The underlying ascriptive ideal of agnation among Luo is expressed unambiguously and in its most condensed form in a range of predominantly reference terms: from that for "my (real) brother" (*owadwa*), to *jakakwaro*, "someone of (our) common great-grandfather", to *jadhodwa*, "my agnate" of any level of lineage segmentation up to that of maximal exogamy, and including other terms. The freely negotiable ideal entailed in friendship is expressed most poignantly in the term of reference *osiepna* (my friend) and in the term of address *janam* (man of the lake, i.e. fellow-countryman). Between these two poles of a continuum depicting the relative strengths of structural and personal obligations is the term of address and reference, *omera*. The connotations behind the use of *omera* may "spread" from the middle of the continuum outwards in either direction: towards the ascriptive pole, as when an unrelated friend becomes or behaves like an affine or relative; or towards the freely negotiable pole, as when a relative or even affine establishes a relationship of balanced and equal reciprocity and discards appeals phrased in the moral idiom of kinship and affinity.

Frake asserts that "the anthropologist's distinction between 'terms of reference' and 'terms of address' represents a naive and incorrect typology of speech acts" (1975, p. 36). He wants to break down terms of address into greetings, summonses, tags, etc., and we may assume that he would want to do the same for reference terms. A breakdown of this kind may be necessary for his intensive study, occupying sixteen pages, of the verbal formulae required for entering a Yakan house. But I would argue that this distinction between the usage of terms is still crucial. As the work on the use of *tu* and *vous* and comparable pronominal address terms has shown (Friedrick, 1966; Brown and Gilman, 1972; Ervin-Tripp, 1972; Lambert, 1972, and others), terms of address are what we may call speech acts of potential face-to-face confrontation. That is to say, by your very choice of term you acknowledge either the superiority and power of the addressee, or his junior and weak status, or, sometimes cross-cutting these, a relationship of trust and even intimacy. Or, you may use a neutral term which implies equality, with or without intimacy. How you refer to someone behind his back and out of earshot need not affect your relationship with him, for he may never hear about it. But how you address him presents him directly with your definition of the relationship as being either hierarchical or egalitarian; and either warm, neutral, or hostile. Among Luo, the use of personal names and *janam* normally ensures equality and some warmth. *Omera* clearly connotes warmth and equality in the early stages of a friendship but later it can presuppose the "generosity" of a kinship superior (Sahlins, 1965, p. 147).

As wives, sisters, or daughters, women are central in this continuum of role definition and redefinition. It is around the status of women that agnatic obligations and the ideal of polygyny are preserved. Yet it is by and through women that particular relationships are being redefined. Many of the changes in personal relationships occur in that large area of ostensibly free and unfettered association which we, as much as Luo, recognize and which I can only translate as friendship. Yet, in its possible movement towards becoming classified as kinship or affinity, friendship is also subject to checks on the extent to which it really does offer a free choice of associates, behaviour and activities. In addition, it is through friends acting as go-betweens that men continue to subscribe to customary marriages, including the requirement that rules of lineage exogamy be observed and that a valuable bride-wealth be paid. The conservative element in friendship is thus very much greater than many Luo realize.

Polygyny and agnation are part and parcel of the Luo ideal mode of self-perpetuation. The search for friends is seen by Luo to threaten this customary ideal if it leads to the neglect of agnates but to support it if the friends become affines through marriage to their sisters or daughters. Associating with friends to the neglect of agnates (and to a lesser extent, kin generally) arouses the same kind of moral disapproval as does favouring one child's education and neglecting that of others. Both are said to arise from too much "pride" (it may be said of a man that he is proud, *sunga* or *osungere*) and to create unnecessary jealousy (*nyiego*). While polygyny and agnation emphasize a collective mode of self-advancement and perpetuation, the search for friends and for education in a system of meritocratic rewards are individualistic modes: it is largely illusory, but friends seem to Luo to offer "escape" from the demands and expectations of agnates, including the customary one that "surplus" cash can be invested in more wives and thereby more children than in education for a limited number.

This current conflict of expectations, one customary and the other of recent origin, arose as men, and subsequently their families, spent more time in town, and became economically more dependent on urban cash incomes. In the next chapter I show how the conflict developed among Luo in Nairobi. I describe the conditions under which polygyny has persisted to a remarkably high degree. Parallel with this development, however, Luo men have increasingly switched from what was a small but growing niche of self-employment and entrepreneurship to work instead as clerks and skilled men for non-Luo employers, both public and private. This switch has been accompanied by a marked emphasis on the value of education as the key to success in these white-collar and skilled occupations. Thus, while polygyny continues as one customary form of social investment by men, education provides another in some respects competing one. Paradoxically, as men have left self-employment, the persistence of polygyny has offered wives the chance to engage in petty urban trade, usually under the auspices of their husbands. There is here a sense in which the persistence of polygyny binds men to traditional Luo ideals more than it does their womenfolk. For, as we shall see, it is men's urban wages which have enabled polygyny to persist and so, with increasing bridewealth payments, they have become increasingly dependent on these wages.

4

The Seeds of Uncertainty

Wage Dependency and Female Dependants

In the last chapter I distinguished between the strong persistence of agnatic ties and of friendship in choosing lodgers. Agnatic obedience and friendship are depicted by Luo as potentially in conflict: to please a friend you have to limit your obligations to an agnate; to fulfil a customary duty to an agnate you have to neglect a personal favour to a friend. We have already seen how the agnatic ideal is linked to that of polygyny in the Luo system of polysegmentary lineage organization, and how even today, Luo townsmen respond to this linking of factors by continuing to marry polygynously and by placing obligations to agnates highest on their list of moral priorities. An important obligation in the urban context, among full brothers especially, is to provide education. A man may eventually have to educate not only these brothers and other relatives but also his own children. And yet to provide limited education for many rather than a higher level for a few is a poor investment in an employment market saturated with moderately educated young job-seekers. The expansionist and yet egalitarian ideals associated with polygyny and agnation thus conflict with those of an educational meritocracy aimed at selecting and rewarding only a few individuals. How did this conflict arise? And how has it affected women's status, on which the perpetuation of polygyny depends?

To answer these questions we must first look at the occupations in which Luo in Kaloleni are found.

From trader to clerk

Comparing the four main ethnic groups in Kaloleni, Luo household heads show two distinctive features (see Table 12): first, they have the smallest proportion of unskilled workers; and second, their proportion of self-employed is almost that of the Kikuyu, who, as other surveys indicate, and as is well known, otherwise dominate this growing sector.

TABLE 12

Occupation by ethnic group in Kaloleni

	White-collar (%)	Blue-collar (%)	Un-skilled (%)	Self-employed (%)	Un-employed (%)
Luo (333)	36.3	38.1	10.2	13.2	2.1
Luyia (222)	30.2	39.2	24.3	4.5	1.8
Kikuyu (122)	39.3	23.8	21.3	15.6	—
Kamba (133)	27.1	43.6	23.3	5.3	0.7
Others (42)	30.9	40.5	19.0	4.8	4.8

Unskilled workers among Luo still tend to be short-term migrants, who alternate between trying to find a better job in another town, perhaps more befitting their education, or trying their hand at a rural business and even farming. Kaloleni, it will be remembered, includes Luo household heads who have lived for many years in Nairobi and this is the main reason why so few of them have unskilled jobs, compared with the household heads of other ethnic groups in the estate. Also, though it cannot be shown by these figures, Luo have become increasingly reluctant to take on unskilled work in Nairobi: among both household heads and their lodgers, there are few unskilled workers in their twenties. This reluctance to accept unskilled work, even in the face of diminishing opportunities for employment of any kind, is ideologically tied up with the growing value placed by Luo in recent years on education as the prerequisite for clerical or at least skilled work.

We can see something of this growing emphasis on education and clerical work by looking at the differences between older and younger household heads in Kaloleni (see Table 13).

TABLE 13

Luo occupations by age and education in Kaloleni

Number of Luo household heads	Age	Average number of years formal education	White-collar employment %	Skilled and semi-skilled blue-collar employment %	Un-skilled %	Self-employed %	Un-employed %
145	Over 40	5.8	38 (26.2)	53 (36.5)	17 (11.7)	32 (22.1)	5 (3.5)
188	Under 40	8.8	83 (44.1)	74 (39.4)	17 (9.0)	12 (6.4)	2 (1.1)

We see also that accompanying the emphasis on education and clerical work, there has been a corresponding decline in jobs of a self-employed nature such as trader, market-stall holder, shopkeeper and freelance artisan. For most of the self-employed Luo are actually in their forties and fifties and began to work on their own in Nairobi from about 1952. This is when the Kenya Emergency was declared by the colonial government. The government launched Operation Anvil in 1954 and imprisoned, detained, or restricted Kikuyu men on the grounds that the Mau Mau nationalist movement was led by them. In Nairobi, Kikuyu were removed from ethnically mixed housing areas, including Kaloleni, and concentrated in guarded areas on their own. This gave Luo a much greater opportunity among Africans to trade or work in a self-employed capacity in Nairobi and other East African towns from which Kikuyu were forcibly repatriated by the colonial government. The clientele of these by now expanding Luo traders, stall-holders, and craftsmen extended beyond fellow-Luo to include also many Luyia (who are very under-represented in trading in Nairobi) and Kamba as well as those Kikuyu families dispossessed of their menfolk and lacking traders of their own ethnic group. There is even evidence from life histories that a number of Kikuyu traders, who had been forced into detention, temporarily awarded guardianship of their enterprises to Luo "friends", sometimes encouraging marriages with a "sister" so as to cement the "partnership"; the Kikuyu and Luo saw themselves at this time as being allied as Africans against the colonialists, and their respective political leaders worked hard on each others' behalf.

So, from 1954 to 1959 Luo traders and self-employed had a short period of ascendancy in African petty commerce. Their main enterprises were trading in fish, which were caught and brought to Nairobi from their home shores of Lake Nyanza, and tailoring. To these were now added the wholesaling and distribution of African foodstuffs generally and the purchase and re-sale of clothes and materials. It has to be acknowledged that, even at this time, European and Asian shops and stores still controlled much of the commercial expansion that might otherwise have been possible for the Luo. Nevertheless, the period did mark something of a heyday in Luo entrepreneurship in Nairobi, as Luo themselves observe.[1]

It does not appear that many trading licences were actually revoked by the city authorities during the Emergency. At any rate, when the Emergency was ended in 1959, and indeed a little before this when restrictions on Kikuyu were gradually lifted, Kikuyu shop and market licencees returned to resume their licensed trades. Other Kikuyu also came to the city and set up businesses or moved into low-paid "unenumerated" (i.e. officially unrecognized or unlicensed) self-employment, which grew considerably in the second half of the 1960s (Leys, 1975, p. 233). They had the advantage of being near to their own rural cash crop growing areas and of catering for an increasingly large ethnic clientele in Nairobi. Luo traders reverted to their two main activities of fish selling and tailoring.

If we look at the four city council markets in Eastlands we can see clearly the changes and trends in entrepreneurial activity among the four main ethnic groups in Nairobi. Two markets, Bama (or Shauri Moyo) and Kariokor, were established before the Emergency and Operation Anvil in 1954. Bama was made available in its present form in 1947, and Kariokor, which was established in 1924, was last extended in 1946. The other two, Kikomba and Uhuru, were established after independence in 1964 and have been extended since then. As we might expect, the two new markets are predominantly Kikuyu. In Uhuru the proportion of Kikuyu stall holders, though a simple majority, is under represented for their whole Nairobi population, a fact deriving from the large numbers of non-Kikuyu living near Uhuru market. In Kikomba market they are hugely over represented,

---

[1] Scott MacWilliam tells me that the period 1954–57 saw the registration of an disproportionately large number of Luo voluntary associations and it is tempting to see these two facts as connected.

reflecting their high residential concentration there. In Kariokor market, which was built before Operation Anvil, Kikuyu are also over represented for their population in Nairobi. Nearly all the Kikuyu stall holders in Kariokor have taken on stalls since the ending of the Emergency, having displaced a smaller number of Kamba, Luo, and to a much lesser extent Luyia stall holders. The most dramatic instance of this transfer can be seen at Bama market, which is across the road from Kaloleni estate and close to Shauri Moyo and Ziwani estates. These residential areas still have a disproportionately high number of non-Kikuyu but, like Kaloleni, have seen a steady increase in the Kikuyu proportion, almost entirely at the expense of Luo. In Bama market itself, Luo stall holders were 52 per cent of the 245 or so occupied stalls just before the Emergency ended. By 1969, this had dropped to 38 per cent while that of Kikuyu increased over the same period from 22 per cent to 38 per cent.

TABLE 14

Current ethnic proportions of stall holders in the four city council markets in Eastlands

Market	Kikuyu	Kamba	Luo	Luyia	Others	Number of stall holders
Bama (established 1947)	38.0 (93)	18.4 (45)	38.0 (93)	3.6 (9)	2.0 (5)	($N = 245$)
Kariokor (established 1924/1946)	70.7 (145)	12.7 (26)	14.6 (30)	2.0 (4)	—	($N = 205$)
Kikomba (established 1964)	72.5 (547)	10.8 (82)	12.5 (94)	3.7 (28)	0.5 (4)	($N = 755$)
Uhuru (established 1964)	49.8 (558)	19.3 (216)	21.3 (239)	8.7 (97)	0.9 (10)	($N = 1,120$)
TOTALS	57.7 (1,343)	15.9 (369)	19.7 (456)	5.9 (138)	0.8 (19)	($N = 2,325$)

The Luo in Kaloleni who are aged over forty and who have been self-employed since at least Operation Anvil in 1954 are said by Luo themselves to be the remaining number of a much larger category of

Plate 3a. Luo cobbler working from home in Kaloleni.

Plate 3b. The mixed market of "Bama" (Shauri Moyo).

Luo traders and market stall holders. The life histories of these and of other older men, no longer self-employed and in some cases settled in Luoland, do suggest that the actual proportion of Luo in self-employment was larger in the fifties though the actual number throughout Nairobi may not have been much greater than now. Even so between a quarter and a fifth of the Luo household heads over forty living in Kaloleni are full-time self-employed and this is by no means an insignificant proportion.

It is well worth while for men over forty continuing to trade in Nairobi. Their educational levels are almost half the average of all household heads. They have never been equipped for clerical work, which in Nairobi requires the use of English, nor have they undergone formal training in or an apprenticeship for a craft. Just under a fifth of them are, it is true, experienced artisans, including tailors, most of whom have been informally trained through working for Asian employers. These men could, under duress, obtain alternative employment with Asians but are able to earn more by working independently. The other Luo are traders, including those already mentioned who deal in fish brought from Nyanza to Nairobi in trucks owned by fellow Luo and then sold in markets throughout the city. The average monthly income of all the self-employed Luo is Shs.528/– which is well above the statutory minimum of Shs.167/– for men in Nairobi in 1969 (Leys, 1975, pp. 234, f. 39) and represented (it became apparent during my survey) a considerable understatement of true incomes, which are also less likely to be assessed in full for tax purposes. Even so, this average monthly income of self-employed Luo compares very favourably with those of other occupations which require secondary education, a knowledge of English and sometimes a formal training. The average white-collar salary among Luo in Kaloleni is Shs.714/– while that of trained artisans who have undergone apprenticeships and obtained City and Guilds certificates or their equivalent is Shs.515/–.

These full-time Luo traders and self-employed artisans often have business connections in their rural homelands. They constitute the elite of Luo petty entrepreneurship who have managed to keep a viable foothold over the years in catering for a rapidly growing, largely Luo clientele in Nairobi. But many of them invested in education for their children. Their own sons and sometimes daughters are therefore either at school or have taken on clerical or skilled work, or, if they are unemployed, have not engaged in trade. In this they are part of a Luo trend.

In so far as self-employment ceased to offer Luo the opportunities it once had, the switch in emphasis from this to clerical and skilled wage employment can fairly be ascribed to the return of Kikuyu to their previous positions in Nairobi at the ending of the Emergency. The stress on education for clerical and skilled work appears to have been accelerated by this factor; seeing the prospects for self-employment as increasingly less attractive in Nairobi, Luo concentrated their aims on acquiring formal education qualifications for themselves and their children on the understanding that these would at least secure "respectable" middle-range jobs of a white-collar, professional or skilled nature. Such expectations cannot always be achieved and, in the contracting field of employment, are more and more frustrated. But the minority of successful cases can still continue to fire the new ideology of urban clerical respectability and qualified craft status.

Luo wives in trade

The Luo view that clerical and skilled work now offer better prospects than self-employment in Nairobi has not resulted in their completely abandoning private enterprise of a limited kind, as is clear from their significant proportions of all stall holders in the four markets in Eastlands. Rather, they have adapted to the new situation as I shall explain. It should be pointed out that Luo showed commercial acumen in such towns as Kampala in the late fifties and sixties (Parkin, 1969, pp. 157–64) and do so in Kisumu at the present time (though many do wryly remark on the growing proportion of Kikuyu traders and shopowners in even this, the Luo capital), and Luo themselves still see self-employment extending into some form of entrepreneurship as an ideal way of securing economic independence. This remains an ultimate ideal but is simply not now regarded as easily attainable in Nairobi. As one 30 year old Luo put it: "Nowadays we aim to get education, then a 'big man's job' in Nairobi, and then a business in Kisumu [the capital of Luoland]." This represents a tacit admission that the Kikuyu are now the "host" people in Nairobi and that other ethnic groups, even if born or resident there most of their lives, are essentially migrants.

Alongside this general Luo acceptance that few of them will establish themselves as highly successful entrepreneurs and traders in
Nairobi, there has developed a tendency among men to regard trading
as a sideline or supplement to his "main" job: a clerk or artisan can
run a market stall through his wife. Thus, over recent years, Luo in
Nairobi have moved away from anything approaching full-time entrepreneurship and closer to a form of part-time trading, usually from
market stalls and usually through or aided by a wife.

We see this when we compare the two older markets of Bama and
Kariokor with the newer ones of Kikomba and Uhuru. The Luo stall
holders at Bama and Kariokor still contain a large proportion of men
who have been trading since Operation Anvil or before. Male Luo
stall holders heavily outnumber women. But in the two new markets,
the number of Luo women stall holders approaches that of Luo men
much more closely (see Table 15). The new markets have thus captured this new Luo trend of greater involvement by Luo women in
market retailing.

TABLE 15

Luo men and women as full-time market stall holders

Market	Men (mostly married)		Women (all married including a few widows)	Joint (husband and wife together)
Bama Kariokor	($N = 123$)	65.8 (81)	22.0 (27)	12.2 (15)
Kikomba Uhuru	($N = 333$)	51.1 (170)	36.3 (121)	12.6 (42)

There has been no shift in the kinds of retailing done by men and
women. Men tend to dominate the more lucrative tailoring and
second-hand and new clothes selling, and food retailing, and completely control shoe making and repairing, while women tend to dominate fish retailing (see Table 16). A fair number of men and women
also share market stalls. Otherwise there is clearly great inter-
changeability. This is consistent with the recent tendency for women
to take on a husband's stall or to take on new stalls which, a few years
earlier, would have been run by husbands.

TABLE 16

Types of retailing/trade by Luo men and women in the four markets

	Men		Women		Joint	
Fish ($N = 201$)	34.8	(70)	51.2	(103)	14.0	(28)
Tailor/clothes (109)	74.3	(81)	6.4	(7)	19.3	(21)
Fruit/vegetable/						
General store (102)	59.8	(61)	33.3	(34)	6.9	(7)
Cobbler (21)	100.0	(21)	—		—	
Other (23)	78.3	(18)	17.4	(4)	4.3	(1)
TOTAL	54.4%	(251)	33.4%	(148)	12.2%	(57)
Grand total = 456						

It should be emphasized here that, at this stage of Luo women's in-creasing involvement, men still tend to provide their wives with the initial capital, and the stalls are usually registered in the husband's name. Exceptions are widows, who are very few in Nairobi. Luo women stall holders are still under an expectation to declare their earnings to their husbands and to channel some profits into the family budget. It is in this sense that I speak of these stalls as being under the nominal and partially effective control of husbands who themselves have full-time wage jobs but may help in running the stall when they are available. As yet, very few Luo women are truly independent re-tailers or wholesale traders.

This contrasts strikingly with Kikuyu. Kikuyu men have not re-jected self-employment even while they have expanded into clerical jobs requiring education (Leys, 1975, pp. 201–2). There are propor-tionally more Kikuyu men in trade than their womenfolk, as com-pared with Luo. But there are also proportionately more Kikuyu than Luo women who retail and trade, though more so in the so-called informal or unenumerated sector. These Kikuyu women operate their stalls independently of men, after acquiring the capital from a sister, mother, or even daughter. They are under little if any obligation to contribute to a common family budget though, of course, may do so as a matter of preference. Since polygyny has given way to monogamy or to matrifocal family units, there are fewer conflicts involved in con-tributing than in Luo polygynous families.

During this increasing involvement of Luo women in trade under the nominal control of husbands, then, Luo men in Nairobi have placed more and more ideological emphasis on education and clerical work for themselves and their children. They have put aside trading or have taken only a part-time role in it through their wives. With exceptions, the supplementary money earned from it is not considerable but it has significant implications for the status of Luo women. Looking back again at the people of Kaloleni, we can see how this is occurring.

When Kaloleni became predominantly Luo as a result of Operation Anvil, self-employed Luo were more easily able to bring their wives and children from their rural homes to live with them in the estate and in the other few areas of Nairobi where the withdrawal of Kikuyu made family housing available. Wives were then brought into the businesses as assistants. But, since the husband was able to devote his full time to the enterprise, his wife or wives rarely assumed a central role in its running. For those middle-aged self-employed Luo still in Kaloleni, wives continue to occupy this subordinate position.

This contrasts with the role of wives in the smaller businesses which are operated by a husband as a supplement to his wage job. Indeed, these enterprises are sometimes begun on the initiative of a wife whose children are now growing up and requiring less of her attention. The capital is usually given by the husband and he and she refer to the business as his. But, simply because the wife is able to devote much more time to it and acquires an up-to-date expertise which frequently exceeds that of her partially absent husband, her role becomes more central. Not surprisingly, wives demand a substantial share of the proceeds of the business and usually get it. Since some of the money is contributed to a wife's own children's school fees, clothes and sometimes even food, as well as used for her own clothes, most husbands are happy that wives should take a larger portion. On the other hand, they recognize the implications for "independent" female status that trading expertise can bring. Men's comments reflect the ambivalence of this new "power" enjoyed by wives who trade under the nominal authority of husbands. They may say: "A wife, and especially a co-wife, is more content this way, and is less troublesome." "We men know that wives who trade do not always declare truthfully how much they have earned, but since most of it goes on the family, we do not mind." And less positively, "The main problem is to know whether they are meeting lovers and spending the money on them instead of bringing it home." "I cannot know how much money she sends to her parents." "The problem is that my wife spends most of the money earned from our business so that I cannot use it to set up another one at home [i.e. in the rural area]." And, as women pass beyond the child-bearing age, they may gradually assume full control over enterprises which they have been running. Sometimes they continue in Nairobi, and sometimes in the husband's rural home area.

A fifth of the 235 currently resident wives of Luo household heads in Kaloleni were working for cash incomes in Nairobi at the time of my survey (late 1968), most of them at market stalls licenced in their husbands' names, and an disproportionate number of them men's senior co-wives. Though their proportion is under a half that of Kikuyu women in Kaloleni who trade, which was well over 40 per cent, these Luo women constitute a small but important reference group for other, usually younger Luo women, just as they themselves privately and discreetly instance the "freedom" enjoyed by many Kikuyu women to trade and do other work independently of their menfolk as an ideal to be aimed at.

We can see from all this that it is possible for a wife as she gets older to move from a subordinate to dominant role in trading in Nairobi which was initially under the nominal control of a husband. More importantly, since Luo males ceased being full-time traders to the extent that they used to and turned instead to part-time trading, more women have been able to move towards the centre of the family enterprise, however small, and eventually to secure a modicum of economic independence in later life. This has been the pattern for some generations in rural Luoland, where women channel their income directly into their own "house" in the compound polygynous family. But it has only developed among Luo women in Nairobi over the last 10 or 12 years, as family settlement became possible and as their Luo menfolk have turned to education and clerical work rather than full-time entrepreneurship as a feasible career pattern in the city. Thus, ironically, the return of many Kikuyu men to full-time trade and self-employment after the Emergency has deterred Luo men from similar pursuits in Nairobi but has indirectly offered their women the chance to step on the entrepreneurial ladder at the lower rung of petty trading. Kikuyu women are well established in both this and high-level trading in Nairobi and, significantly, are often held up by Luo women as worth emulating in this respect.

There is, however, one crucial impediment to Luo wive's shifting completely to the centre of Luo entrepreneurial activities in Nairobi. This is the simple fact that they move from town to country and back again, on average about every six months, as I explained in Chapter 1. A husband is of course helped in this if he has two wives, who can alternate in management of a market stall. A husband with one wife will need a currently unemployed relative to stand in for his wife during her absence. He can at least find this easy solution to her absence. A wife, by contrast, constantly leaves the business at the point when she may be expected to have built up her own full expertise and personal clientele. Thus, Luo women acquire the trading needed for economic independence in Nairobi, but are then required to transfer their expertise to their husband's rural home, where they may continue to trade, and at the same time arrange for the flow of fish and, to a lesser extent, other food, back to the stall in Nairobi.

This system sustains the centrality of the husband's role in Nairobi and, though it gives his wife some limited economic autonomy, does not eliminate her dependent status on the family of which he is head. It is, economically, a betwixt-and-between status. This kind of half-way status is most evident when a man has two wives, for he is under even greater obligation than with one wife to ensure that each wife alternates in equal periods of residence between his urban and rural homes. This is not a result of the machinations of men but rather of the customary expectations surrounding the conduct of polygyny and family relations. Again there is a contrast here with Kikuyu.

Very few Kikuyu men are polygynists, and Kikuyu women generally are articulate and effective in their opposition to the institution. The few young Luo women who have received senior secondary education are still at a premium and successfully oppose polygyny. But the many young Luo women with less education, even if they privately voice objections, in the end accept it.

From a limited formal survey and from numerous informal conversations, there consistently occurred the following interesting contrast between Kikuyu and Luo women. Kikuyu women outspokenly opposed polygyny regardless of educational level and economic status, whether or not their husbands were present. Their reasons were that a man could not possibly share his attention between two or more co-wives any more than between his own wife and a "temporary" wife or mistress. Many Kikuyu women saw polygyny, and monogamy with an outside mistress, as tantamount to the same thing and as inevitably

leading to quarrels and separation. With only the partial exception
of a few who were highly educated, and regardless of whether they
were market traders, Luo women rarely voiced any opinion on the
matter in the presence of husbands, either laughing off the question
or conversational topic, or simply and briefly saying something like,
"This is a matter for the husband to decide". When their husbands
and other close relatives were not present these women would mildly
state a preference for monogamy but might add, with remarkable
frequency, that town life offered a husband the temptation of outside
sexual liaisons which could harm the family, either through the mystical affliction *chira* or through "disease", and that under such circumstances, it would be better for him to take a second wife. Luo
wives also saw as reasonable that a husband's need for many children,
or at least a balanced sex ratio of children, should be fulfilled, through
polygyny if necessary. They recognized an obligation to his lineage.
Finally, whereas Kikuyu women were inclined to elaborate on the
topic by, for example, giving vivid illustrations of how polygyny or a
man's infidelities have disastrous consequences, Luo women, when
they offered an opinion at all, made seemingly abridged and stereotyped comments. Adapting Bernstein's distinction between elaborated
and restricted codes (1971, pp. 144–61), the responses of Kikuyu
women were elaborate and characterized by a low degree of lexical,
syntactic and semantic predictability, while those of many Luo
women were highly predictable: one could more easily guess not only
what, if anything, they were going to say, but also the words they
would use to say it.

It should also be noted here that Kikuyu men's and women's preferences for children were much lower than those of Luo, with a
median range of between three and four (cf. pp. 64–7).

Luo women, then, tend to accept polygyny even if, in private conversational contexts, they may sometimes oppose it. Mature women
whose own children are growing up now have an opportunity to acquire some slight degree of economic independence through market
stall selling, as I have explained. Their marriages have long been
settled and their personal prospects of partial economic self-reliance
are at their best. They have little reason to "campaign" against polygyny at this stage of their lives on behalf of younger Luo women,
while the little educated among the latter have no weapons of their
own, not even the cultural mandate nor verbal power to argue with

men. Undiscussed between women and men and between women themselves, and therefore unchallenged, the practice of polygyny has been free to adapt to the changes in occupational opportunities affecting Luo and has become more dependent on socio-economic factors emanating from Nairobi itself.

The persistence of polygyny

In spite of the shift in emphasis from self-employment to clerical jobs among Luo men, with blue-collar work only slightly more emphasized, this change has not brought about any marked difference of income between male household heads in Kaloleni above and below 40 years of age. The median wage of the 144 over-forties is Shs.518/– while that of the 188 under-forties is Shs.512/–. The large proportion of clerical workers among the under-forties (see Table 13 earlier) might lead us to expect them to have higher wages than this. But many of these younger men are in junior clerical jobs which yield less than is earned by the older, longer-serving clerks, artisans and self-employed men. Included also among the under-forties is a substantial number of men in semi-skilled employment who are as well qualified as older men in better paying clerical or skilled work but have been unable to obtain anything comparable in the recent period of diminishing employment opportunities.

The general trend among Luo towards clerical employment and away from self-employment is reasonably well reflected among polygynists, though there is also a stronger trend for younger polygynists to be blue-collar rather than white-collar workers (see Table 17).

TABLE 17

Occupations of Luo polygynists in Kaloleni by age

	White-collar (%)	Blue-collar (%)	Unskilled (%)	Self-employed (%)	Currently unemployed (%)
70 polygynists over 40 years of age	26.8	35.2	9.6	23.9	4.2
33 polygynists under 40 years of age	36.4	42.4	9.1	12.1	—

Similarly, the general trend towards increased education is even more faithfully represented among polygynists (see Table 18).

TABLE 18

Education among Luo polygynists and monogamists in Kaloleni

		Median level of education (years)
Over forties	Polygynists (70)	5.8 yrs
	Monogamists (72)	6.0 yrs
	Currently unmarried (3)	not significant
Under forties	Polygynists (33)	8.6 yrs
	Monogamists (134)	8.7 yrs
	Unmarried (18)	9.9 yrs
(3 n.a.)		

These figures are remarkable in showing that, though Luo in Kaloleni have placed increasing emphasis on the value of education, the higher level of education among younger household heads has made no difference as to whether or not they become polygynists. It is of course perfectly true that Kaloleni does not include university graduates or even a significant number of persons who have undergone 12 to 14 years of education to senior secondary level. And it is possible that among these formal polygyny is disappearing. But they constitute no more than a minute category of the Luo population in Nairobi, of which the residents of Kaloleni are much more typical.

Together these figures show that the kinds of Luo who become polygynists are not very different in terms of their jobs and education from men of their own age groups who remain monogamous. Polygyny has thus not become the preserve of the uneducated, or of the unskilled or blue-collar worker. For clerks with some secondary education are almost as well represented as monogamists as a proportion of their age groups. What, then, distinguishes polygynists from monogamists and unmarried men? Polygynists generally, both those above and below 40, have much higher monthly incomes. For unmarried household heads, who are nearly all in their twenties (and who are, incidentally, among the most educated), it is only Shs.483/–; for monogamous heads it rises to Shs.520/–; while for polygynists it reaches Shs.603/–. Moreover, men with three or four wives earn more than those with two wives. In other words, the more wives a man has, the higher is likely to be his monthly income, which has not, incidentally, been taken to include money earned by wives. As particular cases show, it is not having two or more wives which produces this difference of monthly income. Rather it is the other way round, with men earning higher than average incomes acquiring second or subsequent wives.

There is nothing unusual about this, which accords with a general pattern underlying the prevalence of polygyny in Africa: traditionally in rural areas the men with the most cattle, land or other property had the most wives. What is distinctive about the feature I am describing here is that this marked difference of income between polygynists and monogamists is based on *urban* wages.

Interestingly, life histories strongly suggest that this differentiation of polygynists and monogamists of the same age by urban income began in the early fifties from about the time the Emergency was declared when, as explained, Luo suddenly found themselves in a position of relative socio-economic dominance in the African population of Nairobi.

Because dating is involved, it is difficult to get precise figures. But Luo polygynists in Kaloleni over 50 have generally married their wives before, say, 1952, while those under 50 have married second or subsequent wives since then. Comparing the present median urban incomes of Luo household heads of three different age categories, we can see that there is indeed very little difference in urban income between polygynists and monogamists over 50, while for men under this age there is a consistently wide gap in income (see Table 19).

TABLE 19

Median incomes of Luo polygynists and monogamists in Kaloleni by age

		Median urban income
Household heads 50 years of age and over	18 monogamists 23 polygynists	Shs. 467/- 495/-
Household heads between 40 and 49 years of age	54 monogamists 47 polygynists	485/- 631/-
Household heads under 40 years of age	137 monogamists 33 polygynists	543/- 660/-

These are differences of current income. Nevertheless, differentials within the age categories of this order seem to have existed when marriages occurred.

It is, then, among men under 50 that polygynists earn considerably more from their work than monogamists. Looked at another way, this suggests that "surplus" urban incomes among the better paid have consistently been channelled into acquiring more than one wife since the early fifties. Life histories bear this out.

As noted in Chapter 1, only 15 per cent of the Luo household heads in Kaloleni have actually bought land and, though they invested a little in petty commerce in Nairobi in the short period from 1954 to 1959 when Kikuyu were restricted, they also continued to invest bridewealth in acquiring a second or subsequent wife. That is to say, they tried to maintain two investment spheres. The reason given for this is that an extra wife enabled a man to manage an urban business as well as his rural family land, while enabling him to continue in urban employment. By contrast, after 1959 especially, increasing numbers of Kikuyu invested *all* their surplus urban wage incomes in businesses, though rarely land, to the exclusion of second wives. The political and economic "opportunities" open to Luo in Nairobi during the period of Kikuyu restriction are today spoken of as such by many Luo themselves and were noted by government at the time (Sandbrook, 1975, p. 105). But Luo men's cultural preference for two or more wives as a means of managing an urban business and family land while remaining in full-time wage employment in Nairobi is logically consistant as an emic response. Unlike the increasing numbers of landless Kikuyu, few Luo heads were at that time without, or unlikely to inherit, a few acres of land, which, while it is unlikely to do more than supplement wage earnings, is valued as an ultimate security. If this interpretation is correct, then landlessness among Luo would have had to reach critical proportions before a shift occurred in cultural preference from two wives as a means of straddling rural-urban interests, to one wife and a commitment to full-time urban self-employment. The "lost" opportunity was, then, quite understandable in retrospect, and so explains the investment of surplus urban income in second wives from the early fifties onwards by men with higher than average wages.

Giving the ideological gloss to this cultural preference for more than one wife was, as now, the sanctions and pressures brought by parents and close agnates to produce children for the "name" of the family and lineage and as a means of protecting its land from encroachment by others. The commitment to polygyny was and is more than a means of securing economic and political advantage. It is also a preferred, custom-hallowed method of doing so which is not necessarily the most efficient economically and politically, for alternative arrangements are certainly possible. As such it contains within itself the seeds of cultural inconsistencies: it has diverted cash away from Luo investment in trade; it now conflicts with a new wish of some Luo to invest in education for few children; and it presupposes women's continuing tacit acceptance of polygyny, an assumption which may stand on the threshold of being challenged. Polygyny, as a customary preference, has ridden rough-shod over such emerging cultural inconsistencies. It is not simply that special economic and political circumstances have perpetuated polygyny. Rather, it is the cultural demands behind the practice of polygyny which have exploited the availability of "surplus" urban income for its use as bridewealth. This pattern developed most rapidly during the temporary economic demise of Kikuyu men, and has not been reversed since then in spite of growing unemployment among younger Luo.

There are two questions to ask here. First, why is it that polygynists and monogamists working in Nairobi before about 1952 did not have significantly different urban incomes? And second, why did men becoming polygynists after this time have higher incomes than monogamists?

As seems to be a general development in Africa during recent generations, an increasingly larger proportion of bridewealth has taken the form of cash rather than kind. The value in 1969 was at least Shs.3,500/–, including or in addition to a few heifers and a bull. The tendency before the early fifties was for men earning in Nairobi to contribute a large proportion of their urban income towards the purchase of the 12 to 20 bridewealth cattle, or to send remittances home in exchange for first option, so to speak, on any "surplus" bridewealth cattle arising from the marriage of a sister in the homestead. As mentioned, there was limited family accommodation in Nairobi at that time and so men worked as bachelors in the city, often by migrating to and from home to town for a couple of years or so. Their general orientation to the rural home was substantiated by these factors. In turn, rural elders thus entrusted as guardians of urban migrants' property secured a degree of control over the migrants' choice of wives and the timing of their marriages. Urban migrants were to this extent dependent on the uses to which rural people put the earnings entrusted to them. This part dependence on the homespeople made differences of urban income between migrants have a less direct effect on whether or not they married polygynously. Added to this is the unlikelihood, anyway, that urban incomes before the early fifties occupied the wide range which they did later.

The rural orientation of most Luo migrants in Nairobi before the early fifties meant that it was there, in the rural areas, that men kept their families and subscribed, as lineages had done before them, to the view that it was the function of a married couple to produce as large a family as possible. Then family accommodation became available for Luo in Nairobi, first following the effects of Operation Anvil in 1952, and later in 1960 when a number of new family housing estates were built, and so something approaching family settlement became possible. Nairobi now became an important and increasingly primary locus for the expression of traditional aspirations and beliefs surrounding children and wives. From this time it was to Nairobi that a Luo townsman would bring his children—for schooling and for employment; it was in Nairobi that many, sometimes most, of a married couple's conjugal and family relationships were now carried on; and it was there that many of the day-to-day problems of disease and nutrition among children, or the more enduring problems of sterility and barrenness among men and women were encountered, explained and dealt with.

The extent to which men could settle their families successfully in Nairobi and cope with the expenses of larger rented accommodation, school fees, an acceptable diet, and traditional and modern medicine, both more costly in Nairobi than at home, depended on a man's urban rather than rural income. Polygynists have more wives and children to provide for and so need corespondingly higher urban incomes. It was, therefore, as a consequence of a policy of family settlement in Nairobi that wealth differences between Luo polygynists and monogamists became expressed as differences of urban income.

In these circumstances, we might have expected the polygyny rate to have dropped rapidly in the face of the extra urban expenses involved and, increasingly, scarce family accommodation in the nineteen sixties. Yet, as I have shown in previous chapters, the polygyny rate among household heads in Nairobi is dropping very slowly, if at all. Men and their families are still prepared to lodge with relatives and friends in an attempt eventually to acquire rented family accommodation of their own. The continuing Luo preference for family settlement in Nairobi is surely linked to their emphasis on education and urban clerical and skilled employment as providing the most ideologically acceptable alternative. It is not, from the outsider's point of view, necessarily the most economic alternative. Urban unskilled work by unattached migrants operating rural farms through their families at home would probably incur fewer economic costs. But the potential benefits do not match most Luo aspirations, for few of them have access to large, commercially viable tracts of land.

Conclusion

In this chapter I have shown how growing Kikuyu dominance of petty commerce has encouraged Luo men to commit themselves to, and increasingly depend on, urban wage employment rather than full-time self-employment in Nairobi. Paradoxically this has meant that their wives can themselves acquire the beginnings of economic independence by operating small market stalls under the nominal but not total control of their husbands. Polygyny facilitates the arrangement by which these urban interests can be combined with rural ones.

The persistence of polygyny into a period of urban family settlement by Luo is an example of a key institution adapting to changing external political and economic circumstances. Before the early fifties, it took the form of a rural compound polygynous family and was still probably linked to the localized polysegmentary lineage system of Luo by acting as its prototype in the manner discussed by Southall (1952). Thereafter the polygynous family, while retaining a rural compound base, became split into revolving rural and urban components, with different co-wives and young children alternating in residence with the husband in Nairobi, as explained in Chapter 1. The polygynous family certainly retains meaning for most Luo as a method by which family land at home can be defended. In the wider political and essentially urban context, it is also frequently referred to as demonstrating Luo "strength" in competition with other ethnic groups. To have many wives is to have many children which is somehow to provide an

F

answer to the apparent diminishing influence of Luo in Nairobi: the more children you have, the more you can educate and the greater the chances of at least one of them reaching a genuinely influential position. The same man or woman who provides this ideal picture will at other times acknowledge that his limited budget might be better deployed in educating three or four rather than, say, eight children. But, while acknowledging this, he may also point to the hazards of disease and death, of misfortune, including the witchcraft of jealous relatives and friends, afflicting a particular child while at school, and of producing a child whose "character" is ill-disposed to his parents. The uncertainties surrounding the likely development of one's children are indeed considerable and it is easy to see how they link up with the political uncertainties of Luo as an ethnic group in Nairobi and form the basis of an ideology which enjoins Luo to have large families, through polygynous marriage if necessary. In other words, domestic uncertainties to do with children and wives have linked up over the years with political uncertainties among Luo in Nairobi: to have and educate many children is seen as an attempt to solve a problem arising from an uneven ethnic distribution of power.

The uncertainties surrounding the desirability of many children through polygyny, combined with the limited trading opportunities recently acquired by Luo women themselves, produce an ambivalence in the status of women: it is only through women's tacit compliance that the ideal of polygyny for many children can be realized; yet it is through polygyny and men's increasing dependence on urban wages that women are able to turn to their own limited forms of self-employment, which are privately admitted by both men and women to contain the seeds of female economic independence.[1]

In the next chapter I show how this ambivalence in the status of women in Nairobi corresponds neatly with an inconsistency in the stated and diagnosed causes of a mystical affliction incurring childlessness and family sickness and death. Luo men and women both state that adultry with a married woman with children will afflict her own children and the man's own wife, children, and even patrilineage

---

[1] A few examples have already been documented in Kampala, Uganda, in which some Luo women have become independent of male control by "becoming" Ganda, the Host cultural grouping of the city (Obbo, 1972; Halpenny. 1975). It is interesting, however, that even here the price of such independence is in effect the self-denial of these women's identity and birthright. To my knowledge there is no comparable process in Nairobi of "Kikuyuization" by Luo women (cf. also Potash, unpublished).

with the debilitating and often fatal disease called *chira*. Adultery
with an unmarried, childless woman does not, however, bring *chira* to
either of them, even if the man is married with children: the bias of
likely blame is tilted against married women. In practice, actual cases
of *chira* are diagnosed by a diviner as due not to adultery but to transgressions by men of the rules of family and lineage seniority. In other
words, the verbalized belief in *chira* puts the main blame on the "sin-
fulness" (*rochruok*) of women's adultery; but the diagnosis of actual
cases by diviners (both male and female) place blame not on a wife
but on her husband. Women are said to have a mystical potential for
ending their husband's family lines, but this is an unrealized, unseen
potential. Rather, it is men who are seen, through diagnoses which inevitably become public knowledge, to have these powers of their own
and their family's destruction.

5

The Control of Domestic Uncertainty

Men's Power and Women's Potential

There are two overriding areas of domestic uncertainty in Nairobi which affect Luo husbands and wives in their capacity as fathers and mothers. First, there is the problem of providing education for their children. This is largely a father's concern. He controls the household budget and has the major say in any decision concerning where the children shall go to school and precisely how much money to spend on each of them. In a polygynous household co-wives inevitably influence his decision, as explained in Chapter 2, as do wives who earn money from trading on their own. But, unlike the many Kikuyu women in Nairobi of independent status and means, Luo wives generally remain subordinate to their husbands' authority in this sphere. Fathers, then, assume responsibility for deciding how much of a family's income can be invested in education, and at what point it is appropriate to terminate a son's or daughter's education, with no certain guarantee that the investment will yield commensurate rewards in the job market.

The second great area of domestic uncertainty concerns the fertility of the marriage and the "inexplicable" sickness and possible loss of children.

From a purely "physiological" viewpoint, in so far as this can be emically distinguished (see the section below entitled "Incompatible blood"), there is still a tendency, as was traditionally always the case (Southall, 1973, p. 345), for a wife to be blamed first for a sterile marriage. In Nairobi the traditional male or female doctor (*ajuoga*) starts out from this assumption, and it may not be until a man has married a second or even third time, and still has no child, that the conclusion may be drawn that it is he who is sterile.[1] This emphasis on female accountability for childlessness is hardly surprising. A woman's status in marriage still rests on her ability to produce children. A barren woman's husband can take a second wife, but a barren woman has no equivalent option.

Whether the husband or wife is regarded as physiologically inadequate, their unfortunate condition is still seen as amenable to further explanation. Like the Azande who know full well that a granary falling at a particular place and time is the physical instrument of a man's death but who also reasonably wish to know why it had to be that particular man, so the Luo usually require this fuller kind of explanation, especially if the case of sterility is seen not as an isolated misfortune in a family or lineage but as one of a number. Early childlessness, and death and sickness in a family occurring after children have already been born are almost certain to require thorough explanation and appropriate remedies. In Nairobi, "Western" doctors, hospitals, and medicines are normally used alongside the services of the traditional doctor. One reason why so much money is spent on traditional methods of diagnosis and cure, even though treatment at a major Nairobi hospital is free, is that many sicknesses are seen as unresponsive to "Western" medical treatment alone. The husband foots these family medical fees.

As outside analysts we often coventionally distinguish these different kinds of medical diagnoses and therapy, i.e. non-physiological and physiological and "traditional" and "Western", as mystical and non-mystical. They are convenient terms of general description and will remain so. But, as has been shown by the detailed work on the semantics of medical diagnosis and healing, these distinctions arbitrarily conflate etic and emic levels of explanation and so obscure our understanding of how the people themselves relate cause and effect. A quite different analytical distinction is that between a people's total emic classification or "world view" of the causes and cures of family sickness and death, and the areas within this classificatory grid which are most used for diagnosis and therapy in particular cases. This view

[1] Blount goes as far as to suggest that "Male sterility is a completely alien concept to the Luo" (1973, p. 326), but neither Southall (1973, p. 345) nor I (1973, pp. 336–8) found this.

enables us to discern an interesting puzzle among the Luo. Both men and wives are held to be capable, quite unintendedly and unconsciously, of bringing ill-health and death to their own families and to the localized lineages in which, if men, they were born, or, if women, into which they have married. This is the level of pure statement and, as far as can be judged by impression, is generally if not always consistently "believed in". But in actual cases diagnosed by men or women diviners, it is men, either as a husband or as recognized agnate of the husband, who are most often deemed responsible. Men's sins of commission and omission fall into two categories: those that reverse "natural" relations with women or involve "excessive" use of them; and those that flout customary rules of family and lineage seniority among both men and women.

Let me now show in detail the four main folk-concepts which Luo men and women in Nairobi use to explain sterility, sickness and death in their families, and some of which we, as outsiders, label "mystical". From them, we see the distribution of male and female accountability for family health, welfare and continuity. The fourth, concerned with the affliction called *chira*, has assumed inordinate significance in Nairobi as a Luo explanatory concept. It is the one that is most used in the diagnosis of actual cases and has imposed a heavier burden of accountability on men than on women as Luo families settled in the city.

In this latter sense the ecological factors of urban settlement and wage dependency shape the relevance and relative significance of these emic explanations. That is to say, the explanatory concepts have adapted to the particular economic and political constrains and directives of family settlement in Nairobi. But there is a second, complementary level of adaptation. For they are also shaped by other key concepts in the Luo segmentary lineage culture with which they must be seen by Luo to remain logically consistent in order to be effective. In discussing *chira*, the most important of these folk-explanations, therefore, I note its general semantic equivalence in a range of other Bantu cultures which strikingly contrast linguistically and/or in other ways with the Luo. It can be seen that this underlying sharing of concepts under the one basic term constitutes a cross-cultural semantic domain which, as among the Luo, adapts to a particular culture's dominant paradigm of ideas.

Explanations of misfortune

INCOMPATIBLE BLOOD

This theory argues that, if a man or woman's "blood" is stronger than that of his or her spouse, then it is difficult for them to have children, even though each may have children by other partners whose "blood" is of approximately equal strength. This strength or weakness of a person's blood is sometimes seen as determined by his or her age in relation to the partner's. One mature woman put it thus: "When two people are married but one (the wife) is very young and her eggs are still weak, then a child may only be conceived when her eggs become stronger." A young married man similarly suggested that, "if an old man marries a young girl [for example as a second or subsequent wife in a polygynous union], his sperms are stronger than the young girl's [eggs]", implying that this may prevent conception. Conversely, a middle-aged married man explained: "If a mature woman marries a young man, he grows thin because she gets fresh blood from his "blood" [referring here to semen]. This is understandable, because the sperms are made from blood, so that he is constantly giving his stronger blood to her." Both a woman's "eggs" and a man's semen may be interchangeably referred to as blood (*remo*), even though there is a specific term for semen, *nyodo*, and a euphemism, *lac*, primarily meaning urine (Parkin, 1973, p. 336).

The two themes, that a husband may not have strong enough semen to impregnate his wife or that "their blood cannot agree", are also reported as explanations of sterility among the Meru of Kenya (Njeru, 1973, p. 76). There is also a widespread African belief that sickness and even death will befall a child who continues to be breast-fed by a mother who has become pregnant. Among the Sukuma of Northern Tanzania, as among the Luo, this sickness is sometimes explained as having arisen because "the blood of the two children mixes" (Varkevisser, 1973, p.234). Varkevisser also makes the interesting observation that the concept "mixing of blood" has a further sexual connotation which extends to incest: for the resultant sickness is most dreaded when successive children are of different sex, i.e. that the blood of a brother and sister are unnaturally mixed through a mother's breast-milk. We are not told whether the Sukuma word for blood can also refer to a man's semen and to a woman's "eggs", as among Luo. But, clearly, there is a common underlying idea among both peoples, as among the Meru, that the sterility and children's sickness and death which result from an improper ordering of relationships may be phrased in the idiom of unnaturally discrepant sexual and physiological strength between men and women. It is likely that culturally varying versions of these themes are found in many parts of East Africa. The overriding Luo explanation is that age differences between a man and woman may cause sexual and physiological discrepancies. We shall see that this fits in with a more general and dominant Luo motif about the problems which arise when seniority is abused.

For the moment, it is important to note from the typical Luo statements given above that it is not only the "understandably unnatural" relationship of older woman and younger sexual male partner which may sometimes prevent conception, but also the perfectly normal case, as in a polygynous union, of an older man taking a younger wife. This may serve to indicate that, though polygyny is in many respects an ideal to be attained, there is underlying recognition of its ambivalent consequences: on the one hand polygyny is a means by which a family and lineage may be strengthened through the addition of many children; on the other hand its practice by older men deprives younger men of women of their own age and forces them to marry later. This latter consequence has particular significance in Nairobi where Luo young men far outnumber Luo girls of their own age and where, in default of full bridewealth coming to them, they must often use their own cash earnings as a contribution, if they are employed. And if a young man is unemployed, then somehow his father should make the major contribution. This implicit reminder that fathers have duties to sons, as well as the other way round, is expressed in the second kind of explanation of domestic misfortune.

LAPSES OF PATRIAL PIETY

The sins of fathers may be visited unto many generations, usually in the form of afflictions brought by "spirits" (*jochiende,* sing. *jachien*). The sterile man or woman is said to be "disturbed" by the ghosts of persons who have been wronged by the man or woman's forefather and who are now avenging themselves on the sinner's innocent descendant. The possible sins committed by the forebear are in fact homicidal and include the killing of a young child or pregnant woman, a "brother", or "father". In town, the sin of homicide may be seen to take effect immediately and affect the living: Onyango, the taxi-driver, accidentally knocked down and killed a schoolchild. It had not been his fault and he was exonerated from blame and so dismissed it as a regrettable incident. He should, however, have gone immediately to an *ajuoga* (traditional doctor) for special medicine (*manyasi*) to be purified. As he failed to do this, his own son died a little while afterwards, quite suddenly. Onyango then went to the *ajuoga* for purification and has had no subsequent domestic misfortune. At a wider "political" level, the assassination of Mboya in 1969 was followed by a collective purification of the whole Luo community as represented by an important *ajuoga* in Nairobi, and under the auspices of the Luo Union, the assumption being that in the event of the assassin being a fellow-Luo, his sin would be prevented from being visited upon them all. These examples illustrate that what is at issue in reversing such sins is the perpetuation of a line of descent; of a single man and his family and lineage in the one case, and in the other of the whole Luo collectively as distinct from non-Luo ethnic groupings. In so far as the belief emphasizes duty to one's children and their descendants by averting their mystical harm, the basic responsibility can be referred to as that of "patrial" piety.

LAPSES OF FILIAL PIETY

The only consistently reported sin of omission by a son towards a dead father or grandfather or other male or female forebear is the refusal to comply with the ancestor's wish (uttered in a dream) to name a newly born son after him or her (a number of males carry female names as a result of an ancestress's wish). This sin of omission may cause sterility in a man or his wife and/or the death of their children. But while there is respect for one's dead forebears, this in no way amounts to worship. Thus, as explained in the preceding paragraph, it is the dead enemies rather than the ancestors themselves who are most likely to inflict their wrath, against which the protection is not their appeasement but one's own self-preservation through purification. In the world of the living the respect for one's parents merges with respect for an older brother and with respect for a senior co-wife by a junior co-wife and husband, to constitute a single order of seniority, the abuse of which may be regarded as ending a line of descent, as we shall see below under the section dealing with the concept of *chira*. Before looking at this concept, it is appropriate to ask whether Luo beliefs akin to those identified by anthropologists as witchcraft are also used to explain child loss and childlessness.

ENVY AND JEALOUSY

Mitchell's well-known dual hypothesis with reference to Salisbury, in Zimbabwe (Rhodesia), was that (a) the necessity for urban family cohesiveness inhibits relatives from accusing each other of witchcraft in town and that (b) witchcraft accusations are more likely to be found in the competitive environment of workplace among unrelated employees, but that, even there, their illegality in the eyes of the urban administration is likely to suppress their open expression. Certainly, accusations of witchcraft (*juok*) among Luo relatives actually living in Nairobi must be rare, for very few cases came to my attention. Office employees sometimes claim that an unrelated rival is advancing himself by secretly placing harmful medicines (*kingo* or *iro*) on his victim's desk and so causing his work to suffer or even killing him. But rarely do the rivals confront each other openly with these accusations.

Interestingly, the most common context in which a witch (*jajuok*) is cited as the likely cause of misfortune is when a child undergoing education in Nairobi becomes seriously sick or dies. In this case the witch is usually identified as a jealous *rural* neighbour or relative. This conceptual separation into rural cause and urban effect among Luo in Nairobi is curiously at odds with the view widely reported for other African societies that it is precisely such rural malevolence from which urban immigrants claim to be escaping. As described in Chapter 1, the Luo straddle town and country, in some cases by locating their assets in both, and in all cases by constantly deploying their families between them. The Luo view that rural jealousies can have their effect in town is thus consistent with the townwards bias in their system of circulatory family movement. The explanation that it may be jealous rural relatives and neighbours who are harming one's children who are getting education in Nairobi neatly underlines the value that is placed on urban educational investment in children and at the same time reveals the uncertainty that any "profit", in the form of secure wage employment, will ever come from it.

Finally, no urban cases of "evil eye" (*juok wang*), traditionally said to occur only among women, are reported. In Nairobi, it will be remembered, polygynous husbands avoid as far as possible having co-wives living together in one house, preferring instead to keep one in town and the other in the rural home. Nevertheless, as I shall show, rules governing the seniority of co-wives can be broken, even in Nairobi, as is the case between brothers and between parents and children. The repercussions of such breaches of seniority are said to come in the form of the affliction called *chira,* to which I next turn.

Summarizing this section and following the broad lines of Mitchell's hypothesis, we can confirm that witchcraft among Luo in Nairobi is not a dominant mode of explanation of domestic misfortune and that, when it is so used, its origin is conceptualized as rural rather than urban. My strong impression is that in Nairobi the concept of *chira* has assumed an inordinate dominance, over and above witchcraft and sorcery, as a mode of explaining sterility and sickness and death, especially among children.

CHIRA

I did not come across the concept of *chira* until I had been doing fieldwork for about eight months in Kampala city, Uganda, in 1963. Its significance arose spontaneously from fieldwork as I came to know a limited number of families deeply and as my knowledge of the Luo vernacular improved. *Chira* does not fit, either conceptually or semantically, into such "traditional" anthropological categories as witchcraft, spirit possession, and ancestor "worship", for which roughly equivalent verbal concepts can be found in the Luo language. *Chira* is not easily translatable and I have not attempted to do so.[1] It refers to a wasting disease, sometimes culminating in death, which a victim or someone close to the victim has incurred through ignoring (not necessarily consciously) some kind of relationship taboo. The disease arises from an improper mixing of categories which are normally kept distinct. In other words, it arises from a confusion of relationship boundaries. The basic idea behind it has much in common with that of "incompatible blood" which I described above. It will be recalled that where the idea of "incompatible blood" had undertones of result-

[1] Whisson (1964b, p. vi) identifies the diseases caused by *chira* as taking "any form—lameness, leprosy, ulcerated wounds, stomach pains".

ing from incest, which is of course the notion of "confused relations" at its most fundamental. I am merely following the Luo in distinguishing "incompatible blood" and *chira* as separate explanatory concepts for sterility and death and sickness in the family: sometimes comparable misfortunes are explained by the one and sometimes by the other cause, but *chira* predominates in Nairobi.

As a culturally explicit concept *chira* is something of a paradox. At a public level many men (though not women), when asked about it, will scoff at the idea. And yet, in actual cases of childlessness and wasting sickness in the family, it is *chira* which is likely to be diagnosed, especially if other methods of medical treatment fail. The diagnosis of *chira* can be shameful because it implies that interpersonal decorum has been neglected, and so it is not surprising that people are reluctant to admit that it is in their family. It carries some of the dread associated with Western views of malignant cancer, which, even when officially "cured", is almost invariably thought capable of returning, in spite of much evidence to the contrary. Girls or men from Luo families or lineage segments which are known to have recently been beset by *chira*, may be rejected as marriage partners if a respected *ajuoga* so advises. *Chira* is, then, rarely discussed openly by men except by those *ajuoga* who are known to specialize in its treatment, and even they carefully control how much expertise they reveal. Women talk more freely about it among themselves but, again, never by reference to cases of it occurring in their own natal or husband's families. By its negative innuendos *chira* is an element in the evaluative language of interpersonal behaviour and communication, and in making marriage choices.

The word *chira* is of Bantu origin. The neighbouring Luyia have a similar verbal concept, *ishira*. But it is not necessarily the case that the Kenya Luo incorporated the word *chira* in their own language as they migrated southwards through Bantu-speaking Luyia country to their present area. It is possible that *chira*, or more likely a phonologically similar antecedent, entered the Nilotic stream further north in what is now Uganda. I outline in an appendix some suggestions as to the movement and interplay of a set of similar sounding terms and concepts to *chira* in both Nilotic and Bantu cultures, for this gives us some insights into its "core" meaning.

For the present analysis it is enough merely to note that, as found in a range of widely separated Bantu cultures in East Africa, to which

I refer in the Appendix, an archetypal concept phonologically linked to *chira* generally refers to a disease afflicting a mother and/or child arising from adultery on her part or, sometimes, by her husband, during her pregnancy and the period when she is lactating, i.e. nursing a child. It does not appear in any of these Bantu cultures that the disease will come as a result of adultery committed when the woman is neither pregnant nor nursing (unless the adultery happens also to constitute incest). In other words the misfortune will only occur as a result of adultery *within* a closed period: from the time the woman is pregnant until she weans her child. In most cases the prohibition effectively applies to women, for this closed period can be very long and it is recognized that men are unlikely, if they lack other wives, to remain chaste throughout: preventive and ameliorative medicines are probably more easily obtainable by husbands to help offset the chances of affliction. In any event, sexual intercourse between the husband and wife themselves is normally only prohibited or discouraged during the later stages of pregnancy and for a specified postpartum period, all of which is a time when the child is being formed in the womb and later nurtured at the breast and so has total physical dependence on the mother. For a mother who nurses each child for up to two years and produces additional children every two or three years thereafter, the prohibition on adultery can be extended until she ceases bearing. Traditionally, the consequences of such an explanatory concept of disease might have been to reinforce husbands' (and their kin's) claims over the offspring of wives too fearful to commit adultery.

The semantic logic of this archetypal concept would seem to turn on the use of the Bantu root verb, *-kira*, meaning to pass (over), suggesting that the period is one of dangerous liminality, albeit often suspended for a long time, during which the respective "blood" of mother, child, and by extension, of father, should not become "mixed" or "crossed" with the "blood" of someone outside the relationship. Again, the conceptual parallel underlying many notions of "incest" is apparent here. Above all, at this level of pure report or statement, women are regarded as more likely to bring the disease through their adultery than are men.

When cross-cultural borrowing of terms occurs, it is rare for them to reflect precisely the concepts referred to in the donor culture. The fitting of terms and concepts to each other is a constant process of logical and environmental adjustment. The Luo have borrowed the term *chira* and have captured with it the specific Bantu reference to the danger of adultery during liminal periods in the husband–wife relationship. But they have also "added" a whole range of extra family and lineage relationships within which broken prohibitions will bring about the disease. They have also "added" men to women and children as the possible victims. The main emphasis is on the possible threats to a man's family and therefore patrilineage continuity, which makes it logically consistent with Luo cultural notions concerning the unambiguity of women's status as producers of children for men. The total range of relationships and situations within which Luo men, their wives and children can be inflicted with *chira* is very much greater. This widening of a conceptual net characterized by a single term probably occurred before Luo migrated to work in Nairobi. But, as I shall show, the presence in Nairobi in recent years of settled Luo families, with their increasing numbers of urban-reared and urban-educated children, appears to have raised the explanatory power of *chira* there to unprecedented levels. A significant devolopment has been the characterization of men as more likely to have committed the transgression bringing *chira*.

What, then, is the total range of relationships and situations in which *chira* may arise?

Negligence as sin

There are two main areas of transgression, of "sinning" (*rochruok*), which are said to produce *chira*. One is where there has been either what in English we call "incest" or what we call "adultery" at particular stages of a marriage or with unsuitable partners. The other is where there has been an abuse of family or agnatic relationships of seniority. *Chira* can only afflict Luo, including those incorporated as Luo, and can only result from relations between fellow-Luo.

Let me list the causes of *chira* as they have been variously given independently of each other, by over 60 mostly married men, and a slightly larger number of mostly married women. All these people live at Kaloleni and knew me, in some cases well. These were responses to my direct, open-ended questions and, as we shall see, miss the emphasis on adultery as a main *cited* cause in Nairobi. Rather, this emphasis comes out in the spontaneous conversations of crises or special events.

Before presenting the list I should point out three differences in men's and women's discussion of *chira*. First, women were in fact more articulate about its causes and consequences and more inclined to elaborate on them by referring to examples which they claimed to know about. By contrast, men tended to give briefer and rather more stereotyped comments. Husbands would often themselves urge me to check with their wives for a fuller and more detailed account, being happy to acknowledge that women knew more about *chira* than themselves. We may note, here, how this is the converse of the situation regarding evaluative discussions of polygyny which I outlined in the previous chapter and which showed women as much less inclined to talk about it in any detailed way. Second, and related to this, women did on the whole give a slightly wider range of possible causes of *chira*. Men had a rather more restricted "knowledge". Third, within the range of knowledge common to both, women tended more to cite illicit sex and men broken rules of seniority as possible causes of *chira*.

These second and third differences between men and women were slight and the overall impression was of general agreement. This suggests that, since a young groom and bride are usually given advice separately on how to avoid *chira*, there is some joint discussion of its causes between males and females at some stages of their respective life-cycles. Whether this is, say, between parental man and wife, or young brother and sister, or whether the joint knowledge comes from participation in diagnoses of victims by the *ajuoga*, I do not know. All we can say is that *chira* comprises a domain of knowledge shared by both men and women, but with women acknowledged by both as better informed.

The listed reasons are:

1. Sex by a man with: a married woman with children; a father's wife; the wife of a living brother; "someone you call sister"; an unpurified widow (and, in some responses, any uninherited widow); the same unmarried girl as "used" by your father or your own sons; an unmarried girl whose child has died; a junior co-wife to the neglect of a senior wife; an unmarried girl on your father's bed; your wife on either of your parent's beds.

2. A father or mother sleeping in a son's or daughter's house and/or on his/her bed (some responses gave sleeping under the same roof as enough to cause *chira*, while a few qualified this by saying that only sleeping in the same

room would cause it); a man sleeping in his younger brother's house; a junior co-wife preceding a senior one into the home after an absence; a man marrying or building his (rural) house before his elder brother; a pregnant woman carrying her own daughter's child; an unpurified widow or widower carrying a child; cursing (*kuong'ruok*) by an elder.

The reasons given under (1) and (2) refer to illicit sex and broken seniority rules respectively. Illicit sex here refers to both adultery and incest. The Luo verbal approximation for "to commit adultery" is *terore*, with *terruok* the noun. That adultery is "sinful" comes out in such general expressions as *ng'ama oterore kod chi ng'ato ojaricho* (someone who has sex with someone's wife is sinful/bad). I have also heard the verb used to refer to sexuality which in English might be translated more as incest than adultery, e.g. *oterore gi nyamin minare* (he has sex with his mother's sister). The word for "incest" (e.g. between an unmarried man and a classificatory sister) is given by Whisson (1964b, p. 28) as *dhoch* and he distinguishes this from "merely ritually dangerous sex", for which the term is *kweo*. Though the terms are distinct, the particular relations to which they refer are not always so clear to a Luo man or woman. It is precisely this uncertainty and overlapping nature of the possible causes of *chira* that makes it such a powerful belief system. For just about any death or serious sickness within a family can be regarded *post hoc* as deriving from this wide range of causes. Reported examples, especially originating from and affecting people in their rural homesteads, are readily available. These represent a repertoire of possible causes of *chira*. But in the particular circumstances of recent and increasing family settlement in Nairobi, only some of them are picked out with any frequency in unprompted conversations and "natural" events.

First, adultery is given great ideological stress. Luo men and women in Nairobi say, with great frequency, that it will arise if a married man who has a child has sex with a "mature woman" other than his wife (*dhako,* presumed also to be married, or to have been married, and to have had a child of her own). It will not arise if his sexual partner is an unmarried, childless girl (*nyako*), or a recently married childless woman (*miaha*), and may not arise if she is much older, though there is then the risk of "incompatible blood" to which I referred above. *Chira* will also strike if a woman commits adultery while she is pregnant or while her child is still suckling.[1] Adultery by a woman with her living husband's brother (a form of "incest") is also stressed as a cause, though if she is young and still fertile at her husband's death, she may be inherited by his brother.

In spite of this spontaneous stress on adultery in these relationships as a cause of *chira* in Nairobi, not a single case came to my attention which had been judged as such by the *ajuoga* (diviner-doctor). Luo might guardedly and privately allude to adultery, including incestuous adultery, as a cause of undiagnosed sickness and death in particular families. But these were not so judged by the *ajuoga* if he or she was summoned, nor openly among themselves by the family's relatives. He always diagnosed broken rules of seniority. Five cases involved families whom I knew personally and I present them as each sufficiently distinct to illustrate the operation, sometimes in combination, of four basic rules of seniority among Luo in Nairobi. Each case can be supported by two or three other reliably reported cases.

Rule 1.   A parent should not sleep in the house of an adult offspring.

CASE 1.   In 1958 the father of a young married man in his mid-twenties came from the rural home and slept in his son's house in Nairobi. The son then had a boy of $1\frac{1}{2}$ years old. From that time the boy and his mother, also in Nairobi, were afflicted with *chira*. First a female then a male *ajuoga* obtained temporary remissions but the disease returned to afflict the second and third children who had been born to the husband and wife. The disease has been with the family for over nine years and has cost them a great deal of money in fees to various *ajuoga*. The second and third children are still weak and unable to talk and walk properly, though old enough to go to school and nursery respectively. The original cause has long been recognized but no amount of purification with the medicine *manyasi*, nor the use of other herbs, either at the rural home or in Nairobi, has significantly improved the situation.

The rule here is that neither fathers nor mothers, nor those standing in the classificatory relationship of father and mother, should be accommodated in sons' (or daughters') houses. This applies to both rural and urban areas. But the rule presents no problem in the former, for

---

[1] Some Luo say that *chira* comes if a woman continues to breast-feed a child after becoming pregnant, but others claim that the disease in this case is called *hero*. The wasting symptom is the same. I may note here also a case reported to me in Kampala in 1963 in which a mother was threatened with *chira* by another woman, who did so by on page 262). Such woman-to-woman threats or instances of *chira* do not normally occur in conversations about the subject, however.

the rural compound family layout provides separate houses for each adult son as well as for their father and each of his respective co-wives. In Nairobi the rule obliges sons to find alternative accommodation for parents who are visiting them in the city. But, as I have been stressing throughout, accommodation is extremely scarce. The problem is all the more acute in view of the fact that parents, whether a father or mother, almost invariably come to Nairobi at little or no notice on a matter of some urgency: someone at home may have died; help of some kind may be needed from the urban member of the family; news may have reached the rural parent that a son or daughter, or their children, are sick and dying in Nairobi. The impromptu nature of such visits by parents concerned to seek or offer answers to such family crises means that a man in Nairobi must have a ready network of friends, or non-agnatic relatives or affines, willing and able to provide accommodation at a moment's notice. Agnates will tend to be of the townman's own generation and so classed by a visiting father as "sons": their accommodation will be unacceptable. A townsman who has failed to keep up a non-agnatic network of this kind, or has simply failed to reciprocate the service, is the most likely to experience difficulty in finding accommodation for a parent outside his own urban home. In the case above, the unfortunate family head in Nairobi had been working for the East African Railways and had experienced frequent transfers from one town to another. His links within Nairobi were therefore fragmentary and fleeting, even though he had been in urban industrial wage employment for some years. He had not maintained a wide and ready network of potential providers of accommodation, and, half-sceptical at the time (as he admitted) that *chira* could really be caused in this way, gave his protesting father a bed in the kitchen of the two-roomed house. He has long since regretted that decision and sadly recognizes his "sin".

Referring back to my suggestion at the beginning of Chapter 1, we can see *chira* as an example of a key verbal concept and its associated semantic domain providing the cultural continuity that links Luo wage earners who move frequently between different towns in East Africa.

Rule 2.   Elder brothers should marry before younger ones.

CASE 2.   In 1964 a man married before his elder brother. He earned a good wage in Nairobi and was able to provide most of his own bridewealth, marrying in defiance of his parents' wishes. His wife soon bore a son. But even by the time the child was three years old he was unable to walk or speak. He is deemed to have been afflicted with *chira,* because his father has reversed the order of marriage between himself and his brother. Not only this, but the elder brother has also become "abnormal" in his behaviour and is also said to have *chira.* The literal translation of the reason given by the *ajuoga* for the *chira* is: "By marrying first, the younger brother stepped in front of his elder, barred his way, and prevented him from seeing ahead. That elder brother is now 'out' [i.e. socially dead], but now the younger brother's children will be, too."

The moral idea behind the *ajuoga's* explanation appears to be that, by thwarting the development of a future lineage of a senior brother, a man runs the risk also of obliterating his own line of descendants.

A younger brother may be more successful in the wage economy than an older one and may be able to marry before him by providing his own bridewealth. This does not often happen but, with younger brothers sometimes receiving more education than older ones, remains a recognized possibility, and one that strikes at the heart of an ideal of agnation and extended family cohesion.

Rule 3. Elder brothers should build their houses on rural home sites allocated to them for that purpose before younger ones.

CASE 3. Another successful wage-earner in Nairobi wanted to invest some of his savings in a semi-permanent house of his own, complete with corrugated iron roof, at the rural family home. His elder brother had been studying overseas for many years and the younger man decided not to await his return before building the house. The elder brother returned after eight years, first staying in Nairobi. Then, he and his wife went to the rural home, staying in the younger man's house. They returned and settled in Nairobi in the high-status area of Kariokor. But he swiftly developed the wasting symptoms of *chira,* and, in spite of being taken to the best doctors and *ajuoga* in Nairobi, eventually died. His wife and the younger brother had by now been taken home and been given the purificatory *manyasi* medicine, and neither developed the disease.

As well as demonstrating that great physical distance between brothers does not free them from maintaining their correct social distance, the case points up the importance of the rural end of extended family cohesion, even for brothers who are financially and educationally successful.

CASE 4. A wife of about 35 years of age, who had produced two healthy children, was troubled by disease for more than a year, suffering haemorrhages and emaciation and finally dying. In this case she and her husband were devout Christians and had refused to abide by Luo prohibitions or to take Luo medicines. After her death, two relatives, including a half-brother of the husband, living nearby in Nairobi, accused the man not only of refusing to go to an *ajuoga* but of having brought *chira* to his wife by marrying before his elder brother many years earlier and by allowing his father's brother to stay with them in Nairobi more recently.

Although an *ajuoga's* specific diagnosis had not been sought in this case, relatives provided a composite explanation of the misfortune which blamed the husband for neglecting seniority rules both within and between the generations.

Rule 4.   The seniority of co-wives must be respected, even with regard to the home in Nairobi.

I have already provided in Chapter 1 cases which illustrate this rule. The following abbreviated version of another such case will remind the reader of their salient features.

CASE 5.   A junior wife came to Nairobi at her husband's request and stayed in his house while the senior wife was still at the rural home. She became thin and apparently barren, and was declared by the *ajuoga* to be afflicted with *chira*.

When moving into or between a husband's houses, it must always be a senior wife who "leads" or precedes junior ones. In the movement of wives between town and country which characterizes polygynous families and provides the useful rural–urban bridging of relationships which I have discussed (see Chapter 1), the normal procedure is for the senior wife to come first to Nairobi and there, regardless of the brevity or length of her stay, to await the arrival of the junior co-wife before returning to the rural home.

I will not reproduce instances from reported "traditional" ethnography to illustrate that these four basic rules of seniority can be seen as variants of rules which were and to a large extent still are fitted to a rural system of compound polygynous family settlement and inheritance, in which status and entitlement are strictly ascribed. These urban variants are clearly adaptations to: (a) the distinctively Luo system of simultaneous urban family settlement and the preservation of rural ties, ideally through the circulatory migration of co-wives and their children; (b) the scarcity of accommodation in Nairobi, in which a network of non-agnatic ties must be maintained in order that visiting parents or parental agnates be accommodated in other than their "sons'" houses; and (c) the opportunities offered by the wage economy during increasing employment for younger, sometimes more educated brothers to usurp the seniority of their elders by marrying or by building rural homes before them.

Why should it remain important for these rules to persist and to become specially adapted to the living conditions of Nairobi? Why should it matter if brothers do marry and build rural homes in the wrong order or allow their parents and paternal uncles to stay with them in their houses in Nairobi? An obvious possible answer is that the rules act as moral sanctions on maintaining family cohesion, and that this stress on family cohesion is a response to the increased pressurization experienced by Luo in Nairobi as the Kikuyu emerge as the dominant ethnic group. This may well be true, for as I have explained elsewhere (1974b), political and economic opportunities are indeed sharply conceptualized as being unevenly distributed between ethnic groups in Nairobi, producing a definite cultural response by Luo. But, strictly speaking, this explanation is undemonstrable, for there are no "before" and "after" situations in which the different responses of Luo families in Nairobi can be compared over time. That is to say, Luo family settlement on any scale in Nairobi is a relatively recent evolving phenomenon which is still working out solutions, so to speak, to the urban ecological problems of scarce housing, limited employment, ambivalent educational opportunities, and the economic and political need to retain rural connections .The Luo conceptualization of an uneven ethnic distribution of opportunity and power provides a necessary wider framework within which fellow-ethnic support is increasingly seen as the *sine qua non* of survival and self-advancement in Nairobi. But, in order to understand why family and close agnatic ties continue to be selected for special ideological emphasis, we have to look internally at this evolving pattern of urban family settlement and continuing rural connections.

Public belief and private diagnosis

The most important development underlying *chira* as an explanation of sterility, and family sickness and death, stems from the distinction made between its two main precipitating causes: particular kinds of adultery on the one hand and abuses of seniority on the other. It will be remembered that at the level of ideal statement both "sins" figured equally prominently as causes of *chira*. But in actual cases dealt with by an *ajuoga* or informally but openly "judged" by relatives, the tendency is for negligence of seniority rules to be given as the cause. That is to say, no one would publicly give a particular example of adultery as being the cause.

At the level of ideal statement, men are regarded as equally likely as women to commit the kinds of sinful adultery bringing about *chira*. In itself, this may represent a shift in emphasis, for there is some evidence that, when Luo male control over their womenfolk was even greater than now, it was adultery by women rather than men which was likely to be most cited as responsible. Certainly, the attribution of *chira* in actual cases to abuses of seniority rather than adultery places the onus of responsibility squarely on men: for it is they, and not their womenfolk, who decide whether to marry or build rural homes before elder brothers, or to allow parents to stay in their Nairobi houses with them, or to ask a junior rather than senior wife to come to the Nairobi house first. These are sins arising from domestic mismanagement by male household heads, and so no blame can be aimed at women members of the family.

At one level of explanation, then, the concept of *chira* has the "function" of constituting the basis of a system of urban family morality, with males primarily accountable for maintaining this morality. At another level of explanation, *chira* can be viewed as the key term covering a paradigm of associated ideas. That is to say, use of the word *chira*, whether to judge a particular case of sickness and death or to refer generally to such misfortune, "unlocks" the two other sets of associations discussed here. First, it is associated with the phenomenon of adultery, and secondly, with that of internal family seniority. Putting this point simply, we can say that when Luo in Nairobi talk about *chira*, they will be led, if they continue talking for long enough, into a discussion of adultery and/or family seniority.

What is the social significance of these two conversational and conceptual pathways? The first thing to remember is that, as I stated earlier, *chira* is not normally a phenomenon encountered in casual conversation. In so far as it refers to a sin committed by someone or other, it is an idea normally communicated only to those with whom one has an intimate or special relationship, perhaps a family member, a close friend or relative, or an *ajuoga* hired for a particular occasion. To acknowledge publicly knowing a great deal about the symptoms and causes of *chira* is to invite the suspicion of having been personally involved in particular cases and perhaps of having been guilty of the precipitating sin. I have many cases of Luo professing to knowing little of *chira* early in our relationship, but later on elaborating on it. Discussion of *chira*, then, occurs in a private domain of relationships based on what Fortes (1969, p. 251) has called the axiom of amity, but including also the contractual but confidential relationship of client and *ajuoga*, that is to say, patient and doctor. Indeed, from the literature it appears that the diagnosis and discussion of *chira* is much less public in Nairobi than was the case in non-urban "traditional" contexts (Dupre, 1968, p. 47; and Whisson, 1964a).

Let me deal with Luo ideas of adultery and family seniority in turn. Though the Luo divorce and separation rates in Nairobi are much lower than for other ethnic groups there, Luo male close relatives and friends warn each other of the dangers of being cuckolded or deserted by a wife in Nairobi. To lose a wife through her desertion or to be cuckolded reflect very severely on a man's honour. Among Luo generally, "honour" in this context equates in intensity with the Latin American concept of *machismo*. It is contained in the term *luor*, roughly translatable as "respect", and is centrally important in the definition of the ideal man.[1] For most Luo, adultery by a woman is almost tantamount to divorce, for it is not normally reckoned that a marriage can survive the dislocation to the husband's honour. Against this, of course, is the question of whether any man who is cuckolded or whose wife leaves him (and who, it is assumed, will also have committed adultery) will wish to reveal the fact in view of his possible loss of honour. It is difficult to know how many cases of adultery or desertion by wives are hidden for this reason. But, unlike, say, the allegedly secret and therefore frequently undetectable acts of witchcraft described in much anthropological literature, acts of adultery or desertion by members of small face-to-face communities can be less easily hidden. Luo men are unlikely to miss this opportunity of cutting their rivals down to size, and so I believe that the few cases of

---

[1] *Duong'* = (literally) bigness, and can mean "respect", cf. *jaduong'*, elder or big man. *Jatelo* is also a term of respect, meaning also a "leader". *Magosi* is a term of address and reference used, especially, at public meetings to introduce a speaker, and meaning "the honourable". *Mikayi* (the term for senior wife) can be used to introduce a married woman, and *nyadende* for an unmarried girl.

female adultery and desertion reported among the close-knit Luo networks making up the Nairobi community and linking up in the rural areas roughly reflect the actual number. The number is not high but particular cases bring together the families of both husband and wife, together with many of their close relatives living in Nairobi and at the two rural homes. Even serious quarrels between husband and wife, which may not by themselves lead to marital breakdown, become matters of such general concern. Men help each other settle marital disputes, retrieve wives, or negotiate the repayment of bridewealth in the event of divorce, ostensibly on the basis of relations of amity, including descent, kinship and friendship. Since the fear of the same happening to themselves is general, it is not unreasonable to assume that they also expect their offers of assistance to be reciprocated should occasion demand. But, to emphasize the important point made earlier, this expectation of reciprocity has to be confined to that ego-centred network of friends and relatives among whom, it is assumed, one's inevitable loss of honour can at least be cushioned, if not actually hidden, from the outside world. In practice, friendships and rivalries alternate over time, as do the conflicting connotations of relationships identified by the term *omera*, discussed in Chapter 3. Any network of relatives and friends mobilized to deal with these private crises therefore inevitably contains one or two who, being untrustworthy like the *jasem* during marriage negotiations, spring information leaks enabling the private drama to become public knowledge.

So, while the reported and probably actual number of cases of female adultery is few, each has inordinate significance as the focus of a network of interpersonal relations, as people rally round in an attempt either to re-establish marital harmony or, if this is not possible, to effect a speedy repayment of bridewealth. The manifest nature of the obligations underlying the recruitment and assistance offered by the network is private, an internal "family" affair in the widest sense covered by the root term, -*mer*.[1] But the likelihood is that the event becomes publicised by individual members of the network.

The ideas of adultery and *chira* are similar in two main respects. Both are seen by Luo themselves to be private matters concerning only family and friends. Also, both can be moved, so to speak, from this private to the public domain. Adultery and desertion, or simply a man's inability to "manage" his wife properly, become public know-

---

[1] Cf. the Neur *mar*, kinship, itself opposed to *buth*, agnation.

ledge through the presence in the network of malevolent rivals. *Chira* can become instanced by an *ajuoga* as responsible for particular cases of family death and/or sickness; but in the few *specific* cases where *chira* is publicly believed, following the *ajuoga's* diagnosis, to have caused misfortune, it is not adultery which is cited as the precipitating sin. Rather, as I explained above, it is men's negligence of the rules of family seniority in Nairobi.

Conclusion

A general belief in the "mystical" affliction called *chira* has assumed considerable importance as Luo families have settled in Nairobi. At the level of pure statement, it is believed that men and women are just as likely as each other to cause it. At this level of pure "talk" about *chira*, women are generally acknowledged to know more about its causes. They are here more "articulate" than men—quite the reverse of their relatively tacit and stereotyped view of polygyny. At this level of undemonstrated belief, women are said to have as much power as their husbands, if not more, to destroy their families through incest or adultery. But in actual cases of *chira* diagnosed by a diviner, it is men's mismanagement of domestic and lineage seniority relations which is cited as responsible. In other words, at the level of pure statement women may be credited with the power to destroy a man's family and ensuing lineage, but in actual cases open to the public view, so to speak, it is men who are seen to wield this power.

The connotations covered by the term *chira* are thus ambivalent. Women's mystical equality to men is posed and then contradicted. This is made possible because the term *chira* floats, so to speak, over the interlinked concepts of incest, adultery, and abuses of seniority, and so facilitates a range of interpretations of the cause of family sickness and death. Here, the mystically ambivalent status of women corresponds with the ambivalent economic status of some of them, as discussed in the previous chapter. The greater knowledge concerning *chira* that women are believed to have links up, in men's conversations, with women's apparently increasing economic and educational status. This itself represents a potential ambiguity in women's status. I do not suggest that men, either individually or collectively, consciously seek to contain this ambivalence. But, for women's status to be logically consistent with the institutions of marriage and bride-wealth exchanged for genetricial rights, it must remain unambiguously defined as concerned with the production of children for men and their ensuing lineages. Hence, in Nairobi, the classificatory nature of Luo lineage segmentation operates by arranging men's marriage "choices" according to precise exogamic and relationship rules. This stress on unambiguity is an implicit meaning and consequence of the remarkable pyramidal structure of Luo lineage associations in the city.

These urban lineage associations are run by men who make up the entire membership. The term *chira* only ambivalently fixes on men as publicly accountable for death and sickness occurring in their own families. But the descent principle, which in the family is constantly "threatened" by *chira*, unambiguously carries the notion of external representation by males to the wider context of lineage associations. It is to this public sphere of Luo social organization in Nairobi that I turn in the next two chapters. It is public, not only in simply involving a more comprehensive group that that of the family. It is also public in providing the basis of overall Luo political representation in Nairobi. For it is through their associations that the Luo organize themselves politically.

We cannot deduce from this, however, that the pyramidal structure of lineage associations "owes" its existence to the political functions its performs. We could as well argue that it owes its existence to the system of marriage arrangements which, in their present form, require precise guidelines and ready-made forums for discussing who may marry whom, and for how much, and who is able to pay. The classificatory aspect of the urban pyramidal structure of lineage associations, while it may be said to be sustained by these institutions, is logically prior to and presupposes them. In these associations polygynists-cum-elders play dominant roles. On the one hand this is because it is they who are most likely to need information for the marriage arrangements of their own children. On the other hand, however, it is simply consistent with the Luo principle of lineage organizations that such men should be seen and heard to lead.

6

The Control of
Political Uncertainty

Two Kinds of Segmentation

From women to men

In the preceding chapter I explained how men are held primarily
accountable in Nairobi for the welfare of their wives and children.
The management of one's family is by no means an entirely private
matter between the husband/father and his wife or wives and their
children. Two domestic events, namely the marriages of one's children
or an outbreak of *chira* within the family, are likely to concern a wide
and more public range of agnates, and affines and other non-agnates.
Senior agnates who have marriageable sons and daughters of their
own have a vested interest in seeing that the rules of lineage exogamy
are upheld. For, as elders unquestionably credited with knowing the
details of relevant genealogical connections, they can use this knowledge to retain control over younger men's marriage "choices". The
most "learned" and therefore powerful of them can influence strongly
the "choice" of lineage into which a man's son or daughter marries.
A senior agnate may also pressure a monogamist with apparently
"surplus" income to take a second wife from an "allied" lineage as
a kind of indirect substitute for an outstanding marriage debt of his
own to an affine. Such elders clearly have competing interests as individuals in such cases, but as a category credited with critically important genealogical knowledge, they stand apart from other men. As
regards *chira*, the families of both a husband and wife or co-wives

wish to eliminate its cause and stop its capricious spread to other victims.

Public male accountability for family welfare extends into the public political sphere in which men much more than women represent the Luo community as a whole. They do this through the many Luo lineage-based associations in Nairobi and through political party branches.

The difference in scope between the work of men and women diviner-doctors (both called *ajuoga*) corresponds with this unevenness of male and female accountability and representation. That is to say, while both men and women diviner-doctors are called upon to diagnose and treat family sickness and misfortune, including cases of *chira*, only male diviner-doctors are summoned to treat public misfortunes or to prepare for events held for the Luo community.

Let me briefly describe some of the social differences between Luo men and women diviner-doctors. I knew of ten male ones in Nairobi, though there were undoubtedly more than this. The most famous is called Agunga. He was even sent on a sponsored demonstration tour to the USA. He lived in Kaloleni and specialized in the treatment of *chira* and was the main (at the time) "war magician" (*jabilo*) to the Luo Gor Mahia football club. Some three other men diviner-doctors also lived in Kaloleni. All such men tend to be in their thirties and early forties, married, and in some cases with a second wife. They have a limited school education and little knowledge of English, though Agunga was the most proficient, and were previously employed in unskilled and semi-skilled jobs. They certainly earn much more from their current practices than from their previous jobs, though precisely how much was difficult to ascertain. With their high income and low education, these men are more like some older Luo in their late forties and early fifties who, though barely educated in many cases, came to Nairobi early enough to be fitted into jobs, often with Asian employers, which eventually provided them with skills now carrying relatively high wages, e.g. tailoring, carpentry, truck driving, vehicle maintenance, welding and fitting, etc.

By contrast, women diviner-doctors do not fit any corresponding social category among Luo women. The five I knew ranged in age from their early forties to late fifties. Three were widows and two divorcees. Three had never produced children, and each of the other two had only one grown-up son. Typical is Grace, also living in Kaloleni. She is in her late forties and originally from Sakwa location. She was married just before the second world war and went with her Luo husband to Tororo, Uganda, where he worked on the railways. She did not produce any children and he took a second Luo wife. He died in the nineteen fifties (of uncertain causes). His second wife thereupon returned to his rural home with her two children, but Grace stayed on in Uganda until 1958 when she came to Nairobi. She claimed to have learned much of her craft as an *ajuoga* in Uganda but emphasized also that her skills were essentially "Luo", with a special knowledge of the problems associated with *chira*. What was particularly noticeable, as with other Luo women diviner-doctors, was (a) the inclusion of some non-Luo women in her predominantly Luo clientele, and (b) her use of excellent (up-country) Swahili. Luo men diviner-doctors cater almost exclusively for fellow-Luo and are not as proficient in Swahili. These men earn more and become public figures within the Luo community, whereas women diviner-doctors earn much less and have much less public status, with their diagnoses and treatment confined to family and personal misfortunes. Interestingly, the women's treatment of some non-Luo women and their greater proficiency in Swahili is not cited as a distinguishing feature in conversations about Luo diviner-doctors. It is not a culturally acknowledged difference. Indeed, when discussing the diagnosis and treatment of sickness and misfortune, Luo men and women use the one term, *ajuoga,* to refer to the diviner-doctor, rarely making it clear in the conversation whether they have in mind a man or woman *ajuoga*. It is as if the role of the *ajuoga* is idealized as "purely" concerning only the Luo and as being above and beyond the social characteristics and sex of the person who fills it. There is not even explicit recognition that women's mystical powers are in practice confined to the domestic domain while those of men diviner-doctors include this and extend beyond it to the public domain.

The use of the one term, *ajuoga,* for both men and women diviner-doctors thus carries within it a tacit differentiation between male and female mystical responsibilities and power.[1] This "hidden" division

---

[1] Abrahams (1972, pp. 116–18) discusses the etymological as well as conceptual links between the words *ajuoga,* diviner, *ajuok,* witch, and *juok,* spirit or god among the Nilotic-speaking Labwor of Uganda. Among the Luo, the terms *ajuoga,* diviner-doctor, and *jajuok,* witch, are similarly linked, with an etymologically unlinked term, *jachien,* for spirit. There is an additional term, *Nyasaye,* for the Christian concept of God. It is of Bantu origin and is used by the neighbouring Maragoli (a Luyia sub-group).

of labour and powers between men and women diviner-doctors corresponds with the open and unambiguous definition of women's status as producers of men's children and so as confined to domestic activities, and of male household heads as political leaders and wage earners. In other words, the same underlying division of labour, powers, and modes of representation are communicated in two different ways, one "mystically" and tacitly, and the other openly.

This open and unambiguous definition of statuses takes us into the public and political field of Luo internal debate between men and to the general exclusion of women. The forums for such restricted debate in Nairobi are the Luo lineage associations of different segmentary levels and the overarching Luo Union. On the one hand, as I have mentioned, these associations are concerned with guiding marriage "choices" and a host of other welfare activities including the repatriation for burial of men and women (but not usually children) who have died in Nairobi. On the other hand, the associations provide ready-made contexts for discussing and, if necessary, organizing Luo politics. Since the associations are first and foremost lineage based, the discussion of and active responses to changes in the political and economic environment are phrased in lineage terms. The two main spheres of interest, marriage and politics, in fact come together: to talk politics is to talk in the idiom of marriage and, by implication, the family and lineage. Internally, this means debating whether a particular family and descent group will make politically useful and financially reliable affines. Externally, it means using both the rural and urban members of lineages as basic building blocks in the formation of a collective Luo political response.

Since the discussion of politics takes place overall within a framework of segmentarily arranged lineage associations under the umbrella of the Luo Union, it predictates a political response in terms of this framework. That is to say, even when the Luo operate through formal political parties, they still recruit, mobilize and engage in propaganda by using lineage ties and lineage elders, the definition of whose status rests on unambiguously defined exogamous marriage arrangements. I shall illustrate this in the present and in the next chapter.

This semantic, conceptual, and organizational linking together of marriage and politics is, then, nicely expressed in the role of the male diviner-doctor who prescribes for a domestic misfortune like *chira* as well as for public misfortunes and uncertainties affecting the Luo as a whole.

We can here distinguish two kinds of public uncertainties with which diviner-doctors deal. One kind is seen by Luo as ultimately controllable at a "mystical" level by the diviner-doctor and at a "secular" level by themselves through a customarily "proper" segmentary organization of their lineage associations. These are the uncertainties arising from soccer competitions between Luo lineages and lineage clusters in Nairobi, and between the Luo as a whole and other ethnic groups. As I shall show, soccer is not to be taken lightly in Nairobi. It is a serious matter. And, as such, the uncertainties of outcome require care and planning, both under the auspices of diviner-doctors and the various teams' organizers. But at least the range of such uncertainties can be calculated in advance: either we win, lose, or draw. This kind of bounded uncertainty entails, like Bernstein's restricted code, a high degree of predictability. Moreover, it is comprehensible in terms of the Luo segmentary lineage structure of associations.

The other kind of public misfortune confronting Luo is quite the opposite. It is random and unpredictable. It hits the Luo community from outside and is seen as originating in a culturally alien environment. The most dramatic of such events was the assassination in 1969 of the famous Luo political leader, Tom Mboya. I shall place Luo public discussion of this event in its wider politico-economic context of ethnic competition in the next chapter. For the moment let me just outline its distinctiveness as an example of random public misfortune afflicting the Luo as a whole. Thereafter I turn, again briefly, to describe the more predictable uncertainties of soccer. We shall eventually see how this contrast between random and controllable public misfortunes corresponds with that between what I call general and specific political segmentation.

Men's definition of public uncertainties

Tom Mboya, though a Luo, was frequently tipped as President Kenyatta's most likely successor, even by many non-Luo. The degree to which his assassination was an organized political act has never been discovered. But Luo certainly interpreted it as directed against their then most powerful fellow-Luo and against the Luo community. It has here to be acknowledged that Mboya's apparent refusal over the years to base his power on a predominantly ethnic following had earned him considerable disfavour among many Luo, who regarded his apparently genuine attempts to transcend "tribalism" as more a form of betrayal than the practice of a liberal political ideology. However, his assassination provided an extraordinarily strong rallying-point among even his worst critics and became an occasion for the expression of open and violent dissent in Nairobi not just against the Kenya government but, largely indiscriminately, against the Kikuyu as a whole. Fortunately, there was no concerted Kikuyu backlash and the situation was under control after a few uneasy days in the city.

The organized Luo response to the tragedy was to call a meeting in Kaloleni Hall under the auspices of the Luo Union. The hall and the area outside were packed with thousands of Luo men and the meeting received full, and, I can witness, accurate coverage in the national press. Acknowledged Luo political leaders, including existing and former MPs, and senior members of the Luo Union addressed the meeting for a whole day. In contrast to the violence which was happening on the streets of Nairobi, these Luo leaders played down categorical accusations directed against Kikuyu as individuals or as a community. Instead they moved to the suggestion that they use "traditional" means to "sniff out" the culprit. A prominent Luo diviner-doctor in Nairobi was called upon to address the meeting with a view to organizing this.

This diviner-doctor was one of a number of the more prominent in Nairobi who are separately called upon to prepare the Luo soccer team (called Gor Mahia) for its matches in the all-Kenya championship.[1] Herbal medicines, charms, incantations, warnings and advice are dispensed. When the diviner-doctor addressed the meeting in Kaloleni Hall, his exhortations, suggestions and, later, methods of divination employed the same techniques and style as are used by him and other *ajuoga* on the soccer field. An ostensibly public political affair such as this meeting is linked to the organization of Luo soccer in another way. Just as many ordinary Luo saw Mboya's assassination as the result of inter-ethnic conflict between Luo and Kikuyu, so

[1] I have on rare occasions heard such men referred to as *jabilo* in Luo and "magician" in English. The traditional usage of *jabilo* differs from *ajuoga* in referring more to a specialist in "war" magic, which might actually seem more appropriate to soccer.

were the heated soccer matches between their team and, say, the Luyia or Maragoli Union.

In other words, inter-ethnic conflict is a crucial component of the Nairobi dweller's world view and provides a conveniently general explanation for any ethnic misfortune. Sandbrook (1975, p. 17) notes that enduring political support in Kenya rests on the basis of what he calls "ethnic consciousness". It is only in specific conflicts between employers and workers that something approaching a trans-ethnic "class consciousness" is manifested. Many previous studies of the role of ethnicity as a system of conscious classification have emphasized people's perception of the distinctiveness of the different ethnic groups around them in terms of their differing life-styles and work and residential preferences. In Nairobi, the diminishing pool of jobs and housing have altered this perception to include not just differences of custom, occupation and residence, but also of competition for jobs and housing and of the conflict which accompanies such competition.

The public expression of such inter-ethnic conflict then takes two forms. First, there are the sudden and apparently random events such as Mboya's assassination, which, because they do not fall within a regularly controlled system of activities, are potentially more politically explosive. Second, there are those events, such as the Kenya soccer championship, in which inter-ethnic competition is consciously regulated and, to a much greater extent, controlled. Even though inter-ethnic fighting between young men is a constant after-match feature, it rarely continues for more than a few hours and is, in its own way, as "traditional" a feature of the soccer scene as in Britain.

As regards the Luo, the random kind of event or misfortune is most likely to involve an expression of public dissent against Kikuyu, who are popularly conceptualized as having increased their political and economic dominance at Luo expense and as therefore responsible for the misfortune. The more regularized event, the all-Kenya soccer championship, must involve misfortune for some ethnic groups, for only one team can emerge as champion. But as betting agencies are well aware, an element of predictability in the outcome of the event is also recognized by most people, who nevertheless are sufficiently uncertain that the services of a male diviner-doctor are regarded as indispensable. At the time of fieldwork in 1968–9, only the Luo, Luyia, and Maragoli (normally regarded as a major Luyia sub-group) fielded

G

exclusively ethnic teams. But even, as apparently happened in later years, had Kikuku and Kamba teams been entered, the blame for losing matches was unlikely to have been consistently directed at the machinations of one rather than another ethnic group.

Unpredictable ethnic tragedies such as Mboya's assassination are politically much more explosive in bringing about a direct challenge to the supremacy of one ethnic group. But we get a much clearer understanding of how Luo have been organizing themselves politically by looking intensively at their involvement in the soccer championship: in other words by looking at what is on the surface a non-political organization. This is because the Luo associations and titled officers who are concerned in some way with organizing soccer are, on less frequent and less predictable occasions, called upon to organize for more manifestly political ends. It is as if soccer provides a regularly organized set of activities and roles whose political content is kept in store, so to speak, to be released in crises when the Luo community as a whole is under pressure. The prime example of this is an important Luo rural by-election in 1969 which jointly involved urban as well as home people which has been described in detail by Okumu (1969).

Inter-ethnic soccer competition provides the framework within which the Luo associations organize themselves internally. The Luo and Luyia (including Maragoli) soccer teams are offshoots of the respective ethnic unions of these two peoples, which have been strong for many years. By contrast the Kikuyu and Kamba ethnic unions are weakly developed (as at 1968–9) and do not provide the basis for further elaboration into soccer clubs. Individual Kikuyu and Kamba soccer enthusiasts must find a place in one of the very few non-ethnic teams. Inevitably they are under represented in the soccer competition generally and in the Kenya national side.

The organization of soccer matches involves a large number of officers and spectators and so produces considerable interaction both within and between the two ethnic groups. Soccer rivalry between Luo and Luyia is intense: opposed supporters occupy clearly demarcated areas of the city stadium which are crossed at peril; disputed decisions may trigger off fighting between them during or after matches; before and during matches the Luo diviner-doctor and his Luyia counterpart have the job of trying to outwit each other by constantly prescribing different medicines and rituals for their respective teams. Matches between Luo and Luyia are also great money-spinners. The Kenya International Stadium, adjacent to Kaloleni estate, is always packed at these matches. Sufficient revenue is obtained from ticket sales that expenditure on rituals and medicines by each team is considerable, between K£5–25 of it at each match going in fees to each diviner-doctor. This has even been noted by *The Times* of London which, in its February 22, 1971, issue, reported that the Luo team called Gor Mahia, had spent K£1100 (then about £1276) for this purpose during the previous year.

In summary, the public domain is no less full of uncertainties for Luo as that of family life and the welfare of one's children. The Luo diviner-doctor (*ajuoga*) has a central role in both. In this public domain which involves confrontation with other ethnic groups in Nairobi, either of the direct political kind, or more "ritualistically" through soccer, it is men who predominate as organizers. Let me look at the wider, inter-ethnic context within which these uncertainties have developed.

The ethnic framework of political belief and action

Their ethnic associations and their rival soccer teams stress Luo and Luyia separateness. And yet, even as fierce rivals in a common game, they have much more in common with each other than either of them has with the Kikuyu and Kamba. No large-scale organization links the Luo and Luyia to the Kikuyu and Kamba in face-to-face interaction. The Nairobi-based trade unions do tend to represent all ethnic groups in the occupational categories for which they were formed. But they are run by small numbers of people who are mandated to represent their members but who do not need to call frequent, well-attended meetings of them. The scarcity of jobs makes Nairobi very much an employer's market, and trade unions have called few strikes by comparison with those of Europe and North America. Indeed, localized wild-cat strikes appear to be much more common than formal strikes (Sandbrook, 1975, p. 180), suggesting the highly situational nature of "class consciousness". Nearly 60 per cent of the household heads in Kaloleni claimed to be paid-up members of one of Kenya's thirty-eight registered trade unions, but very few ever attended meetings and hardly any claimed to have lost any time through stoppages called by their union. For Kenya generally, Sandbrook notes: "In most unions only about 10 per cent of the rank-and-file actually vote for the branch officials, a small proportion of whom then elect the national officials every three years." (ibid., p. 182.)

As well as being linked through their common participation in the soccer league, Luo and Luyia in Nairobi are linked in other ways. First, they tend to congregate in the same residential areas of Nairobi. as is the case in Kaloleni. Second, marriage may occur between those Luo and Luyia who share a common rural borderland. The number of mixed marriages between them is not high, being less than three per cent of all their marriages in Kaloleni, but it is the highest proportion of all mixed marriages between members of the four main ethnic groups. Finally, though their languages are unrelated, a surprisingly high proportion of Luyia can converse in Luo, amounting to over a quarter of all Luyia household heads in Kaloleni. Only seven per cent of Luo household heads are able to speak Luyia, but their combined knowledge of each other's vernacular is much greater than that which either group has of Kikuyu and Kamba and is a significant indicator of the special, almost alliance relationship between them (Parkin, 1974, pp. 181–3). Swahili is the lingua franca most widely used by all ethnic groups.

The close if ambivalent involvement of Luo and Luyia with each other contrasts strikingly with the social distance which has emerged between each of them and the Kikuyu. The fourth group, the Kamba, are regarded by many Luo and Luyia as relatively "neutral" bystanders in a struggle for jobs and housing between themselves and the growing proportion of Kikuyu in Nairobi. In fact, Kamba are as much affected by these scarcities as any other group and, though I do not wish to give detailed evidence here, they also can be said to have a close if ambivalent relationship with Kikuyu. Their respective languages are very close, there is some intermarriage between them, and they may employ each other in small private commercial enterprises in Nairobi. It would be going too far to suggest that Luo and Luyia on the one hand and Kikuyu and Kamba (together with other associated groups including Embu and Meru) on the other are developing into two "super-tribes" rather than four culturally distinct groups. But in terms of interaction, intermarriage, co-residence, formal organizations, and certain customs and attitudes, each pair does have the makings of a special relationship.

It is interesting that, at a formal political level, these four ethnic groups had quite different relationships to each other in the years immediately before and after Kenya's independence in 1963. Before independence there were two main political parties, KANU and KADU. KANU wanted a unitary, non-federal Kenya and consisted largely of Kikuyu and Luo, the so-called "dominant" groups, and of Kamba. KADU wanted a federal Kenya and was made up of a large proportion of Luyia, and a number of other numerically smaller groups, including those collectively called nowadays the "Kalenjin" and such coastal peoples as the Mijikenda. Ethnic size was a dominant and certainly recognized and much argued factor in the confrontations occurring between these two political parties. It is not something read into the confrontation by outside analysts. KADU won the pre-independence "election" and constituted Kenya's government for a year, but it was KANU who won the "real" election at Independence. KADU shortly thereafter disbanded ostensibly in the interests of national unity in 1964.

KANU was not the sole political party for long however. In 1966, the KPU was established. It was purportedly left-wing in ideology and not initially ethnically based. Though it drew most of its support from Luo it also had some from certain Kikuyu and other groups. But gradually the party became increasingly associated with Luo. It was banned in 1969 by the ruling KANU government of which its Luo leaders had once been prominent members but which now had a strong Kikuyu element. At present KANU remains the only effective political party and is the ruling one.

Kikuyu and Luo have been in many ways politically the two key ethnic groups in Kenya's history. From a situation, then, in which Kikuyu and Luo cooperated before and immediately after independence in the formation of KANU, we now have a situation in which Kikuyu and Luo are seen as opposed to each other by most people in the nation. Neither Luyia nor Kamba can now be said to be *politically* allied with either Luo or Kikuyu: their respective leaders are very conscious of the primary need to develop the interests of the people of their own regions. But, as I have indicated, a special relationship does exist at a domestic and cultural level between Luo and Luyia on the one hand, and between Kikuyu and Kamba on the other. Excepting the unchanged positions of Kamba, this is a reversal of the formal political alliances making up KANU and KADU at around the time of independence:

ᵃ There was also the short-lived Kamba-based African Peoples Party (APP).

Fig. 3. Changing ethnic alliances.

People in Nairobi use these generalized facts as *broad* outlines when discussing ethnic relations. But within the outlines there are the many details which refer to relations between the various sub-groups making up an ethnic group. To take just a few examples, the Luo in Nairobi from the administrative locations (or "sub-tribes") of Alego and Gem are sometimes accused of monopolizing the leadership of the Luo Union; the Maragoli entered their own soccer team in the Kenya championship in the late 1960s in opposition to the overall Luyia team of which they were formerly members; people from Kangema division of the Kikuyu district of Murang'a call themselves Rwathia and have recently established a number of small businesses under this name, inviting both admiration for their success and indignation at their exclusiveness from many other fellow Kikuyu from other divisions within the district, while at a more inclusive level considerable rivalry is expressed between the Kikuyu from the allegedly dominant Nyeri district and those of less advantaged Murang'a; the Kamba of Machakos draw a sharp, yet from the outsider's viewpoint hardly perceptible, distinction between themselves and Kamba from Kitui. There are many other examples of this micro-ethnicity in Nairobi. It is also found all over the world in poly-ethnic urban migrant communities in which the constituent ethnic groups have reached a sufficiently large size for home-based divisions to become significant units of urban identification and interaction. One's very village may achieve this significance. Yet, these ethnic segments close ranks in opposition to unrelated or more distantly related groups.

There is, in other words, a general principle of segmentation likely to operate in any proportionally large migrant ethnic group which is conscious of itself as such and which is seen by its own members and by others to stand in an opposed relationship to other like groups. This is the general principle to which M. G. Smith referred when he spoke of the segmentary nature of *all* politics: ". . . . political action is always and inherently segmentary, expressed through the contraposition of competing groups and persons." (1974, p. 27.) We can call this the general principle of political segmentation.

But ethnic groups differ in the extent to which they make use of segmentation as a culturally explicit "special" rather than general principle of their social organization. Lineage segmentation is, of course, the prime example. Variations in the degree of political co-extensiveness of segmentary lineages have been widely documented in social anthropology (e.g. Fortes, 1953; Middleton and Tait, 1958; Sahlins, 1961). Throughout, however, there is common recognition of the principle by the people themselves, though of varying intensity. Whether we call it an ideology or simply an emic system of political rules, a segmentary lineage system is anywhere an explicit cultural construct, peculiar in its referential details to a particular culture.

The distinction then is that between (a) the general principle of segmentation inherent in all politics, which is rarely culturally sanctioned nor made explicit by the members of the political community and may even be denied in periodic assertions of political unity; and (b) the specific principle of segmentation which is expressed in its most culturally explicit form in societies based upon constantly expanding, polysegmentary lineages, and which is recognized as such by the people themselves. The classic East African example is that of the Nuer (Evans-Pritchard, 1940, 1940b). Recognition may take the form of discussion or argument about the appropriate genealogical relatedness to each other of competing lineages or segments, or in the form of everyday proverbs, as in the Arab one provided by Abner Cohen: "I against my brother; I and my brother against our cousin; I and my brother and my cousin against the outsider." (1974, p. 31.)

The distant Nilotic cultural affinity of Luo and Nuer is not, of course, any justification in itself to draw cultural inferences one from the other. An obvious major difference is that Nuer lineages are not localized in the way that many Luo ones are. But the facts speak for themselves in Nairobi, in which we do find Luo making conscious use of their distinctive segmentary principle in setting up their urban ethnic associations for recreational and political purposes in a climate of increasingly uncertain inter-ethnic relations. I shall describe these Luo ethnic associations. From the description it will be seen how the ideal of male control of the public domain is further expressed in the proportionally high number of polygynists who are members and leaders in the associations.

Specific segmentation and polygyny among urban Luo

In their rural homelands in western Kenya both the Luo and the Luyia have superficially similar systems of land tenure and family organization which derive from a segmentary arrangement of many localized lineages of varying sizes. In Nairobi this special segmentary principle is not stifled but operates in modified form to produce among each of these two peoples roughly a three-tiered structure of ethnic associations which represent maximal exogamous lineages (or "clans" as they are called in English) and a few lineage segments at the bottom, "sub-tribes" at the intermediary level, and an all-inclusive Union at the top of the pyramid.

Given the segmentary nature of Luo urban associations, the Luo high polygyny rate compared with other urban ethnic groups, and the predominant position occupied by Luo polygynists in these associations, we may ask to what extent any interconnectedness of these features of urban social organization draws conceptual inspiration, so to speak, from the rural setting, and to what extent the rural setting most closely represents for urban Luo a reservoir of "traditional" ideals.

The Luo in common with many African peoples are better characterized as traditionally having had a polysegmentary rather than simply segmentary lineage system. For, as Southall demonstrated (1952), segmentation among the Luo really begins in the compound polygynous family where *each* of the wives of a single family head acts as a focal point for the eventual development of a distinct lineage. In other words the segmentary "blueprint" is not simply that each of a man's sons will one day become the progenitors of separate and partially opposed lineages: structurally prior to this is the separation into opposed lineages of the sons of each of his wives. As Southall puts it, ". . . Luo regard every segmentary relationship as having its symbolic prototype within the compound *polygynous* family" (p. 6). Wives, then, are prior to sons as reference points for the formation of future lineages.

Southall's work shows how lineage segmentation and polygynous family relationships are aspects of the same process. We typically think of lineages as involving interaction between "groups", and families as made up of close interpersonal relationships. And in terms of actual numbers of people involved it does seem reasonable to characterize lineages as essentially "group-like" and families as made up of a relatively few close, face-to-face relationships. Nevertheless, as Southall emphasizes, Luo may conceptualize even wide-scale lineage relationships in terms of family ones, and conversely refer to family relationships as having implications for future lineage developments. Each is an idiom for the other. In rural areas contemporary land enclosure schemes have taken account of rather than ignored lineage boundaries and so it is easy to see why even today most speak of the ideal Luo family as "a man with more than one wife, each of whom has more than one son" (p. 7). This conceptual linking together of polygynous family and lineage is evident not only in the formal Luo terminology for kinship and spatial relations but also in their more general verbal and non-verbal behaviour, as I shall later illustrate.

What is the relevance of all this for a study of Luo in Nairobi? First, we see that here too Luo make use of a special segmentary principle in the organisation of their ethnic associations. Second, Luo have a much higher polygyny rate in Nairobi than other ethnic groups.

How are these two features of Luo social organization in Nairobi connected? The most settled urban families tend to be the polygynous ones, with at least one of a man's wives resident with him in town and the other(s) at his rural home. These polygynists tend to be key figures in Luo activities in Nairobi: they have lived there longer than average, they have secure accommodation and jobs, with above average incomes, and can act as "gatekeepers" to new, young migrants seeking employment in the city. These polygynists are, as might be expected, also older than the urban average. They outrank monogamists of their own generation in terms of income and so make up a select sub-category of the important urban generation of older men who, though much less educated than the present younger job-seekers, have otherwise benefited from the easier times of earlier migrations.

What is particularly distinctive about Luo polygynists is that they show a very strong tendency to be multiple members of Luo ethnic associations, which are based on exogamous lineage and administrative locations (frequently coterminous with traditional "sub-tribes"). In other words, whereas a monogamist is more likely to be a member of not more than one of the three or so levels of associations, proportionally few polygynists are this confined. Polygynists are not, however, especially prominent in the large and internationally known Luo Union itself, which is led by a mixture of very high status Luo, younger aspiring men, and elders. The influence of these polygynists operates first in the intermediary and lower level associations and thereafter feeds into the activities of the Luo Union.

The segmentary organization of Luo ethnic associations in Nairobi is not a direct institutional reflection of the "traditional" rural segmentary lineage system analysed by Southall. But it is surely a partial product of it in that it is organized within a segmentary framework of lineages of different size and scale, of "sub-tribes", and the whole Luo people. Nor do polygynous families in Nairobi "function" in exactly the same way as do the rural compound polygynous families intentionally described in traditional terms by Southall. The point here is that empirically there is no such thing as a concrete "traditional" rural family and a distinct urban one. Regular urban migration has been a way of life for generations and the simultaneous development of both rural and urban interests is increasingly the norm. What polygynists do in town is bound up with what they or their wives and relatives do in their rural homes. Similarly, the activities of a lineage or sub-tribe association in Nairobi affect and are influenced by what goes on in the particular rural areas represented by each of these associations. It is not surprising therefore that the symbols, language, and behaviour which are depicted in the literature at traditionally linking together family and lineage also operate in modified form to link Luo families and ethnic associations in Nairobi today. In other words certain key Luo concepts have persisted over at least a generation of settlement in Nairobi. My interest is to see how these key concepts have continued to link family relationships and the activities of ethnic associations as the latter have developed and adapted to the demographic, political and economic changes and uncertainties of Nairobi and Kenya.[1]

Specific and general segmentation in Luo urban associations

Leach's distinction (1954) between two alternating modes of political process among the Kachin of Burma, the hierarchical *gumsa* system and the egalitarian *gumlao* one, can be regarded as a master exemplar of the divergent tendencies existing within any organization, whether that of the conventional anthropological "tribal" society, or a wholly institutionalized commercial corporation. The Luo Union in East Africa has, apparently throughout its existence, exhibited these same conflicting tendencies.

Increasing numbers of Luo males have migrated to towns from their rural homes since the building of the East African railway at the turn of the twentieth century. It is claimed by a number of current Luo leaders that the Luo Union itself was established in the 1920s (see Chapter 7). Certainly, since the second world war, the Luo Union has constantly adapted to the growth in numbers of Luo employed in urban and other wage-earning centres throughout East Africa. With its headquarters in Kisumu, it has established branches in main towns. In later years, when sectional associations based on home divisions of location and localized lineage came into being, the Luo Union came to be regarded as the corporate embodiment of their collective identity. Thus, though such sectional associations might seem at first to be based only on parochial interests and to display rivalries reflecting these interests, the irregular general meetings of the Luo Union within any one town bring their members together. The undeniably fissive tendencies within the Luo community, frequently said to be due to *nyiego* (jealousy), are, indeed, counterbalanced by the important role played by the Luo Union with regard

[1] There are two main sources of information on the number and spread of welfare associations in Nairobi. One is the Registrar of Societies office to which I did not have access. Scott MacWilliam has information derived from this and his work should contribute substantially to our knowledge. The second source is the one I have used, namely a 100 per cent sample of Luo household heads in Kaloleni, who not only gave me information on the associations of which they were members but in some cases allowed me to sit in on meetings of them held at Kaloleni. M. Tarmarkin's work on Luo associations in Nakuru suggests similarities with the Nairobi structure.

to matters affecting the Luo people as a whole, both town and country dweller.

This sounds like a structural-functionalist explanation of an organization held in equilibrium. In the sense that the sectional tendencies have always prompted Luo Union leaders to try and check this fragmentation by appeals to unity and trust in their leadership, i.e. by appeals to hierarchy by concensus, this is true. But the Luo Union, its branches and their subordinate associations have changed in their individual forms and have taken on and discarded a range of different functions. One association may have started out as a burial society, developing into one providing welfare of a more general nature, and emerging later as an urban-based home investment organization, possibly operating an urban business as well. If we look at any one association, over time, therefore, or of a number of different ones coexisting at any point in time, we see a range of different functions being emphasized. We even find some associations purporting to represent what is clearly to be seen as a localized lineage in the rural area, while others claim to represent fellow members of a home local area, not necessarily bound to each other by lineage or kin ties. A few associations combine common home origins with another purported qualification of membership such as age or socio-economic status. The extended, "modern" use of *nyiego* as meaning jealousy in the general sense, and not in the specific sense of referring to co-wife relations, is frequently given as causes of association splits. It is interesting, therefore, to note how the term *nyiego* has thus shifted from reference to a culturally explicit specific principle of segmentation to the more general one.

Beneath these surface variations arising from a general process of segmentation, there are four consistent features. Thus, as I have already indicated, a pyramidal structure of associations is recognized by Luo themselves to be based on their own "specific" segmentary principle; the associations are viewed as substantiating men's accountability to each other as custodians of ethnic welfare and morality, including the status of women as wives, daughters and sisters; and polygynists are over represented as members and leaders.

A fourth relatively consistent feature is that the leaders or officers of the larger associations, including those of sub-tribes or major lineage clusters and the Luo Union itself, tend to be of higher socio-economic status than leaders of associations of exogamous lineages of lower levels of segmentation. This was also a very pronounced feature of the ethnic pyramid of Luo and other associations in Kampala, so much so that it was possible to say quite definitely that the three tiers of Luo Union, sub-tribe, and lineage associations were each led by high, middle, and lower status townsmen respectively (Parkin, 1966, pp. 153, 157–8). The correspondence is not that clear-cut in Nairobi. It is still the case that members generally are well above the Kenyan, and probably Luo, wage-earning average. But the larger number of Luo in the city, and the wider scale of their activities and degree of social differentiation, have made for more diversification in the socio-economic characteristics of the leaders of associations at the three levels.

Even the division into three tiers is arbitrary to the outsider. For so great is the number of Luo associations in Nairobi that at least five levels could be distinguished etically: (1) the Luo Union at the top; (2) a few associations based on rural administrative "divisions", some of which may have traditional significance as lineages or lineage clusters; (3a) those "sub-tribe" associations which are identified by Luo as roughly coterminous with an administrative "location" and comprising clusters of major and maximal exogamous lineages; (3b) associations based on such lineages which may or may not coincide with contemporary administrative locations; (4) associations based on maximal exogamous lineages which may or may not coincide with an administrative sub-location; and (5) associations based on smaller lineages of a lower order of segmentation which may or may not coincide with the whole or part of an administrative sub-location. To these could be added a sixth and seventh category including (a) those few Luo associations which are ostensibly based on a rural home area or centre (e.g. a school or market), and (b) those very few which ostensibly open up membership to all Luo regardless of local home area and lineage and which do not fit into the segmentary pyramid. Apart from a few short-lived "youth" associations, I have only limited data on these.

These complexities stand in contrast to the less ambiguous associational structure found in Kampala among a much smaller Luo population. But, to repeat, we have to recognize that one relatively persistent feature is the general correspondence between level of socio-economic status and level of leadership in the hierarchical pyramid of Luo associations in Nairobi. This is evident not only from a simple head-count of leaders. It is a feature spontaneously referred to by Luo themselves, some who have never lived in Kampala and so cannot be said to have internalized the Luo associational structure existing there and to have superimposed it on the Nairobi one.

I shall return in the next chapter to my distinction between general and specific segmentation by analysing a series of events involving the Luo Union and other associations. I shall show that while fissive tendencies lead to uncontrolled and random fragmentation with different kinds of associations splitting off from each other with widely contrasting aims and personnel, a more controlled form of segmentation is constantly bringing these associations back into line, so to speak, as leaders appeal to and make explicit definitional use of putatively traditional sub-tribe and lineage relationships. These appeals for unity through the discipline of descent are often linked to the Luo ideal of polygyny as a mode of regulated population growth and, traditionally, territorial expansion. Thus, polygyny is believed (falsely) to increase the size of the Luo collectivity but, through the house-property complex, imposes a systematic ordering of the descent lines ensuing from a family; similarly, the numbers of Luo and of their associations are increasing in Nairobi but the relationships to each other of these associations are, by and large, identified and regulated by a combination of common home area and descent, under the overall cover of the Luo Union. Finally, those leaders who make these appeals for unity are themselves commonly polygynists.

Before turning to this next stage of analysis, however, I have to give more details and some figures to back up my claim that Luo associations in Nairobi are (a) organized in a segmentary pyramid; (b) led by higher and lower status men at the top and bottom of the pyramid; and (c) led at the second and third tiers of the pyramid by a disproportionate number of polygynists.

The segmentary pyramid

While recognizing that five levels of Luo associations could be distinguished, I shall retain the broader division into three, which most closely approaches that of Luo themselves who, in English for instance, may speak of (1) the Luo Union, as distinct from (2) a "location" or "division" (a cluster of locations) association, as distinct again from (3) a "clan" or "sub-clan" association. In the Luo vernacular the names of lineage ancestors or rural place-names are used to identify the associations but, except when these are also names of administrative areas, they do not always delineate clearly a specific number of tiers making up the pyramid. Nevertheless, in conversation, Luo themselves point out that their associations make up this type of three-tiered segmentary pyramids. It is an order with which they are culturally well acquainted. A non-Luo from a contrasting culture lacking this specific segmentary principle might be expected to see and define these associations differently, perhaps by stressing home areas rather than descent as the primary idiom of their relationship to each other. Though both criteria apply, Luo certainly put the emphasis the other way round: most associations are founded on the notion of common agnatic descent.

The general three-fold distinction between types of Luo association is further justified by one other important criterion which is used by Luo themselves to distinguish between third-tier urban associations based on so-called "clans" or "sub-clans" and second-tier ones based on larger territorial units which are or were based on administrative areas, which have or had traditional significance in Luo segmentary organization.

When, in English, Luo use the word "clan" to identify an urban association, often by including it in the association's title (e.g. Kabar Clan Association), they refer implicitly to two features: that it is based on a rural localized lineage; and that this lineage is exogamous. Thus, to take the example just given, the people of Kabar "clan" (in East Kano) cannot marry each other. They frequently marry the people of their rural neighbours, of Kamagaga "clan", who may themselves form an urban association. In town as much as in the rural areas, differing interpretations of who may marry whom may bring such associations into dispute with each other or may have brought about their existence in the first place through segmentation from a supposed genealogically higher-order association (Parkin, 1969, pp. 119–27). Noting, then, the importance of exogamous marriage choices underlying the distinction between lineage-based and other associations, let me now describe the formal features of each of the three tiers of association.

THIRD-TIER ASSOCIATIONS

The lineages on which such associations are based are not necessarily those of maximal exogamy. The term "clan" in English is a direct translation by Luo of the term *dhoot* which can refer to rural localized lineages of any segmental level. Luo use of the English term "sub-clan" is uncommon and simply distinguishes an association based on a lower order of segmentation from an existing "clan" association. In fact, both "clan" and "sub-clan" are terms only meaningful in relation to each other in particular instances and both refer to exogamous lineages. In general, it does seem that most so-called "clan" associations are based on maximal exogamous lineages (of from nine to 13 telescoped generations depth) but this is an impression and is not confirmed in every case. For simplicity. I shall refer to them all as lineage associations, only identifying different segmental levels in particular cases.

From a survey of Luo in Kaloleni I identified 87 of these third-tier lineage associations, of which about a dozen were in fact associations based on even lower orders of segmentation from existing lineage associations. It would complicate the analysis to call these a fourth-tier in the segmentary pyramid, though this is in fact what they are. More important is to recognize that they are themselves offshoots of a parent lineage association, and that this latter may itself have split off from, or at least see itself as a territorially—if not genealogically—based segment of a second-tier association which is not defined by exogamy. This illustrates the continuing process of segmentation among the expanding Luo population of Nairobi. Though this process is made possible by numerical increase, actual fission may arise from conflicting interpretations of the precise limits of exogamy or from disagreements over the organization of the parent association and the allocation of its resources, i.e. the funds it raises through subscriptions and special collections.

The distinctive feature of third-tier associations, then, is that they are much more likely to be based on localized rural exogamous lineages of varying segmental level than on government administrative areas. There were considerable administrative boundary changes in 1963, as there have been before then. The Kenya Census 1969 (vol. 1, p. 2) notes this in commenting that comparisons of administrative areas between the 1948, 1962 and 1969 censuses are for this reason difficult. It implies also that the administrative boundaries will alter according to whichever information the district commissioner has from the elders summoned to advise him or his officers. The Luo, like other peoples, have, however, a persisting notion of what they will call "traditional areas, not all of which coincide geographically with current administrative ones. The names of "traditional" rural areas which were formally used by the government administration may continue to be used by rural Luo. They are also used by urban Luo for associations set up when the names were in currency. For these reasons, the current list of urban associations at the third-tier level and, to a lesser extent, the second-tier administrative "location" and "division" level (see Fig. 4, opposite page 196) includes some names of rural areas which no longer appear in the 1969 census. But, to repeat, this is much more likely to be the case at the second-tier level, while third-tier associations are identified through persistent use of "traditional" designations of lineage area and membership. It is true that a rural lineage boundary is often also that of an administrative sublocation; thus, of the 87 lineage associations which I identified, 18 had names which were also those of sub-locations, suggesting broadly coterminous boundaries. But only six third-tier associations were based on a sub-location which included more than one exogamous lineage.

To sum up, then, third-tier associations, frequently referred to in English as "clan" associations and much less commonly as "sub-location" associations, are mostly based on exogamous rural localized lineages or segments of them. Second-tier "superordinate" associations are based on current or former administrative areas which nevertheless have "traditional" segmentary relevance and consist of different but neighbouring lineages between some of whom marriage may be permitted (with the exception of Karachuonyo which is an exogamous lineage of nearly 100,000 people comprising two locations, and one or two other South Nyanza locations).

Let me abstract from this contrast to make it even simpler: (1) members of both third- and second-tier associations are men; (2) within a third-tier association fellow members cannot marry each others' daughters and sisters; (3) within a second-tier association, this is generally possible and in many cases preferred.

SECOND-TIER ASSOCIATIONS

Luoland consists (at the time of fieldwork and as listed in the 1969 Census) of three *districts*: Kisumu, Siaya, and South Nyanza. Two of these districts consist of four and one of five *divisions*. Each division has two to five *locations* depending on the extent of its population or area. Each location has anything from two to 17 (East Karachuonyo) *sub-locations,* but the median is between six and seven. It is part or current administrative divisions and locations which may form the basis of the second-tier or intermediary urban associations. Again, the spatial relations of many of these locations (especially those dating from earlier administrations) are thought of by Luo in terms of an original segmentary lineage model (see also Southall, 1952, pp. 14–15). Some of these second-tier associations are based on a combination of locations and divisions.

I came across seven associations which were based on a home area whose boundaries were at least coterminous with those of an administrative division and in some cases went beyond them by spanning more than one division. Let me briefly describe these seven.

(1) Bondo Association and (2) Boro Association are each based on a division. Two associations, (3) Algenya Progressive Society, and (4) Riwruok Mamwalo Pinje Abich (The Five Lowlands Society) have particularly wide areas of recruitment. The title, Algenya, is an abridgement of the two principle "traditional" areas of Alego and Ugenya. The area of Alego is almost entirely coterminous with that of Boro division,[1] while that of Ugenya takes up almost all of Ukwala division.[2] To complicate matters still further, there are separate associations for each of these: (5) Alego Ragar Association, and (6) Ugenya Association. The people of Alego and Ugenya are neighbours from the north-eastern area of Luoland. They abut the Bantu-speaking Samia and other Bantu peoples. Their language reflects this. They are numerous in Nairobi and stress what they regard as their distinctiveness from other Luo. Yet another example of micro-ethnicity. In these respects they are like the people of Gem, another "traditional" area, now made up of the three locations of North Gem, East Gem, and West Gem, and reconstituted as the administrative division of Yala. Their association in Nairobi is the Gem Union. Thus, though the Gem Union's area of recruitment is coterminous with that of Yala division, this administrative designation is not the label by which the association is called. Only one informant referred to it as the Yala Union. The Riwruok Mamwalo Pinje Abich (The Five Lowlands

---

[1] Three of the four locations of Boro division are in fact called East, West, and Central Alego. The fourth, Usonga, has a minute population.
[2] Three of four locations of Ukwala division are called East, North, and South Ugenya. The fourth, Uholo, has a separate urban association from that of Ugenya.

Society) draws its members from the whole district of South Nyanza, which is made up of five divisions which are, again "traditionally", the five areas referred to in the association's name. The people of South Nyanza are very few in Nairobi and they, too, are regarded by themselves and by others as distinct from other Luo (see also Southall, 1952, p. 15, for a description of the descent relationships to each other of some of the lineage locations known as the *Jook* group).

There is in all these associations a mixing of administrative and "traditional" names and areas of recruitment, e.g. Algenya, and, separately, Alego and Ugenya, instead of Boro and Ukwala divisions, Gem instead of Yala division, Riwruok Mamwalo Pinje Abich instead of South Nyanza district; but also Boro Association and Bondo Association (both based on administrative divisions).

Though "traditional" and administrative areas and names are here mixed, the "traditional" ones come through as the most frequently and persistently used. A man will normally speak of himself as a "Gem man" (*jagem*) or "Alego man", rather than as a Yala or Boro man. It is true that, for example, a split in the original Alego Ragar Association resulted in a breakaway association initially calling itself Boro, but this represented a difference of title and not an attempt to recruit from any other than the "traditional" Alego area.

As might be expected I discovered a larger number of associations which were based on administrative locations (or on areas broadly coterminous with that of a location) than on divisions. There were altogether 20 such associations. However, 11 of them are based on locations in South Nyanza. There are very few Luo from South Nyanza in Nairobi compared with the other two districts, Siaya and Kisumu. Indeed, there are so few that only three South Nyanza location associations have segmental third-tier associations, and even then only one each (West Nyokal, Karachuonyo, and Kasipul, with their respective subordinate associations of Kanyadoto,[1] Kanyiker, and Kodera—see Fig. 4, opposite p. 196). Moreover, a number of these South Nyanza locations are in fact exogamous lineages. This, together with their small potential membership in Nairobi, combines to make their organization and standing much more like the lineage associations of other more heavily represented locations in Nairobi.

I have said that, strictly speaking, the Nairobi associations of Alego,

[1] Kanyadoto was in fact itself a location in early colonial administration (Evans-Pritchard, 1965, pp. 207–8) and has retained its traditional distinctiveness.

Ugenya, and Gem each caters for a district, or at least most of it. But the areas represented by these names have considerable traditional significance and, though no longer exogamous lineages, are thought of as each comprising related lineages. They are, in this sense, more like the other location associations, which are similarly thought of as comprising related lineages and, in the case of some South Nyanza locations, as still exogamous. As Evans-Pritchard put it (1965 (1949), p. 208): "These locations correspond approximately with the old tribal (for which read sub-tribal) areas of the Luo." He notes a few exceptions in that the peoples of Gem, Ugenya, and Kano, though then divided into two locations, nevertheless each constituted a single "tribe", i.e. traditionally a politically autonomous unit among many making up the Luo people as a whole. Nowadays, as mentioned, the areas of Gem and Ugenya have been subdivided still further into three locations, as also has that of Alego, which at the time of Evans-Pritchard's fieldwork (1936) still constituted only one administrative location. It is for this reason that in earlier publications I referred to what I am here calling second-tier associations as location associations. For it is the administrative locations as they were first delineated by colonial government which were broadly superimposed on traditional Luo political units, including maximal lineages, and it is these same units which, though altered by internal and external population movement and changes in the limits of exogamy of constituent lineages, retain broad significance as large-scale segments of the overall pyramid recognized by Luo as their society (see also Ogot, 1967, pp. 111–12).

I do not want to imply that the segmentary pyramid of Nairobi associations described in Fig. 4 and in the text here, will show an exact correspondence with the segmentary lineage systems depicted by Evans-Pritchard and Southall. I have reproduced, from a partial and by no means statistically representative sample of Nairobi, a segmentary pyramid of associations in the city as my Luo informants themselves saw it. As is well known to anthropologists, even in so-called traditional times there was never total agreement among elders on all genealogical connections (see also Blount, 1975, pp. 117–35, for a detailed contemporary rural account). In Nairobi, much later and among an essentially migrant population drawn from different parts of Luoland, it is therefore surprising to find so much agreement, where comparisons are possible, with the pictures given by Evans-

Pritchard and Southall. The main points about the modern Nairobi pyramid are (a) that what I have called third-tier associations are based on exogamous lineages at home and this is a relevant feature of their organization, and (b) that second-tier associations, i.e. "location" associations, are less likely to be exogamous but do each consist of exogamous lineages, some of which are intermarrying at any one time out of mutual preference, and use the basis of common home areas as a principle of identity in a wider urban classificatory system which also incorporates lineage membership of different segmental levels.

The mention of urban associations as constituting a classificatory system raises the question of what the associations actually "do" for their Luo members and for Luo generally. There are three main "functions" of the whole associational framework: first, its segmentary arrangement constitutes a kind of cognitive map for placing other fellow Luo and, in this capacity, provide guidelines for marriage choices; second, it provides a range of potential recruitment bases, from small lineage to large location or district, on which to organize common interests, including welfare projects, repatriating deceased members of the lineage of an association, setting up business, and organizing for elections; third, the associations keep Luo in communication with each other, both within and between cities, and between town and country.

Potentially, of course, a Luo is a member of as many associations as are represented by different segmental levels. The range of interests represented by the different associations for him at any one time may be correspondingly wide: a small lineage association provides him or his go-between (jagam) with information as to an appropriate marriage choice for himself or his children, and may at any time intervene in an unstable marriage; a larger association mediates disputes between affines, or organizes the collection of money to repatriate a deceased member; a location association has plans to set up a soccer team and to link this with setting up a Harambee (self-help) school back home; and the Luo Union keeps a man informed, at its mass meetings, of political and other developments affecting Luo in Nairobi as a whole. Any Luo is by definition a potential member of the Luo Union: most would say that all Luo are automatically members regardless of whether they have paid subscriptions to the Union.

Let me now present a brief example of how marriage, welfare, and politics, link lineage and location associations with each other and with the Luo Union. In this case-study, most of which is reported, I wish to preserve the anonymity of the actors and their lineages and home areas.

Seven thousand men, women and children of the exogamous Konguto lineage live in X location in a rural district. Another 800 or so men of the lineage and a smaller number of women and children live and, in the case of the men, work on nearby plantations or in distant towns. In Nairobi there are probably about 150 of these men, some 70 of them married. Thirty of these married men are acknowledged elders (*jodongo*), with almost a half of them polygynists. Ten of them, including six polygynists and up to six younger married men arrange monthly meetings of the Konguto association in Kaloleni Hall. These are attended by another 25 or so other men, most married but not always the same men from meeting to meeting. In 1968 two separate issues engaged the association's attention. One was political and one marital. To take the political issue first, the Konguto people were dissatisfied with the way the current Member of Parliament for the rural constituency in which Konguto falls was conducting his affairs. This MP was identified as belonging to another localized exogamous lineage in the rural constituency and was believed to favour his "brothers" to the exclusion of other constituents. He was said to have helped find jobs for his lineage-mates, or to provide them with rural trading licencies, but to have failed to bring "development" to the area.

One Konguto youth was offered the chance to study abroad. He had received a letter of acceptance from a British further education college, arranged by a friend there who had also agreed to accommodate him in Britain. The Konguto youth's lineage held a series of festivities to raise the money for his fare and promised further support while he was in Britain. The youth now only needed his MP's support to get a passport. The MP was apparently uncooperative, never got round to arranging for the passport to be made out, and the chance was lost as the youth failed to get to Britain by the enrolment date.

This incident spurred the Konguto association into encouraging their most up-and-coming Konguto man, highly educated and in his mid-twenties working as a middle manager for a para-statal organization, to consider standing at the next general election which was expected at any time. The manager had until then rarely attended meetings of the Konguto association but came to this and subsequent ones. The general election did not in fact take place until 1974 (long after I had left the field), though, by spending two short periods in Nairobi in 1971 and 1972 and through correspondence thereafter, I was able to follow developments until then. Through the organized efforts of his fellow Konguto, who persuaded people of the constituency other than those of the MP's own maximal exogamous lineage to vote for the manager, the manager was elected the new MP. During his rise to success, the manager had also become more closely involved in the Luo Union. But at meetings of the Konguto lineage association he continued to defer to his sponsors, the Konguto elders.

One of the manager's tasks in the Luo Union was to help organize inter-location soccer matches. He became secretary of the location association which comprised, among others, his own lineage, Konguto, and that of his future rival, the current MP, who did not involve himself much in the location association. The manager did not, he said, ever discuss his political prospects with other members of the location association but concentrated instead on the job of getting up a location soccer team. He never came into personal or public conflict with the current MP. That, he said, was an "internal" matter. Nevertheless, since he did the job well and earned praise for his dedication from people of the location, we may infer that his efforts on the location association's behalf were at least partly rewarded by his later election success.

The second incident involving the Konguto lineage association occurred in mid-1969. It concerned a man of the manager's location but of a different exogamous lineage to himself, and the man's first wife (he had two). This wife was a successful trader in fish at a stall in Nairobi registered, as is normal, in her husband's name. She had four children, the youngest of whom was eight, whom she had helped considerably in their education during her years as a market-stall trader. She was not, apparently, yet past child-bearing age, a point of some relevance as will be seen. She expressed resentment at her husband's demands to know her earnings and receive a contribution to the common household budget, i.e. food, rent, and electricity, and suspected that her younger co-wife, who had young children and did not trade, encouraged him in this attitude. She took her chidlren to live with her in the house of an older widow friend, who was past child-bearing age and whose children had grown up and left her. She, too, was a market trader in Nairobi.

The husband tried in vain to retrieve his wife. His threats were to no avail. Eventually, however, the manager in his capacity of location association secretary, and by talking to both the husband and wife separately, reconciled the couple. He had gently pointed out to the wife that she was, after all, still able to produce children, though she had not done so for some years, and so was still under some obligation to her own and her husband's families. The manager had also gently advised the husband to send his younger co-wife back to the rural home, earlier than the husband had intended, so as to lessen the jealousy (*nyiego*) between the two co-wives. For this demonstration of mediatory powers, and for his organizational abilities generally, both of which are customarily valued as qualities of older leaders such as *jaduong maduong'* (great elder), *okebe* (rich man), and *ruoth* (chief) (see Southall, 1973, vol. III, p. 345), the young manager was widely acclaimed by people of his own location, and not only by those on his lineage, as a future great Luo leader. It should be noted, also, that it was at this point that his patronage was sought even more strongly. He, meanwhile, invested in the purchase of a few houses and small businesses in Kisumu and Nairobi which thrived on his now captive clientele.

This is an example of the pyramid of Luo associations operating in an integrative manner. It contrasts with the cases which occur of associations which are formed by breaking away from parent associations. Let me give an inevitably complicated example (names used are here genuine).

Asembo location ("sub-tribe") association was set up in Nairobi either just before or just after the second world war (there was disagreement as to the precise date). In the early nineteen fifties, the people of Omiya maximal exogamous (?) lineage in Asembo (comprising the four lineage segments, i.e. minor lineages, of Kokise, Konyango, Koyoo, and Kochola), accused Gor, then the administrative chief of Asembo location, of favouring the people of Kalee, a maximal exogamous (?) lineage in north Asembo, comprising the minor lineages of Kolal, Kabonde, Kakia, Kochieng', and Kanyigoro. The Omiya people further complained that chiefs of Asembo always came from the north. This dispute was expressed in Nairobi in the formation of two separate associations: Asembo Omiya and Asembo Kalee. Much later, in 1966, the two were reunited as the Asembo Progressive Society, but with separate internal sections and a rotating general chairman.

By the time of reunification, however, separate associations had been formed in Nairobi of some of the constituent minor lineages of Omiya and Kalee. A reason given for having four separate Omiya lineage associations in Nairobi was that there are two "stranger" (*jodak*) lineages (Kasabong' and Kanyang'wa) living in the rural area of Asembo Omiya, and that the "true" lineages of Omiya needed "private" opportunities for meeting together in Nairobi to discuss problems arising from marriage choices and the welfare of their "own" members. The four "true" lineages had therefore split off from the previous Asembo Omiya association. But they quarrelled among themselves, accusing each other of improper use of funds, and decided to set up four separate associations in Nairobi. At first they each regarded themselves as independent of any other association. But when, in 1966, a young man and girl from Kokise and Konyango fell in love and wanted to marry, i.e. within the same maximal exogamous lineage, they agreed to sink their differences both with each other and with the Kalee people and, while retaining their separate associations, to reunite at a higher segmentary level (and including the two unrelated *jodak* lineages) as Asembo Progressive Society. The Asembo (location) Progressive Society now meets as a need arises, e.g. a funeral (there was a big one in May 1969) or for special fund-raising "tea-parties", such as are held to send sons and daughters abroad to study. By contrast, Kokise lineage association meets monthly. There are 60 Kokise men in Nairobi, with about 20 regularly attending meetings. Six hold titles, and twelve are "committee members". Four of the office holders are referred to as *jodongo* (one only hesitantly so), two of whom are polygynists. The office-holders show a broad spread of socio-economic status, with three quite well-off. One of them, who is now an "accountant", a young man, was able to complete his secondary education partly helped by funds provided by the association. Another, in his late twenties, had married a non-Luo in his early twenties before joining the association. The bridewealth was negligible and he was severely "blamed" for this "folly"—"she will run off with your children". The wife was under so much pressure that the prophesy was in danger of fulfilling itself. The man joined the association, contributed heavily to it and became an officer in it. His wife became fully accepted as a Luo. The twelve committee members average slightly lower socio-economic status than the officers.

In this case we see that, eventually, breakaway associations (and breakaway individuals) cede their 'independence" and redefine their relationship with other associations (and other individuals) in terms of the segmentary lineage model, even suppressing the genealogical intrusions of *jodak,* i.e. non-lineage members or "strangers", by incorporating them in the Luo segmentary pyramid of associations. Luo recognize well that not all rural areas at home can be fitted neatly into a segmentary lineage model but, as this and many other examples show, they find it convenient to treat them as if they do. At the apex of the pyramid stands the Luo Union, with its own limited segmentary structure of headquarters in Kisumu and branches in towns throughout East Africa.

THE PYRAMIDAL APEX: LUO UNION

Okumu, a political scientist, emphasizes the Luo Union's political involvement through "clan elders". He shows how the success of the then recently formed KPU party in 1969 in the Gem parliamentary by-election in defeating the KANU candidate was due to the way it had taken over the previous organizational link between KANU and the Luo Union. He writes: "Although branches were established at location and sub-location levels in keeping with the administrative structure, they were very closely connected with the structure of the Luo Union, and it was not uncommon to find a neat overlap in the leadership of KANU and that of the Luo Union. This brought a major link between KANU leadership and the clan authority with which the Luo Union was itself connected." (Okumu, 1969, p. 11.) When the KPU political party was formed in 1966 its Luo Union leadership, in Gem at least, thereafter gave it their support and abandoned KANU. Thus, while political parties may come and go, the Luo Union persists by virtue of its links with localized lineages or "clans" and traditionally significant locations.

As mentioned above, the Luo Union in Nairobi, as in other towns, exists as an umbrella organization nominally over and above the subordinate associations. The main features of the Luo Union are the relative independence which its many branches throughout East Africa have of the Kisumu headquarters, their heavily attended annual meetings and occasional ones called to cope with crises affecting Luo either nationally or locally, and their low paid-up membership as a proportion of urban Luo, who are by definition all eligible to join. Regarding the latter characteristic, many Luo remark that there is little point in being a regular paid-up member of the Luo Union. It is better, they say, to subscribe to one's lineage or location association, within which one has more direct interest in its affairs. However, the Luo Union does raise large sums of money at its well-attended meetings, whether they are of a manifestly political or welfare nature, or to do with the various soccer competitions. And the Luo Union has always been central in the organization of modern Luo politics, drawing, like the soccer competitions, on traditional segments of Luo society as Okumu's example, cited above, shows. A final feature is that, like the subordinate associations and the Luo community itself, it is faction-ridden. In the mid to late nineteen sixties this factionalism resulted in formal splits in the organization of soccer, which has great internal political significance, and in which first the Luo Sports Club emerged in opposition to the Luo Union and then later, within the Luo Sports Club, a rival soccer club was set up. This latter was Gor Mahia, which means literally "Gor (the name of a venerated war hero) the reckless". It is these splits and the factionalism preceding them which illustrate the two types of segmentation, general and specific, at work in the Nairobi Luo community, and which I describe in the next chapter.

We may at this point illustrate the three-tiered segmentary pyramid of association in Nairobi. Note that I have only shown the genealogical relationship to each other of the third-tier associations of Asembo location which figured in the last case of the preceding section. I have simply listed the third-tier associations of other locations, though they too would show similarly complex interrelationships. (Fig. 4).

THE PYRAMID OF ASSOCIATIONS AS A MODE OF MICRO-ETHNIC CLASSIFICATION:

EASTERNERS, WESTERNERS, AND SOUTHERNERS

This illustration of the pyramid of Luo associations reflects the way in which Luo in Nairobi themselves classify different segmental levels of area and descent relationship with each other. Apart from the levels of district, location and lineage which I have already described, there is also an over-arching three-fold division between "Easterners", "Westerners", and "Southerners". I had noted the use of this same initial classification in Kampala, where it was used for a variety of purposes and particularly at public meetings of the Luo Union, attended by hundreds of Luo in the city (Parkin, 1969, pp. 203–14). This three-fold classification largely coincides with the administrative one between the three districts of Kisumu, Siaya, and South Nyanza. When speaking English, these three terms may be used in addition to those denoting the eastern, western, and southern areas of Luoland. But, when speaking DhoLuo, other expressions are used, such as *jo wang' chieng'* (people from where the sun rises, i.e. the east, *ugwe*), *jo podho chieng'* (people from where the sun sets, i.e. the west, *imbo*), and *jo milambo* (the people of the south).

The rural populations of Kisumu, Siaya, and South Nyanza are, respectively, 400,643, 383,188, and 663,173. If rural population was a main determinant of a district's emigré urban population, we would expect Luo from South Nyanza to be the most numerous in Nairobi. In fact they are the fewest, numbering only 6,691, with Luo from Kisumu district by far the most numerous with 23,553, and next those from Siaya, with 18,675. These figures do not account for the district of birth of some 1,605 Luo in Nairobi for whom the information was not available, nor do they refer to 12,341 Luo, presumably mostly children and adolescents, who were born outside Luoland and, we may assume, mostly in Nairobi itself. Nevertheless, these figures on district of birth from the 1969 Census that we do have clearly have significance as rough indicators of the district origins of Luo in Nairobi: Kisumu 47.5 per cent, Siaya 38.5 per cent, and South Nyanza 14 per cent. Putting this another way, in the classificatory terms of the Luo themselves, Easterners only outnumber Westerners by about a quarter, but are well over three times the number of Southerners. The two key groups in this initial classification are, then, Easterners and Westerners, with Southerners a small minority but big enough, should the occasion arise, to hold the balance of power. We shall see the significance of this in the discussion in the next chapter of the factions underlying the development of the Luo Union.

When we turn to consider the distribution of these three groups among the Luo of Kaloleni, we find a quite startling unrepresentative distribution: instead of being the most numerous as they are in Nairobi, Luo Easterners are only 18 per cent, while Westerners are an extraordinary 72 per cent. Southerners are, more consistently, a mere 10 per cent. Thus, just as Kaloleni estate is famous for being predominantly Luo with only a minority of Kikuyu and so reversing the ethnic demographic pattern of Nairobi as a whole, so it achieves similar distinctiveness among the Luo themselves in catering for a particular section of Luo. Is this simply a demographic accident? Figures from other residential areas of Nairobi showing the internal distribution of ethnic groups (technically deducible from the census returns) would probably show similar cases of micro-ethnic chain migration from particular home areas, not just among Luo but generally. This need not surprise us if we recall that, unlike the situation in Kampala in the early sixties where the allocations of public housing was more strictly controlled on a first-come, first-served basis, so precluding much ethnic clustering, public housing in Nairobi is generally sub-let, sometimes at several removes from the original tenant, beyond the knowledge and control of the authorities. As I explained in chapter four, home-based ties can therefore more easily be used by men and their families to find accommodation as lodgers in Nairobi. Thus, though most "lodgers" are relatives of one kind or another who come from small common home areas, even so-called friends are likely to come at least from the same district. Once again, we note that, though friendships are often formed in town, the pattern of home-based relationships shapes even the "choice" of these, while the partial fiction is preserved by Luo that they are formed quite independently of rural ties and obligations. Up to a point they are, but only up to the point at which a potential friend is either a Westerner, Easterner, or Southerner. For not only are acknowledged urban friendships for Easterners and Westerners, and to a lesser extent Southerners, generally contained within these groups, so are marriages. That is to say, Easterners, Westerners, and Southerners in Nairobi each show a high rate of endogamy. It may be recalled, also, that though most of these townsmen's marriages are eventually "arranged" in the rural home area, the initial advice and introductions are through urban friends, the go-betweens. We see, then, how "choice" of friends in town and "choice" of wife from the rural area via urban contacts constitute two mutually reinforcing spheres of interaction. That is to say, they are logically consistent in terms of Luo culture.

TABLE 20

Sample of Luo marital unions showing incidence of "district" endogamy

		Wife's area (district) $(N = 124)^a$		
		Westerners (Alego, Ugenya, Gem, Uyoma, Asembo, Imbo, Uholo)	Easterners (Nyakach, Kano, Kisumo, Kajulu, Seme)	Southerners (Rusinga, Karachuonyo, Nyokal, Kasigunga, Kasipul, et al.)
Husband's	81 Westerners	77	4	0
area	31 Easterners	6	22	3
$(N = 110)^b$	12 Southerners	3	2	7
	124 unions	86	28	10

^{a} This number excludes 13 wives who are non-Luo (mostly Luyia).

^{b} That is, 14 have two Luo wives: this low polygyny rate results from the unsystematic nature of this particular sample, which was taken late in fieldwork and, for various reasons, includes a disproportionately large number of young monogamists.

It might be argued that choosing urban friends and spouses from within one's own rural district is only to be expected of such large categories of urban population, who continue to be involved in rural interests and property through the circulatory movement of their wives and their children. This is perfectly true, and surely characterizes all ethnic groups in Nairobi to some extent. But it receives particular emphasis among urban Luo as a result of their segmentary arrangement of district, location, and lineage associations. That is to say, each exogamous lineage association emphasizes whom one may *not* marry, while location and district associations, representing lineage clusters between some of which marriage is permissible, begin to offer "choice" in marriage and so, in effect, point out eligible spouses. The even wider district-based distinctions between Easterners, Westerners, and Southerners has significance for Luo in lumping together their constituent locations as in some way related by common interest as well as tradition. Thus, even when a man from Gem takes a wife from outside this "location" he is likely to marry a woman from

Ugenya or Sakwa, that is to say, a fellow-Westerner. Similarly, a man from Kano who takes a wife from outside is likely to marry a fellow-Easterner, from Nyakach or Kisumo locations. Of 134 marriages, 46 were between spouses coming from the same location, while 86 involved the man taking a spouse from outside. Of these 86, only 18 Luo wives and 13 non-Luo wives were from outside their husbands' districts. Finally, the Luo Union itself substantiates this three-fold classification by providing an arena in which competition for office is often fought along the lines of it.

I am not worried that the preponderance of Luo Westerners, i.e. from Siaya district, makes Kaloleni demographically unrepresentative of Luo generally in Nairobi. Given the chain migration of Luo to Nairobi from particular rural locations and districts, most housing areas in the city will show biases of this kind. It is precisely such biases which give added significance to the distinction between Westerners, Easterners, and Southerners, who also show very minor differences of DhoLuo pronunciation and vocabulary and even, allegedly, of custom (cf. Stafford, 1967, p. vii). Kaloleni was one of the earliest public estates built. The large number of Westerners there may reflect their earlier migration to and family settlement in Nairobi. It may be that a smaller number of them were sufficiently more numerous than other Luo in 1952, when Kikuyu were evicted in Operation Anvil, to expand their numbers even more.

The point here is that, as Mitchell (1967, p. 31) has warned, it is virtually impossible to get statistically a representative locality (whether an urban housing estate or rural village) of a large socio-cultural group. Kaloleni is no exception. It does, however, have emic significance as a locality for all Luo in Nairobi. They recognize that it has an inordinately large Luo population in the city, and they regard it as their "headquarters", with its many association meetings of Luo drawn from all over Nairobi and its proximity to the city stadium where the top Luo soccer teams play. As this implies, Kaloleni is not a bounded sociological unit. Rather, it is a focus of Luo activities and has significance in being regarded as such by all Luo, whether Westerners, Easterners, and Southerners.

Obviously, the preponderance of Luo Westerners in Kaloleni means that I have more information on them, including their numbers of associations, than on other Luo. Had I worked in an area which had more Easterners than Westerners, then the reverse would have been the case. It is for this reason that Mitchell warned against arguing statistically from such biased samples to the formulation of social facts.

Of the 333 Luo household heads in Kaloleni, only 133 or 40 per cent are not at present members of any of the three kinds of association: Union, location, and lineage. But a number of these have at some time in the past been members and/or, on the evidence of their own and other life histories, are likely to be so again. There is, in other words, a fairly rapid turnover of some individual members of associations as a result of disputation, some remaining behind to constitute a continuing core, especially those who have many children occupying a wide age-spread and so successively reaching marriageable age. The turnover of members does not, then, reduce the actual number of associations in existence at any one time, so that the overall structure may be said to persist. By membership I mean here regular participation in the running of these associations which meet once a month or more in the hall or one of the rooms of the Kaloleni community centre, or, less often, in another housing estate in Nairobi. The fluctuations of membership make it difficult to state at any one time precisely how many members an association has. But between 10 and 30 would seem to be a median for lineage associations, and 20–50 for location and district associations.

So far so good. Now, when we look at Table 21, we encounter a puzzle.

TABLE 21

Proportionate membership of the three Luo association types

Association type	Lineage	Location	Union	Total
Number of members	124	123	34	281 (i.e. includes 81 cases of multiple membership)
As a proportion of all 200 Luo household heads in Kaloleni who are members of associations	62%	61.5%	17%	

This Table drawn from Kaloleni's Luo household heads suggests that the lineage and location associations both have the same size of membership (i.e. 62 per cent and 61.5 per cent). And yet, since a location has within it a number of lineages, there should be many more lineage associations and therefore many more Luo claiming membership of these than of location associations. The puzzle is resolved when we look back at Fig. 4 (opposite p. 196) and focus on the "genealogy" of associations of the Westerners only. The Westerners, it will be remembered, are by far the largest Luo group in Kaloleni. It is among them that we find, as we would expect to find, the fullest evidence for the polysegmentation of urban associations: altogether 87 lineage associations of different segmental levels are instanced, stemming from some twenty location and district associations; 66 of these lineage associations and nine higher-order ones comprise Westerners. Among the Easterners and Southerners, their smaller numbers in Kaloleni mean that associations of the widest units of rural identity, i.e. the district or location, are likely to be represented among the household heads, but not those of their lineages, whose smaller numbers are more thinly dispersed outside Kaloleni in other parts of the city.

We can say that though the figures drawn from Kaloleni household heads are biased in favour of Westerners, it is nevertheless possible to see, precisely in this preponderance of one large grouping coming from a common home area, the fullest extent of the segmentation of their urban associations. For it is clear, from ordinary observation if not from systematic samples, that the Easterners, and to a lesser extent the Southerners (in view of their smaller overall population in Nairobi), also have undergone comparable processes of associational segmentation.

This is the point at which to reiterate that I have followed conventional anthropological practice in simply using the figures from my survey of Kaloleni households to back up empirical impressions gained generally about Luo in Nairobi as a whole. I am satisfied that, at the level of generalization I have been working at, the Westerners do not differ significantly in the facts I have described from other Luo in Nairobi. My task has been (a) to identify the segmentary nature of the pyramid of Luo associations, while acknowledging that the list of them is by no means total, and (b) to show how this pyramid is organized.

The high number of Westerners in Kaloleni nicely illustrates their distinction from Easterners and Southerners, which is, as I said above, the initial and over-arching three-fold classification of Luo as represented by their pyramid of associations in Nairobi, and within which are the further sub-classifications of district, location, and lineage of varying segmental levels.

Socio-economic status of association members

Since more and more of them have settled in Nairobi, Luo now speak of there being two main categories of household heads. First, there are those who came in the immediate post-war years of urban migration, usually after military service in the British Army, and who took jobs and found housing in Nairobi or some other town and stayed on as townsmen to become central figures in the organization of housing, job-hunting, and the plethora of Luo associations. Second are those who have come to Nairobi since about the ending of the Kenya Emergency in 1959 and who now (1969) are sufficiently established in Nairobi to have families of their own but who are clearly regarded as "younger" than the "old-timers". The ending of the second world war in 1945, the beginning and ending of the Kenya Emergency in 1952 and 1959, and Kenya's independence in late 1963, are watersheds in the development of Luo settlement in Nairobi, as I have described. These events are also convenient ways of dating people's careers. Luo use the beginning of the Emergency to distinguish "older" married men (jodongo) from younger married men. The old-timers are generally forty years of age and above, while the "younger" men are between twenty-five and forty. The eviction of Kikuyu in Operation Anvil in 1953 made Kaloleni the earliest preponderantly Luo area of family settlement by allowing new "waves" of Luo into the estate. But the original Luo also stayed on and it is these who are included among those defined as old-timers (i.e. jodongo or elders). Of all 333 household heads, 44 per cent are forty or over, and nearly all migrated to town before 1952, while most of the 56 per cent aged between twenty-five and forty came to towns after that date.

The under-forties are slightly more highly represented as members in location than in lineage associations, and the over-forties more numerous in the latter. But the difference is slight. The claimed membership of the Luo Union is roughly equal for both younger and older men. Given the fact, then, that elders do not seem to be any

H

more numerous in any of these tiers of association than younger men, what are we to make of the many claims by Luo of different ages to the effect that, "Elders dominate the lineage ('clan') and location associations"? I was struck by the frequency of this claim and, through observation of actual meetings of associations, by the prominent role taken by senior men in making proposals and taking decisions. The verbal claim seemed to be borne out by observation and I first assumed that these figures, which had been collected to cross-check this, must in some way be innaccurate. But a much more important feature in the figures then showed itself—a feature which was also borne out by observation. This was that men over forty were much more likely to be members of *both* lineage and location associations. I call this multiple membership since it sometimes includes involvement in a couple of lineage associations (i.e. one of a lower segmental level) as well as in that of a location and, in a few cases, in the Luo Union. Single membership, of course, refers to that of only one association of any tier. Table 22 shows clearly the tendency for elders to be members of more than one association.

TABLE 22
Multiple association membership of elders

	Non membership of associations	Single membership	Multiple membership
Elders (40 and over)			
145 (100%)	63 (43%)	46 (32%)	36 (25%)
Young men (under 40)	73 (39%)	87 (46%)	28 (15%)

In other words, though there are more young men than elders and though a young man is just as likely as an elder to be a member of at least one association, it is the elder who is likely to straddle, so to speak, a number of them. In fact, there are, in absolute terms, more cases of multiple membership among elders even though their total number is fewer than young men. How is this borne out by observation? If you go to a meeting of, say, Asembo location association, you are likely to find the most prominent speakers are elders and that these same men are also the most prominent members of their respective lineage associations as well. If we confine the figures to lineage and location associations only, and exclude consideration of the Luo Union, we find an even stronger tendency for elders to be multiple members: twenty-nine are active members of both location and lineage associations, while only eight under-forties are.

The picture, then, becomes clearer. These figures can only show a tendency. But it supports statements by Luo themselves and my own observation that elders play dominant roles in *both* lineage and location associations, almost to the point of monopolizing them. We must not, however, think of such elders who are multiple association leaders as die-hard "traditionalists" tied only by ideology to rural-based custom. They are themselves well above the average in income and include a fair proportion who are white-collar workers with above average education. They know well the advantages of economic strategy and it is partly for this reason that they straddle both their location association and the constituent lineage ones. As men over forty likely to have marriageable daughters and sons themselves, or as paternal uncles of eligible brides, or simply as potential husbands of second or subsequent wives, they are centrally involved in the bridewealth negotiations preceding a marriage. Since bridewealth among Luo is so valuable, there is much to lose or gain.

I have mentioned in a previous chapter that younger men attempt to control the urban negotiations concerning their own sisters' marriages in the absence of a father. This can create conflict between such men, and, say, their father's brother(s) if he happens to be in Nairobi, and makes further sense of the tendency for elders who have been in the city longer to try and extend their monopoly over leadership positions in both lineage and location associations. For, as I have explained, while lineage associations stress the exogamy of their members, location associations represent a higher-order level of segmentation at which the possibilities of intermarriage between lineages are advertised, so to speak, with reference to a common home locality. In short, location associations offer the possibility of intermarriage between lineages which are nevertheless close neighbours in the rural area, and which may also be represented by associations in Nairobi. To be able to play a key role in both types of association gives an elder access to any information about eligible spouses for his "dependants" or himself and draws him, willy nilly, into arguments concerning other people about the admissibility and advisability of prospective marriages between couples of closely related lineages.

Elders also need to substantiate their authority over younger men and women. Those who earn have little difficulty with those who are unemployed, for they control them financially. But symbolic reminders of the dangers of ignoring parental wisdom are necessary if elders are to influence and control young men who earn. At a meeting of Kakan (Alego) maximal lineage association, its chairman reported the facts of the following case as an example "from home" (i.e. the rural area) of how important it is for elders to supervise the marriages of the young. From an analytical viewpoint, it also illustrates the interconnection of three factors: the fruitfulness of a marriage; the economic significance of bridewealth as an investment in children and in perpetuating the lineage; and the harmful effects of the young disregarding the rules of incest.

A man in his late twenties of Kakan met and fell in love with a girl from Kagombe maximal exogamous lineage, also in Alego. But it was pointed out that the man's mother herself is of Kagombe, though the girl and mother had never met each other and the relationship between them could be traced only with difficulty. The prospective groom claimed that the link was too distant to constitute incest, but his parents and his father's brothers and those of the girl disagreed. His father refused to contribute towards the bridewealth, "not even", as it was put "to the extent of leading two heiffers and a goat from his homestead to that of the girl's parents." To do this, it was feared, would bring *chira*. But the son took the girl without formal ceremony to live with him in Nairobi and proceeded to pay the bridewealth out of his urban wages to the girl's parents, who did not refuse it.

It happened that the expansion of Siaya township forced the new husband's father's senior brother to abandon his homestead site and merge with that of his younger brother, i.e. the new husband's own father. This senior brother then became head of the merged homestead. Thereafter death and sickness hit children within the larger family. The homestead head, the new husband's senior paternal uncle, claimed that this was the *chira* that had been brought by the incestuous marriage and which threatened to wipe out not just the son's own prospective family but also the local lineage segment (*anyuola*). The men and women had to undergo extensive purification by *manyasi* medicine, but people darkly observe that the *chira* can still return at any time.

The eligibility of a spouse rests on three main questions:

1. Are the prospective bride and groom from lineages which are genealogically distant enough to preserve an exogamous rule, or sufficiently free of close matrilateral and cognatic connections (i.e. marriage into a mother's and her mother's maximal exogamous lineage is banned as with anyone firmly regarded as "my relative" (*watna*) in

order to eliminate the possibility of the union being regarded as "incestuous" (*marach*, i.e. "bad", and see p. 154 above in Chapter 5).

2. Can the prospective husband and/or his agnates be relied upon to pay the bridewealth and can a mutually acceptable "bargain" be struck between the two parties to the transaction?

3. Connected with these negotiations, do the girl's personal and family histories suggest a fruitful marriage, free of disease, death, and *chira*, and preferably with an equal proportion of boys and girls?

The second question about bridewealth is of a direct economic nature, and is certainly recognized as such by Luo, but cannot in practice be dissociated from the third about whether the wife will produce children. And even the first question, concerning the limits of exogamy and the definition of incest may, in borderline cases, be invoked as *post hoc* explanations of a fruitless marriage. To repeat, then, as seekers of spouses for their grown-up sons, daughters, or other dependants, or as seekers of second or subsequent wives for themselves, elders are more likely than younger married men to require immediate answers to such questions, and are helped in their quest and in controlling the marriage choices of younger men and women by becoming active and involved members of both lineage and location associations. This is not to say that all elders are multiple members and leaders, as is clear from Table 22. It is only that an disproportionately large cluster of them have assumed such key roles.

There is another outstanding difference between single and multiple association members. Multiple association members include an disproportionately large number of polygynists (see Table 23).

All but seven of these polygynist multiple members are over forty (i.e. are *jodongo*). In other words, not only is multiple membership generally a feature of the over-forties, it is also inordinately represented among polygynists. Putting the matter even more simply, the figures depict a tendency for Luo who are prominent members of more than one association to be over forty and to have more than one

TABLE 23
Single and multiple association membership by monogamy and polygyny

	Non membership of associations	Single membership	Multiple membership
103 Polygynists (100%)	41 (40%)	35 (34%)	27 (26%)
204 Monogamists (100%)	78 (38%)	93 (46%)	33 (16%)

wife. Once again, from observation of the activities of the most prominent men in lineage and location associations, this is certainly the impression.

Bringing together all the characteristics I have mentioned, we can
say that Luo men who are leaders in both their lineage and location
associations are likely to be over forty and each referred to as *jaduong'*,
and to have more than one wife, a higher than average income and
education, a white-collar job, and to have lived in Nairobi since at
least the beginning of the Kenya Emergency in 1952. It is, I have said,
precisely such men who are likely to have vested interests in securing
financially sound arrangements for the marriages of their dependants.

These men constitute a kind of non-conscious leadership elite at
the level of lineage and location associations. They are not, I should
point out, likely to be as well represented at the level of the Luo
Union, whose leaders are often of even higher status. But then the
Luo Union is not normally concerned with providing guidelines for
marriage choices and bridewealth negotiations, which are the underlying interests of such men. They are not an elite, however, in the
strict meaning of the term. For they are not aware of themselves as a
single category with common interests, even though they combine
seniority through age, honour through polygyny, and prestige
through above average socio-economic status—all critical measures of
Luo notions of worthiness which neatly combine "traditional" with
contemporary features. Rather, as I have said, their significance as a
social category comes through from observation of association activities and has been borne out by a quantitative analysis of a restricted
sample.

When we turn away from such men and look generally at all
claimed members of the two main types of association, we see that,
here too, socio-economic factors are important differentiators.

Taken as a whole, members of lineage associations have lower
socio-economic status than those of location associations. This can be
seen from a comparison of average income, educational level, and
occupational span (see Table 24).

We may note here that household heads who are not currently
members of any association are very similar in socio-economic status
to members of lineage associations. It is, then, members of location
associations who stand out as being consistently above the socio-economic average.

TABLE 24

Socio-economic status of lineage and location association members

	Educational level			Occupational span		
	Average income	Under 8 yrs	Over 8 yrs	White-collar	Blue-collar	Un-skilled[a]
Lineage association members ($N = 121$)	Shs. 525/-	46%	54%	35%	51%	14%
Location association members ($N = 120$)	Shs. 640/-	39%	61%	45%	47%	8%
Household heads not currently members of any ethnic association ($N = 133$)	Shs. 530/-	50%	50%	35%	53%	12%

[a]Including 6 currently unemployed.

Nevertheless these figures show that, while it is generally true that lineage association members have lower socio-economic status than members of location associations, there is clearly considerable overlap. For Luo men themselves, however, the ranking of associations is more clear-cut than that. Their spontaneous comments reveal the view that lineage association members are "poorer" than those of location associations, with the leaders in the Luo Union among the wealthiest and most influential. In other words, just as Luo emically distinguish three tiers in their pyramid of associations, when in fact, as I have explained, an outsider might distinguish four or even five, so they attach to this hierarchy a corresponding emic three-fold ranking of members and leaders, as "poor", "well-off", and "wealthy". The structure of associations, then, provides a socio-economic as well as genealogical blueprint.

There are only thirty-one household heads in my sample who claim to be "paid-up" active members of the Luo Union. On the other hand, as we see from my next chapter, other men make voluntary contributions at one or more of the Luo Union's many collective appeals for funds. And "active" member has the same nebulous connotation. Unlike location or lineage associations, with their clear membership lists and regular subscriptions, the Luo Union is, by its very inclusive nature, regarded as automatically for "all" Luo. Nevertheless, the thirty-one members of my Kaloleni sample who claim to "active" and "paid-up" membership does suggest some greater sense of involvement on their part. The number is too few for any significant quantitative breakdown. It may be noted, however, that they have mixed socio-economic status characteristics. Thus, their incomes are about average for all Luo household heads, as is their distribution by the three main occupational categories, but their educational level is high. This socio-economic mixture does show the wide range in social statuses of the active members of the Luo Union, as I show in the next chapter. The high educational level is due to a proportion of young men in their late twenties and early thirties who are well educated but do not yet command very high incomes. Otherwise, the average income and occupational spread is due to the counterbalancing inclusion of elders who, though they are less educated than their younger fellow-members, nevertheless exert considerable influence as long-settled townsmen who have above average incomes and more than one wife. There is, then, in the Luo Union a juxtaposition of young, educated, and, as yet, monogamous men in white-collar jobs with less educated older polygnists in a range of jobs, all headed, formally or informally, by the most powerful men in the Luo community.

Summary and conclusion: individualism and collectivism

In the last chapter I discussed the paradoxical way in which, at the level of stated belief, wives and husbands are equally held to be responsible for any sickness and death mystically afflicting their families, but that in actual cases involving diagnoses by male and female Luo diviner-doctors, husbands are more likely to be blamed. I interpreted this difference between men's observable power to destroy their own families and women's putative but undemonstrated power, as conferring ultimate moral accountability for the perpetuation of a line of descent on husbands rather than wives. Women may suffer with men, though more so than men, the *general* stigma that it is their adultery which destroys their husband's family and his ensuing line of descent. But, in actual cases which inevitably get gossiped about, it is men who are seen to wield this perverse power, though through "negligent" breaches of seniority rather than through "sinful" adultery. In other words, the future of men's families is seen to remain in their own hands, with women presenting a latent challenge, so to speak, to this male control of a fruitful marriage and its lineal destiny.

Lineages and lineage clusters based on localized rural areas continue to be politically important for Luo both within Nairobi and between Nairobi and their rural homeland. This emphasis on the lineage principle puts men firmly in control of public political affairs. Luo political activities and personnel overlap those of Luo associations, which organize welfare schemes, soccer competitions and provide ethnic political platforms. The wider inter-ethnic framework of competition and conflict, particularly between Luo and Kikuyu, provides the external pressures and uncertainties which constantly "politicize" the meetings and activities (e.g. soccer and fund-raising for the homeland) of the Luo associations. The pyramid of Luo associations owes its internal, segmentary structure a great deal to the system of marriage choices, for lineage exogamy is still observed.

In this chapter I have shown the importance of marriage choices in maintaining the Luo pyramid of associations in Nairobi. I have described the three levels of association: Luo Union at the top, location ("sub-tribe") in the middle, and exogamous lineage at the bottom. I have compared the socio-economic, generational, and marital statuses of their members and leaders. Lineage association members are generally of lower socio-economic status than those of the more inclusive location or "sub-tribe" associations. But many leaders are common to both. These multiple leaders tend to be polygynous "elders" (i.e. middle-aged), of above average socio-economic status. Young monogamists, especially those of below average status, are not normally leaders.

In addition to men of the Luo top elite, the leadership of the Luo Union includes well-educated, relatively young monogamists in white-collar jobs but also less educated polygynists working in a variety of jobs. Both categories have above average incomes. The juxtaposition is not, in reality, that clear-cut, but is spoken of in these contrastive terms by Luo themselves. Phrased thus, this contrast echoes two other oppositions referred to in the preceding paragraph: between young man and elder, and between monogamist and polygynist. In the contrast between "educated" or "less educated", and "white-collar" and "mixed occupations" (i.e. not exclusively white-collar), there is a partial echo of the main socio-economic differences in the membership of "sub-tribe" and lineage associations.

Taking the association leaders and members as a whole, it is clear that above average socio-economic status on the one hand, and generational seniority, including polygynous status, on the other hand, are the two criteria which, singly or together, are used by Luo to create a hierarchy out of their pyramid of associations and to distinguish leaders from members. Let me put this more strongly and say that these are the two main underlying forces in contemporary Luo society. We may call them simply socio-economic status and generational status, with the implicit understanding that this is also likely to include polygynous status. These may divide persons or be combined within the one person. Thus, differences of socio-economic status need not by themselves have anything to do with people's age, social seniority, or whether they are polygynous or monogamous. Nor need a polygynous elder necessarily have high income, education and a prestigious occupation; though, as we noted in Chapter 4, men with more than one wife do tend to be well above the average in urban income.

Taking generational status first, I have already described how, quite unconsciously, becoming a polygynist propels men into defence of the principles of agnation and of those Luo "customs" which ensure the circulation of valuable bridewealth. One aspect of this protection of agnation is, of course, preservation of the principle of lineage exogamy and of broad notions of marriage eligibility between approved lineages. The identification and preservation of such demarcatory lines is very much at the basis of the formation of the lineage and location associations in Nairobi, in which polygynists play important roles.

On the face of it, socio-economic advancement, centred as it is on individual achievement through education, job skills, and earned income, would seem to propel men away from the conforming restraints exacted by strict adherence to agnation and lineage exogamy and the implication that these are most fully expressed through polygyny. And, indeed, such conflicts are strongest among young men who have education and who wish either to advance themselves socioeconomically or to do so through their children, and who calculate that one wife and a limited number of children may achieve this aim.

As my earlier chapters have indicated, this may be regarded as a conflict of values and expectations confronting a man and, sometimes, his wife, in the early stages of their family's development. As we shall see in the next chapter, this same conflict of values and assumptions is expressed in the most collective and public of activities involving Luo in Nairobi: the annual general or extraordinary meetings of the Luo Union. At these meetings, whatever the manifest issue under discussion, the underlying assumptions of socio-economic status are expressed as initially lavish displays of prestige competition through cash donations known variously as *gisungore* (literally "they are being proud or boasting"), or *gichamo nyadhi* ("they are eating *nyadhi*"— meaning unknown), or *pakruok* ("praising", usually by giving money to a traditional lyre-player who sings songs in praise of the donor's family, lineage or sub-tribe). This kind of pot-latching, while it draws attention to particularly generous individuals who make cash donations to the Luo Union, is nevertheless channelled through the "traditional" units of "sub-tribe" and lineage, for it is in the name of such units that the generous donor makes his contribution. And these lineages and sub-tribes are, of course, used to classify exogamy and marriage eligibility. Thus, through competitive acts of generosity, rival marriage groups are distinguished.

We come back at this point to the distinction I drew in this chapter between specific and general segmentation in Luo urban social organization. I want to suggest that competition arising from differences of socio-economic status divides individual Luo leaders and may drive one or more of them to form a rival association which is clearly not in the first place based on recognized traditional segmentary principles. Thereafter, and once established, this association may claim traditional credibility, so to speak, by referring to a venerated ancestor as linking it genealogically to the "parent" or "brother" association. Here, the specific "cultural" principle of Luo segmentation is brought in to legitimize the breakaway association. The overall process is similar to that described in many ethnographies of rural African societies organized through segmentary lineages. The distinctive feature in Nairobi is that the arguments preceding fission are to do with competing claims for socio-economic status and prestige and the disposal of the association's funds, rather than with, say, the ritual right to officiate at ancestral shrines in a society "with few distinctions of rank and wealth and little difference of authority other than within the family cluster" (Middleton, 1960, pp. 74–6). The socio-economic idiom of fission among Luo is consistent with the underlying reality of urban wage dependency, which inevitably fosters a ranking of people and values which must often be at variance with that deriving from generational and genealogical position.

7

Paradigms of Leadership:

Generation and Socio-economic Status

We can talk about the "objective" reality of socio-economic status and of generational status: some men do indeed earn more, or are better educated and have more prestigeful jobs than others; and some people are clearly older than others. But the last chapter has shown how tidier subjective assumptions are superimposed on such measurable "objective" differences. Thus, Luo claim that the pyramid of Luo associations in Nairobi has three ranked tiers, while an outside analyst, broadening the criteria, might say five. The Luo also claim that these ranked tiers have members and leaders who are correspondingly "wealthy", "well-off but not wealthy", and simply "poor", when in fact this is no more than a tendency. Similarly, their statement that "elders dominate lineage and location associations" does not refer to the total distribution and proportions of elders and younger men throughout the membership, but really refers to an disproportionate share of control exerted by a relatively small number of elders who, as well as tending to be polygynists, are leaders at two or more levels of the associational pyramid. It is these "subjective" or, better, emic differentiations emanating from socio-economic status and generational status which provide the most immediately relevant yardsticks in interaction. Their general etic accuracy is sharpened to a point of emic precision.

Emic dualisms

Whatever terms we use to identify them, and at the risk of reification, emic considerations of socio-economic status and those deriving from generational status are accompanied by a series of other dualisms. Thus, the recognition among the Luo that socio-economic status is most easily observed and measured through the achievements of an individual rather than a group is expressed in the concept *sunga* (a proud person). This is the common root of both the personal noun and of the verb *-sung*, to boast, as in the term *gi-sungore* used to refer to competitive donations made at meetings. Gossip and backbiting are inundated with the use of the term *sunga*. Unlike the term *moluor* (respected person) or *jaduong* (big man, elder) which unambiguously denote an admirable personal quality, the significance of *sunga* derives from its ambivalence. Thus, on the one hand *sunga* can be used to express disapproval of breaches of the Luo egalitarian premise: a man who neglects relatives in favour of friends may be called *sunga,* an accusation which may even precede accusations of sorcery or *chira* on the part of the aggrieved relatives. On the other hand *sunga* may also denote a sneaking regard for an individual's urban successes: for those who neglect relatives are also those who no longer need them. The late Tom Mboya was very much held in this light. He was condemned for his alleged neglect of the Luo community as a whole through his tribally transcendental policies, yet he was admired for his powerful intellect, articulate use of English, achieved wealth, sartorial elegance, and sheer personal style.

At a lesser level the socially aspiring young monogamist who seeks education for himself, his children, and sometimes even his wife, and who is condemned for neglecting kin, especially agnates, in favour of friends, demonstrates this same clustering of features. This comes out consistently in Luo conversations with each other, in spite of each person's own situationally varying position. An individual is normally only referred to as *sunga* in small groups or dyads. It is as if the term's ambivalence represents the private uncertainties most Luo have regarding the advantages and disadvantages of adhering to collective Luo customs as against the possible benefits of individual achievement.

The contrary view explicitly and unambiguously condemns "damage" done to the Luo community by individuals who disregard kin and custom in the name of personal socio-economic objectives. This comes out most strongly at public meetings when voiced by elders. This is the view which, while strongly urging the benefits of education to help Luo as a whole, demands that this be done collectively through publicly subscribed funds. From 1971 onwards large sums of money were raised by the Luo Union to build a proposed higher learning institute, the Ramogi Institute of Advanced Technology in the Luo capital of Kisumu (Mutiso and Godfrey, 1972, p. 11). (Ramogi refers to a Luo ancestral founder: see Malo, 1953; Whisson, 1962; Ogot, 1967, p. 142.) There are many other examples before this time of public fund-raising for similar purposes.

The sums of money are raised through the competitive donations made by representatives of rival groups, each usually conceptualized as based on common descent. A way of referring to such display is, I have mentioned, *gisungore* (they boast). This expression, unlike the "private" use in gossip of the personal noun *sunga* (a proud man), suggests *no* ambivalence as to the appropriateness and worthiness of these conspicuous donations. In other words, *sunga* (and, less often, *osungore, he* boasts) refers to individual display. But the plural verb form, *gisungore* (and sometimes *gichamo nyadhi* or the abstract noun *pakruok*, as mentioned above), denotes public and open display by traditionally accredited groups, even though it is actually an individual who makes the cash donation. Use of the singular personal noun *sunga*, then, reveals the uncertain delights and dangers of uncontrolled individual freedom through achieved wealth and status. Use of the plural verb form *gisungore* legitimizes the acquisition of socio-economic status by expressing it through traditional group membership.

The customary value of polygyny is also implicit at these public meetings in sensitive discussions on the need for Luo to remain at full numerical strength with Kikuyu. This political consideration may be used to justify the continuation of polygyny as a way of providing families with many children. Objectively, the apparently increasing size of Kikuyu relative to Luo in Kenya may well derive from the gradual Kikuyu repudiation of polygyny in favour of monogamy, which, as I mentioned at the beginning of chapter three, actually increases individual women's and therefore their group's chances of producing many children.

On the one hand, then, we have a conceptual paradigm linking (a) individually achieved urban socio-economic status; (b) alleged preferential treatment to friends to the neglect of relatives; and (c) a stated preference by young men for monogamy rather than polygyny as a means of educating few children to a high standard rather than many to mediocre levels. On the other hand, there is a contrary paradigm which links (a) collective efforts by the Nairobi Luo community as a whole at self-help in education and rural welfare; (b) a continuing emphasis on the control of "random" fissionary elements among Luo associations through the dogma of rural-based segmentary descent; and (c) public appeals, both explicit and by innuendo, for the preservation of Luo "custom", including the value of polygyny and of prior obligations to family, lineage and rural home locations.

The first paradigm, which we may crudely call that of individualism, equates with general segmentation: it predicates the apparently random and unregulated aspect that accompanies any fissionary process. Thus, leaders quarrel and one or more of them takes it upon himself to set up an alternative association, a process reminiscent of the way a disputing elder in the rural area may "hive-off" to form his own lineage. The second paradigm, that of collectivism, equates with the special principle of segmentation. For this "hiving-off", while clearly a response to a quarrel between individuals and based on an individual's decision, eventually becomes legitimized as an act which is perfectly consistent with their culturally distinctive segmentary lineage system which all Luo recognize and can talk about through the use of specific terms.

Let me now give flesh to these abstract distinctions by describing and then briefly analysing a series of linked events involving the Luo Union in Nairobi during the period of urban settlement there by Luo families.

Charisma through emic contrasts: Odinga and Mboya

While a full history of the Luo Union has yet to be written, some Luo leaders in Nairobi gave me consistent accounts of some important recent events.

Some Luo elders in Nairobi say that, almost since its alleged "foundation" in the 1920s (sic),[1] the Luo Union in Nairobi has been riven by factions, though no more than two at any one time. Some middle-aged and older Luo still refer to the traditional two-part division of their society into *Jook* (the Outside People), referring to those involved in the earliest and most southerly migration, and *Joiye* (the Inside People) who mostly live north of them (cf. Southall, 1952, p. 15; Evans-Pritchard, 1965, p. 208).

Whether the successive and differently termed divisions within the Luo Union originate from this or have independent origins is difficult to say. It should be noted, however, that most Luo in Nairobi are not *Jook* (Southerners) but are *Joiye*, and that the big division between them is that of Westerners and Easterners, as I described in the last chapter. It may be assumed, however, that any enduring organization like the Luo Union has a tendency to split. It is interesting, then, that this tendency appears to have been kept in check for so long in the Luo Union. Indeed I would suggest that this is the logic of Luo culture operating according to a principle of internal opposition which holds factions in changing but balanced complementarity—a kind of schismogenesis, to use Bateson's concept (1958, pp. 175–8).

Luo say that there was a general call for unity at the declaration of the Kenya Emergency in 1952, with some reformation of the internal organization of the Luo Union in 1953, initiated by Oginga Odinga.[2] But then, in 1962, factionalism recurred. First, leaders of the rival factions in the Union accused each other of trying to oust one another from office. There seems little doubt that, even at this early stage, actually before Kenya's independence in December 1963, the factions began to align themselves behind either Oginga Odinga or Tom Mboya, the two most prominent and internationally known Luo political leaders.

On the surface, factionalism within the Luo Union has been based on so many different issues and involved such changing sets of per-

---

[1] Possibly referring to the Young Kavirondo Association of Maseno of 1922, or the Kavirondo Taxpayers' Welfare Association of 1923 (Lonsdale, 1963; Rosberg and Nottingham, 1966, pp. 60, 88, 90 ff.). Okumu (1969, p. 10) states that it was formed in the mid-forties, citing Nyanza Archives ADM8/31. However, Oginga Odinga does refer to the existence of the Luo Union based only in Nairobi when he was a schoolboy, which would corroborate the above report. He was born in 1911. From 1946, however, he helped set up branches all over East Africa (Odinga, 1969, pp. 86–7).

[2] Rosberg and Nottingham (1966, p. 316) also refer to reorganization of the Luo Union by Oginga Odinga during 1953–7.

sonnel that it is difficult to identify any consistent underlying "cause" or set of causes. Indeed the search for a single "cause" or consistent set of them is likely to be a chimera, if only because, at one level of analysis, the constant factionalism is a changing expression of a fundamental principle of emic opposition which operates within any self-consciously "united" organization or social collectivity. For a collectivity can only define itself and its external boundaries by reference to its internal structure, and this invariably involves a notion of internal conflict however ephemeral it may sometimes be and however much it may be played down in the presentation of a united front to the outside world. This point need hardly be laboured, except to note that among the Luo, the notion is a permanent cultural feature which is made especially cognitively salient in conversation between fellow Luo though the use of such terms denoting "traditional" conflict (*nyiego*) and structural opposition (*libamba*), which I have referred to in previous chapters.

Odinga and Mboya were the most constant expressions of opposed factions. This was more than arbitrary and rested on more than an historical accident of their contemporary prominence. In political policy, parliamentary constituency, personal philosophy, age, region of origin, and leadership style, they could not have contrasted more vividly. It can be surmised that it was partly this contrast which threw them into opposed "charismatic" prominence by enabling them to act as distinct rallying points within the Luo community. Two men of similar characteristics could not have provided such clear-cut focal points of internal dissension. The point here is that charisma is less a matter of personality strengths and more a product of relevant emic cultural contrasts.

Odinga is a "true" Luo elder. He is often referred to as Jaramogi. As mentioned above, Ramogi is the name of a (some say the) Luo ancestral founder, and so Ja-ramogi means the Man of Ramogi, i.e. the leading Luo elder. Odinga dresses in allegedly traditional Luo style and is regarded by many Luo as having had fewer years' formal schooling than Mboya, though in fact the difference between them is slight. Odinga's political constituency is in Luoland itself. He is himself a "Westerner" born in Sakwa location but is normally regarded as transcending Luo sectional interests. He is accused by his rivals and by non-Luo opponents of taking a "tribalist" stand in politics. His supporters retort that he is no more than a *Luo* "nationalist", with links with the great Luo *Piny Owacho* movement (literally: "the (Luo) country says", i.e. governs itself), dating from the early nineteen-twenties (Odinga, 1969, p. 65). The political party founded by Odinga in 1966, the Kenya People's Union (KPU), was purportedly left-wing, though this was for the most part a rhetorical identification (see Scott MacWilliam's discussion of the Luo Thrift and Trading Corporation, unpublished manuscript).

Mboya was only in his early thirties at the time of Kenya's independence in 1963, yet had already become an international figure as a forceful Kenyan trade unionist. He bore no special Luo nickname, traditional or otherwise, though in his later years I heard his admirers and supporters refer to him as Moluor Tom ("Tom who is respected"), which is a title of esteem which can be attributed to a prominent young man as well as an elder. He addressed public meetings in superbly tailored suits. His constituency was both urban and non-Luo, being Pumwani, a polyethnic, predominantly Swahili-speaking area of Nairobi. He himself had been brought up outside Luoland, in an area predominantly farmed by whites. There were many who denied that he was a "true" Luo, for his family home was Rusinga Island in an area of Luoland which fairly recently contained Bantu-speaking peoples before Luo traversed it in their southward migration. This family home is, moreover, in South Nyanza which, as we noted from the figures given in the previous chapter, has far fewer emigrants in Nairobi than either western or eastern Luoland. Mboya's polyethnic constituency mirrored very much his political position as one who had to repudiate any organization or philosophy which suggested ethnic self-preservation or advancement. He therefore had no truck with the KPU, instead dedicating himself to the ruling party, KANU, until his assassination in 1969. He was also a strong supporter of a mixed economic and political system including both capitalism and "socialism" (i.e. social democracy), as was illustrated in his famous statement of KANU policy, Sessional Paper No. 10: African Socialism (May 1965).

I want to emphasize that these contrasts of style, status, age, origin, and political philosophy, between these two great Luo leaders were very much the focus of discussion among Luo themselves. They are not slight differences merely exaggerated by my analysis. Indeed, it is clear that these two leaders each represented a symbolic condensation of contrasting characteristics which periodically divide Luo from each other.

Odinga represented (a) elderhood, (b) Luo genealogical purity (e.g. as in his nickname, Jaramogi), (c) "true" Luo traditions, (d) continuing rural involvement in the Luo heartland (i.e. his constituency is rural though, of course, his political stage is in practice as much urban), and (e) a purportedly socialist political philosophy expressed through KPU.

In contrast, Mboya represented (a) "youth", (b) mixed Luo–Bantu origins (i.e. he came from Rusinga Island), (c) an accentuated Western style and an explicity "non-tribal" stand, (d) urban involvement (i.e. through his Nairobi constituency and, of course, through Kenyan trade unionism, for which he was most famous), and (e) a mixed economy, but essentially capitalist political philosophy expressed through KANU.

It is said that by 1965 it became public knowledge among Luo in Nairobi that the factions within the Luo Union leadership were aligned behind Odinga and Mboya (see also Mutiso and Godfrey, 1972, p. 4). The minority pro-Mboya faction, allegedly coming mostly from South Nyanza and from Kisumo and Seme locations, wanted to change the name of the Luo Union in Nairobi to the Luo Sports Club. This minority argued that the organization's activities were recreational, i.e. soccer, as well as welfare-oriented, and that to continue with the name, Luo Union, was falsely to emphasize a "tribalist" organization potentially in political conflict with the "non-tribal" state of Kenya, represented by the ruling party, KANU. We see how close was this argument to Mboya's own philosophy. This minority faction registered the rival Luo Sports Club as sole representative of the Luo in the Kenya National Soccer League. Mboya himself donated valuable sports equipment. The Luo Sports Club began to poach active members from the parent Luo Union, whose new chairman was a vociferous supporter of Odinga.

That this division into two factions with contrasting philosophies meant a great deal to ordinary Luo is instanced by the anger and violence exchanged between their respective supporters during and after the well-attended general meetings held by the Luo Union at Kaloleni Hall at the time. It is also interesting to note the consistency with which Luo report how in many cases the factions actually had a divisive effect on affinal and even sibling relations. Thus, X, living in

Kaloleni, supported the Luo Union and quarrelled over the issue with his brother-in-law, Y, who lived in Starehe and supported the Luo Sports Club. Neither would visit nor speak to each other. Nor was Y's wife "allowed" (*sic*) to speak to her brother X. X was a Westerner from Ugenya and Y an Easterner from Seme. There are also cases in which relatives, affiines or friends from the same location or region became divided by the issue. Indeed, regarding the cast just mentioned, I should point out that it is only since a recent organization of administrative locations and districts that the people of Seme have come to be regarded as Easterners rather than Westerners. Whether such disputes occur among people of the same or different locations and districts, the point is that the Odinga–Mboya rivalry, the differences between these two men, and the factions aligned behind them, together constituted separate and contrasting sets of issues, any one of which might be used to explain a quarrel between structurally close individuals. We are, therefore, unlikely to find any consistent "pragmatic" or material basis of each faction, even though, as we shall see, particular issues may produce material incentives. What is more significant is that the Odinga–Mboya contrast represented a summation of alternative ideological possibilities. Odinga ostensibly stood for the collective defence of the Luo community through both "corporate" radical thought and Luo conservatism. Mboya represented a Western-style meritocracy through the transcension of ethnic conservatism and through individual achievement. Once again, then, we find the paradigms of collectivism versus individualism, and by extension special versus general segmentation, ranged alongside the social representations of Odinga as against Mboya.

It is consistent with the way Luo explained this split that, thereafter, key soccer players of the Luo Union (e.g. Arudhi, Rabuogi, Chege, Yongo and Okeyo) were allegedly "bought" by the Mboya-led Luo Sports Club or, some would say, threatened with loss of job if they did not join it, the reference being to the central influence wielded in the government employment sector by Mboya.[1] The explanatory theme, in other words, was that the Luo Sports Club recruited its team by individual appeals backed up by material reward

---

[1] When the Luo Sports Club was registered in 1965 Mboya was Minister for Justice and Constitutional Affairs, and by 1966 was Minister for Economic Planning and Development.

or the threat of material loss, while the Luo Union relied on collective appeals phrased in terms of a communal obligation on the part of Luo Union players.

It was not long, however, before the Luo Union, too, saw the advantage of material enticement. Its leadership was not without men of influence who allegedly made fresh deals with the key players who had joined the Luo Sports Club. Though the Luo Union, Nairobi, was no longer eligible to field a team in the all-Kenya league (because the Luo Sports Club was already registered for that year), it secretly enticed a number of its original players, now with the Luo Sports Club, to play for another Luo team based in the Luoland capital of Kisumu. This team was the formidable Kisumu Hot Stars.

In late 1965, Luo Sports Club and Kisumu Hot Stars played at the Nairobi Stadium in a match which is still talked about today with avid enthusiasm. But the content of the talk is less to do with the soccer played than with the opportunity the match provided for a clear expression of the Odinga–Mboya split within the Luo community. I will here simply reproduce a partial account:

Both Odinga and Mboya attended before a packed stadium. The Kisumu Hot Stars were in peak form. The two factions occupied distinct areas of the stadium, one chanting Odinga's slogans, and the smaller faction chanting Mboya's. The prize was the Mboya Cup, paid for and presented to the competition by its namesake. Kisumu Hot Stars, with some top players "regained" from the Nairobi Luo Sports Club and with the support of most of the crowd, won. When Mboya presented his cup to the victorious team, which was now clearly identified with his "rival", Odinga, there was a great deal of abuse hurled at Mboya. Mboya became angry and rebuked the crowd. Significantly, he spoke in Swahili, which visibly pleased the small but noticeable number of non-Luo there, principally Luyia, but drew hostile calls from many Luo. Incidents followed the match, including an attempt to assault Mboya in his car as he was driven away, and numerous arrests. Among those arrested were two of the star soccer players originally poached from the Luo Union and on this day playing for the Kisumu Hot Stars.

The Luo Union achieved great prestige in the eyes of ordinary Luo by getting both released on bails of Shs.5,000/– (£250 at the time). But it was still the Luo Sports Club and not the Luo Union which was registered to play in the Kenya national league, and the Luo Union leaders now prepared a "plan" as they called it, to reverse this situation.

In 1966, a new development occurred in Luo politics which might on the face of it seem unconnected with these events, but in fact mobilized the same two factions. Odinga was foremost in setting up the Kenya Peoples Union (KPU) which, as I mentioned earlier, opposed KANU, the party of government. With its leftist views KPU was not ostensibly created to cater only for Luo, and indeed its early leadership included such a prominent non-Luo as the Kikuyu Bildad Kaggia. But it swiftly and increasingly became identified as such and had the support of most though not all Luo. And therein lies the parallel. On the one hand, Mboya headed a minority faction within the Luo community of Nairobi, represented by the Luo Sports Club, and was also representative of those increasingly few Luo who, for a range of reasons, continued to support KANU. Mboya was even tipped as a likely successor to Kenyatta as President of Kenya. On the other hand, Odinga continued to be associated with leadership of the majority Luo faction, represented by the Luo Union in opposition to the Luo Sports Club, while at the same time strengthening his increasingly unambiguous Luo following through leadership of the KPU in opposition to KANU.

I cannot demonstrate quantitively that those who supported Mboya and Odinga were, respectively, the same Luo who supported KANU and KPU. But, though there were, as always, cases of individual changes of allegiance resulting in somes partial overlap at any one time, there does seem to have been this general coincidence. Put simply, then, the internal politics of recreation among Luo in Nairobi, based on the opposition between the Luo Sports Club and the Luo Union, was an expression of the more manifestly formal political conflict among Luo between KANU and KPU. Both these were in the first place national rather than purely ethnic parties, but KPU grew much less so and could soon reasonably be termed an almost exclusively ethnic one. As time went on it became almost a form of ethnic treachery to show support for KANU[1] and, because of the parallel, for the Luo Sports Club. But that was a later development.

1 Okumu (1969, p. 13) notes that the KANU candidate at the by-election for Gem in 1969 became known as an "illigitimate" son of Gem because of his apparent close relationship with a Kikuyu leader.

Here, let me return to the plan that the Luo Union leaders prepared in 1965–6 to destroy the Luo Sports Club and regain for themselves the registered right to represent the Luo of Nairobi in the
Kenya soccer league. They noted that the Luo Sports Club had no
special lines of communication with the many Luo location associations in Nairobi. By contrast these constituted the very essence of
the Luo Union. So, it is claimed, Luo Union leaders visited the
officials of "all" (*sic*) location associations in Nairobi. They claimed
to find general opposition among them to the Luo Sports Club's
"undemocratic" (i.e. non-elected) abrogation of the "right" to represent Nairobi's Luo in the soccer league. They further claimed that,
at their instigation, officials in location associations who did support
the Luo Sports Club were dismissed from their positions by other
officials. It is said that many of them recanted by renouncing the Luo
Sports Club, recognizing that the latter was not designed to help
them financially as are location associations and that, anyway, to be
rejected by "one's own local people" (*sic*) was extremely shameful.

This process of eradication and reconversion was continued into
1967. The "plan", it transpired, was for the Luo Union to revive its
importance as a centralizing organization by setting up an inter-
location soccer championship (in this context referred to by the
Swahili word for locations/districts, *majimbo*, itself a rallying call
used by the former political party, KADU, which had been opposed
to KANU when the latter included the Luo). I have reported a
similar use of inter-location soccer by the Luo Union in Kampala
in the late fifties (Parkin, 1969, pp. 155–7).

The inter-location championship was an immediate success, so
much so, apparently, that its matches drew more attention from Luo
than those featuring the Luo Sports Club. The inter-location matches
were played three times a week not at the City Stadium, but on an
ordinary municipal pitch adjoining Kaloleni estate. There was no
charge to spectators, who came from all over the city. The matches
proved a good training ground for talented players who could then
be recruited into a newly constituted Luo Union team. Meanwhile
the Luo Sports Club became weaker. The Luo Union was now
stronger and ready to re-register in the new season for the Kenya
national league.

By late 1967, Mboya is said to have anticipated the imminent
collapse of his Luo Sports Club. More charitably, one might argue

that he wished to end the undeniably vehement friction between Luo. In either event, he tried to arrange for the main Luo Union officials (Opondo, Dange, Ramogo, and Ogutu) to meet those of the Luo Sports Club (Oiro, Nyandega, and Ager). No private meeting was agreed to, and so the Luo Union called a general meeting in Kaloleni Hall of all Luo in Nairobi.

Two issues were voted on. First, a new set of officials were elected onto the Luo Sports Club. The former were deposed and the new ones included existing members of the Luo Union. The second issue was to decide on the actual name of this soccer club within the Luo Union. Three names were proposed: the existing Luo Sports Club (LSC); Luo Union (LU), and a completely new name, Gor Mahia, based on a traditional Luo war hero and magician (*jabilo*) and meaning "Gor who dares". The Luo Union received most votes, Gor Mahia second, and Luo Sports Club last. While this clearly reinforced general withdrawal of support for the faction once associated with Mboya, it raised the old question as to whether a name like Luo Union was too "tribalistic". Most Luo present were persuaded that this was a danger. Others argued that in other towns, the names of local teams included the word "Luo", and that, for many younger Luo, a name like Gor Mahia meant very little. But the fear of being dubbed a "tribalist" team eventually prompted general agreement to use Gor Mahia. Thereafter a short period of quite clearly discernible unity characterized Luo internal politics.

First, a strong Gor Mahia team was easily recruited from players in the inter-location championship. Gor Mahia and Luo Union each retained separate officials but the football club was now regarded as under the wing of the Luo Union, and not in opposition to it. The strength of Gor Mahia now attracted many more Luo spectators to the City Stadium than had its predecessor in the national league, particularly in matches with the ethnic rivals, Abaluyia United, or Maragoli Club. This inevitably detracted from the attendances at the inter-location matches. So, in June 1968, this intra-Luo competition was changed to include a much smaller number of teams based on administrative divisions rather than locations. There was no disagreement with this decision.

A second expression of Luo unity in Nairobi at this time was the decision early in 1968 of both Odinga and Mboya to attend a Luo Union meeting jointly, and each to present a cup to be played for in two inter-location (a little while later, inter-divisional) champion-ships.[1] They each preached collaboration among Luo, explicitly re-ferring to the need among Luo to take advantage of the opportunities to buy and manage shops and small businesses in Nairobi, many of which had suddenly been vacated by Asians as a result of the govern-ment's drive to Africanize petty commerce. A third explicitly stated development, which was stated by Luo themselves to express their unity, was the decision to leave the running of Gor Mahia in the hands of recognized elders (jodongo), who were reputed to have had relevant experience and some of whom I had, indeed, known in Kam-pala in the early sixties, where they had also, as younger men, helped reorganize Luo soccer from the fifties onwards. One special qualifi-cation attributed to these elders in Nairobi, as to other elders in Kam-pala, was their understanding of the appropriate magic and medi-cines necessary for success in soccer. They might be referred to as jobilo themselves ("war magicians"), and/or they might summon the help of diviner-doctors (the ajuoga referred to above), and, finally, the correspondence was always being made between this involvement in the use of magic and Gor himself, reputedly a jabilo of extraordinary talents.

Why should Luo in Nairobi adopt this united front? There were increasingly glaring differences among them of income, and oppor-tunity, and the proportions of jobless, homeless, wifeless, and family-less were growing all the time. They could hardly be more internally divided by socio-economic factors.

The promised availability of jobs and homes following the ex-pected departure of Asians was, as mentioned above, a main factor. It was recognized that Kikuyu were numerically well placed to take over, as indeed they did for the most part, and that Luo should not compete with each other but with non-Luo.

A second factor prompting unity was the disqualification of KPU candidates at the Nairobi city council elections in July 1968. The disqualification was defended by the returning officers on legalistic grounds (i.e. that the ballot papers had been spoiled) but, not sur-prisingly, few if any Luo accepted this explanation and saw it, rather, as an attempt to smother the growth of the KPU. Much later, in late 1969, the KPU was indeed banned, ostensibly on the grounds of sub-version and following the overwhelming defeat of a KANU candidate

[1] Odinga's was to be played on a points basis, and Mboya's as a knock-out competition.

by a KPU one in what became for Luo everywhere the famous by-election for the rural constituency of Gem in Luoland (Okumu, 1969, and referred to in the last chapter).

The show of unity was not long-lived. Early in 1969, Gor Mahia suffered its first setbacks. Luo generally gave two reasons for this. First, that the elders had been usurped by younger officials, who lacked the necessary magic, and that the spurned elders had used their magic against the team. Second, that a prominent member of the deposed Luo Sports Club faction had been employing a diviner-doctor (*ajuoga*) to secure the team's recent "inexplicable" defeats. As one Luo put it, "In recent matches against Feizal and against Kisumu Hot Stars, Gor Mahia was in front and good scoring chances kept coming its way, but it still did not win because magic was being used against it." The power of elders must be respected.

Family and lineage idioms of restricted, internal debate

We see from the account that factionalism was reasserting itself. But, this time, it first became expressed not as the Luo Sports Club versus the Luo Union but, within the Gor Mahia club, of Easterners (*jo wang' chieng'*) against Westerners (*jo podho chieng'*).

Two former members of the now disbanded Luo Sports Club went to the Chairman of the Luo Union to complain that, by their estimation, K£880 (*sic*) of the money held in trust by the Gor Mahia officials was missing. They further complained that the Gor Mahia was dominated by Easterners, which they specified as including in this case people from the locations embracing Nyakach, Kano and parts of South Nyanza (i.e. including some Southerners). They appealed to the Chairman of the Luo Union, a very respected elder from Western Kenya, known by the honorific Luo title of *Ker*, for an enquiry into the loss. *Ker* suggested that a general meeting of Luo in Nairobi should decide on this and should, if the Luo wanted it, elect new officials for Gor Mahia. The meeting was set for the 3rd July, 1969.

It should be noted here that the two complainants were, respectively, from Seme location and from Kendu in South Nyanza and so were, in effect, complaining of domination by a wider group, the so-called Easterners, of whom they themselves might in some contexts

be regarded as members. Seme location was, however, only transferred from the western Siaya district to the eastern Kisumu district
after independence. Thereafter Seme people have expressed ambivalence as to whether they wish to regard themselves as *jo podho
chieng'*, Westerners, to which they have become accustomed, or as
jo wang' chieng', Easterners. Inevitably, Seme people tend to be
situationally selective in their affiliations. Similarly, people from
South Nyanza, while subscribing to the view that the main division
among Luo in Nairobi is between Easterners and Westerners,
are themselves so few in the city that they are able to attach
themselves to either half according to situation. Persons whose ambivalent regional origins and identities allow them to straddle
opposed sections of a society in this way have the potential for claiming non-regional, unitary qualities of leadership, like prophets in
many religious movements. With this factor in mind, I believe, on
the basis of discussion and observation, that the two complainants'
attack on the domination of Gor Mahia by Easterners was the prelude
to the offer of their own leadership of all Luo in Nairobi regardless
of district of origin. It is important also to note that, as I have indicated above, Tom Mboya himself also had this quality of non-
regional identification by virtue of his having been brought up outside Luoland and later being clearly urban based. The two complainants were themselves former officials in "Mboya's" Luo Sports
Club, and it is difficult to avoid the conclusion that they, with Mboya,
represented an element among Luo in Nairobi which does not fit
neatly into the overarching contemporary classification of Luo into
Easterners and Westerners.

They do, indeed, represent a "random" element which can be said
to parallel other such elements: the Luo who refuses to join KPU;
the leader(s) of a breakaway lineage association; or, at a domestic
level, the man who resists his family's attempts to get him to marry a
second wife; or the unmarried woman who resists pressures to become someone's second wife; the Luo accused of favouring friends
over kin; and the man accused of disrupting rules of family seniority
among Luo in Nairobi and so bringing *chira* upon his wife and
children.

I mention all these as conceptual parallels, because Luo themselves
will frequently exemplify one by reference to another. The meeting
of the 3rd July, 1969, was an excellent example of how the random

element was both referred to in different ways and eventually tamed through incorporation in a collective Luo demand for order.

The events of the meeting, which I attended, were as follows:
1. The two complainants arrived at the meeting very early and, together with supporters, sat in the chairs put out beforehand for the officials of the Gor Mahia.
2. The hall gradually filled to capacity. There was a striking air of confusion. People asked each other whether the Gor Mahia leaders had been changed.
3. As is customary, the "real" officials of Gor Mahia came only after the packed hall had been waiting for some time. The chairman strode to the rostrum with hardly a moment's hesitation. Pointing at the self-installed "leaders", he firmly asked the assembly whether or not it wished them to conduct the meeting, to which the cry was an equally firm "No".
4. The pretenders refused to move and the next five minutes were taken up with having to eject them physically from the hall. One Luo in the hall commented that though they had done well to raise the question of possible embezzlement and of district monopoly (i.e. by Easterners) within Gor Mahia their whole strategy was wrong, and that it is not customary for Luo to usurp one another in this crude manner.
5. The secretary then said Christian prayers (a normal procedure by which meetings are opened), and an agenda was announced, which included items on the suspected embezzlement and on the question of whether there should be an election of Gor Mahia officials.
6. The chairman then respectfully asked *Ker*, the chairman of the Luo Union in Nairobi, to speak. At this point, the ejected pretenders were allowed back into the hall and quietly joined the assembly. *Ker* preached unity among all Luo, emphasizing that the contestants were all his "children" and that he had absolute parental authority over them. As such, he affirmed that an election of Gor Mahia officials would only take place at the next annual general meeting at his command. He selected a committee to enquire into the alleged embezzlement (which was, later, never proved) in place of the current atmosphere of accusation and counter-accusation by what he referred to as rival factions based on the old Luo Sports Club/Luo Union differences. *Ker* then left the hall.
7. The Luo Union, represented by *Ker*, had been seen satisfactorily

to perform its mediatory role in an argument between rival factions affecting a subordinate Luo association in Nairobi. The chairman of Gor Mahia condemned the two complainants for subversion and disruption, to the agreement of the assembly which loudly called the more prominent of the two, "traitor Tshombe[1]—X (i.e. the name of the complainant)". To this X managed to retort that his sole aim had been to awaken Luo to the alleged embezzlement and to stir up Luo interest in their own affairs.

8. The final phase of the meeting took the form of the competitive donation of cash, referred to as *gisungore* or *gichamo nyadhi*, this time between divisions rather than locations or lineages as would be the case in other, usually smaller and sectional, meetings of Luo.

The chairman of Gor Mahia appealed for money, ostensibly to buy oranges for the players to eat at half-time in their matches. He chose a well-known orator-cum-cajoler from Kisumo location to exhort and comment. The first donor was a clerk of average socio-economic status, not especially well-known, who was from Bondo division (Uyoma location), a Westerner. He paid Shs. 20/–. He was followed by another Bondo man (from Asembo location), this time a well-known senior administrative officer in Nairobi University who paid rather more. The commentator expressed admiration for Bondo and called on the assembly to recognize it as the "husband" of all other divisions, having now "married" (into) them all. Then, two people from Nyando division, Easterners, again of average and the other of high socio-economic status from Kano and Nyakach locations respectively, paid in excess of these sums. The commentator thereupon praised Nyando and referred to it as now "ruling the house", with the implication that it now had the most wives and, from them, the most children. The commentator declared that no one in the hall was now allowed to speak without Nyando's permission. A Bondo man from Sakwa then paid a larger sum, once again incurring the commentator's praise in the idiom of changing power relations achieved through accumulating wives. These competitive donations and banter continued until the chairman of Gor Mahia called a stop after a quarter of an hour, as smaller and smalled sums trickled in. Shs. 424/– were

---

[1] The former Prime Minister of Zaire (then Congo Kinshasa) who had died the previous month and who in 1960 had announced the secession of the mineral-rich Katanga province in which the multi-national (mainly Belgian) corporation, Union Minière du Haut-Katanga, had considerable interests, and where Tshombe himself was born.

contributed by between 200 and 300 people, some of them paying very little. This is, in fact, a small sum compared with others raised at meetings called to discuss external crises affecting Luo as a whole. It was, after all, ostensibly only for buying oranges. At the meeting held after Mboya's assassination, to which I shortly turn, the issue was infinitely greater and the sum much larger.

Even this limited competitive display clearly involved rivalry between Easterners and Westerners, even though, at this meeting, the commentator did not explicitly refer to it, identifying instead the donors' divisions. The meeting had, after all, reached for consensus by repudiating the complaint that Gor Mahia was run by Easterners to the exclusion of Westerners.

The point is that though the donations were referred to by the commentator as alternating between different administrative divisions, which they did, underlying them all was still the general alternation between Eastern and Western divisions, as with the initial donations which I described. Since donors are not only of different divisions, but are also of different locations, then, within this general alternation of Easterners and Westerners, we have a clear example of a segmentary framework in operation. Many other examples could be given of this, including ones at the meetings of location associations, in which alternation at different levels actually occurs between exogamous lineages, again in the polygynous idiom of "paying for wives" and "ruling the house".

Further, it may be noted in the meeting which I have just described that in the initial reciprocal prestations, at least, there is a tendency for donors to alternate between average and high socio-economic status. The later, much smaller offerings will include some made by men of low socio-economic status. The whole institution of *gisungore*, then, both gives expression to and yet accommodates two principles of contemporary Luo social organization: on the one hand the different segmentary levels by which Luo continue to organize marriage and their associations; on the other hand their internal socio-economic divisions. The first legitimates divisions among Luo because they are seen to occur within a customarily accepted framework of Luo segmentation. As a legitimizing principle, it rests on some degree of collective approval. The second, that of division by socio-economic status, may evince private and personal admiration for, say, the self-made man of wealth. But, in the urban context of joblessness and

homelessness, no one is likely to speak up at a formal **Luo meeting**
and publicly express approval for a continuing division of Luo society
by socio-economic status. For Luo will recognize quite openly that it
is precisely over discrepant incomes, jobs, and education, that quarrels among them arise. The debate is, in the end, a restricted one,
whose course and conclusion are highly predictable.

Family and lineage idioms of political speech

We should at this point note the ease with which factionalism had
been erased at the Gor Mahia meeting of the 3rd July, 1969, and the
conciliatory yet authoritative role played by *Ker*, the Luo Union
chairman. There is little doubt that, with an increasingly heightened
political consciousness due to the events which I mentioned concerning the fate of KPU and its followers, this was indeed a period of
relative internal Luo unity. It is also interesting to note that, at the
meeting, the old factionalism involving the Luo Sports Club, associated with Tom Mboya, and the Luo Union itself, associated with
Odinga, was effectively declared dead. Neither Mboya nor Odinga
were present nor were they hardly referred to.

It is therefore ironic that the second day after the meeting, on
Saturday, 5th July, Tom Mboya was assassinated, at the very point
when the two Luo factions expressed through the rivalry between
him and Oginga had fallen into abeyance.

A few days later, on the 7th July, the Luo Union, chaired by *Ker*,
held probably its most emotional and heavily attended meeting to
date. This proved to be a dramatic collective Luo response to the
assassination. Kaloleni Hall was packed with, as a conservative esti-
mate, some 2,000 Luo, all males, and many more thousands outside.
One newspaper report suggested that "almost the entire Luo population of the capital gathered in and around the hall. . . ." (*Daily
Nation*, 8th July, 1969, p. 13), and, from observation, I do not regard
this as greatly exaggerated as regards adult males (some 25,000? out
of a total Luo population in Nairobi of 62,865 in 1969).

The stated objectives of the meeting were (a) to raise money for
an appropriately ceremonial repatriation of Mboya's body from
Nairobi to Rusinga Island, his birthplace in Luoland; and (b) to ar-

range to discover the assassin's identity through customary means, including the use of Luo diviner-doctors (*ajuoga*).

There were two main speeches. The first by *Ker*, the Luo Union chairman, was again conciliatory and urged Luo not to take the law into their own hands. This referred to fights which had broken out in Nairobi between Luo and Kikuyu immediately after news of the assassination, for many Luo assumed that the assassin must be a Kikuyu. As in the last meeting, *Ker* preached unity, ironically against a background of shouts from the hall of *"Dume"* (Swahili for "bull"), referring to the sign given by supporters of KPU, to which Mboya had been so resolutely opposed but which had steadily been acquiring almost total Luo support. *Ker* managed to quell most of the shouting by appealing to his role as the respected elder of their community in Nairobi. But the hall remained unsettled and individuals continued to call for some kind of immediate action to discover the assassin.

At this point *Ker* called the then perhaps third most politically important Luo in Kenya, Achieng Oneko, the publicity secretary of the KPU. As a younger man, Oneko had himself played a significant part in the independence struggle against the British (see Odinga, 1969, numerous references). He was not much older than Mboya but now politically akin to Odinga, and his apparent heir. His intervention was appropriate, for, with skilful rhetoric and style, he calmed the crowd by declarations subtly turned into proposals. First, he declared that Odinga himself was going to spend the night at Mboya's house, said to be a customary act of respect by one important elder for another. Oneko put this forward as a demonstration of current Luo unity. We can argue also that, by unambiguously conferring the status of "elder" on Mboya, who was one month short of 39 years of age at his death, this "customary" act lessened the otherwise most obvious and talked-about difference between the two rivals, that of age. Not only was Odinga nearly 58 at the time, but he had himself played a major role in building up the Luo Union from an organization based only on Nairobi in 1946, to one with branches throughout East Africa, alongside the commercial development of the Luo Thrift and Trading Corporation (Odinga, 1969, pp. 86–7).

Secondly, and even more subtly, Oneko reincorporated Mboya in the Luo "moral" community. That is to say, without specifically referring to it he played on the sentiment that many Luo had expressed before his death that Mboya had "forgotten" his fellow Luo by refusing to join the KPU and by attacking it as a "tribalist" political party. Oneko brought Mboya "back" to the Luo by the following words: "When a child is born, he or she belongs to the father or mother, and when adult he belongs to the country [*piny*] [i.e. leaves the home], but when he dies he returns to his father's and mother's land [*gweng'*]. So it is with Mboya. He was ours when young, and when he became adult he became Kenya's Man [with an emphasis justifying the capital M and certainly implying eventual succession to Kenyatta's presidency]. Now he is back in our hands. We know what to do. We must raise money to send him home, . . . We must also pay our best diviner-doctor [*ajuoga*] to lead our own, independent 'commission of enquiry' [English term used, i.e. in addition to that set up by the Kenya government]." Oneko sat down.

After this moral reincorporation of Mboya among Luo, there was now no contradiction between the tribute paid to Mboya and the even more vociferous cries of *"Dume!"*. The speech itself was replete with double-meaning and word-play which are lost in the translation from DhoLuo into English. The contrasting terms *piny* and *gweng'* are the best example in the abstract I have given. *Piny* can refer to a location (i.e. sub-tribe), for which *oganda* is also used. But *piny* can also refer to Luoland as a whole and, by implication, the Luo people. It was used in the title, *piny owacho* (literally, "the land says", i.e. "the Luo people say"), of the early Luo political movement mentioned above. At a third, even wider level, *piny* can also be used to refer to Kenya as a whole, or even the whole world, both in a physical or metaphorical sense. In my earlier work among Luo in Kampala I noted the apparently key use in an important meeting of the phrase, *piny ok'ong'e*, "the world is not known", i.e. that life is full of ups and downs (Parkin, 1969, p. 208). By contrast, *gweng'* refers to the land occupied and worked by a family and lineage, for which the term is otherwise *dhoot*. Southall (1952, p. 27) puts the contrast thus: "It is when they have the territorial aspect of a *dhoot* particularly in mind that the Luo refer to it as *gweng'* (pl. *gwenge*). The basic connotation is land, but the social group occupying the land is always implicit in the term *gweng'*." So, a generation after Southall's study, in the middle of a modern, rapidly growing city, among men most of whom have spent most of their lives outside their rural areas of birth or origin, a speech decrying the loss of an international figure turns to key lexical contrasts of this kind to express the sentiment of tragedy.

J

It seems legitimate to interpret this contrast, and the accompanying remarks and parallels in the speech, as indicating a contrast in Luo cultural ideas between the two spheres of domestic (*gweng'*) and politico-jural (*piny*) relationships (Fortes, 1959). Further to this, and taking into account the total context of Luo segmentary social organization, as I have described it, we can also view the two terms as comprising its minimal and maximal segmentary levels. Again, a quotation from Southall (1952, p. 27) illustrates this: "When the Luo have a territorial unit in mind as being the most inclusive of its kind, . . . they refer to [it] as *piny* [country] rather than *gweng'*." (My bracketed substitution.)

Alongside this use of the two terms, there is another contrast deriving from the parable-like content of the speech. Mboya is characterized as a son who after leaving the natal home goes out to the "country" beyond even Luoland to become Kenya's Man, but finally returns to his natal home. *Piny* has here a second superimposed meaning of a "country" (i.e. Kenya) which is beyond Luoland and, in the context of everything else that is being said, alien. Mboya, like the prodigal son, takes to *piny* in this sense; incurs the disfavour of many Luo in his departure including that of the great elder Jaramogi himself (Odinga); yet returns to the Luo elders and the unambiguous Luo roots of *gweng'*. In other words, *gweng'* wins out over *piny* in its extended sense: Luo family and lineage impose order on youthful and random departure from customary Luo expectations. Once again, we see the public expression of approval by elders for specific as against general segmentation.

Appropriately, *Ker* then called for lavish contributions through the competitive *gisungore*, initially aimed as usual at the mock acquisition on many "wives", with the names of a donor's division *and* location called out. Shs. 2,700/– (K£135 or $378) were collected, with individual contributions ranging from Shs. 100/– to 10 cents. Additional sums were collected after the meeting and on subsequent days. *Ker* ended the meeting with a Christian prayer in DhoLuo, which asked God to bless the speeches of the meeting.

It was some months before factionalism among Luo in Nairobi reasserted itself. This time it took the form of Gor Mahia in opposition to the Luo Union, a fundamental switch from the situation at the two previous meetings I have just described in which, as part of the expression of Luo unity, the Gor Mahia officials deferred very markedly to *Ker*, the Chairman of the Luo Union. The first public expression of the new factionalism was at a meeting held on 19th October 1969. A little while afterwards, the KPU was banned by the Kenya government, and Luo public meetings returned for a short while to expressions of unity. The oscillating public expressions of bifactionalism and unity continued thereafter by all accounts. The oscillation is once again reminiscent of the alternation of *gumlao*, "egalitarianism", and *gumsa*, "hierarchy", in highland Burma described by Leach (1954), and here points to a generic feature of societies based on underlying segmentary and egalitarian premises yet confronted by dominant external hierarchies: Shan state systems in the case of highland Burma; an urban socio-economic hierarchy based on increasing wage dependency and urban family settlement, in the case of Luo.

Summary: two paradigms

In the conclusions to the last chapter I introduced a distinction between socio-economic and generational status. I showed how the segmentary pyramid of Luo ethnic associations in Nairobi is based on a combination of these two statuses. Elders, who tend also to be polygynists, monopolize leadership positions in the lineage and location associations by straddling both. In this way they have access to and control information on eligible and profitable marriages. At the same time these elders are above the socio-economic average and include those who have lived and worked longest in Nairobi or other towns and whose jobs are relatively secure. The general relevance of socio-economic factors is also apparent in the tendency for lineage association members to be of lower status than those of location associations.

The membership of the Luo Union, by contrast, encompasses a broad spectrum of socio-economic status. This is largely a matter of definition, however, for all Luo are regarded, and normally regard themselves, as members of the Luo Union, differentiating among themselves only in the degree of active involvement. For the same reason Luo of different age ranges, and monogamists and polygynists, are accommodated within the general and active membership.

Looking at the Luo Union and its activities as a whole, we find these broad ranges of income, occupation, and age or seniority in many ways represented as socio-economic status on the one hand, and generational status on the other. For example, sometimes a leader seems to achieve his recognition by virtue of his high-ranking job and superior education, but sometimes he or another leader, who is not necessarily of high socio-economic status, makes public appeals to Luo on the basis of his seniority as an elder. In location associations, which are the next tier down in the pyramid from the Luo Union, socio-economic and generational status may also alternate as idioms of appeal and authority. But the essentially rural localization of lineage clusters denoting their urban membership places a greater premium on legitimacy incurred through generational seniority. In lineage associations, the emphasis is even more marked in favour of generational seniority: thus, even when, say, a prosperous Member of Parliament plays an active role in a lineage association, he presents himself as an elder first and foremost, in one or two cases being obliged to stretch the notion of "elderhood" beyond what is normally acceptable.

Though variable, then, the contrast between socio-economic and generational status has an underlying conceptual significance at all the segmentary levels of the Luo associations. Luo talk about this contrast in a number of different ways. For example, the word *sunga* ("a boaster/proud/arrogant man") is normally a term of disapproval confined in its use to gossip or conversation between two or three people. In Nairobi, it almost invariably denotes an individual's socio-economic success, variously shading into condemnation of a man as a "snob" or "upstart". However, *gisungore* ("*they* are boasting/lavishly competing with each other") normally refers to the public donations made in a spirit of approved rivalry at Luo association meetings by representatives of administrative divisions, locations or lineages, for the purpose of some collective interest or rural self-help enterprise. The activity is regarded as requiring the support of Luo elders, as "referees" or even as "treasurers" and is dramatized as the accumulation of many wives, children, and domestic control.

The contrast between the socio-economic and generational aspects of status is most poignantly and publicly expressed among Luo at Luo Union meetings. For this reason, in this chapter, I analysed in detail a succession of events and public meetings of Luo in Nairobi spanning a few years. I started with a contrast used by Luo to depict factionalism among themselves: that based on alleged political, personal, and generational differences between the two leading Luo political personalities, Oginga Odinga and the late Tom Mboya. I noted that there were never more than two factions at any one time and that the issues on which the factions were based constantly changed as did, to a lesser extent, the membership of factions. Even when the contrast between the two rivals, Odinga and Mboya, ceased to have relevance when the latter died, bifactionalism reappeared. The underlying principle of internal opposition characteristic of all cultural groups is additionally consistent among the Luo with their culturally explicit principle of lineage segmentation and is, for this reason, reinforced in its various expressions.

The contrast between Odinga and Mboya was vivid and may, I suggest, partly explain their respective prominence in public life over and above their individual abilities, for the attributes of the one threw into such glaring contrast those of the other. Odinga was and is unambiguously regarded as an elder. His nickname and "pure" genealogy characterize him as a Luo "father". He visibly supported Luo tradition and transformed his rural political base into a national political party, the KPU, which eventually became identified as a left-wing party of the Luo to the exclusion of other ethnic groups in Kenya. Mboya died before reaching the age of 40. He might be called *moluor* ("he who is eminent/respected") but rarely *jaduong* ("elder"). In contrast, also, were his polyethnic urban, and trade-union political base, his allegedly mixed Luo-Bantu genealogy, his apparent preference for Western life-styles, a manifestly "non-tribal" political philosophy which he expressed as a foremost leader of the ruling party, KANU, and which was essentially capitalist.

I want to emphasize that these are the differences which Luo themselves attribute to Odinga and Mboya, whatever their respective preferences. Taken as idealized summations of characteristics, Odinga represents customary rural Luo culture, while Mboya represents non-customary, urban developments. Abstracted still further, Odinga represents the cultural continuity of the Luo collectivity, and Mboya individualistic and random elements operating beyond Luo cultural constraints.

This interpretation is aptly supported in a speech given at a Luo meeting held immediately after Mboya's assassination. There, Mboya was likened to a son who had left his home lineage (*gweng'*) for the outside world (here, *piny*), but had finally returned to his natal home.

This contrast between cultural order and its random counterpart is reflected also in the two-stage process by which (a) discontented members of an association in Nairobi may form their own association, after what appears to be a random quarrel, but, later, (b) re-establish themselves as part of the Luo segmentary pyramid of associations by justifying their split on the basis of their role as rightful representatives of, say, a particular lineage or location.

We return here, then, to the original distinction between general and specific segmentation. In this chapter, as in previous ones, we have seen the continuing relevance of some key Luo cultural concepts, expressed in such words and verbal contrasts as *chira, nyiego, jaduong', ker, jo podho chieng', jo wang' chieng', sunga, gisungore (gichamo nyadhi), gweng', piny*, as well as a range of kinship and friendship terms of address and reference. The wider referential meanings of some of these terms has been modified. But their "core" meanings still only make full sense if thought of and talked about in terms of the specific Luo system of rural localized polysegmentary lineages. Further to this, it must be emphasized that the continuing relevance of these concepts in Nairobi can be said to be *not* despite, but a partial result of (a) increasing Luo dependence on urban wage employment and (b) their increasing commitment to family "settlement" of the dual rural–urban kind which I have described.

The main point about these concepts, and others, e.g. "marrying many wives" or "ruling the house" (i.e. domestic control) as in *gisungore*, or "neglecting relatives in favour of friends", is that those which are used publicly to discuss political issues both within the Luo community and outside it derive from the domestic domain. To put it simply, to talk politics in the language of domestic achievements, control, and obligations is to confer upon the speaker and his words the greatest likelihood of their being acceptable to a large Luo audience. We saw this clearly in the successful appeal for Luo unity made by *Ker* and Achieng Oneko at the meeting held after Mboya's assassination. *Ker* spoke of the rights and obligations of elderhood, and Achieng Oneko morally reincorporated Mboya among the Luo in an idiom reminiscent of the parable of the prodigal son. Other examples could be given. This is not to say that the use of such words and expressions having primary reference to domesticity are by themselves enough to sway an audience. For a start, the speaker must already be held in high regard. More important than the individual's own status and choice of words, however, is the structural situation in which he or others find themselves speaking. For example, on the one hand the highly emotionally charged meeting following Mboya's assassination contained pleas for internal Luo unity which reflected the sense of Luo tragedy at the loss of a great man. But, on the other hand, that same great man had also for some years been regarded as the representative of a range of forces which "threatened" the Luo cultural continuity: he opposed Odinga and the KPU; he stood for an urban polyethnic constituency and not a rural Luo one; he regarded manifestly "Luo" causes as "tribalist", and so on. In the eyes of senior Luo, Mboya here represented the random nature of general segmentation. The successful public pleas for unity and his posthumous moral reincorporation in the Luo community in the idiom of domestic control can therefore be interpreted as a triumph by specific over general segmentary processes.

Conclusion

In this chapter, then, I have shown how an initial analytical contrast between socio-economic and generational status can be seen to correspond with a range of other emic contrasts, including that based on general and specific segmentation, frequently expressed through key Luo words and expressions. Socio-economic status and general segmentation are both seen by Luo to involve random and relatively unpredictable forces, which may drive individuals away from group expectations and constraints. Generational status and specific segmentation emphasize continuity of customary authority by concensus.

It is this continuity of custom in modern Luo social organization to which I now turn in the next chapter. It can be regarded as the Saussurian *langue* which both regulates and yet is sometimes seen to be threatened by men's and women's unpredicable inventiveness, that is their individual *paroles*. I ask what are the constituent features of Luo culture which provide this continuity. Cultural continuity implies cultural distinctiveness and a level of analytical abstraction which must, for the moment, ignore cultural borrowing and the common underlying links between cognate or neighbouring cultures. Cultural continuity also implies that, since the constituent customs making up any culture are systematically and not randomly related to each other, the culture may be said to enjoy a degree of autonomy, comparable to and indeed interconnected with the autonomy we ascribe to individual ideologies. As Cohen puts it, "In his earlier work, Marx . . . recognized the fact that the symbolic order [i.e. comprising culture and ideology], which he labelled as 'superstructure', was not completely determined by the power order, which he labelled as 'intrastructure', but that it had an autonomy of its own." (1974, p. 135, my bracketed inclusion.) When we conventionally identify a people as sticking tenaciously to their culture, we are ascribing to that culture a high degree of autonomy.

Why do some cultures appear to exhibit more resilience and autonomy than others? Is the answer to be found only in the dialectic relation between a culture and its external social and environmental conditions, or can we identify certain cultural features which are, in any external socio-technical environment, particularly resilient and ideologically autonomous. The Luo in Nairobi can be regarded as exhibiting an intrinsically high degree of cultural autonomy. This is based on an emic logical consistency of three main institutions. That is to say actors interpret the meanings of these three institutions as presupposing each other. One institution is the exchange of valuable bridewealth, which has proved to be equally tenacious under urban as well as rural and "traditional" conditions. Another is polygyny which seems most likely to undergo both formal and substantive change through the efforts of women. Mediating and, so to speak, disciplining these two is that of the Luo segmentary lineage structure which, as we saw in the last chapter on the formation of Luo urban associations, has remarkable ideological flexibility.

8

Cultural autonomy and the status of women

What are the bases of Luo cultural autonomy which I defined, following Nadel (1951, pp. 258–65), in the Introduction and in the previous chapter as the emic logical consistency of institutions recognized by a particular group or groups; and how may we expect this autonomy to "change", i.e. to undergo alteration of its constituent sets of presuppositions governing institutional activities? Here, following Nadel again (1951, pp. 387–8), I must distinguish this view of cultural autonomy from that once followed by proponents of "culture pattern", essentially Gestalt, theory (e.g. Benedict's distinction (1935) between Apollonian and Dionysian "moods" or "biases"; and Kardiner, 1945; Linton, 1945; Opler, 1945; and others). These are studies which deal with a total configuration of "values", one or some of which may assume a disciplinary dominance. This concern with the priority of "values" or "themes" is essentially *psychological* and falls within that sphere that Bateson (1958, pp. 29–33) calls the "ethos" of any cultural group. It is not primarily concerned with the *logical* pattern of institutional presuppositions and activities shared by a group and identified by Bateson as its "eidos". This distinction between ethos and eidos is critical. A concern with different ethoses alone does not lead to any logical classification, for it is only at a subjective level that we, as analysts, can contrast, say, "greed" as a dominant cultural value with "generosity". A concern with cross-cultural analysis of ethoses alone can only lead to "an infinite variety of cultural configurations, each possessed of its own irreducible individuality" (Nadel, 1951, p. 393).

A concern with eidos, however, considers the logical bases of cognitive processes, depicting the classificatory framework within which sentiments are articulated. That is to say, it distinguishes within a culture the alternative but limited possibilities presupposed by a particular institutional activity. Putting this yet another way, it outlines the sequential rules within a particular culture for saying and/or doing things. It is for this reason that Nadel (1951, p. 392) equates Bateson's concept of "eidos" with his own "logical consistency". I suggested in the Introduction that we regard this concept as a cultural group's emic classification of the mutually implied meanings and unintended consequences of its institutional activities. Here, then, we do have some method of making broad cross-cultural contrasts, for what we contrast are not sentiments but systems of classification. As such, they may be regarded as comprehensible in terms of a limited range of logical possibilities, depending on the level of analytical abstraction.

Let me adapt and expand on one of the many examples from the work of generative semanticists to illustrate the essentially "linguistic" nature of this view of cultural logic. I will put the matter simply. G. Lakoff (1971, p. 333) distinguishes between a language speaker's extralingustic presuppositions and the grammar of the language he is speaking. A phrase like, "John told Mary that she was beautiful and then she insulted him", is odd. In the conventional sense it is grammatically perfect but is (or was at the time) culturally inappropriate for Euro-America. But, if we may speculate a little, let us assume that, in order to eliminate all sex-based presuppositions, the women's liberation movement exerted sufficient pressure that it did indeed generally become an insult for a man to call a woman beautiful to her face. In that case the phrase cited above would no longer be semantically inconsistent, just as, in Middle East Islamic culture a woman in purdah might culturally be disposed to reciprocate John's statement with an insult or at least to regard it as such.

Speakers, then, are cultural actors who normally presuppose institutional consistency. But their presuppositions may undergo transformation, as suggested above, and may then figure as contrasts in another culture or at a later period in the same culture. As contrastive features, cultural presuppositions are comprehensible in terms of what Lakoff calls "relative grammaticality", and which we may gloss as the logic of all cultural logics.

The contrast which I have outlined in previous chapters between

(a) specific segmentation as an explicit organizational rule of a particular culture like that of the Luo or Nuer, and (b) general segmentation as an implicit organizational rule of all social life, can be viewed in the same light. Specific segmentation presupposes institutional consistency and a retention of Luo cultural autonomy, while general segmentation presupposes forces which separately and together both threaten this consistency and yet may bring about a radical reformulation of the existing cultural paradigm. The two paradigms may be logically inconsistent with each other in specific situations (e.g. a lineage association among the Luo must be seen and said to split from a parent association along the lines of agnatic descent rather than socio-economic status), but represent logical alternatives rather than inconsistencies at a higher level of abstraction and comparison (e.g. in one culture, or in one particular domain within a culture, associations may split along lineage lines, but in another culture, or cultural domain, it may be customarily acceptable for them to split on the basis of occupational, educational, or wealth differences).

Apart from the example just given, that association splits should be talked about as genealogically consistent rather than as the mere result of differences between richer and poorer men, the socio-economic basis of general segmentation among Luo is further expressed when an individual questions the expectation that he should give preferential treatment to agnates or other relatives over friends. He may also question the value of having more than one wife and many children, few of whom can become highly educated, as against the value of having one wife and fewer children who may, ideally, reach a higher educational standard.

By contrast, a stress on authority by age and on the value of the culturally specific Luo segmentary system of relations go together with a high rate of ethnic endogamy and polygyny. That is to say, elders tend to be polygynists who will have "chosen" their wives on the basis of a segmentary system of exogamous lineages, a system which they perpetuate when it comes to helping choose spouses for their daughters, sons, and wards. This recurrent nature of the system inevitably has the overall effect of retaining Luo women for Luo men and so continuing the very high rate of ethnic endogamy. To break out of this circulatory system would require foregoing valuable bridewealth.[1] Thus, a Luo man pays dearly for rights in his wife, including all rights to children born to her. He is then hardly likely to forego the "repayment" of bridewealth one generation later at his own daughter's marriage to a fellow Luo. He may be perfectly happy not to have to contribute to a son's bridewealth if that son happens himself to be in well-paid employment. But, whether he or his son contributes, one of them will have to, for in this circulatory system the son will have responded to the pressures described in Chapter 2 and chosen a Luo girl whose own father expects bridewealth.

Bridewealth and investment

The continuing Luo stress on generational status and specific segmentation as the legitimate bases of authority rests heavily on the circulatory nature of valuable bridewealth transactions over generations. Had Luo in Nairobi invested "surplus" cash over the years in, say, private enterprises, rather than extra wives (see Chapter 4) as did the Kikuyu, then one may speculate that the cycle of cultural constraints might have been disrupted. But this is really to beg the question of *why* Luo did not, then, invest "surplus" urban incomes more heavily in trade rather than wives during the period of the Kenya Emergency when Kikuyu control of African petty commerce was temporarily withdrawn.

Since the ending of the Emergency in 1959, there has been increasing Kikuyu domination of Nairobi in politics, commerce, education, and white-collar occupations. In fact, as Leys (1975, pp. 201–3) has explained, Kikuyu advances in these spheres go back to their early confrontation with colonial authority, who, in protecting White settler farming, restricted Kikuyu agricultural production. Before then, Kikuyu had a strong tradition of pre-colonial trading and entrpreneurship with the Maasai. Later, in competition with White settlers for agricultural production, their modern capitalist orientation and preponderance among wage workers in Nairobi inevitably gave them political and economic advantages. In spite of the restrictions on Kikuyu during the Emergency, Leys seems to argue that these advantages were sufficiently strong not to be permanently offset

[1] With the partial exception of marriage to the neighbouring Bantu-speaking Luyia, among whom bridewealth is quite valuable and secures comparable rights.

by the restrictions. He suggests that the Swynnerton Plan, which was implemented as an attempt to "pacify" African unrest, in 1954 at the height of the Emergency, was particularly favourable to the Kikuyu. It provided them with capital for growing cash crops like coffee, for licences, and contract work for the government, a trend which continued into the period of independence from 1963. By 1964–5, in the farming areas formerly reserved for white settlers 120 of the 158 cooperatives were composed of Kikuyu farmers. By 1966 Marris and Somerset noted (1971, p. 71), 64 per cent of industrial loans and 44 per cent of commercial loans went to Kikuyu recipients. And, inevitably, in view of their entrepreneurial advances, Kikuyu traders most benefited from the 1967 Trade Licensing Act, which prevented non-citizens (i.c. mainly Asians) from trading in rural areas and the non-central areas of town in an increasing number of goods. As regards education, by 1962, three years after the ending of the Emergency, 56 per cent of Kikuyu children of primary school age had received or were receiving education, compared with 38 per cent of Luo, 34 per cent of Luyia, and 21 per cent of Kamba. The relationship between secondary school education and white-collar wage employment shows similar trends. During the 1960s there was a six-fold increase in secondary school enrolment, while up to 1965 there was a rapid expansion as well as Africanization of white-collar jobs. Kikuyu most took advantage of this development. But from 1965, there was a dramatic decline in the rate at which white-collar jobs were provided. Jobs become even more precious resources of political patronage and the popular view developed more strongly than before that the structure of socio-economic opportunities was controlled on ethnic lines, with the Kikuyu dominant.

In fact, as the dates given above indicate, the seeds of Kikuyu political, commercial, and educational dominance go back to before independence in 1963. The reasons are indeed partly political and economic, e.g. the Swynnerton Plan of 1954 and, before that, confrontation with and, paradoxically, adaptation to the white settler capitalist mode of production. But they are also "cultural" in the sense that the Kikuyu were expert traders with the Maasai before the colonial period, living in a kind of economically and ecologically symbiotic relationship with them. The Kikuyu lived (and live) on small thin ridges of land separated from each other by valleys, and their social organization into small lineages (*mbari*), which easily lost contact with each other after fission, reflected this. The Maasai lived (and live) on the vast open plains of the rift valley. While the Kikuyu grew surplus crops on their fertile hillsides, the Maasai kept surplus cattle, sheep and goats. In the exchange of vegetables and grain for the produce of cattle, the Kikuyu emerged as the dominant traders. It was they who ventured into the Kikuyu–Maasai border-lands, took Maasai wives, and ventured beyond.

It is of course difficult to speculate why the Kikuyu and not the Maasai should dominate, for there are many examples in the world of cattle herders becoming dominant traders in neighbouring agricultural regions. But the argument by Marris and Somerset (1971, pp. 26–9) is convincing. Land was plentiful, and though land rights were granted according to lineage membership, sons could take their share of a father's estate as they became adult. In some areas of Kikuyuland at least, the lineage head could not control how much an ambitious son took of his father's estate. Once they had it, sons were even able to sell or lease land. Though it was customarily possible for the seller to buy his land back, this rarely happened. This highly individualistic pattern of land tenure thus occurred in an area where land was plentiful and so allowed for it. The terrain of fertile hillsides and narrow ridges further permitted lineage fission and settlement on a separate ridge from that of the parent lineages at almost any period of the lineage's growth.

This combination of individualistic land tenure and sale and possible early lineage fission and dispersal are hardly ideal conditions for the formation of an all-embracing system of localized, land-holding segmentary lineages, such as characterized the Luo. For the Luo moved southward through Western Kenya "like a line of shunting trucks, each tribe driving out the one in front of it to seek compensation from one yet further in front. . . ." (Evans–Pritchard, 1965, p. 209), and recording their genealogical relations with each other in largely unambiguous spatial terms. While the Luo present a picture of "perpetual" lineage segmentation, the Kikuyu present one of "drift" lineage segmentation from early times, to use Fox's distinction (1967, pp. 128–30).

How in all this do we distinguish culture from politics and from economics? In what sense are economic and political factors exclusively external to culture? Pre-colonial, and post-colonial factors of all three kinds have interrelated. In the end we are left with different histories of the development of two quite distinct cultures, that of the Luo and that of the Kikuyu, most of whom now *see* themselves as in political and economic competition.

Let me here return to my question of why the Luo did not heavily invest in business in Nairobi during the Emergency instead of continuing to invest in extra wives. From the above it is clear that we are entitled to regard the relative distinctiveness and autonomy of Luo culture as having existed long before most Luo and Kikuyu saw themselves in confrontation as at present. Luo cultural distinctiveness and autonomy has been sharpened by this confrontation, but it was not moulded by it. On the contrary it was already there and has played a dominant part in shaping the Luo people's perception of the causes of what has for them become a diminishing environment of political and economic opportunity.

The question can then be rephrased. The Luo recognize clearly that having two wives enables a man to continue in urban wage employment while retaining a rural home and land. But, in view of the valuable bridewealth required, this is an expensive way of straddling town and country. If the economic gain is sufficient, there is no reason to suppose that other culturally approved methods could not be emphasized instead, e.g. through retired parents or unemployed brothers, between whom conflict is essentially a cultural notion derived from rules of inheritance which could, if people always acted in the most "rational" manner, always be changed to avoid conflict. The East African Asian small businesses owe their strength to extended family cooperation.

But people do not necessarily calculate "rationally" in the same way as each other. Emic rationalities are not just culturally approved ideas held in isolation. They are presupposed by and in turn presuppose other ideas, and frequently require demonstration by deed and word. So, the Luo preference to continue to invest in extra wives and not in trade when the conditions were ripe, and thereafter, has to be seen as one of a mutually reinforcing cycle of institutional preferences, arranged in terms of an internal logic of Luo culture. The logic is not without its weaknesses and contradictions as we shall see.

This cycle of institutional preferences among Luo is their high rate of polygyny, a high value placed on bridewealth (increasingly of cash more than cattle) in exchange for rights over a wife's children, and a rural-urban emphasis on segmentary organization based on a model of rural localized polysegmentary lineages which tends to perpetuate a high rate of ethnic endogamy. Moreover, the Luo have retained these preferences through two main changes of political rivalry and alliance. Immediately before and after independence Luo were allied with Kikuyu and in opposition to another main Kenyan people, the Luyia; and more recently they have clearly been seen to be opposed to Kikuyu, repeating, it seems, a much earlier pattern in Nairobi during the colonial period (Mboya, 1963, p. 71). Thus, from situations both of ethnic strength and ethnic weakness there has been no break in the Luo cycle of institutional preferences. What is also significant is that this cultural resilience and consistency has occurred during increasing urban wage dependency by Luo.

There is some evidence that, during their alliance with Kikuyu during the Kenya Emergency, a few Luo men in Nairobi informally cohabited with unmarried Kikuyu women, whose own menfolk suffered detention or restriction. But the unions were rarely formalized by a customary exchange of bridewealth and so the offspring of these unions remained with their Kikuyu mothers when cohabitation ceased towards the end of the Emergency, and effectively lost contact with their Luo genitors. There are even cases of Luo men taking over market stalls previously run by Kikuyu men then in detention, and of handing them back at the Kikuyu men's return, in whose names apparently the stalls were licensed.

The appropriate strategy for Luo to have continued in these businesses would have been for them to attempt formally to marry into Kikuyu society and then convert such "permanent" marriages into secure trading partnerships. But there are cases then and now showing how much individual Luo may be dissuaded from marrying into cultural groups with regulations relating to the custody of children somewhat different from their own. Similar cases were recorded in Kampala in which Luo men were dissuaded both from marrying Ganda women, whose bridewealth and child custody rules are in striking contrast, and from forming business partnerships with men of the Ganda and culturally similar groups (Parkin, 1969, pp. 97–103). In Nairobi, the Kikuyu and Luo do not contrast in these respects to anywhere near the extent of the Ganda and Luo. But the difference is big enough to be critical.

There is great variation in the value of bridewealth among Kikuyu today. The Kikuyu term for bridewealth may first be glossed as *ruracio*. It may include some goats and heiffers and will certainly include cash, and is frequently exclusively of cash. The girl's father may receive anything from a few hundred to a thousand or more shillings, but this may be drawn out, and may also, but need not, be supplemented by extra amounts, ostensibly according to how much the new husband can afford and in practice as a result of negotiation between himself and his father-in-law. The value of the *ruracio*, then, from the cases I have looked at in Nairobi, is highly variable, and on average considerably less than that of the Luo. In many cases a Kikuyu father-in-law contributes most of the bridewealth he has received towards the couple's wedding expenses or as wedding gifts to them. Increasingly it is the wedding ceremony rather than the actual amount of *ruracio* transacted that is becoming important. The marriage is, however, made customarily "legal", with the man obtaining the right to be called father of his children, by his ceremonially slaughtering the *ngurario* ram. This "childbirth payment" ceremony does not take place until some time after any payment of *ruracio*. A number of the Kikuyu husbands I knew had been married for ten years or so and had children but had not yet slaughtered the *ngurario* ram. Other couples had separated after a few years, irrespective of whether children had been born to them and before the husband had slaughtered the ram. Though the *ruracio* payments are technically recoverable, many men do not bother to do so after separation if these are small amounts.

This variability in the value and customary legal functions of modern Kikuyu bridewealth and the distinction between its *ruracio* and *ngurario* components, lead Luo to believe that marriage with a Kikuyu woman and the rights over any children she produces are based on uncertain foundations. And, indeed, the separation and "divorce" (a concept which nowadays becomes difficult to define in customary terms) rates among Kikuyu are undoubtedly higher, especially in Nairobi.

From direct questioning and from impression, Kikuyu estimates of ideal family size are lower than those of Luo men and women. Kikuyu men and women nowadays also reject polygyny as a worthwhile institution. Given the practical and ideological pressures on Luo men by parents, agnates and, indirectly, other kin and friends to produce many children, and the uncertain foundations, in their eyes, of Kikuyu marriage, it is not surprising that few Luo accepted any possibilities that occurred during the Emergency, nor since that time.

In other words, Luo cultural notions regarding the desirability of more than one wife and many children impinge on individuals and oblige them to forgo potentially profitable trading partnerships with non-Luo. This is the Luo cycle of institutional "preferences" acting as a set of constraints on the individual. Its logic is that (a) a rural localized polysegmentary lineage system presupposes and is presupposed by (b) a high rate of polygyny which, in the resultant competition for scarce women, presupposes (c) transactions of valuable bridewealth in exchange for genetrical as well as sexual and domestic rights in women; and that these three constitute a tenacious syndrome of interrelated phenomena and make for the high degree of Luo cultural autonomy.

Each of these three institutions has of course "changed" in adaptation to increasing urban wage dependency by Luo men in the ways that I have described. But they have not "changed" in their logical relationship to each other. They still are mutually reinforcing. For the logic to be broken, so to speak, one of the three would have to change in such a way that it no longer presupposed the other two. Let me now speculate on the effect of future possible changes on each other.

Constancies of cultural change

LINEAGE POLYSEGMENTATION

Would the Luo polysegmentary lineage principle fade in ideological significance if their increasing rural population and successive fragmentation of land holdings could not be contained within it? As a long-term development this seems likely. But how long-term may this be, for we must recognize the tenacity of the lineage principle to adapt itself. Thus, the Luo response to land registration was different from that of the Kikuyu: whereas the Kikuyu accepted the administrative consolidation of dispersed land fragments with little regard for lineage (mbari) connections, Luo elders insisted that wherever possible neighbouring parcels of land, even if registered in the names of individual family heads, should be allocated with due regard at least to close lineage ties (Sytek, 1965, 1966). This different Luo response from those of other Kenyan peoples has often been noted (see Dupré, 1968, pp. 81, 91, 92, 176 for references). The precise Luo terminological distinction between *dhoot,* the abstract *idea* of a lineage which is not necessarily localized, and *gweng',* a lineage which *is* localized, may well have facilitated this distinctive Luo response. For all the differences between segmentary lineage systems identified by Middleton and Tait (1958, pp. 1–32), the essential common features "are the 'nesting' attribute of segmentary series and the characteristic of being in a state of continual segmentation and complementary opposition" (ibid., p. 7). Among many segmentary lineage-based peoples, this pyramidal structure of different levels of lineage inclusion and exclusion provides an abstract but simple mnemonic containing potentially complex taxonomic information about how to order people in relation to each over wide distances of time and space and over a range of changing local conditions. It suits agriculturalists and mixed farmers who expand their occupation of territory while retaining coordinate lineage relations with each other, as well as nomadic or transhumant peoples such as the Nuer, Somali, and Bedouin.

What is relevant for my analysis is that this formula also systematically prescribes relations between people who are socio-economically differentiated as well as geographically dispersed and who may number millions. As compared with the classificatory formulae required for cultures undergoing "drift" lineage segmentation or for those with non-unilineal descent groups, this pyramidal lineage mnemonic may therefore rank as one of mankind's great cultural inventions, for it can impose considerable classificatory order and consistency over large numbers of people through relatively little conceptual effort.

Among modern Luo, the segmentary lineage principle is thus a ready-made classificatory mode of political mobilization. Politicians use it for recruiting followers as we saw in previous chapters, for its all-embracing segmentary character gives it an ideological existence which operates beyond and above immediate territorial attachments. The widespread movement of Luo between and within towns all over East Africa can remain ordered by this all-embracing segmentary character. Finally, and most importantly, it helps sustain parents' and elders' control over younger Luo. For, through elders' unchal-

lenged knowledge of exogamic boundaries and genealogical relationships, they may "guide" younger men's and women's marriage
"choices". In short, then, the Luo segmentary lineage principle seems
likely to operate, though in modified ways, for a long time yet in
both urban and rural conditions.

THE HIGH POLYGYNY RATE

Let me now look at the second important institutional sphere making
up Luo cultural autonomy, namely the high polygyny rate. This
would seem to be very much shorter-lived. It will persist only so long
as young men and women continue to accept it. With many young
women married to older men, young men are obliged to marry on
average eight years later than women of their own age. Young men
do sometimes express a preference for one wife and few children. But,
as I explained in Chapter 2, they portray quite incorrectly the second
and subsequent younger wives of older polygynists as likely before
marriage to have had sexual relations in town with many younger
men like themselves. This view unintendedly depicts "town girls"
generally as of this kind and therefore as unsuitable as their own first
wives, and so ensures a steady supply of young wives for older polygynists. In other words, young men themselves create and subscribe
to an urban "myth" which has the consequence of perpetuating
polygyny.

Polygyny is not, then, effectively opposed by young men. And yet,
under modern conditions, it is difficult to envisage formal polygyny
continuing beyond, say, a couple of generations. It may then be followed by formal monogamy plus plural "marriage" arrangements
of an informal kind unaccompanied by bridewealth transactions.
Goody (1973, p. 179) cites cases given by Clignet (1970, p. 31) from
other parts of Africa in which urban polygyny has in fact increased,
and concurs with Clignet's view that, in spite of this increasing rate,
the education of women to a relatively high standard is the factor
most likely to reduce it eventually. I think that this may also apply
to the Luo. But it does not fully apply to the Kikuyu. Why is there
this possible difference?

Early educational facilities in Central Province, Kenya, may indeed be partly responsible for the reduction in the polygyny rate
among the Kikuyu over the last couple of generations. The Kikuyu

household heads in Kaloleni in Nairobi are almost all monogamous, as they are elsewhere in the city. Some households are headed by women of independent means—the so-called matrifocal family units (Nelson, unpublished, 1977). Many of these women have little or no education. Some of them were among the earliest to settle independently in Nairobi, and so in their case increased education was not, by itself, responsible for the reduced polygyny rate and eventual rejection even of formal monogamy. A second set of causal factors may be the increase in rural population in Central Province, family and lineage land fragmentation, some landlessness, and, latterly, family dispersal during the Kenya Emergency. But we must note also how the cultural definition of Kikuyu women's status contrasted in some respects with that of Luo women. This contrast takes us, temporarily, into a further discussion of bridewealth differences between the two peoples.

Among the Luo the payment of bridewealth did and still does secure an unambiguous transfer of all genetricial and uxorial rights in a woman from her natal to her husband's agnatic descent group, resulting in her complete and, again, unambiguous incorporation in it. Among the Kikuyu, the very semantic distinction between the two payments at marriage which I outlined earlier in this chapter, namely the uxorial payment (*ruracio*) as distinct from the childbirth one (*ngurario*), mirrors the element of ambiguity in Kikuyu women's status as reproducers of children for men. The distinction explicitly raises the question: should the woman produce for her husband's agnate, or, if he fails to make the childbirth payments, for her own natal descent group? The Luo make no such initial distinction. At divorce when the bridewealth is returned to the husband's family, the Luo do make proportionate deductions for any children produced by the wife during the marriage, which they then keep. But otherwise they see bridewealth, any of the terms for which (e.g. *dhok* (cattle), or *pesa* (cash) *keny; nyombo;* and, according to Evans–Pritchard (1965, p. 238), *miloha*) cover payment for both uxorial and childbirth rights, as facilitating an unambiguous transfer of a woman's reproductive power from one group of men to another.

The semantic distinction among the Kikuyu offers them a wider range of interpretation as to the destiny of these reproductive powers or at least the timing of their transfer, as some of my brief examples indicated. Going further, it can be argued that the distinction has the potential for introducing not only a customarily acceptable ambiguity but also negotiability regarding a woman's uxorial as distinct from reproductive role. Men might traditionally do the negotiating but the split nature of the marriage payment meant that the Kikuyu wife might, for some time until the childbirth payment was made, be neither fully incorporated in her husband's descent group nor fully disassociated from her natal one. This betwixt-and-between status surely offered the woman herself a chance to play one descent group off against the other, thereby giving her some degree of control over her own negotiable status. Fitting this into a wider context of, first, pre-colonial entrepreneurship and mobility among Kikuyu men as I described above, and, later, the dramatic political and economic effects of land loss to white farmers and forced physical dispersal during the Emergency, we can see the further opportunities open to Kikuyu women for pursuing trade and for living relatively independently of their menfolk. Nelson reports that even as early as the beginning of this century, independent Kikuyu women were living in Nairobi (personal communication, and see also Bujra, 1975, p. 217).

I would suggest that these cultural political and economic factors combined to give Kikuyu women the power, especially when they moved into trade on a large scale in recent years, to reject polygyny. Their rejection of polygyny was not especially articulated by the most educated among them. Rather, it was rejected because women achieved the economic rather than simply verbal power to do so.

Among Luo women, even though they have engaged in rural trade for generations, the nexus of political, economic, and cultural factors is quite different, as I have outlined, and men have generally retained control over the unambiguous definition of women's status. I have shown in various chapters that this control is to a large extent expressed through the illocutionary force of formalized speech at particular events. It may therefore be through a countering power of verbal argument acquired through superior education that Luo women are most likely to spearhead any significant rejection of polygyny and so redefine their own statuses, possibly within new or additional modes of cohabitation. Individual cases from Nairobi illustrate this, but they refer still to only a small minority of Luo women who have senior secondary education.

Nevertheless, the few cases we have may be pointers to the future, for they illustrate how superior education for Luo women is more than simply a means to a job. It also gives them access to a power of verbal argument which can circumvent the more restricted logic of time-hallowed customary argument. The first case below illustrates some of this power but also shows, paradoxically, that educated women may still compete with each other on the basis of assumptions of the worthwhileness of traditional notions of co-wife seniority. The second case shows further that educational differences among women can create disputes among them which, again paradoxically, are reconciled only through appeals by other women referees to the domestic virtues of the status of wife. That a wife's education is seen by both men and women as a potential usurper of men's customary authority over women comes out in both cases. It is also evident in an observation I make below of a man who is torn between giving his wife professional training and his fear of the independence this may bring her, and who is then pressured, anyway, into taking a second wife rather than invest in his first wife's further education.

Case 1: The potential of women's verbal argument

Otieno (a pseudonym), a man with senior secondary education, from Alego location, married a girl with the same level of education from Gem in 1958. They had a church wedding as well as a customary marriage. Otieno went in 1960 on a scholarship to Spain to study for a degree. He left his wife in Nairobi with their two children, where she continued to teach at a primary school. Though they wrote to each other consistently during the husband's four years' absence, the wife did not tell him that she had two new children by other men, a fact which he discovered on his return to Nairobi in 1964. She also managed to keep the fact from her own and her husband's parents. During their visits to Nairobi from the rural home, she always arranged for the children to stay with a non-Luo woman-friend. Informants insist that the wife did not, however, attempt to hide them from her husband when he came back. As they put it, "she did not fear him". The husband angrily ordered her back to her rural home. Members of his family and other agnates in Nairobi expressed sympathy but urged him to recognize that "according to Luo traditions" the children (a boy and girl) were his and, though the family might undergo purification with *manyasi* medicine, they were too valuable to "throw away" and that, anyway, he could not expect his wife, left alone in Nairobi, to "endure" his four years' absence without "sleeping" with other men. They argued that she was not unhappy in the marriage. The couple were then ostensibly reconciled within a month of his arriving back from Spain. The wife had played an important role in arguing that having children in his absence was indeed in accordance with Luo custom, for she herself regarded them as his. She also denied precise knowledge of their biological paternity.

Then Otieno suggested to his wife that they visit their respective parents in their rural homes. He loaded all his wife's and their children's clothes and other personal effects into his newly bought car. But instead of driving first to his own parents, he went instead to his parents-in-law. They were shocked to learn of the two new children. The husband insisted that the wife and all four children stay at the parents-in-law's home to await further discussion of the affair between himself and the two respective families, but excluding the wife. The girl's parents agreed and considered this proper, "for it was not the wife who had received the bridewealth, nor had she paid any". The wife herself was also shocked by this, having thought that they were reconciled. She was literally speechless. The husband left for his own parents' rural home. The girl's own father admonished her severely, arguing that, if the husband wanted to divorce her and demand his bridewealth back, then she must marry whichever man (or one of them) who had produced the additional children.

The husband's comments on reaching his own parents' homestead are particularly interesting. They asked him where his wife was. He said: "I have been thinking that I should marry but have not yet found a suitable one for marriage. That is one reason why I am here, to arrange for one to be found". The parents repeated their question, this time saying, "But where is *mikayi* [i.e. the first wife]? He replied: "But I have never been married. The one to whom you refer was not really a wife. She was a false one and is in her own home, with some other children to prove that she is not my wife". He then gave his parents the story and repeated his request that they arrange for the return of the bridewealth and find him a new wife because he was soon going abroad again.

But the parents protested that he should first consider retaining all four children, since they were, "according to Luo tradition", his, and that he should also consider keeping his wife, for she needed to bring them up, and that he could then acquire a second wife in due course. But the husband said that he did not wish to bring up "bad" children in his home (referring to another Luo belief) who might inherit their mother's character.

His parents, however, went secretly to the wife's parents and discussed the matter with them. Both sets of parents agreed that it would be better to prevent divorce. The wife was asked her version of the story, which she gave and in which she confessed her wrongdoing. She further argued that anyone could be lured by "temptation" when living alone in Nairobi and that she should be allowed now to keep all four children in her parents' home and get a job teaching. But both parents insisted that she return to her husband in his parents' rural home with all four children. She did this but was immediately brought back to her parents by the husband. The husband and wife then saw nothing more of each other until the husband went abroad again after less than a year. There in Britain he met a trainee-nurse from Alego and married her in a registry office. He had told the girl about his earlier problems but claimed that he was now unmarried. In 1967 he returned to Kenya, still married to his first wife from Gem, for no bridewealth had been returned nor had he undergone a "legal" divorce under civil marriage law. His first wife heard about his second civil law marriage and successfully got a (magistrate's grade 3) customary court order for him to reinstate her as his wife in his home. (There was no attempt, incidentally, to charge him with bigamy, which is technically a criminal offence under civil marriage law and should be prosecuted at a higher court.) After this and out of court, the husband insisted that the first wife would now have to become his second wife and be referred to as *nyachira* and not *mikayi*. She refused. The other wife, who he married second and was now with a small child, was also angry at the situation and accused the husband of falsely claiming that he was unmarried. She fought the man, claiming that now that she had a small child, "her freshness is finished" and she could go nowhere else but as another man's second wife. Each wife thereafter insisted on being called by the title of *mikayi*. The first wife took the matter back to the customary court and presented them with her dated wedding certificate, arguing articulately that under civil rather than customary marriage law her husband could be charged with bigamy. The elders noted that threat and, while not pressing the charge, ruled in her favour that she should indeed be called *mikayi*, the first wife. The husband left Nairobi and took a teaching position nearer home in Yala High School, while the two wives also followed their professions nearby, having accepted the ruling. The husband's parent's home remained their and their children's base.

This case demonstrates the power of verbal argument. The first wife moved through three phases: (1) in Nairobi, she successfully articulated an appeal, backed up by the husband's agnates, to Luo custom as demanding that the husband keep her as his wife; (2) brought back by her husband to her parents' rural home, the affair was taken out of her own hands at the husband's suggestion and placed in those of the two sets of in-laws, leaving her with no further voice in it; (3) much later, she perceptively seized upon the unusual but technically illegal and criminal nature of the husband's second marriage and, by persistent verbal approaches to the court magistrate and elders, and by demonstrating her own knowledge of civil as opposed to customary marriage law, succeeded in regaining the title and status of first wife. In other words, she transferred the matter of Luo custom from the level of unquestionable statements to that of debatable propositions, which was no small achievement.

The case also, of course, shows how, in spite of its unusual nature, and the unusual degree of verbal involvement and initiative by the first wife, in the end a modified version of the polygynous family was created and preserved. The deterrents to divorce on the part of a wife are (a) immediate or eventual loss of her own children; and (b) marriage as "only" a second wife to another man. Interestingly, neither woman considered the alternative of setting up an independent matrifocal family unit. The main deterrent to this is the loss of their children. These women's jobs might have provided them with sufficient independent incomes to repay the bridewealth by which they were married. But even assuming that elders agreed that each wife should settle her own divorce in this way, she could not retain her children, for whom she would be required to make appropriate deductions in the bridewealth returned to her husband's family. Parental ostracism is also a deterrent, for it means loss of the right to live in one's natal home ever again. In this case the ensuing, somewhat occupationally dispersed polygynous arrangement located more in country than town represents the extreme to which most highly educated and professional women contemplate going. In this case, then, female verbal articulateness, reinforced by high education and a professional, income-earning status revealed a power of women which further modified but did not destroy polygyny. But it gave us a glimpse of such possibilities: had the second wife not already borne a child, it is almost certain that she would have insisted on divorcing the man and attempting to marry elsewhere as a first wife.

Such glimpses are evident, too, in everyday situations. One man had long and frequent discussions with agnates, other kin, and friends with him in Nairobi, but not, significantly, affines, about whether his wife, who had long since left school after getting good grades in the Certificate of Kenya Primary Education (eight years) and had continued to read and write, should take typing and short-hand lessons at a secretarial college in Nairobi. She was twenty-nine and had three daughters. Her husband was quite keen on his plan but was also unsure as to whether acquiring secretarial qualifications and a job would enable her to undermine his "authority", especially since, under pressure (he said) from his parents, he would soon marry a second wife in order to beget sons. It is relevant here also to note that he is the only son of his mother who is the senior of his father's two wives. In the end he did take a second wife, but his first wife never went to secretarial college. The elders' argument against investing in her education and for getting her husband a second wife instead was that the "name" of his family and lineage would die if he did not marry again. To her sister also living in Nairobi, the first wife expressed great disappointment but received rebukes and no sympathy from her husband's and her own parents.

I have mentioned some of the constraints on the effectiveness of women's verbal argument as well as its potential. A main point to make here is that it is only the collective articulation of such female views as those expressed above that could give them the organizational quality needed for implementation. In the instances just cited, sisters or fellow-women friends who can visit and help each other frequently in Nairobi provide the private relationships in which women separately exchange opinions which may contravene custom and men's authority. But there is no evidence of these relationships being brought together in a single women's "movement". Indeed, we cannot even assume that the expression of apparent grievance, or of a wish to redefine women's roles, is really that great. That would be ethnocentric. Nevertheless, educated and professional women do express a wish for and sometimes attempt to create what they regard as non-traditional ("modern") conjugal role-relationships, and it is legitimate to assume that this small minority is beginning to articulate verbally the underlying forces of change in women's relationships to men.

However, for the moment the emerging awareness of some women as a female elite, worthy of emulation, creates conflict between women conceptualized as "educated" and "uneducated". The same conflict exists among men. But it is constantly played down through the idiom of fraternity and ultimately common descent at any level of agnatic segmentation. This idiom overrides educational, occupational and wealth differences between men, as I have shown. Women have no such idiom.

Case 2: Women divided by education (reported by men and women neighbours and relatives)

Three men (two of Gem and one of Sakwa), of different occupations but equivalent status, working in the railways, are friends. Their wives, all of whom have children, also know each other well. They are each from Gem, Alego, and Asembo, and are, respectively, a primary teacher, a secretary, and an as yet unemployed trainee seamstress, being trained by the welfare organization, *Maendeleo ya Wanawake* (Women's Progress). The teacher and secretary have both received senior secondary education and speak English fluently, but the trainee seamstress received only four years' primary education and speaks no English. All live in Landimawe railway housing estate, but the secretary and seamstress and their families live in one house. The secretary and her husband are the recognized lodgers.

The teacher and secretary became especially close friends to the partial exclusion of the trainee seamstress, and spent more time in each other's company. Between themselves they criticized the third woman's domestic untidiness and her "stupidity" and inability to manage the domestic budget, and further claimed that she "stole" charcoal, paraffin, and small household items from the kitchen stove when the secretary was at work. The teacher urged the secretary to get her husband to speak to the trainee's husband to chastise the woman and to get their own house. She said that the seamstress's behaviour would drive away visitors, which would be "shameful" to the wife and husband. She summarily dismissed the seamstress as "dirty", "uneducated" and "disrespectful" to visitors (i.e. being ignorant of European-style hospitality).

Previously the secretary had been closest in friendship to the seamstress. One day the seamstress overheard the criticism and burst in and lengthily accused the teacher of ruining her friendship with the secretary. She later told her husband but he "refused to listen to women's affairs". She appealed to the secretary not to receive nor visit the teacher and asked whether the teacher had ever bothered to help accommodate her, as she, the seamstress, had. One day one of the seamstress's hens strayed over to the nearby teacher's house. The teacher called for one of her children to take the hen back to the area round the seamstress's house. The child did so but was slapped by the seamstress, who asked what she was doing near the house. The child said nothing, and her mother, who was within earshot, demanded to know what was wrong. The seamstress replied that "a witch cannot go where a good person is" (*jajuok ok nyal dhi kuma ng'ama ber nitie*). That evening the teacher came to her secretary friend and demanded that the three of them should discuss what had caused the quarrelling. But the seamstress hurled further abuse at the teacher, including threats of such mystical sanctions as *chira* to destroy her children. The teacher accused the woman of acting from "jealousy" (*nyiego*) and of being a "primitive" (English word used). The secretary and, soon, other women neighbours intervened and the three calmed down and resumed their uneasy relations with each other. The turning point in reaching reconciliation was the appeal by one of the neighbour women: "You [the secretary and seamstress] have been together a long time. You are all [all three] Luo, and your husbands are friends. You should solve these problems by discussion, leave the past, and come together again."

It is clear that women do have the potential for resolving these kinds of disputes, but their idioms of reconciliation concern the honour of husbands. Husbands' friendships are at risk, and they should not be "shamed" by poor hospitality to visitors. The idiom of ultimate common descent("you are all Luo") is conceptually linked with the preservation of men's friendships.

Education for women, then, promises much but at present divides more than it unites them. We see this also in the increasing frequency with which educated young couples view church weddings as prestigious marks of their status. Church weddings were not, and are not, exclusively associated with "educated" status, but the tendency in this direction is strong. Just as people's definition of what constitutes an "educated" person varies considerably, so do church wedding expenses. However, for all except the elite, they do not normally amount to more than a few hundred shillings. In the rural area a church and customary wedding may make up a single ceremony. But some couples have a church wedding in town and a separate rural customary ceremony (of which there may in fact be a number alternating between the bride's and groom's homesteads and, ideally at least, culminating in a final one at which the *riso* bull is handed over to conclude all marriage payments). In so far as they can be distinguished from each other, the customary ceremonial costs are normally greater than those of the church wedding. The costs of a church wedding supplement but do not supplant the ceremonial ones. Similarly, though there has been an increase over the past generation or so in the proportion of church weddings, especially among educated couples, all marriages are also accompanied by an often long drawn-out customary transfer of bridewealth which, however much it may consist of cash, will include at least some animals. Nor does a church wedding ensure a monogamous marriage.

Most of the 103 polygynist household heads in Kaloleni married their wives in customary marriage with due payment of bridewealth and without church weddings. But 25, or nearly a quarter of them, married their first and senior wife in church as well as customarily. The period of their church marriages ranges from 1937 to 1957. Only two men first married customarily and then married a second wife in church. Clearly, then, the fact that a wife has been married in church does not mean that she will not be joined at a later time by a customarily married junior co-wife. However, it is extremely rare to find a polygynist whose co-wives have both been married to him in church. This is technically bigamy. Although, as we saw in a previous case in this chapter, a Luo is unlikely to be charged in a customary court for this offence, the possibility acts as a deterrent. It follows from this that a first wife is assured of, if not monogamy, then at least a distinctive status for herself in a polygynous marriage should she have been married in church, for no successive co-wives can achieve this status. In this way the customary status of first wife, *mikayi*, receives extra support. It is in this light that we should regard the relatively high proportion of Kaloleni's monogamists, 43 per cent, who have undergone a church marriage in conjunction with a customary one. That is to say, it clearly does not prevent the men from taking a second wife in customary marriage alone, as the case of the generally older polygynists has shown, but a church marriage does satisfy a first wife that, should she ever be joined by co-wives, then her seniority is doubly reinforced by civil as well as customary law. Moreover, as far as I can judge, second co-wives do nowadays tend to have dropped out of school at an earlier stage than senior ones married in church. In general, then, church marriages create a further element in the rivalry between co-wives and, by themselves, do nothing to dislodge men's progress from monogamous to polygynous marriages.

It would similarly be a mistake to assume that the growing emphasis on church marriages for first wives reflects correspondingly greater involvement in church activities and worship. Most Luo household heads in Kaloleni claim some kind of Christian religious denomination: none claimed Muslim and few a "pagan" or "traditional" one. Moreover, polygynists and monogamists show an almost identical distribution. Among the 306 married household heads in Kaloleni taken as a whole, the proportions are 4 per cent "traditional", 42 per cent Catholic, 37 per cent CMS (Anglican), 8 per cent Seventh Day Adventist, and 9 per cent African independent churches and movements of various kinds and predominantly Luo and, in some cases, also Luyia, such as Nomiya, Revival, Africa Israel, Legio Maria, Johera, Jomera, and Church of Christ in Africa, which charateristically involve individual or group spirit possession (Ogot and Welbourn, 1966, pp. 73–113). In spite of these extensive denominational claims, only a small minority of men and their wives are in any way involved in church organization, and there is no apparent tendency for people to marry within these denominations. The partial exception to this are the independent churches which, though they involve only a minority proportion of all Luo, do attract the lesser educated men and women, many of these latter joining independently of husbands. Otherwise the significance of formal Christianity at present is not in offering prolonged worship, but rather the possibility of roughly denoting a couple's "educated" and by implication secure socio-economic status through a church wedding. Though it is logically plausible, only time will tell whether the increase in the number of church weddings for first wives links up with an increase in these same women's education to produce the basis of their effective opposition to polygyny. To date it has not. Similarly, though church weddings indirectly highlight the desirability and believed advantages of education, the costs of the weddings have not yet reduced the importance of bridewealth as the customarily effective means of securing a Luo husband's rights over his wife's children (perhaps even less likely with the repeal of the Affiliation Act in 1969), nor its rising value.

VALUABLE BRIDEWEALTH

Since it has frequently been brought into the preceding discussion, let me consider only briefly the third institutional sphere making up Luo cultural autonomy: the transaction of valuable bridewealth in exchange for genetricial as well as uxorial rights in women. I repeat that its value is no less than K. Shs. 3,500/– (in 1969) plus or including at least two heifers and a bullock. There are various well-known hypotheses by anthropologists on the question of whether marriages are most "stable" when valuable bridewealth is exchanged for the right of a husband and his kin to any children born to the wife (Gluckman, 1950; Fallers, 1957; Leach, 1961b, pp. 114–23; and others). Luo divorce and separation rates are relatively low after the birth of a wife's first child. As we have seen from the preceding case material, this stability partly derives from the reluctance of a wife's family to have to return the valuable bridewealth should the marriage break up. Moreover, it is her parents who might have to support a divorcee who has had a few children (called *nyasigogo*), for her chances of remarrying are slim. A wife is, then, encouraged by her family and agnates to become fully incorporated in her husband's extended family and descent group. On the other hand, should a wife force a separation, her children will remain at her husband's home to be brought up by his own local descent group. There are many cases in which a wife has first left her husband and then agreed, after pressure from kin and in-laws, to return to him and his family for the sake only of the children. Indeed, I came across no cases in which a wife has been prepared to forgo her children by leaving her husband. Since, with modifications in particular cases, courts generally support the entitlement to father-right through payment of bridewealth, there really is little that women with children can do to contest either the custom as such or the high value of the bridewealth if they wish to. Similarly, young men are unable to circumvent the high bridewealth payment and, if they themselves eventually have daughters of their own, will clearly benefit from it as older men.

Increases in the value of bridewealth, dowry, or simply wedding expenses have been noted in a number of African societies (Goody, 1973, p. 4), often persisting informally in the face of government attempts to curb them. Societies of the Luo type may be characterized by rights to a woman's offspring unambiguously secured by bridewealth; patrilineal inheritance of both movable and immovable property by sons; a compound polygynous family system incorporating a house-property complex; and an all-embracing system of segmentary lineages, frequently localized. In them, as among Luo, the value of bridewealth under modern conditions has rarely fallen behind the general rise in the cost of living. It has frequently advanced ahead of it, sometimes including an informal system of graded values according to a daughter's level of education.

The partial or full conversion of bridewealth content from, say, livestock to cash has not altered this trend to higher value. Nor are the attitudes of women themselves unequivocally opposed to high bridewealth. Most young Luo women justify high bridwealth values as fair compensation to their parents for the loss of a daughter, and for having raised and possibly educated them. The loss of a highly educated daughter is seen to represent a loss of potential earning power. Even some highly educated girls argue that a prospective husband's respect for the bride herself can be measured by his preparedness to transact valuable bridewealth.

To summarize: of the three institutions showing a high degree of logical consistency among the Luo, that of valuable bridewealth in exchange for a wife's reproductive powers as well as her sexual and domestic services seems the most likely to persist through a variety of different external political and economic changes. It may be that even a severe economic depression resulting in a drop in the absolute value of the bridewealth would not significantly lessen its relative value compared with, say, payments for land, labour, or medicines. Similarly, though predictions about the lineage principle cannot be long-term, it too has a capacity for persistence. It is literally grounded in rural territorial arrangements. Yet it has sufficient ideological autonomy as a system of ideas about how, say, fellow-townsfolk may be classified and married or rural voters recruited for it to be stretched to accommodate changes in the make-up of descent groups which straddle the rural and urban contexts of Luo activity.

Formal polygyny is the most likely of the three mutually implied institutions to undergo dislocative change, such that it no longer presupposes nor is presupposed by valuable bridewealth nor a modified polysegmentary lineage system. As indicated also in the work of other scholars in Africa, we may expect an increasing number of educated Luo women to oppose formal polygyny and even to initiate changes in new patterns of marriage and cohabitation. But, given the very small number of Luo women who have the education and salaried occupations necessary for this, even polygyny may be expected to continue at its high rate among, say, the current generation of Luo men newly married for the first time. Similarly, as I explained in Chapter 4, most Luo women who run independent market stalls in Nairobi or at their rural homes are already mature in years and remain married. They have less interest in resisting polygyny at that age, and may welcome it as a way of freeing themselves from some domestic duties. Younger Luo women stall holders are not financially independent, for they are obliged to contribute at least part of their earnings to the domestic budget. The bridewealth that keeps them tied to their husbands via their children also obliges them to run their market stalls as family enterprises. Husband–wife market stalls are far more common among the Luo than among Kikuyu and Kamba and, to a lesser extent, the Luyia. That said, the movement by Luo men from trading to clerical work in Nairobi, which I described in Chapter 4, has at least enabled proportionally more Luo women to manage their family enterprises effectively on their own. Though they still operate within the context of family obligations, the increasing trading experience of Luo women may conceivably, under the influence of a catalytic factor, provide an eventual basis of greater "independence".

Women as potential agents of cultural change

The three main institutions making up Luo cultural autonomy, namely bridewealth exchange, polygyny, and lineage polysegmenta-

K

tion, bridge rural and urban relations. Co-wives can alternate in residence between town and country and so enable a man to retain and develop his land while remaining in urban wage employment, as I explained in Chapter 1. Urban friends act as "go-betweens" in enabling fellow-townsmen to choose an ostensibly rural bride. Together with lineage elders and their urban associations, they help ascertain the legitimacy of a potential marriage and may advise and referee transactions of valuable bridewealth. As well as impressing upon any individual Luo the segmentary nature of potential marriage and affinal relations, the polysegmentary structure of lineage and regional associations in Nairobi draws for its manifestly political activities on the very symbolism of marriage alliances and oppositions between lineages, as I showed in Chapters 6 and 7.

Unlike the Kikuyu in Nairobi who have increasingly invested much earned cash in a whole range of commercial enterprises rather than in polygyny, the Luo there have invested a large proportion of their cash in a second or subsequent wife and, latterly, in education for their children.

The more marriages there are concerning Luo in Nairobi in their capacities as grooms, fathers, brothers, agnates, and in-laws, the more this sustains the activities of their Nairobi associations. In this sense, polygyny keeps the Luo segmentary pyramid of associations in business. The political significance of the pyramid is undeniable in a period of intense inter-ethnic competition. But this is a "function" grafted on, so to speak, to an autonomous organizational and ideological structure which would almost certainly take this segmentary pyramidal form even if Luo dominated Nairobi politically and economically, as it does in the Luo home town of Kisumu, which they certainly dominated at the time of fieldwork.

This comes across as a tightly circular model depicting Luo cultural autonomy. Thus, a system of lineage polysegmentation entails polygynous families as its own prototype, which presupposes a competition for necessarily scarce women predicating valuable bridewealth transactions between exogamous lineages. In turn a continuing system of lineage exogamy requires that, under urban conditions, marriage choices and information on the eligibility and availability of possible spouses be constantly "advertised" and regularized by a comparable segmentary structure, conveniently through formal associations frequently headed by older polygynists. The current urban situation in which older townsmen are more likely to have jobs than their sons, further substantiates elders' control of family resources, including prospective bridewealth. Finally, as I have shown throughout, the appropriate use of key verbal concepts, by older to younger men, and by men to women, both legitimates and imposes conceptual order on these institutional areas, each of which is changing, but in constant relationship to each other.

Through women as potential agents of change, formal polygyny is the weakest link in this cycle of verbalized institutional entailments. Put another way, this means that if women wished and were able significantly to challenge and erode the rate of polygyny by using the power of organized verbal argument acquired through, say, superior education and backed up by true economic independence through careers or trade, then the cycle would eventually break. Monogamy entails fewer marriages and exchanges of bridewealth (though, conceivably, more informal modes of cohabitation without bridewealth), less control by elders, and, as a consequence, less "business" for the segmentary pyramid of urban associations which provide the forums for the numerous formal speeches in which is vested elders' control of the means of communication. As a result of monogamy, the lineage principle might then be radically modified. It does not seem likely that marriage payments would cease. However, with a greater voice by women in the affairs of their own marriages, bridewealth might take the form of "indirect dowry" (Goody, 1973, p. 20). That is to say, payments made by the husband and his kin might go to the wife herself or to her via her parents for her to use within the marriage at her own discretion. Women might also be expected informally to rewrite the clause in the marriage contract, so to speak, which entitles a husband and his kin to her children in the event of divorce.

This is necessarily speculative but logically plausible. The importance of such prospective innovations by women is in highlighting the possibility of other developments which might then be unleashed but which are at present held in abeyance, like female "independence" itself. In other words, if and when women gain significantly greater control of conjugal relations and their own children, then other social innovations affecting men may be expected to occur.

The biological basis of the culturally sanctioned control of women by men is the simple fact that the women have the children, and so are expected to rear them. The controls exerted by men on women through their children are indeed the very pivot of the cycle of institutional entailments making up Luo cultural autonomy which I have described, i.e. polygyny, polysegmentary lineage formation, and valuable bridewealth. By looking at the way controls on child-rearing are applied by men, for the most part unintendedly or without awareness of their consequences, we can pick out the frailties, division and differences among men themselves, for men are by no means agreed as to, say, what is an appropriate number of children, in view of the potential benefits of superior education for a few. These divisions between men are the other potentialities for change which might accompany a shift to a greater degree of female control. First, let us look again at the controls exerted on women through their children.

I showed in Chapter 5 how even within the domestic domain in Nairobi, as well as in the political, men rather than women are held responsible for its affairs and destiny. Within the domestic domain this is most clearly seen in the beliefs and practices associated with the mystical affliction *chira* which causes sterility and harms or kills children and mothers, in particular, and agnates of the husband. The explanatory ideology in Nairobi is that adultery involving married women with children, terminologically and conceptually subsumed under "incest", is most likely to cause the disease *chira*. But the actual urban cases for which I have evidence indicate that it is men's transgressions of co-wife, family, and lineage seniority rules that are said by a diviner to bring *chira*. That is to say, at a purely ideological level married women with children are regarded as a central cause of *chira* which arises from adultery. But when it comes down to actual cases presided over by a diviner and the couple's kin, it is men who are held responsible. Thus, almost as an unconscious concession, women are ideologically ascribed the power of life and death over their own and their husband and his lineage's offspring, or over those of some other man with whom they have adultery, but it is only ever men who are seen to wield this power. In so far as both men and women appear genuinely to believe, nevertheless, that adultery involving married women with children does cause *chira*, the consequence is an apparent reluctance on the part of such women to risk committing it. By contrast, the breaches of seniority rules committed by men, even when they are diagnosed by a diviner as having caused *chira*, can easily be excused as "understandably" caused, for example, by a parent on a quick visit to town having to stay overnight in a son's urban house (see the case in Chapter 5, p. 155). Purification by *manyasi* medicine can remedy either kind of transgression but it is not foolproof, for *chira* can recur, and so the element of risk is always there.

On the face of it, then, women are subordinate to men politically, economically, domestically, and even mystically. Though wives may influence particular husbands, it would be inaccurate to regard this as representing "hidden" control of men by women, as is sometimes reported in other societies superficially exhibiting male control. A continuing high rate of polygyny, of valuable bridewealth transactions, and the perpetuation of the lineage principle, all depend on this tacit compliance on the part of females. Yet it is precisely over children that there is an emerging inherent contradiction in Luo values. As I explained in Chapter 2, in recent times younger Luo men and women have seen an investment in children's education as the key to economic security and even prosperity. But, they also regard this aim as best achieved through having few children by one wife. A new value placed by both men and women on financial investment in their children's education thus contradicts an older value placed principally by men on polygyny; for men now see practical as well as ideological benefit in having at least two wives, one of whom can at any one time look after land at home while enabling her husband to keep his job in town and lead a "normal" nuclear family life there.

I have already indicated that the few highly educated Luo women already oppose polygyny, an observation also made with regard to educated women in other parts of Africa. Young men, too, show themselves at best ambivalent as to the continuing advantage of polygyny in view of the presumed better educational rewards from a monogamous marriage with fewer children. They are, however, caught in the cycle of institutional entailments and beliefs which I described and so do not effectively oppose polygyny, but instead eventually become polygnists themselves. The institutional restraints reach out beyond the question of the choice between monogamy and polygyny. There is a complementary stress on obligations to agnates and kin in preference to unrelated friends: we saw in Chapter 3 how, compared with other ethnic groups in Nairobi, Luo were much more likely to provide accommodation for agnates, other kin, and in-laws. Yet, as far as one can judge from observation and people's statements, friends are genuinely valued as a refuge from the exacting demands of these relatives. Relatives impose themselves as lodgers and almost certainly drain a household head's budget. By contrast, friends almost invariably contribute to it.

Even here, however, the choice may not remain that clear-cut. For the Luo definition of kinship is broad, and after a while a friend may take on the "sponging" characteristics of a relative. The common term of address and, to a lesser extent, reference for a friend, *omera*, with a basic meaning of "my brother" facilitates this conceptual role-shift in certain friendships, particularly where, as is often the case, the friends come from a common home area broadly associated with a particular major or maximal lineage. Moreover, since a best friend may act as a man's marriage go-between (*jagam*) for first and subsequent marriages, he plays an indirect role in perpetuating customary expectations even though the friend is explicitly regarded as offering freedom from them.

In such situations of contradiction (i.e. the assumed economic advantage of monogamy as against that of polygyny), and of ambiguity (i.e. concerning the status of "friends"), the pyramid of segmentary lineage associations stands out as relatively fixed and constant. Its terminological designations of agnatic as opposed to non-agnatic status are unambiguous even if they blur the precise lines of genealogical depth. Association leaders may quarrel and split up into rival associations but eventually legitimize their break by claiming to represent one or the other lineage segment. The structure of associations provides relatively unambiguous guidelines as to who may marry whom. At the wider political level in assumed confrontation with the government and other ethnic groups, it is again the segmentary structure of associations culminating in the Luo Union which provides the platform on which Luo unity is expressed over and above internal divisiveness, as we saw in Chapter 7 regarding the contrasting roles played by and with regard to the rival leaders, Odinga and Mboya.

The contradiction between the economics of monogamy and polygyny and the ambiguities surrounding obligations to (putatively) socio-economically useful friends as against relatives are the mainsprings of what I called general "random" segmentation. The retention of polygyny, of valuable bridewealth, and the structure of urban lineage associations are the disciplined and predictable responses to the specific and explicitly recognized segmentary organization of Luo society and culture. In the latter the status of woman is of fundamental significance. Should her status change, say through superior education or genuine economic independence, to the extent that she is able to redefine any of these institutions, the most likely of which would be polygyny, then we may expect the expression of cultural autonomy among Luo to be radically altered. We might expect ethnic endogamy to cease, some matrifocal family units to emerge, and the development of inter-ethnic "marriages" more controlled by women, such as has already been documented among an increasing number of women in Kampala, Uganda (Halpenny, 1975; Obbo, 1972, 1975), Lusaka, Zambia (Shuster, 1976), other parts of Africa and the Third World (Tanner, 1974), as well as among some Kikuyu and others in Nairobi itself (Nelson, 1977).

It is in this sense that we can view general segmentation as expressing the latent power of women, and the specific segmentary lineage principle of Luo society as expressing the publicly acknowledged power of men. Early in this chapter I said that general segmentation is most obviously expressed in socio-economic divisions and differences, while specific segmentation is expressed through generational and genealogical authority. These two interpretations are perfectly consistent. In the context of growing urban wage dependency in Nairobi, "random" quarrels and conflicts among Luo are inevitably over problems of differential access to jobs and housing, or arise from accusations of improper use of resources (as in associations), or are over conflicting interpretations as to the economic worthwhileness of polygyny as against monogamy, or of relatives as against friends. This is an aspect of general segmentation which is seen by Luo themselves as constituting a threat to the solidarity of all Luo. In the same way, but, seemingly at a much less conscious level, the possibility of women's "independence" and their redefinition of marriage patterns is seen to constitute a complementary threat. It, too, is then an aspect of general segmentation from the male viewpoint and also that of many mothers who wish to preserve traditional roles for their daughters. It is ultimately only by appeal to the unquestionable legitimacy of the specific lineage principle of the Luo with its distinctive regulations governing bridewealth and exogamy that men can continue to exert formal, informal and mystical controls over women and so curb what are seen to be their "random" and potentially destructive tendencies.

To summarize: at one level there is an apparently increasing generational difference of opinion between older men who wish to preserve, say, polygyny, and younger men who question its value if it diverts a family's resources away from educating a smaller number of children. But young men tend to become polygynists themselves as the over arching Luo segmentary lineage organization works upon them and tames their "deviant" aspirations. Specific triumphs over general segmentation.

At another level, men of all ages exert the controls I have described over women in both the domestic and political domains, and even, in modified form, in trade. Once again, their control is legitimated by reference to the rules emanating from the Luo mode of segmentary lineage organization, expressed through the use of key verbal concepts in the formal speech of family discussion, advice, and dispute settlement. Here, too, specific "smothers" general segmentation, expressed as yet in the tacit threat of women's changing status.

To conclude, older men may indeed control younger men indefinitely under these conditions of rapid population growth, increasing rural land density, growing urban unemployment, increasingly valuable bridewealth, and a continuing high rate of polygyny. But for how long can men control women? A few Luo women with superior education have already shown some possible redefinitions of marriage patterns and male/female role-expectations. Influence also comes from the many Kikuyu women in Nairobi who have little or no education. By setting themselves up independently in petty commerce in low-income areas of the city, they have radically redefined traditional Kikuyu relations between men and women in both the domestic and public political domains. It can be hypothesized, then, that the high degree of Luo cultural autonomy rests principally on the relatively unchanging status of its women in relation to polygyny, bridewealth, and exogamous lineage organization. Further, we may expect women to have a similarly pivotal status in other societies of the Luo type, which, even under the conditions of rural–urban migration and dual settlement, continue to combine polygynous families with a patrilineal house-property complex, the unambiguous exchange of valuable bridewealth for genetricial as well as sexual and domestic rights in a wife, and an overarching polysegmentary lineage system. Let me now suggest that cultures can differ in the consistency with which their institutions emically presuppose each other, by briefly comparing the

Kikuyu in Nairobi, some of whose historical background I have already sketched, with the Luo.

Cultural inconsistencies: Kikuyu by contrast

The Luo "traditional" view is that the compound polygynous family household is the prototype of future lineage polysegmentation. As men have become more dependent on urban wages, this view has remained consistent with the way Luo nowadays see the three main institutional spheres as entailing each other. Thus, Luo haggle in individual cases but generally agree on the content, high value, and duration of marriage payments for unambiguous rights in women's children and services. They see the continuing high polygyny rate in Nairobi as evidence of men's preparedness to invest heavily in wives and children as a way of perpetuating their names in future lineage relationships as well as for more immediate practical purposes. A modified segmentary lineage model, expressed in the formation of urban associations, is seen as regulating men's marriage choices of scarce women from appropriately "allied" exogamous lineages, and as therefore providing the most customarily acceptable framework of political recruitment between town and country. "Their" emic view makes perfect sense to the "outside" analyst as a logically consistent paradigm of institutional meanings and consequences. The outside analyst simply stands a better chance of looking at the paradigm from a distance and, by comparing it with similar situations elsewhere, picking out some emerging inconsistencies. But individual Luo themselves will, as I have stressed, point out for example the contradiction between acquiring many children through two or more wives and trying to invest in their education, or in a business. Individual Luo can certainly analyse their situation as well as the outsider and so cannot be said to be "mystified" by the forces beyond their control which induce them, often reluctantly, to take a second wife. They recognize the external pressures and, sometimes, the compelling inner motives for honour and self-perpetuation. But, like those women who oppose polygyny, such men have not come to articulate their views within a consistent contrary paradigm. We may say that they are "undecided". Indecision, however, is often, as here, the inability to articulate a new cultural paradigm under the constraints of the existing one. Part of these constraints is the view that to change the system implies a change in the status of women and a loss of male control over marriage and children generally.

We may briefly compare this with the Kikuyu among whom there is considerable variation in the nature and value of marriage payments, with variations increasingly along the lines of socio-economic status rather than, say, district of origin; there has been the rapid and almost total elimination of polygyny, corresponding with the emergence of many politically articulate and economically independent Kikuyu women; and there is now considerable variation in the extent to which "traditional" marriage rules based on lineage exogamy are followed.

The external political and economic pressures on the Kikuyu have, as I outlined earlier, differed from those to which the Luo were subject, and these may partly account for the open expression among Kikuyu of internal socio-economic differences among them, and of corresponding, emerging socio-cultural ones. But the Luo also are similarly divided along socio-economic lines: they, too, have their rich and their poor. But such differences, while recognized, are constantly played down in subordination to lineage relationships of varying segmental levels. Since Luo elders play a key part in maintaining the Luo premise of equality, we may here begin by looking at the different relationship between the Kikuyu lineage system and Kikuyu elders' roles.

Kikuyu elders living in both town and country do hold important roles in rural, sometimes lineage-based, farming and trading cooperatives (Ferraro, 1971, pp. 110, 160–5), but they do not represent lineages and lineage clusters of different levels in a segmentary pyramid. Rather, the position of Kikuyu elders *per se* is more structured by a system of age-grading. This system is far removed from the traditional one but has modified and more immediate modern significance than lineage relations, as Ferraro observes (1971, pp. 118, 140–1, 160). Put simply, Kikuyu elders operate within their nuclear families relatively independently of each other and of the urban fellow-members of their rural lineages, and do not "advise" people to marry or organize politically within a pyramidal framework of perpetually segmenting lineages.

From the literature it is clear that the Kikuyu have never conceptualized their compound polygynous family as the prototype of an expanding system of lineage polysegmentation (Middleton and Kershaw, 1965, pp. 20, 23–7). It does not appear that a patrilineage (*mbari*) segment formed by the sons of a lineage founder's co-wife would normally be known by that co-wife's name, as among the Luo. From early times land-holding segments of different lineages were interspersed, sometimes as a result of settlement in another lineage's area through land purchase (ibid., p. 26), making it difficult for a consistent notion to develop of coordinate lineages of increasingly more inclusive levels in a state of balanced, segmentary opposition. It was even possoble for men of different lineages to band together, buy or clear unclaimed land, and found a "new" lineage named after an important ancestor of one of the founders and sometimes after "an important powerful man, not related in any direct sense" (ibid., p. 25). Contributing to this dispersed and "drift" segmentation of Kikuyu lineages were (a) the existence of large, widely dispersed, non-exogamous clans (*mihiriga*), which have not for a long time, if ever, been associated with particular places (ibid., p. 24); and (b) the named, corporate age-sets and the named generation-sets (both called *marika*) which cut across lineage and clan affiliations, and between and within which kinship terminology was used, as well as between "real" consanguinal kin and affines (ibid., pp. 35–8).

None of this is to suggest that the Kikuyu did not think of themselves as having common ancestry. Nor that they were unconcerned with population growth. Far from it. It is only to suggest that, in spite of once having had compound polygynous families based on a flexible version of the house-property complex (i.e. in which sons receive family property from a father via their mother as his co-wife), they did not verbally conceptualize the family's internal roles and relationships as a future model of extensive segmentary lineage relationships, nor as a model of their society generally. Indeed, pursuing what has been said above, the following quotation shows that generational differences take priority over internal family relations as the model by which Kikuyu saw themselves as ultimately bound by common kinship:

For a proper understanding of the Kikuyu view of kin, reference must be made to some aspects of their world-view. The Kikuyu conceive of individuals, institutions and the people as a whole, as they are living in the present, embodying the past as well as the future. The living male person is his grandfather, he is also his grandson [i.e. I have the same generation-set name as my grandfather, as also with my grandson—we are each called, say, *Maina*]. The generation-set in office is [i.e. was] the generation-set alternating above, as well as the as-yet unformed set alternating below. A woman giving birth to her children thus brings forth her parents, so does a generation-set give birth to the next, which is its own parent set. The thought of giving birth, *guciaruu*, as the means b which the present re-creates the past and the future leads to the view of people and institutions as units in descent in which people are kin. (My bracketed inclusions.)

Middleton and Kershaw, 1965, p. 38

I am not trying to explain present Kikuyu institutions and values solely in terms of the past. But I simply want to point out why today in Nairobi or more distant towns the Kikuyu have nothing comparable to the Luo polysegmentary lineage organization of associations and marriage. A principle of patrilineal descent which lacks the discipline, so to speak, of a relatively strict segmentary "nesting" system is bound to lead to considerable variation in separate families' interpretations of its relevance and range. And so it is among Kikuyu in Nairobi who, even as putative members of a common named *mbari* (lineage) of more than a few generations' depth, may differ widely among themselves as to its exogamous limits, and its genealogical and consanguinal relationships to other lineages.

Similarly, as I explained earlier, families vary among themselves considerably as to the amount of bridewealth (*ruracio*) payable at a marriage (though it is much lower on average than that of Luo), the duration of its payment, and the rights and duties that go with it. The separate ceremony involving the slaughter by a husband of the *ngurario* ram, which secures for him rights in his wife's children, is often not carried out for years if at all. Many factors, including land scarcity and the removal of men during Operation Anvil, have contributed to the currently very low polygyny rate among the Kikuyu in Nairobi. But certainly, these highly variable interpretations as to the value of and customary expectations attaching to bridewealth have played a major part. In turn these factors are linked to the increasing numbers of Kikuyu women who live and work in Nairobi independently of any one male, husband or otherwise, and whose stable matrifocal family units consist of a mother and her children, sometimes with sisters and, in some cases, with the mother's mother living nearby (Nelson, 1977). In Nairobi these matrifocal Kikuyu families usually live in so-called low-income areas of unauthorized settlement, but are also found in the privately owned and rented buildings of permanent construction in Eastleigh. But there are also "conventional" stable nuclear Kikuyu families comprising a man and his one wife and children as found in housing estates like Kaloleni. These are in striking contrast and are part of the variations in Kikuyu family patterns in Nairobi.

If a Luo says that the polygynous family is his society writ small, we can understand precisely what he means by observing the remarkably consistent process by which male-dominated urban nuclear families have expanded into polygynous ones and so provide the model of future lineage growth. Even in the few areas of unauthorized settlement in Nairobi in which Luo live, there are hardly any matrifocal families. But a Kikuyu has two contrasting types of urban family to "choose" from: the conventional nuclear one, and the "new" matrifocal one. Which, we may ask, is he or she to think of as a microcosm best representing total Kikuyu society?

The matrifocal family and the nuclear one among the Kikuyu do not each unambiguously represent contrasting incipient "classes", i.e. with the matrifocal family a product of the "culture of poverty" and the nuclear one a product of a comfortable urban "labour aristocracy", though this is a tempting first assumption. Kikuyu men and women themselves often speak of matrifocal and nuclear families as premissed, respectively, on "low" and "high" socio-economic status. Nelson shows, in fact, that some female heads of matrifocal families have climbed to positions of economic and political strength, while it is also clear that some wage-earning male heads of nuclear families are very poor.

This internal Kikuyu contrast between matrifocal families and male-headed (though not necessarily male-dominated) nuclear families is best seen as representing the current, ongoing dialectic in relations between Kikuyu men and women in Nairobi. Again, to refer to Nelson's material which my own observations certainly corroborate, Kikuyu men and women are firmly explicit in their judgements and criticism of relations between men and women. Not all Kikuyu women express a wish to head their own families independently of any man, but enough do for us to say that, among Kikuyu, the debate about women's status is well under way.

There is no such open debate among the Luo, just as there is no significant contrast among them between matrifocal and male-headed families. Just as the Luo family is conceptually and verbally linked up with the wider segmentary organization of Luo society in the way I have shown, so men's and women's relations are covered by a consistent set of verbal assumptions. Individuals may sometimes disagree as to the merits of these persisting family and lineage relations and obligations. But their disagreement has not reached such proportions that there has developed a contrast between matrifocal and male-headed families, or even an end to the process leading from monogamy to polygyny nor that the Luo cease to think and speak of the family and lineage as implying each other. Among the Kikuyu the two main family types offer a woman some area of "choice"; she may start out as the co-wife of a polygynist, which is rare, or as the wife of a monogamist in a nuclear family headed by him, but may then leave her husband and set up her own matrifocal family. But even here "choice" does not end, for there are cases of women heading matrifocal families who eventually marry or permanently cohabit with a man in a stable nuclear family household. I qualify use of the term "choice", for it is often factors beyond women's control which induce them to move from one to another family type, and possibly back again. In other words, the range of family types and modes of cohabitation and child-rearing is much less limited for Kikuyu women, or for Kikuyu men for that matter, than it is among Luo. This means that, compared with Luo, we cannot specify which family type in Nairobi is most characteristic of the present-day direction of Kikuyu culture.

The continuing high rate of Luo urban polygyny is, as I have shown in previous chapters, highly interconnected with two other institutional spheres in Nairobi: valuable bridewealth in exchange for children born to a wife, and the overarching segmentary pyramid of associations. It is because of this highly integrated presuppositional logic of their culture and the consistency with which Luo identify it as such through verbalized concepts that I speak of it as having a great deal of autonomy of changing external political and economic circumstances. This is not simply a matter of Luo culture being either suited or unsuited to, say, entrepreneurship, or of being intrinsically conservative. It is quite clear that Kikuyu have enjoyed certain historically derived political and economic advantages in Nairobi compared with Luo. But, as I showed earlier, we can exaggerate the significance of those advantages in explaining the rise of Kikuyu entrepreneurship and political ascendancy. Just as the Kikuyu individual is less limited in his "choice" of family type, so he is less restricted by a consistent interconnection of family kinship and lineage constraints to pursue individualistic kinds of economic investment. A Luo man and woman are generally confined in their "choice" of marriage types to monogamy probably leading to polygyny; they are more constrained to spend surplus income, whether earned, inherited, or received as bridewealth from a daughter's or sister's marriage, as bridewealth for a son's, brother's, or for their own wife or second wife; and, because of the continuing importance of lineages in defining exogamy and in facilitating rural–urban political communication, they are constantly brought into regular interaction with those designated as agnates and reminded of the polysegmentary lineage classification of relationships: even those urban individuals designated as "friends" and valued as personal refuge from the dictates of agnation, eventually steer a man back into the arms of agnates by involving themselves as urban go-betweens in customary rural marriage arrangements.

It does not, therefore, seem likely that, in competition with modern Kikuyu in Nairobi, whose manifold interpretations of the appropriateness of different marriage or family types and kinship obligations can be used by individuals to justify a range of alternative enterprises, the Luo are likely to thrive in an economy characterized by *laissez-faire* entrepreneurship initially set up by individuals independent of family constraints. This is not a contrast between an "innovating" and a "conservative" culture but that between different cultural responses. The forms of Luo entrepreneurship most likely to succeed would probably operate first within the pyramidal classification of lineage relationships, and, second, within maximal exogamous lineages providing a pool of labour and investors but with an internal blurring of the lines of its constituent segments, of the kind described by Watson (1975) for the Hong Kong Chinese huge commercial lineage network called *Man*. But for Luo this transition must surely be difficult in an economy already dominated by a culturally contrasting group. It may well be that, just as a radical change in women's status seems most likely to alter the Luo cultural paradigm, so it is through women as traders and, eventually, political voters, that Luo may expand economically in an otherwise contracting environment of opportunity.

Although Kikuyu can interpret their family and kinship customs and obligations in different ways, so enabling the individual more choice, this does not imply that the Kikuyu as a whole are not able to express cultural distinctiveness. They do so, however, not by picking on relatively precise kinship, lineage, and marriage rules underwritten by a segmentary organization, as do the Luo. Rather, they appeal to highly generalized symbols. Examples are the person of President Kenyatta himself, who is both a national and Kikuyu hero; the famous traditional Kikuyu dancing at KANU political rallies at both national and local levels; and, on occasion, widely dispersed "secret" Kikuyu oathing ceremonies, some of which were reported in 1969 to have been taken by "virtually every adult Kikuyu" (sic) (Leys, 1975, p. 236). This latter followed the Luoland Gem by-election victory of the opposition KPU candidate (see Okumu, 1969, and Chapter 6 in this book), which was interpreted by many Kikuyu leaders as a growing threat to KANU and to Kikuyu hegemony (Mutiso and Godfrey, 1972, p. 6). The use by Kikuyu leaders of such highly generalized symbols on repeated ad hoc issues can temporarily overcome the internal variations of cultural interpretation and foster some sense of cultural distinctiveness, while facilitating individual choice and specialization in new fields of economic enterprise.

In this sense, it is precisely the "inconsistencies in the logic of cultural expression", to parody my citation of Leach (1954, p. 4) given in the Introduction to this book, that facilitate the growth among the Kikuyu of separate sub-cultures corresponding with marked socioeconomic differentiation. Though the Luo are also sharply differentiated internally by socio-economic factors, it is the prevailing consistencies in the logic of cultural expression among the Luo that currently restrain the development of separate sub-cultures. In a Third World economy which is dominated by international factors and interests, the transition from "tribal" to peasant to industrial dominant modes of production is universal in its most fundamental aspects. The divergent responses of the Kikuyu and Luo suggest, however, that the wider logic of this transition can only be understood at the level of emic statement, belief and response in terms of the logic of contrastable, and therefore inverse cultures.

Conclusion

I have argued that the weakest link in the chain of institutional entailments among the Luo, i.e. of polygyny, valuable bridewealth, and a patrilineal polysegmentary organization of marriage and politics, is the prospective status of their women in relation to polygyny. We cannot with any certainty assume *a priori* that Luo women are poised, so to speak, to break the chain. Women do not consistently express dissatisfaction with the *status quo,* and it would be ethnocentric to assume that they do. We can only note the few cases where women have articulated opposition to polygyny. These are largely confined to a relatively small number of women with higher education and do not as yet include Luo women traders (see Chapter 4). We must recognize the generally tacit or at most culturally structured nature of Luo women's views about their status as co-wives, as producers of men's children, and even as potential entrepreneurs still under husband's control (cf. M. Strathern, 1972, pp. 270, 314; E. Ardener, 1975 (1972); S. Ardener, 1975). Luo women are not tacit about everything: they are more articulate than men in discussing causes and effects of the mystical affliction called *chira.* But this is a culturally structured articulateness. For one of the causes of the disease frequently cited is adultery, for which women are held as much as men to be responsible. Nevertheless, women's articulateness has here introduced an ambivalence in their status even if it does not explicitly question that status.

Women are best seen as potential rather than certain agents of Luo cultural change. But when, if ever, will Luo women generally move from the tacit to the explicit and pose new questions? This may happen for instance if the Luo women members (who are not numerous) of some Christian religious sects in Nairobi (Aoko, 1974) institute marriage and family changes, including the rejection of polygyny, which coincide with those articulated by educated women, and which coincide also with less dependence on their husbands by Luo women market traders. What has been demonstrated to date, however, is the resilience of Luo culture, the logical consistency of which has been based on a largely unquestioned asymmetry of male and female moral accountability in domestic and political affairs (cf. Rosaldo and Lamphere, 1974, p. 8).

In spite of some general stated beliefs blaming women as well as men, it is men who are *seen* to be held mainly accountable for any harm to their families. That is to say, a husband is seen to be primarily responsible for the perpetuation of his own family and, by extension, the lineage of which it is a prototype. Similarily, in the public, political sphere, it is men who decide through the Luo Union and its affiliated associations what action to take regarding the destiny and self-perpetuation of the Luo people. Yet, cross-cutting this "traditional" mode of cultural self-perpetuation which depends on producing many children, is the new interest in education for a few. It is here that the interests of some Luo men as well as women coincide. For the new view credits, though to a largely illustory extent, education as the key to an individual family's socio-economic success. But this common interest of randomly distributed individual men and women comes out only in occasional comments. It has not overcome the structural contrasts in men's and women's roles. In this sense, it is like the unanswered questions regarding Luo women's status. That is to say, the equation that few children equals superior education equals socio-economic success remains culturally tacit: the diffuse ideas of casual conversation have not yet become unambiguously attached to key terms and so leave unchallenged the key verbal concepts of male elders' authority.

At this point it is appropriate to draw a conclusion in prospect. Much of the book shows that the persistence of polygyny binds men to traditional ideals more than their womenfolk. It is men's urban wages which have enabled them to acquire two or more wives. So, with increasing brideweath payments, men have become more and more dependent on these wages. Since one way in which older men exert their authority regarding polygyny and the status of women is through the use of key verbal concepts in speech, they are stifling discussion of their own increasing urban wage dependency through their use of formalized speech. Formalized speech may, then, be more than a reinforcer of authority, which is the hypothesis advanced by Bloch (1975, p. 23). It may also obscure the creation of relations of external dependency among those who control the verbal means of endocultural communication. An extended hypothesis applied to an "encapsulated" group is that under the cover of the authoritative use of custom, verbally legitimized through the use of key terms, external forces of radical change can be "smuggled" in and create internal discontinuities and contradictions in the logic of its culture (cf. Parkin, 1972, pp. 98–103; 1976, pp. 183–4).

Conclusion

The Dynamics of Cultural Autonomy

From cultural conversation to open debate

I have analysed an unusual process of urban family settlement in Nairobi. The Luo from western Kenya continue to marry two or more wives. With only the partial exception of the top elite, the higher a man's urban income, the more likely he is to take a second or subsequent wife as he gets older. Their urban family settlement is unusual in that a Luo man ensures that each co-wife alternates in spending an equal time during the year in town and at the rural home, supervising the family smallholding. In this way men can retain certain economic interests while remaining in full-time urban wage employment and while living within an urban nuclear family of one co-wife and her children.

Luo recognize this practical advantage in having two or more wives. This usefulness has developed over a period of twenty-five years or so, since the end of the second World War, when men migrated in increasing numbers to Nairobi as bachelors and later, when urban family accommodation became available, with their wives and children. The practical advantage of polygyny has become merged with a traditional ideological stress on the value of many wives and many children. The new usefulness and the old ideology support each other as justifications for the persistence of polygyny. That is to say, they both fit comfortably within the existing cultural paradigm.

The beginnings of a contradictory paradigm have appeared in the view that educating one's children is the key to a family's socio-economic success and that, because of the expenses of education, men should have only one wife and few children. But men who have expressed such views frequently continue to take a second wife and beget more children. They do so for the practical and ideological reasons mentioned above.

The circulation of valuable bridewealth is linked with the persistence of polygyny. A high polygyny rate entails: a scarcity of marriageable women for men of their own age; late marriage for men; and the likelihood that high bridewealth will not decrease in value and, in the conditions of an expanding cash economy, will become inflated in line with the rise in the cost of living. Previously, Luo bridewealth consisted of cattle. Now it mostly consists of cash, exclusively so for second and subsequent wives. Most of the cash for bridewealth comes from urban wages. It gives a husband full rights over his wife's children, who continue to be regarded as vital family "assets".

Valuable cash bridewealth received for a sister's or daughter's marriage is "earmarked", and is not normally used for any other purpose than another marriage. Middle-aged men who control much wage employment in a city of considerable unemployment can together exert pressure on younger recipients of bridewealth to use it in this customarily acceptable way. These Luo "elders" have a mutual interest in finding financially reliable husbands for their own daughters and younger sisters. They have strict rules about who should marry whom, including those of lineage exogamy and the avoidance of incest.

The circulation of bridewealth and the mutual interests of recipients are regulated and expressed in a segmentary pyramid of associations in Nairobi which are based on exogamous lineages and non-exogamous lineage clusters, with the Luo Union at the top of the pyramid. For this system to be perpetuated, elders must control young men and men must block the development of women's aspirations for an end to polygyny. In addition to the economic controls which facilitate this, there are mystical sanctions arising from fears of death and sickness eliminating a man's family, which impress upon male doubters the desirability of many wives and children. And reinforcing both the economic controls and mystical sanctions is the continued use in speech by elders in authority of key verbal concepts which draw on traditional ideas more appropriate to past conditions yet still possessed of great illocutionary force.

At the same time that Luo have become increasingly dependent on urban wage employment, they have seen themselves excluded by the dominant Kikuyu from a previously large share in the political control of Kenya, a process most dramatically portrayed in political activities in Nairobi itself. Recurring themes in the speeches at public meetings of Luo organized by the Luo Union in Nairobi concern the defence and social and cultural self-perpetuation of the Luo people. Here, the metaphor of the polygynous family as the key to self-perpetuation is constantly stressed. The polygynous family is regarded as the prototype of the lineages which make up the internal segmentary structure and delimit the boundaries of the Luo people and their culture. Luo public political views and strategy are thus based on a cultural definition of the worthwhileness of the polygynous family.

This Luo culture has shown remarkable consistency as a system of key terms used in speech to refer to ideas about customary practices. It has persisted as a system of modified practices overlaid by traditional terms and ideas through some short-term dramatic changes of an external political and economic nature. For this reason, and after a comparison with Kikuyu, I concluded the preceding chapter by ascribing to Luo culture a relatively high degree of autonomy as a self-regulating system of key terms, ideological assumptions, and practices. That is to say, the three Luo institutions of polygyny, bridewealth transactions, and segmentary lineage organization, making up the logical chain of presuppositions and consequences which we call Luo culture, have each "changed" internally through adaptation to these developing external factors. But the institutions have not changed *in relation to each other:* they still presuppose each other. Certain key verbal concepts are the most continuous and predictable elements of Luo culture. They help sustain its emic logic by denying the existence, so to speak, of the emerging inconsistencies and contradictions in Luo culture concerning the desirability of education against that of many children, and the potentially ambivalent status of women as providers of children and of independent incomes.

I have suggested that, in this sense, Luo cultural continuity depends on the continued and unquestioned and therefore tacit acceptance by Luo women of their role in perpetuating the polygynous family as the model and linchpin of Luo culture. The corollary of this is a continuing control of the traditional means of communication by those who control marriage, namely middle-aged men, especially the polygynists among them. We may hypothesize that it is precisely under the cover of their control of customary verbal concepts which blandly summarize and so obscure changes in customary practice, that these men become increasingly dependent on the urban wages which pay for polygyny.

In a number of chapters I have concentrated on the way sets of contrasting key verbal concepts (a) represent forces of "disorder" and "order" in opposition (i.e. "order" from the veiwpoint of the Luo establishment and of Luo cultural autonomy); and (b) contain a dialectic. Let me list some of these semantic antinomies.

Forces of disorder	*The ordered response*
nyiego = (a) Jealousy between Luo co-wives, (b) jealousy between fellow-Luo men in relation to the outside world.	Imposition of the seniority implicit in the terms for first, second, and third co-wives: *mikayi, nyachira*, and *rero*, and the term for polygynist, *jadoho*. Imposed metaphorically in public meetings as well as literally in family ones.
Jasem = The "friend" who undermines friendship by sabotaging advantageous marriage payments.	*Jagam* = The "true" friend who ensures advantageous marriages.
Omera = The friend who seems to offer freedom from kin yet who is close like a brother. He may however become too much like an over-demanding kinsman.	*Owadwa, jokakwaro*, etc. are some of a number of relatively precise segmentary agnatic terms of address and/or reference which, when contrasted with specific terms for friends, e.g. *osiepna, janam*, reduce the ambiguities inherent in *omera* and clarify the critical distinction between agnates and friends.
Chira = The "mystical" afflication about which women are more articulate than men in expressing a knowledge.	But men are shown by both male and female diviners' (*ajuoga*) diagnoses actually to have the mystical power of afflication.
Ajuoga = Both male and female diviner-doctors for domestic misfortune.	*Ajuoga* = Male diviner-doctor only, for public political misfortune, thereby restricting to the domestic domain women's mystical influence.

Sunga = The singular term for a "proud man" or "upstart" and connotes individual success and pride acquired to the neglect of agnates and other kin. But ambivalently connotes also a tacit admiration for the self-made man that the term sometimes implies.

Gisungore (or *gichamo nyadhi*, etc.) = Plural forms which negate individualistic achievement by referring to the potlatch-like, competitive money-raising displays between lineages or lineage-clusters, expressed in the idiom of segmentary opposition.

The significance of these terms is that they occur repeatedly in conversations and, especially, that they appear strategically to punctuate speech in the many formal meetings which characterize family crises and those crises which affect the Luo as a whole and are discussed in their lineage and lineage-cluster associations. I have not attempted in this book to show their further linguistic embeddedness which gives them illocutionary force, for this would require more detailed analysis of speech events than is appropriate in this book. But I shall suggest in this concluding chapter some further implications of the anthropological analysis of key verbal concepts in a holistic study.

For the moment we may return to the two lists of semantically opposed concepts. Looked at emically, such contrasting verbal concepts of ambivalence and threatened disorder on the one hand, and of unambiguity and order on the other, characterize every culture as a relatively bounded system of communication. Looked at etically, it is clear that the first set of concepts in column 1 fit together sufficiently logically to be regarded as an alternative system of cultural order-in-the-making which, as an emergent paradigm, threatens the established one depicted in column 2.

In a strict sense, the emergent paradigm is not really a "new" one, though it is convenient to speak of it as if it is. That is to say, the Luo concepts of disorder did not take on significance only in the last generation or so. Rather, what we see and hear now is the modern expression of the pre-existing counterpart to the dominant paradigm: in other words, a dominant paradigm must always presuppose an opposite, however shadowy and variable in expression the latter is.

The idea that a dominant cultural paradigm presupposes and so effectively generates an opposed one leads to the idea of every culture or cultural complex containing within itself the seeds not of its own destruction but of its transformation.

This notion of paradigms contradicting one another raises the question: if culture is a system of communication, then how and what is it communicating? For Leach the younger (1954), ritual and myth, i.e. culture, make statements about differences of status and power. The later Leach (1976) sees culture essentially in the Levi-Straussian sense of both communicating and resolving at a subliminal level man's most fundamental philosophical and psychic problems centering on his obscure origins and destiny. For Gluckman (1965, pp. 223–4), Turner the younger (1957), and Cohen (1969, 1974), culture as ritual, myth, and symbolism, is seen less as a system of communicating messages and more as a mechanism resolving conflicts of power and interest, either of groups or of individuals set within group contexts. That is to say, culture is seen less as having message-carrying properties, i.e. as having transactable meanings, and more as having materially functional ones, i.e. as "doing things". Cohen (1969) sophisticatedly applies this view when he shows the power of symbolism, i.e. culture, in keeping together an economic interest group which loses its formal political autonomy. That is to say, culture "does" for the group what its formal political system used to.

In this study I have viewed culture as the implicational meanings rather than simply functions of institutions. This is essentially a difference of emphasis, for Cohen is perfectly aware that culture can only direct people's actions if it has sufficient meaning for them to belief in it. But where Cohen sees the messages conveyed by culture mainly as directives, dressed up in religious or customarily acceptable idioms, about how to defend or advance economic interests and political autonomy, I see them as live exchanges in what Bloch neatly calls "the long conversation between and within the generations that we call culture" (1976, p. 231). What, then, is this conversation about and what is the logic governing its conduct? It is not necessarily nor even normally about whether the group is losing or winning a political and economic contest with other socio-cultural groups, though this may be the "reality" which we see as outsiders. The conversation is as likely to be about whether values held to be important by the group, or by some members of it, are threatened. Indeed, by definition, much of the conversation we call culture goes on within and not between socio-cultural groups, and the threats to established values are often seen by those in authority to come from the enemy or sinner within. After all, it requires a special externally imposed crisis for internal ranks to close sufficiently that the conversants stop bickering and engage in harmonious chorus. "Politics" are, then, the justifications, exhortations, questioning, and, occasionally, reformulations of a broadly self-defined group's "moral" code and scale of worthwhileness, whether these come from inside or outside the group.

We see the relevance then of the opposed Luo verbal concepts. From one analytical viewpoint those concepts threatening disorder represent the enemy or sinner within and those imposing order represent the cultural continuity cherished by those in authority and with vested interests in maintaining the *status quo*. But another view is to see these opposed forces of emic order and disorder as attempts to turn the long converation between generations into an open debate, a debate that may invite participants from outside the culture. Thus, some young Luo men and women prefer monogamy, few children, lower bridewealth payments, and thereby more money for education for themselves and their children. And they may give examples of "successful" Kikuyu couples who have followed such preferences. But they are accused by the elders in authority of undermining Luo cultural continuity. Their views are muzzled and so there is no debate. Furthermore, through the replication in different institutional contexts of core symbolic values and meanings, the same would-be dissidents themselves unknowingly conform: friends turn out to be false allies in the attempt to escape kin by becoming go-betweens in traditional marriages, and so link lineages and perpetuate the segmentary system; young men refuse to marry young "town" girls as first wives and so ensure older men of a ready supply of second and subsequent co-wives, so perpetuating polygyny, which is seen as the prototype of lineage segmentation; young men struggle to evade heavy bridewealth payments but demand high ones when their own daughters or sisters are eligible to marry, so perpetuating the unambiguous definition of women's status as producers of men's children, on which the segmentary patrilineage system depends. And so on.

If cultural debate among the Luo is stifled in this way, we may legitimately ask what is so special about the Luo case. Is it the particular external environment? Thus, Luo men have become increasingly dependent on urban wage employment; they have developed a powerful interest in education for their children and in clerical work; yet their opportunities for further expansion in these fields have been reduced as unemployment hits all Kenyans generally and as the Kikuyu in particular acquire an increasing proportion of jobs and education. While it is true that the Luo and Kikuyu generally see each other as, and to some extent are, in competition, this fact is by itself inadequate as an explanation of the Luo cultural response. For, increasing wage dependency is part of a global Third World transition from pre-peasant or "tribal" to a combination of peasant and industrial modes of production and distribution. Moreover, most Kikuyu are as subject to this transition as Luo, and their cultural response has been different. The Kikuyu interpret very broadly the value of, and rights secured by, bridewealth; there are wide variations in women's status, and different modes of marriage and cohabitation coexist among them. One form, the urban matrifocal family unit, is in some senses the obverse of Luo urban polygynous families. The latter consists of a "stable" husband working and living in town while his wives alternate in residence between town and country. The urban matrifocal family among some Kikuyu, by contrast, consists of a stable female household head and a succession of "husbands" who pass through the household, perhaps in some cases alternating between rural and urban situations and interests. This obverse parallel is by no means exact but gives some idea of the contrasting cultural responses to a broadly similar process of proletarianization.

I am not arguing that cultural differences *determine* contrasting responses in a common politico-economic or ecological environment, but that (a) they play a critical part in shaping responses which, between interacting and competing groups, take on an exaggerated contrastive nature, and that (b) we are bound, therefore, to consider the logical bases of cultural contrasts.

The stifled cultural debate among the Luo (what is sometimes called the "mystification" of inequalities or "false consciousness") is, then, here to do with certain inherent logical properties. I suggest that the Luo frequent use of key verbal concepts emanating from the domestic domain which impose cultural order on disorder corresponds with a series of other emic unambiguities characteristic of what Fox (1967, pp. 128–30) has called "perpetual" (as distinct from "drift") lineage segmentation, and what Radcliffe-Brown (1950, p. 40) and Southall (1975b) have called a polysegmentary lineage system such as those of the Luo, Tallensi, Nuer, Tiv, and other well-known

African examples, together with the Chinese cases so far documented and which I have mentioned. Even among the peoples of New Guinea, whose descent systems have been contrasted with those of Africa, at least one scholar feels able to apply to one of them, the Melpa, the "classical" notion of a "nesting" segmentary lineage system (A. Strathern, 1971, p. 27).

Perpetual or polysegmentary lineage systems tend to be pyramidal in shape through the recognition of genealogical connections at different levels of segmentation up to the highest superordinate levels. It is as if in this kind of system few or no "gaps" can be tolerated in the genealogical pyramid and that, moreover, there is a drive to preserve the symmetry of coordinate lineages at any level of segmentation. Elders may well "fix" genealogies to conform with ground-level changes of descent group territory, power or wealth. But they do so in conformity with and not in defiance of the overall pyramidal "shape" of their segmentary lineage system. In this sense the classificatory pyramid is unambiguously defined: it is only groups of people who are moved around in it. This overall classificatory unambiguity presupposes unambiguity at all levels of lineage segmentation right down to the family, where this be monogamous or polygynous. The unambiguously defined relations between brothers, and between half-brothers, as expressed through their mothers as a father's co-wife, presuppose their distinctiveness as progenitors not just of separate lineages but of lineages which retain the coordination of these original family relationships. This further presupposes an unambiguous distinction between sons and brothers on the one hand, as eventually perpetuating the segmentary lines of descent, and daughters and sisters on the other hand as eventually producing the children necessary for men to reproduce their lines in this way. Perpetual segmentary lineage systems may differ in some of their diagnostic features, as is well known especially with regard to Africa (Middleton and Tait, 1958, pp. 1–32), and I need not outline them. For example, the Tallensi lack a house-property complex of the kind originally proposed by Gluckman (1951, p. 198) and do not use co-wives' names as lineage eponyms as among the Luo. But there is the same critical importance in polygynous families of matricentral units as future points of lineage segmentation and demarcation (Fortes, 1945, pp. 198–202).

The imposition of cultural order through the use of key verbal concepts among the Luo, then, has to be seen in the light of these unambiguous definitions of descent rules and women's status. Those concepts which threaten order through their ambiguous connotations are, precisely because of this ambivalence, most likely to introduce into Luo culture new ideas and practices from the "outside" and so to redefine it from within. The Luo cultural conversation controlled by elders is, therefore, about how best Luo may preserve the customary unambiguous definitions of men's and women's statuses. The debate that threatens to take place is about these statuses in relation to each other.

Would-be participants in the Luo cultural debate inevitably look to the Kikuyu in Nairobi for support for their arguments depending on their position. Thus, Luo elders decry the independence of many Kikuyu women who set up matrifocal families and control all rights in their children. On the other hand, some younger Luo men and women point approvingly to the absence of polygyny among the Kikuyu and the prevalence of monogamy, with the men drawing a line at expressing approval for matrifocality itself, and with women at most ambivalent. We move here to the realization that, just as there may be said to be the beginnings of a cultural debate among the Luo concerning the advantages of polygyny versus monogamy and the implications this has for women's status, so there is already under way a parallel debate among the Kikuyu concerning the advantages of monogamy as against matrifocality. As a whole the Luo and Kikuyu peoples see themselves in opposition to each other, yet it is clear that the "old" and the "new" models or paradigms of Luo culture already presuppose a partial movement in the direction of those of the Kikuyu. We may characterize this wider structure as follows:

Luo 1 $\longrightarrow$ Luo 2
polygyny   monogamy
           Kikuyu 1 $\longrightarrow$ Kikuyu 2
           monogamy   matrifocality

In other words, the generalized opposition between Luo and Kikuyu is really another way of talking about the opposition among Luo themselves concerning polygyny versus monogamy and the old and new cultural paradigms represented by these two systems of marriage and family: specific as against general segmentation and, more narrowly, perpetual as against drift lineage segmentation. Meanwhile the Kikuyu have their own, open cultural debate regarding the worthwhileness of male-headed monogamy versus matrifocality which I have only touched on in this book but which clearly has implications for a further possible movement from the drift patrilineage segmentation traditionally characteristic of Kikuyu culture to a system of cognatic descent or even, though it is unlikely, matriliny.

The diagram above is not meant to imply that the transition is necessarily one way. Logically, there is no reason why the direction should not be reversed. There are many examples throughout world history of political regimes insisting on a return from what they interpret as "loosely" structured to "conventional" unambiguously defined family life. In Africa it is at least possible, though unlikely, that some future regimes might attempt to curb the matrifocal families that are associated with increasing urbanization in favour of male-headed monogamy and even polygyny. At present the stifled Luo cultural debate means that polygyny is held up as the ideal prerequisite of political leadership and response. That is to say, Luo politics are talked about in the approved idiom of polygynous family relations. By contrast, the more open discussion of internal differences among the Kikuyu has brought politics into family relations in the form of an explicit confrontation between the sexes. The openness of this "sex-war" in Nairobi is well demonstrated by Nelson (1977). Thus, while Luo male elders talk and act politics in a domestic idiom, Kikuyu men and women discuss and organize domestic relations in "political" terms: they can refer to the contrast between male-headed monogamous families and "poorer" matrifocal ones either as a confrontation between the sexes or as a difference and sometimes conflict between socio-economic status groups and even "classes". But, to repeat, these are primarily ways of talking about and so defining relationships, and, over the inevitably long period during which smaller economies and polities are becoming increasingly dependent on and dominated by larger ones, the direction of this process of emic classification may well be reversed, and reversed again. To that extent it is a process which enjoys considerable autonomy as a wider system of transformable cultural paradigms.

Custom as word, deed, and concept

Let me now give the theoretical perspective on the emphasis in this book on culture, i.e. customs, as consisting of the three interacting variables of word, deed, and concept.

Cohen's broad equation of "custom" with "symbol" (1969a, p. 219; 1974a, pp. 66–75, 93) has usefully enabled him to compare such widely varying socio-cultural groups as the endogamous, co-resident, occupationally specialized, ethnically distinct Hausa of Ibadan (1974a, pp. 103–5), the residents of a new South London suburb (op. cit., pp. 27–8), and the people who work in the City of London financial square mile (op. cit., pp. 99–102). Each group interacts frequently enough to establish common conventions or customs, which, like symbols, become unquestioned by its members, or, if they are questioned, are justified as having usefulness (the individual versions of which may vary greatly) which places them beyond further criticism. These shared customs are thus the symbols of the group's autonomy and distinctiveness.

The hypothesis would seem to be that as a group develops common economic interests which cannot, for whatever reason, be protected by government or other formal political means, then the unquestioned and often unrecognized symbols (i.e. customs) correspondingly develop a strength and intensity which exert emotional control over members of the group. If the group's economic interests are threatened and the loyalty of its members in jeopardy, then the symbols may adjust accordingly and exert control over members by drawing on new, powerful ideas to engage their emotional and therefore unquestioning attachment.

This self-regulatory nature of symbolism is why Cohen is able to ascribe to it an autonomy of the group's *immediate* economic interests and political position. While recognizing that symbolism by no means always "saves" a group from economic and political annihilation, I subscribe to this general view of its self-regulatory autonomy. I would ascribe an even greater degree of autonomy to symbolism, to the extent of suggesting that complexes of verbalized and non-verbalized ideas may be kept in store, so to speak, for almost indefinite periods of a group's existence, and brought in and out of storage over long periods. It is even possible for such complexes of ideas temporarily to "float", as it were, over and above and between related groups.

In criticizing this kind of view, Hanson omits to consider the diachronic relationship between cultural ideas and their receptivity or temporary rejection as blueprints for action by members of groups

(Hanson, 1975, p. 101, on Schneider, 1968, p. 7). As I understand them, Turner (1968, p. 7) and Geertz (1966, pp. 7–12) seem to find no difficulty in the view that cultural ideas may at one time appear to be redundant anachronisms but may yet be revived as blueprints for action after relatively long periods in unexpressed "limbo" (Parkin, 1975a, pp. 138–9). A possible case of some cultural ideas being kept in temporary conceptual storage occurs in Southall's analysis of the complex of divine concepts of *Jok Rubanga*. These underlying ideas about divinity and the lexicon for them are shared, but not consciously so, by neighbouring Nilotic and Bandu peoples in Uganda, who otherwise regard themselves and have so been ragarded by anthropologists, as culturally alien to each other. We can speculate that, should these otherwise culturally and linguistically "unrelated" peoples suddenly be drawn into expressing strong common economic and political interests, they would bring such shared ideas much more to the forefront of their collective cultural definition of themselves. It may even be suggested that floating complexes of named ideas which are not unambiguously associated with any one culture but are used by a variety of them, may acutally provide the template on which new social groups may later become defined and established (Parkin, 1977).

I would not, however, equate "symbol" with "custom". "Custom" involves the three-fold interaction of terminology (i.e. there is likely to be at least *some* verbalized reference to the custom which may or may not take the form of variable phrases of indirect reference rather than fixed, key terms), concept (i.e. people have variable notions of what the custom means or does), and conventionalized activity (i.e. carrying out a custom necessarily involves interaction with others which is generally if not precisely premissed on precedent). By contrast, though symbols have meaning in social contexts they do not by themselves include activity. Indeed, their polyvalent efficacy rests precisely on their transcendence of activities. A symbol may be an unverbalized idea, as are the many private symbols of our everyday existence (Cohen, 1969a; Firth, 1973) but as are, also, some of the "blank banners" characteristic of mass and therefore public movements whose purpose and direction are often unclear, ambivalent, and varied both among its members and observers (Ardener, 1971, p. xliv). Or the symbol may be the verbalized idea or set of ideas, suggesting a two-fold interaction of word and concept, rather than the three-fold interaction of word, concept, and action that makes up custom.

The term symbol is used in so many different ways within and out-side of anthropology (see Leach, 1976, pp. 10, 17) that I had here better make clear that I see it as broadly similar to Saussure's "sign" (1960, pp. 66f). Saussure's sign consists of the "signifying", i.e. the "word" and the "signified", i.e. the concept. Levi-Strauss also sees sign (apparently used interchangeably with symbol) thus: ". . . signs can always be defined in the way introduced by Saussure in the case of the particular category of linguistic signs, that is as a link between images [i.e. the sound image of a word] and concepts." (1966, p. 18, my bracketed inclusion.) Here, however, I see the relationship be-tween term and concept being reciprocal and not purely arbitrary (Bauman, 1973, p. 105). The Saussurian arbitrariness of the relation-ship is berhaps best viewed as an unchartered area of potential new relationships, as when a new or old term comes to denote for the first time ever a new or old idea, a process which is probably quite rare even in everyday speech. Otherwise, even wide shifts of meaning in a term do not normally lose contact with an "original" archetypal con-notation.

My concern here is with the analogous distinction between people's conceptualization of the custom and the vernacular terms used to identify it. Semiology (the science of signs) turns upon a basic dis-tinction between verbal and non-verbal signs or symbols. Non-verbalized objects, images, and practices, as well as verbalized ones stand at various levels of homology or opposition. Similarly, we can speak loosely of there being such a thing as non-verbalized custom. That is to say, a particular conventional practice is assumed by the ethnographer to have some meanings for the people engaging in it, but this practice is not verbally identified in any consistent way. It is a convention (i.e. a practice, deed or action of conceptual significance) but it is not neatly labelled with words. It is equivalent to the signi-fied concept without the signifying word-image.

In fact, any culture has these "tacit" conventions together with neatly labelled ones. Moreover, the dynamics of any culture consist in part of the tacit becoming explicit and, though it is surely less easy to detect, of the explicit becoming tacit. This is not a unidirectional process of nature being progressively labelled by expanding cultural taxonomies, but a two-way process of (a) conventional activities losing

L

their verbal labels yet continuing to stimulate intellectual and emotional responses predisposing to further action; and (b) new but unlabelled, or old and delabelled conventions becoming clearly and consistently verbally identifiable.

The emphasis here is really on the *degree* of consistency of verbal identification. That is to say, as I noted above, there is likely to be at least some variable and indirect reference in people's speech to the conventionalized activities in which they are engaged. We can use the distinction between set words and variable phrases (Parkin, 1976, pp. 176–188) to show how new conventions become labelled, and old ones relabelled or delabelled. In the early 1970s in Britain, there developed such a unprecedented demand for houses that for the first time on any scale, estate agents would accept higher offers on behalf of a vendor even after a would-be purchaser had already had his offer accepted and had incurred expenses. This practice did not fall into a previously known category. It was sometimes described as unethical, and sometimes as ethical (i.e. the estate agent trying to do his best for his client) and merely an unfortunate practice. The mass media described it by a multitude of various phrases until, finally, the new (as far as I know) term "gazumping" was applied to the practice.

A contrary process, taking much longer, has occurred in the virtual disappearance from ordinary speech in much of Britain of the single term "courting" to describe a conventional practice which was seen as a possible prelude to formal engagement, itself prior to formal marriage. The term courting was superseded by such variable phrases as "going steady with" or "going out with". Increasingly perhaps, the practice may not be verbally identified at all, it being tacitly assumed that a plurality of boy–girl relationships will eventually narrow down to one culminating in marriage or quasi-permanent cohabitation. The social deformalization of the stages of courting, engagement, and marriage has thus been accompanied by a verbal shift from the use of set words to variable phrases and tacit assumptions. By contrast the consistent use of the term "gazumping" developed in correspondence with the recognition of the practice as having become institutionalized. The originally American terms "gerrymandering", i.e. the political manipulation of constituency boundaries for electoral advantage, and "filibustering", i.e. interminable parliamentary or Senate opposition speeches, are set terms to describe institutionalized practices which were probably preceded by variable phrases to depict "new" conventions (Elliott, 1969, pp. 156, 178).

Such apt and isolated illustrations of this dynamic relationship between word/phrase, concept, and convention can be picked out easily from any culture. Our task should not be just this, however, but should be to show within a culture or between cultures in interaction some key verbal interconnections on the one hand, and some approximately corresponding, interconnected conventional practices on the other. We have to note the gaps and inconsistencies in the possible correspondence between word and practice, and then show the social and conceptual significance of shifts to and fro between the use of set terms and variable phrases.

The ethnographic semanticists have shown close correspondence between the systematic use of referential terms and semantically distinguishable domains of activity and of cultural "thought", e.g. events like weddings, the collection of firewood, plants and medicines, the diagnosis of disease, the use of colour categories, and of kinship terms, to cite a few, familiar early examples. But they have looked at such correspondences as synchronous. They have not tried to relate shifts in the verbal categories to social processes of institutionalization and de-institutionalization, as I am advocating. Not even one of the most recent and sophisticated analyses by "new ethnographers" has attempted this (Manning and Fabrega, 1976).

Among the Giriama of Kenya, for example, the two roles of "diviner" and "doctor" came to be performed by two quite distinct social categories of people: diviners are now either young men or women, while doctors are only old men. Previously, the two roles were performed by the same person, usually a mature man, known simply as a *muganga* (diviner-doctor), the tacit assumption being that he was master of both arts, divination and therapy, which could only be distinguished in speech by variable phrases. Later, as the social separation into the two types of ritual expert occurred, set terms emerged correspondingly to identify them: *muganga wa mburuga/kitswa/pepo* for diviner; and *muganga wa mukoba/kombo* for doctor. The opposition between the two institutionally distinct roles came neatly to correspond with the use of concise and consistent role-terms to identify each of them. This development corresponded with the emergence of an internal cleavage among the Giriama between entrepreneurial and poor farmers as the society became involved in an international cash crop economy. In this rapidly changing society, the contrary process occurred: some key terms became unhinged, so to speak, from the conventionalized roles and activities to which they once narrowly referred. Thus, at the same time that the roles of diviner and doctor were being verbally distinguished, another term, *mwenye mudzi*, meaning homestead head, was losing its previous specific reference. Previously it referred to a man who was head by virtue of his age and genealogical seniority. In more modern times its meaning has been extended to include men who are relatively young but wealthy enough through cash cropping to head their own homesteads. The old idea that authority was principally conferred by social and lineage seniority with or without wealth has become part of a wider idea of authority as conferred by economic power held by young men as well as elders. In other words, as authority by age and seniority has languished, the key term that used to refer to it has lost its old semantic specificity and has been extended to cover other kinds of authority. As a third example, the "new" practice of entrepreneurship in the modern capitalist sense is not consistently referred to in the vernacular by any key terms, but is referred to either by a variety of phrases formed on the spot, so to speak, or by a foreign loan word (Parkin, 1967, pp. 176–88).

This analysis is thus "holistic" in the sense that it looks at the range of politico-economic and cultural institutions both uniting and dividing the whole society in its relation with the outside world, yet it also considers more microscopically the way in which people's *verbal* identification of key roles could be seen to be dynamically related with the conceptualization and practice of these roles. Comparable is Sansom's analysis (1976, pp. 143–61) of the way in which the Pedi (South Africa) publicly refer to individual amounts of bridewealth as consisting of livestock when in fact these amounts each vary considerably in their proportion of animals to cash and in overall value. Privately, individuals frankly talk about these differences of value in the matter-of-fact phrases of everyday speech, but publicly they use the key terms denoting customary livestock values as a way of playing down wealth differences and preserving the idea of an "unspoiled" egalitarian ethos among them.

A "customary" role, then, like a "customary" practice, in fact consists of three interacting variables: the word or words used to describe the custom; the conventionalized practice of the custom; and the varying meanings and purposes that people may attribute to the custom. The verbal variable involves a potential shift to and fro between key, set words and variable phrases. Or, to put the range of shift more succinctly, in describing activities speakers may shift back and forth between (a) verbal categories which are conceptually condensed and lexically and syntactically predictable, and (b) functionally descriptive phrases which are conceptually more diffuse and lexically and syntactically less predictable. This contrast roughly parallels Bernstein's distinction between "restricted" and "elaborated" codes (1971, pp. 144–61). The second variable is the extent to which people agree on the ideas connoted by terms and practices. Key terms tend to limit interpretation more than variable phrases. But it is also precisely under the "cover" of key terms that new conflicting ideas can break out. The third variable is the conventionalized activity which may or may not be named, and which may alternate between having considerable or limited conceptual significance for other conventionalized activities. For many people "courtship" has lost its previous distinctive significance and does not nowadays clearly demarcate the subsequent phase known as "engagement". Engagement may itself become conceptually blurred with temporary cohabitation and common law marriage, so that, together as a single area of male–female relations, courtship, engagement, and cohabitation contrast with formal, legalized marriage with its more specific role-expectations and sanctions. In other words, a three-part semantic structure has been reduced to two.

Leach's study (1954) of the Burmese Kachin is the best-known early example of an holistic analysis of the dynamic interrelationship of the use of verbal categories and of conventionalized practices in a wider politico-economic context. The whole analysis turns on the meticulous examination of "such key verbal concepts" (op. cit., pp. 100ff.) as the antithesis *mayu-dama* (landlord/wife-giver: tenant/bridewealth giver); *hka* (debts) and its counterpart *hpaga* (trade, ritual); the ritually relevant contrast of *nta* (an ordinary house) with *htingu* (a chief's house); *htinggaw* (ranging in meaning from family to localized lineage of small span); the ranked classes of *nat* (spirits); and so on. These and many other verbal concepts among the Kachin can be seen (a) to be conceptually related to each other in a systematic way even though they refer to different semantic domains which we normally characterize as political, economic, ritual and kinship; (b) to fall, as an interconnected set of verbal concepts, under the over-arching verbal contrast of *gumsa*, denoting a hierarchical political philosophy and system, and *gumlao*, an egalitarian one; and (c) to have such conceptual ambivalence in relation to each other that a term or set of terms can actually "mask" the activities of men. Thus, ". . . while the kinship composition of the community (of Hpalang) had remained more or less unaltered over the past 40 years, there had been radical changes in the internal authority structure. The leaders of the community still used *gumsa* categories to describe the respec-tive status of groups and persons; they attached importance to the notion of aristocracy, to the title of chief (*duwa*), and to the rights of chiefs . . .; they insisted vigorously on the obligations of *dama* towards their *mayu*; they stressed the importance of large and spectacular sacrifices at the *numshang*. But all this was largely pretence. Had the community been organized on *gumlao* principles with no aristocrats, no chiefs and no tributary dues, the *de facto* situation would have been almost the same. This is an illustration of the fact that the con-trast between *gumsa* and *gumlao* is a difference of ideal order rather than empirical fact." (ibid., p. 97.)

I would add also that it is an illustration of the dynamic inter-relationship between the variables of ideal, terminology, and con-ventionalized activity. To this Saussurian perspective can also be added the suggestion that the shift from the use of one key term, *gumsa*, to another, *gumlao*, was mediated by innumerable interven-ing phrases gradually expressing the conceptual change. This can only be a suggestion but does seem likely to have accompanied the quarrels and arguments in the factional feud in the community of Hpalang which finally enabled a headman in it to call himself chief (*duwa*, i.e. a *gumsa* category) in opposition to another "official" chief (also referred to as *duwa*) and, effectively, to stress the principles of lineage independence and equality which are, in fact, *gumlao* catego-ries, even though they were not, for a time, identified as such (ibid., pp. 88–9).

In other words, through the medium of *paroles* of infinite verbal variety but similar conceptual thrust, key terms in a taxonomy may be altered or transposed. But in this process there must be a time-lag during which one key term is used, e.g. *gumsa*, which does not accurately represent the "facts on the ground", which are themselves half-way, so to speak, to becoming renamed, e.g. as *gumlao*.

It is, then, not simply that ideals have to be out of fit with empirical facts in order that diverse socio-cultural groups can continue interacting with each other. It is more that key terms denoting central fields of action must signify sufficient conceptual ambivalence that they can accommodate changes in these fields of action while remaining in use as the interconnected words of a language. The point is that, even after a revolution, people still have to speak to each other in the same language as before. The revolutionary government can ban the use of certain terms or insist on the use of new ones. But old terms have a habit of creeping back in, and new, artificially created terms or usages have a habit of dropping out. Immediately after the French revolution in 1789, the egalitarian "fraternité" converted all terms of address into the mutual *citoyen* and mutual *tu*. But after a few years, people abandoned *citoyen* in address and reverted to the hierarchical usages of *tu* and *vous* (Brown and Gilman, 1972, p. 266). Soviet Union revolutionaries decreed the egalitarian use of the term of mutual respect, *Vy*, but the hierarchical use of *Ty* and *Vy* eventually returned (Ervin-Tripp, 1972, pp. 233–4). As a general rule, the only enduring changes in a language, even those of vocabulary, are the unplanned ones. "Gazumping" in British English was coined because it filled a lexical gap and a conceptual need to identify a new practice. A loan word is sometimes used in this way. "Courting" was dropped because it demarcated a social distinction which had become blurred. Such changes are relatively few and, one may reasonably speculate, are more characteristic of societies undergoing rapid and extensive social differentiation and specialization which are becoming recognized, or made cognitively salient, in people's speech.

Here we may return to the Luo. For, in spite of Luo men's increasing urban wage dependency and internal socio-economic differentiation, these developments have not diverted them from following three key institutional practices: a high polygyny rate, the exchange of valuable bridewealth for rights over the children of a woman as well as for her other services as a wife, and an overarching modified but recognizable segmentary lineage system of urban associations which deal with politics and define marriage choices.

But what is it that is really consistent in their retention of these three customary practices? In normal anthropological parlance, we say that each customary practice has "persisted" because it has successfully "adapted" to changing political and economic circumstances. Thus, polygyny is seen by Luo to be useful because it enables a townsman to keep his urban job and bring up and try to educate his family in town while at the same time continuing to farm land at home. Valuable bridewealth persists, and becomes even more inflated in value, because it is tied in with a cultural notion, which is controlled by older men who want a good "return" on their daughters and sisters, of how best to invest "surplus" income derived from urban employment. The segmentary pyramid of urban associations (a) provides a general guideline as to who is eligible to marry whom, thereby also facilitating the circulation of information about who is financially a good risk as a possible son-in-law and about whether a prospective daughter-in-law comes from a family which has no history of having been afflicted by *chira*; and (b) has been central in the political organization of the Luo as a whole, within town, between town and country, and nationally.

These three major components of Luo culture are, then, by no means analysed as simple transplantations from a traditional past to a modern, metropolitan-dominated national society (*pace* Cohen, 1974, p. 94). They have these modern, practical "functions" and implications which reinforce and are reinforced by traditional ideals of generational and genealogical authority and of the desirability of large families and the demonstration of ethnic strength through population growth.

I now recognize, however, that there is a definitional problem if we regard these three, i.e. polygyny, bridewealth, and segmentary lineage relations, as no more than persisting customary *forms* of Luo culture which have become adapted to new political and economic circumstances by taking on new functions and meanings (Cohen, 1969, pp. 218–20; 1974, pp. 30, 64, 86; Parkin, 1974, p. 144). There is a problem because it raises the question of what precisely we mean by customary forms. If we mean the practice of the custom then here the meaning of "form" becomes inseparable from that of "function": and we have to acknowledge that each of the three institutions has an altered range of "functions", i.e. unintended consequences, as I have described.

The significant continuity is that the three institutions do still presuppose each other. They presuppose each other emically, in the way people identify and evaluate their structural interrelationship. Thus, a Luo says: "You cannot have marriage without bridewealth, or you will lose the children, whom you need to build a strong family and lineage, which requires expansion through additional wives and children." The three institutions also presuppose each other etically in that: a high rate of polygyny tends to create a scarcity of women and so encourages elders and polygynists to marry off daughters and sisters at the best rate; which requires these men to convert their control over urban employment and educational opportunities into control over young men's and women's marriages and marriage choices; which then requires these older men to use their genealogical knowledge of the "precise" lines of exogamy and permissable marriage relations; which further implies the modified preservation of a segmentary lineage framework of classification and activities.

The *forms* of custom, then, are like the constitutent elements of language, whether phonemes, morphemes, or whatever. They are the emes of behaviour and the etics of analysis. The point is that they can only be discussed in relation to each other, but not in isolation. Treated in isolation, we might be tempted to regard the Luo localized polysegmentary lineage structure as no longer greatly concerned with, say, "predatory" territorial expansion and so as having greatly changed over the last fifty years, and to leave the matter at that. But, in fact, in its relationship to the other two key institutions of polygyny and bridewealth, there is a consistent dominant paradigm of family and lineage expansion and segmentation through the accumulation and exchange of women and bridewealth. This cultural paradigm is as much in evidence nowadays as a rural–urban phenomenon as it was fifty years ago as a rural one, in the same way that, fifty years ago, any institutional "changes" noted over the previous fifty years could be seen to have occurred in relatively constant relationship to each other. A shift of paradigm will occur when, say, the above proposition falters: as when, perhaps, women and bridewealth are no longer exchanged and accumulated. The "changing" status of Luo women has therefore to be viewed as either consistent with, or contradictory to, this traditional paradigm. It is only when it is logically contradictory that we shall have a new paradigm.

A continuing paradigm of cultural logic does not have to exist only nor mainly at the level of activities. It also exists at the levels of lexicon and concept. I have explained that the actual "practice" of the three Luo main institutions has undeniably adapted in each case to the particular exigencies of urban housing and wage employment. The surface or "visible" continuity of Luo customs or culture lies more in the interconnection of key Luo terms which summarily refer to people's conceptualization of these customary practices. That is to say, like the verbal categories associated with *gumsa* and *gumlao*, key Luo terms identify the ideas that people associate with polygyny, bridewealth, and segmentary lineages. The terms of identification appear to have remained constant since before Luo became so heavily dependent on urban wages. The ideas connoted by key kinship, family, and lineage terms have, not surprisingly, undergone some shifts as Luo adapted to a dual rural–urban system of family settlement. But they can still be used by male elders in authority in such a way that they presuppose each other: the disease *chira* results from a breach of seniority rules; seniority rules among co-wives, between older and younger men, and between men and women, must therefore be preserved; such seniority rules imply the preservation of rules of agnatic exogamy, and so on.

But alongside this authoritative use of verbal concepts, people inevitably develop their own ideas of what the key terms "mean". As long as the ideas remain at little more than the level of individual interpretation, the authoritative use of established verbal concepts remains unchallenged. This is the area of individual interpretation that characterizes the young Luo monogamist who argues that one wife and a few well-educated children are better than two or three wives and many less educated children, but who responds in the end to family and other pressures, both practical and ideological, to take a second wife and becomes a respected *jadoho*. It is when individual interpretations become associated with sectional interests that they then challenge the authoritative use of key verbal concepts. Neither young Luo monogamists nor Luo women themselves have transformed individual into sectional modes of verbal articulation.

It is this area of individual differences of interpretation covered by the single term and potentially transformable into sectionally opposed differences that takes me back to my elaboration of the Saussurian analogy of "custom" or "culture" as consisting of three interacting variables: conventionalized activities, the terminology referring to them, and the ideas connoted by the terms and activities.

The following schema suggests eight logical possibilities of articulation:

	Fixed	*Varying*
Referential term(s)	A. Key term	a. Variable phrase
Denoted concept(s)	B. Collectively shared meaning	b. Individually and sectionally held meanings
Conventions	C. Changing in consistent relationship with each other	c. Changing in conflict with each other

The eight logical possibilities can be set out as follows:

ABC	*abc*
ABc	*abC*
Abc	*aBC*
AbC	*aBc*

These can be regarded as possible tendencies going on *within* a culture and as associated with one or other social category (e.g. male elders as against young men, or men as against women). Thus, *ABC* roughly represents the authoritative use of key verbal concepts by Luo elders in their domestic or political speeches. It presupposes a high degree of cultural harmony and homogeneity. Its opposite, *abc*, represents chaos, with individuals or emergent sections of a cultural group disagreeing not only about the way activities should be carried out but also about what they mean and how to describe them verbally. At the level of individual differences, it refers to moments out of line with everyday life, a kind of malign communitas, which characterizes, say, the "unreasonableness" of Luo negligent fellow-agnates or of co-wives who quarrel and who must be brought to order through the use of key terms in an attempt to denote precise lines of seniority and obligation. At the level of emergent sectional differences within a cultural group, it may characterize continuing disagreement, resolvable only through a switch to common key terms and/or mutually consistent conventions to reunite them; or to distinct key terms and/ or unambiguously opposed conventions to establish their sectionalism.

ABc represents the kind of situation which may occur if, say, (a) Luo women effectively oppose polygyny, men start marrying at an earlier age, and young couples invest cash in education or a business rather than in bridewealth and many children, while, (b) at the same time, male elders continue to preach through the use of key verbal concepts tied to notions of an expanding segmentary lineage system which is no longer appropriate. I have suggested that this is a possible direction for Luo. *abC* represents the private and variably expressed mutterings of complaint of young Luo men and women who, for their various different reasons, oppose the authority of elders, the obligations to agnates, and the pressures to marry an older man, or a second wife, or to have many rather than few children. The institutional pressures exerted by elders succeed in overwhelming the inarticulate and unorganized.

Abc and *aBC* have to be seen as complementary aspects of a single process by which institutions become renamed, rethought and reordered in logical relationship to each other. For example, if the practice of formal polygyny conflicts with a new economic use to which bridewealth is put and so is rapidly abandoned, we may expect a period during which the term for polygynist, *jadoho*, which is synonymous with a man of eminence, authority, and wealth, will have attached to it a high turnover of different and new meanings, many of which contradict the traditional sense as well as each other. Transferred to a popular Western context the idea of an old or middle-aged man taking a much younger second or third wife exhibits some possibilities, not all of them disapproving nor denigratory! This is the process depicted by *Abc*. Its complement, *aBC*, might be the public acceptance and institutionalized practice of either serial monogamy or formal monogamy plus "outside" wives (cf. Fraenkel, 1964, p. 114), which is, however, for some time described through the use of variable phrases rather than fixed terms. A Luo would probably not apply the term *jadoho* to a man plurally "married" in this way, for the term already presupposes cardinal features of Luo culture. He would have to invent phrases to describe the man's "marital" state.

AbC refers to a conventional activity which is constantly referred to by the same terms but about which there are individual and/or sectional conflicts as to its meaning. Thus, as we saw from some cases in Chapter 8, women identify monogamy, polygyny, and lineage growth as being constantly linked to each other, but are at present often divided by age and/or educational and occupational differences in their views on the appropriate status of women in marriage.

The joker in the pack, or perhaps the ace, is *aBc*. This represents a people's sharing of an idea which is not, however, consistently denoted by word and convention. Such shared ideas are best seen as the outpourings of a consistent archetypal concept of Jungian proportions which underlies a range of distinct and differently labelled Luo conventions. It ultimately characterizes the latent paradigm of Luo culture which I have mentioned and which is at present given no more than shadowy verbal expression in the set of semantic concepts of "disorder", outlined in the preceding section.

As well as depicting tendencies within cultures, the scheme can be used to make contrasts between cultures, though I make the following contrast only generally. The use of key terms deriving from the domestic domain in the formalized speech of Luo in authority presupposes consensus among other Luo as to what the terms mean and the customs to which they refer (i.e. a tendency towards ABC). The formalized speech of Kikuyu in authority tends towards Abc. That is to say, it abridges national with ethnic verbal concepts and acknowledges more frankly some Kikuyu sectional differences, as for example in the contrast between matrifocal and male-headed families, and the implied contrasting notions of the use and value of bridewealth and of the status of women and children. At the time of fieldwork, then, a Luo audience was likely to reply in the formalized idiom with which it was presented, while a Kikuyu one was more likely to include in its reply some language of individual and sectional disagreement (i.e. veering towards abc).

In these ways the schema allows us to depict systematically variations in the degree of formalization in speech and in the responses to it both within and between cultural groups, depending on the level of analytical abstraction and contrast, and over time. Even within a manifestly homogeneous cultural group, new forces may be at work which have yet to be articulated. Thus, Luo men exchange key verbal concepts with each other in the formal speech of domestic crisis and other events and of political meetings; but under the cover of this exchange, individual men and women think, act, and talk in ways that are at variance with the assumptions behind the formal exchange. These are the beginnings of an open debate about the redefinition of existing cultural statuses and, possibly, boundaries.

The problem of cultural self-perpetuation

The control of women as producers of men's children as being at the basis of the perpetuation of a segmentary lineage society is classically illustrated in Meillassoux's study of the pre-capitalist Guro of West Africa (1964). There the emphasis is on the exploitation by elders of younger men, for it is elders who control the land, livestock, the goods that make up brideweaelth, and the genealogical and ritual knowledge deemed necessary for the proper fulfillment of customary obligations.

At first sight there are striking similarities here with the situation described for Luo in Nairobi. But the power that Luo elders wield over young men no longer derives from lineage relations providing the basis of economic production, either in rural or urban areas. Rather, elders' economic power over the young comes from their control of diminishing urban job and educational opportunities and, as a consequence, of bridewealth. Yet these same Luo elders are themselves subject to wider controls emanating from their own dependency on wage employment. This means that, during a prolonged period of expanding employment and educational opportunities, young men might reverse this power of elders as I have described for the rural Giriama of Kenya following the consequences of a boom there (1972), but it would fall to young women to redefine radically their own statuses and, by implication, the existing Luo cultural paradigm.

Such contracting and expanding environments of opportunity are, of course a dominant feature of modern Third World *laisser faire* economies, which are especially vulnerable to the market forces of international supply and demand. Through them, the Luo segmentary lineage framework persists, not as providing the primary units of economic production as among the pre-capitalist Guro, but as a relatively autonomous classificatory system of ideas directing marriage relationships and the circulation of valuable bridewealth, and thereby providing ready-made units of political articulation. As a classificatory system, then, the segmentary lineage framework is here less to do with how a people operate their dominant mode of economic production but more to do with how they conceptualize, if I may use the phrase, their dominant mode of cultural self-perpetuation. This view obliges us to consider the distinctive logical features of this mode of endo-cultural communication.

The problem of cultural self-perpetuation is central to social anthropology. In its negative etic sense, i.e. as really "masking" the destruction or exploitation of a group, a theory of cultural self-perpetuation is implicit in the originally Marxist and neo-Marxist concepts of "false consciousness", ideological "misrepresentation", and "mystification of social inequality", which have entered the language of socio-cultural anthropology (Cohen, 1969a, pp. 220–21; Parkin, 1972, p. 99; 1975a, p. 137; Bloch, 1975b, pp. xiv, 204; Hobart, 1977a, b). But since the foundations of the subject, anthropologists have been dealing with theories of self-perpetuation in a positive emic sense, usually with reference to kinship, and to a lesser extent named age-set organizations linking men with "fathers" and "grandfathers", as consisting of the views of the people themselves as how best they and their customs might be reproduced. Socio-cultural anthropology is based on trying to understand how peoples reproduce themselves (or fail to do so) through their cultures. Hence the importance of kinship in at least a wide sense of the concept as the anchor and *sine qua non* of the subject. In its metaphorical as well as literal sense kinship is not only irreducible but also the generative grammar of all cultural communication, for the analyst as much as for the people he studies. The continuing analytical concern in anthropology with cultural definitions of self-perpetuation in complex societies is nicely instanced in Cohen's use of the metaphor, "the 'lineages' of modern society", as being "the interest groups which compete, quarrel and co-operate in the struggle for power and privilege" (1974, p. 125). The use of the word "lineage" is clearly more than a matter of illustrative convenience. It represents the meeting together of "our" analytical and "their" folk assumptions about the very purpose of human existence: that the individual should play a lineal and therefore indispensable part in the process of collective continuity.

In discussing cultural self-perpetuation we may not assume *a priori* that cultural boundaries are immutable. On the contrary, as scholars have demonstrated in recent years, they are constantly shifting. Before colonization the Luo culture and people were part of a wider interacting set of groups, some of whom are linguistically related (the "Nilotes"), and some not, e.g. the Bantu Luyia neighbours of the Luo and Padhola, and the Bantu Nyoro neighbours of the Nilotic Alur and Acholi. Across surface cultural and linguistic boundaries, ideas were transacted to and fro and came to constitute a common pool of fundamental concepts as Southall demonstrated with reference to the divine concept of *Jok Rubanga* and to folk theories of twinship (1971, 1972), and as I have suggested in Chapter

5 with reference to the concept of *chira*, a word of Bantu origin covering a range of ideas about mortal sin.

The cultural exchange of ideas and words across ethnic boundaries continues. But two factors now impede or retard this. First, colonial authorities imposed permanent administrative boundaries on the impermanent, previously shifting ones of alleged ethnic groups, thereby artificially freezing the rate of population movement and cultural and linguistic exchange between them, and setting up the self-consciously discrete groupings which we first recognized as "tribes" and then as "ethnic groups" (Southall, 1970). Second, thus distinguished as self-consciously discrete social entities, these ethnic groups were bound to provide the primary frames of collective reference in the scramble and competition for jobs, housing, education, and political power in the process leading towards increasing urban wage dependency. As I have shown in this book, the Luo in Nairobi have developed this sense of cultural autonomy and discreteness, as, to a lesser and variable extent, have other ethnic groups. Adopting a conventional analytical approach I have looked at Luo culture adapting in the context of three external factors: the political, i.e. increasing Kikuyu dominance at the expense of Luo; the economic, i.e. Luo men's increasing dependency on urban wages; and the urban ecological, i.e. the late provision of family accommodation in Nairobi and its still later inadequacy, and the availability in Nairobi of a wide range of state and private schools. In fact, we may regard all three sets of external factors, including those of a manifestly political and economic nature, as "ecological" in a wide sense. They together constitute a variable environment of opportunity.

For any particular group, or for "entrepreneurial" individuals in any group, opportunities expand or contract. For the Luo as a whole, though not necessarily for a minority of individual Luo, this environment of opportunity has recently contracted, while for Kikuyu it has expanded. Those few Luo who have discovered potentially profitable "niches" in this otherwise contracting environment of opportunity, e.g. women traders, professional women of superior education, and men who successfully invest in education for their children rather than extra wives for themselves, represent possible breaks in the continuity of Luo culture. Within their contracting environment of opportunity and in the face of these perceived but as yet unarticulated "threats" to their self-perpetuation, most Luo "struggle" as they see it, to reproduce themselves biologically by way of a close adherence to the three main tenets of their culture: polygyny, bridewealth and a modified principle of organization through segmentary lineages.

The cultural responses of such African peoples as the Luo, Luyia, Tiv, and Ibo, each with its localized polysegmentary lineage system, may in fact be broadly similar within a range of contracting or expanding environments of opportunity (Southall, 1975). What about the lineage systems in New Guinea which have been regarded as sufficiently distinctive of "African" ones to be called a New Guinea type (Barnes, 1962)? Is their underlying paradigm of cultural self-perpetuation so different that we cannot expect them also to share a broad range of responses to environmental change? It may be fruitful to consider this question in some detail.

In the preceding section I characterized Luo culture as having operated over at least the past hundred years according to a dominant paradigm of family and lineage expansion and segmentation through the accumulation and exchange of women and bridewealth. The paradigm is nowadays expressed more in the attempt to push one's progeny into acquiring jobs and education than land and cattle, but it is still the ultimate referent of thought, speech, and action.

The alleged differences between the "New Guinea" and "African" descent models have been listed and argued about but in the end it is difficult not to agree with La Fontaine, who in an exhaustive comparison, insists that most of the differences are to do with "the history of anthropological theory rather than the geography of anthropological fieldwork" (1973, p. 41). As analysts, our perception of cultural similarity depends on the degree of generality of our level of abstraction. My paradigm characterizing Luo segmentary lineage culture is certainly highly generalized. But then it has to be, for in a diachronic analysis of the response of a segmentary lineage culture to increasing urban wage dependency within, paradoxically, a contracting political and economic environment, the variables would otherwise be too numerous to handle, and we have a theoretical obligation at least to keep in mind the basic paradigm which broadly characterizes some cultures and distinguishes them from others.

Provided a heuristic model classifies a wide ethnographic range of cultures on the basis of contrasting and complementary rather than simply "different" features, it should be possible to keep under control the tendency for rampant, endless typology-making.

To begin with, then, let us ask whether a New Guinea people like the Melpa or Mount Hagen are, like the Luo, culturally premissed on the paradigm of (a) family and lineage/clan expansion and segmentation through (b) the accumulation and exchange of women and bridewealth between exogamous descent groups. For the Luo these two factors can be elaborated as exogamous descent group expansion and segmentation emanating from the polygynous family as prototype, and the exchange of women and valuables between exogamous descent groups. From the evidence in this book and cited sources, I think it is clear that the Luo "think" of the first process as culturally prior to the second. That is to say, they work out the genealogical range of marriage possibilities and then fit "suitable" marriages into it. This is not to deny that they "fabricate" genealogies nor as individuals seek financially reliable families for intermarriage. They certainly do. But they do spend a great deal of time, energy and resources in ensuring that elders of the different lineages and segments of a "clan" (i.e. maximal exogamous lineage) agree on such matters, as Blount also shows in a contemporary example (1975). In other words, the Luo concern for genealogy decides whether a particular marriage is acceptable: ideologically genealogy governs the exchange of wives and valuable bridewealth between exogamous descent groups. For the Melpa, the cultural priority is the other way round: (a) important *moka* transactions may develop from bridewealth and childbirth payment exchanges between "clans", which require (b) only enough of a notion of family and clan expansion and segmentation to preserve the exogamous principle.

Thus, under (a), exchange marriage between "clans" and *moka* transactions are idioms of each other, and bridewealth transactions and subsequent childbirth payments in other marriages can anticipate *moka* transactions between affines (M. Strathern, 1972, pp. 91, 97); and "big men" achieve their positions through successful *moka* transactions between exogamous descent groups called "clans" (A. Strathern, 1971, pp. 33, 121 ff.), and, through their activities, perpetuate the segmentary operation of descent group structure (p. 28). Under (b), then, Melpa descent groups do operate according to "the classical 'nesting' fashion of segmentary lineage systems" (A. Strathern, 1971, p. 27), even though genealogical connections at the different segmental levels may be unspecified (A. Strathern, 1973, p. 31). Certainly, this "nesting" segmentary operation is more significant in its similarity with Luo than whether we call descent groups and segments of them "lineages" or "clans" and "sub-clans".

Both Luo and Melpa also have patrilineal inheritance and succession, polygyny, and marriage payments which are exchanged among other things for rights in wives' children and which are normally recoverable (though under a narrower range of conditions among the Melpa (M. Strathern, 1972, pp. 96–120, 190, 196)). The Melpa, like the Luo, place considerable value on a wife's child-bearing capacities (M. Strathern, 1972, pp. 99, 186, 193–5).

The Melpa cultural paradigm of self-perpetuation and expansion is, then, the Luo one read backwards: the accumulation and exchange of women and valuables (including marriage, childbirth, and *moka* transactions) is achieved within a framework of clan/lineage expansion and segmentation. The Luo and Melpa operate according to the same paradigm but in each case it is emphasized in the contrasting direction. This simple model based on contrasting and complementary rather than simply "different" features, is a more useful way of initially comparing descent group systems whose unilineal and segmentary natures vary on the surface.

We can go further with the comparison between Luo and Melpa. Critical to both is the position of women which is characterized as "ambivalent" and "inarticulate". Among the Luo the conceptualization of the polygynous family as the prototype of future lineage expansion and polysegmentation locates the ambiguities of female status within the family in the role and person of the co-wife: co-wives produce sons for a husband's lineage but different sets of uterine sons later divide the lineage by forming opposed segments. This future process is implicit in the related terms for jealousy (*nyiego*) and co-wife (*nyieka*), and in the term *libamba*, meaning alternating rivalry and alliance between lineage segments in balanced opposition of the kind deriving from separate fathers or from co-wives of the same father (cf. Beidelman, 1966, pp. 458–9, on Nuer and Gluckman, 1965, p. 224, on Zulu co-wives).

The modern expression of this ambiguity in women's status rests on the emerging conflict, privately expressed by men and sometimes women, between the ideal that a husband should have more than one wife, each producing many children, and the socio-economic advantages of having only one wife, preferably earning money, and a few highly educated children. These are "advantages" which, when transferred to public conversations and men's speeches become re-expressed as the potential instruments of female independence and of the destruction of agnatic unity and lineage growth.

The Melpa observe that "a woman should not make brothers quarrel" (M. Strathern, 1972, p. 265), and co-wife relationships are seen as characterized by jealousy as among the Luo. But though there is a term for head wife, there are none for second and subsequent wives, and they are not formally ranked as among the Luo (pp. 52–3). Moreover, there is no suggestion that Melpa polygynous family relations are conceptualized as prototypical of genealogical growth and segmentation. The ambivalence of a Melpa wife's status is not located *within* the family, polygynous or otherwise, but *between* families, or more specifically between her husband's descent group and her natal one. This ongoing, in-between status of a wife-cum-daughter/sister corresponds with the ongoing nature of material exchanges between the two exogamous descent groups, which may start out as bridewealth and childbirth payments and end up as full *moka* transactions.

It is consistent with this ongoing, in-between status that Melpa wives have a higher chance than Luo women of keeping their own children after divorce. Though it may well be the divorced Melpa women's father and brothers who have formal jurisdiction over any children she manages to keep, she does at least represent the thin end of a possible wedge facilitating the development of increased control by women of the custody of their children, as tends to be the case in cultures based on cognatic and, sometimes, non-segmentary unilineal descent groups (Fallers, 1957; Leach, 1961, p. 119, on Lakher; A. P. Caplan, 1975, p. 31), a kind of incipient if partial "mother-right", such as appears to be developing among the Kikuyu in Nairobi.

However, this is speculative, for Melpa women are still characterized as much less likely than men to articulate verbal arguments advocating the change of cultural paradigm that would result from, say, their insistence that they control whom they should marry and who should have custody of any children born to them (M. Strathern, 1972, pp. 159–62, 266–70). In this respect, the Melpa and the Luo are still much closer to each other than either is to the Kikuyu, among whom matrifocal families headed by politically articulate women have already emerged. There is, however, an interesting parallel be-

tween the Melpa and Luo which points to a possibly similar development.

I have argued that, because Luo men have inflated bridewealth by
investing urban income in it and by marrying more than one wife,
they have become even more dependent on urban wage employment,
even though younger men entering the job market face diminishing
opportunities. But men use their verbal "articulateness" not consciously to "free" themselves from this dependency, but to perpetuate
their traditional control of women's marriages. We can suggest that,
under the "cover" of this male control of the means of verbal communication among Luo, men are increasing their urban wage dependency while women remain at least relatively insulated from it.
Women's possible movement into higher education and trade may of
course push them into comparable dependency. But it may also secure
for them control over what Luo culture dictates a Luo man should
aim for: to be the father of many children and the founder of a
lineage. The implications for the dominant Luo paradigm of self-
perpetuation are radical.

Among the Melpa, too, men's perception of women as inarticulate
in argument and therefore politically ineffectual actually gives women
the "cover" to challenge male dominance by deliberately non-verbal
means, e.g. independently trying to assert marriage choices, sabotaging
ongoing affinal exchanges through divorce (M. Strathern, 1972, p.
314), and by withdrawing from verbal discussion of possible reconciliation (p. 270). A main difference between the two analyses is that
the Luo are seen as subject to a diachronic, global process of increasing
Third World involvement in capital-intensive urbanization creating
high employment expectations and relatively few jobs. It does seem,
however, that the huge increases in *moka* transactions have to be
looked at indirectly as deriving from similar global factors (A.
Strathern, 1971, pp. 107–11, 227–8) which encapsulate and widen
economics previously smaller in scale and which may redefine the
Melpa paradigm of cultural self-perpetuation through changes in the
status of their women under the cover of men's speech.

The problem of self-perpetuation is, then, one of political as well
as ecological struggle and survival. This falls within the variable
identified by Cohen (1974a) as that of power relations, which I have
subsumed in the idea of each socio-cultural group operating within
a variable environment of opportunity. The cultural definition of

M

self-perpetuation, i.e. the key terms in speech and the ideals and conventionalized activities which a people see as best achieving their self-perpetuation, falls within the second variable identified by Cohen as that of symbolism. I have looked internally at the dynamics of this variable, i.e. culture, and so have placed primary emphasis on it. I have broken it down into the three "sub-variables" of speech, cultural "thought", and conventionalized activity. I believe that this breakdown represents an advance on the perennial two-variable preoccupation in anthropolgy and sociology, variously expressed, of ideals and expectations on the one hand, and action on the other.

The three variables interact among the Luo within the constraints imposed by a dominant paradigm that predicates family and lineage expansion and segmentation through the accumulation and exchange of women and bridewealth between exogamous descent groups. A shift in the paradigm can only occur by a reordering of inconsistent or contradictory assumptions which were previously tacit or private but then become explicit and public: in the case of the Luo this could happen if women collectively articulated in thought, word, and deed their control over marriage forms and over the destiny and use, and perhaps number, of their children. As it is, the Luo continue to extract from their culture the idea of polygynous family growth controlled by men as a way of communicating and defining their collective response to apparent threats to their self-perpetuation. That is to say, their very interpretation of changing power relations is part of their continuing system of cultural ideas, key terms, and conventionalized activities. I have only needed to document briefly as an historical fact that the Luo environment of opportunity has indeed contracted.

Were it to expand significantly and without impediment, there are two possible developments.

1. The increased internal differentiation of wealth and socio-economic status that might result among Luo might be accompanied by publicly contrasted and conflicting interpretations as how best they should perpetuate themselves, e.g. whether through monogamy and a few highly educated children or polygyny and many evenly educated children. The Kikuyu in Nairobi already depict this alternative development. They, however, have gone beyond rejecting polygyny in favour of monogamy, and now talk about the main internal cultural contrast as being between allegedly poor matrifocal families and

better off nuclear ones. This is an exaggerated contrast but at least indicates a verbalized consciousness of socio-economic divisions as being between social categories rather than simply individuals. This is the conventional understanding of how an ethnic group becomes divided by "class".

2. But, if, for whatever reason, Luo women do not articulate a demand to control more rights in their own children, during the period of an expanding environment of opportunity, then we could equally speculate that the Luo modified segmentary patrilineage structure could actually be harnessed in the exploitation of more numerous niches and could continue to "smother" the open expression of internal differences of socio-economic status. Watson (1975b) has recently demonstrated the resilience incurred through flexibility of some Chinese segmentary patrilineage systems in both peasant and urban industrial contexts. He shows how men continue to control the destiny of women's children both to secure socio-economic advantages over rival lineage segments and, by adopting non-agnatic children as heirs when lacking their own, to inhibit agnatic rivalries. To this may be added Sahlin's demonstration (1961) of segmentary patrilineages as the most efficient cultural means of predatory territorial expansion in "tribal" (i.e. peasant and pre-industrial) conditions. Through such lineages, population growth and territorial expansion are together premissed on a basic opposition between agnates and non-agnates and on a perpetual "equal and opposite" discrimination and recombination at successive levels of segmentation.

The point here is that it is only by a culturally assumed unambiguous opposition between agnate and non-agnate (however much the anthropologist may perceive actual sliding of kinship identity by individuals (*pace* La Fontaine, 1973, p. 37)), that men can engage in the paradox of perpetuating themselves agnatically through non-agnates, whether adopted children or wives. If preferred, they may do so through the women of fellow-agnates as in many Middle East cultures (Cohen, 1965, pp. 110–14), but this preference for lineage endogamy still turns on the cultural opposition between agnatic and non-agnatic continuity.

We may return at this point to the distinction between two possibilities of lineage segmentation: perpetual and drift (Fox, 1967, pp. 128–30). Drift segmentation occurs when lineage segments "soon" lose genealogical contact with each other, as among the Kikuyu whom I briefly described, or, say, among the Swazi among whom "segmentation has not given rise to any distinctive interlinked lineage structure, . . . the lineages are parallel, unable to trace exact genealogical connexion" (H. Kuper, 1950, p. 87). Many if not most so-called "unilineal" descent group systems are of this kind, but the degree of segmentation does vary. The Luo, by contrast, are characterized by perpetual lineage segmentation, or polysegmentation to use the comparable term (Radcliffe-Brown, 1950, p. 40), for, like the Nuer, Tiv, Tallensi and others already mentioned, their genealogical links are remembered right up to the apical ancestor of the maximal exogamous lineage and beyond.

Logically, there is no reason why a matrilineal lineage system should not also be polysegmentary or "perpetually" segmenting. In Africa the Ashanti seem to be an example, among whom some localized maximal matrilineages may stretch back for up to twelve generations (Fortes, 1950, pp. 254–5) which is about the same as for Luo. But otherwise, as Fox points out (ibid., p. 130), the problem of uterine brothers, or sets of them, having to control the residences of their sisters' husbands as well as those of the sisters themselves, make matrilineage polysegmentation rare. This means that most matrilineage segmentary systems in fact have more in common in this respect with, say, the Kikuyu and Swazi mentioned above, whose "drifting" patrilineages can be visualized as ranged alongside each other but linked if at all by genealogical connections in an uneven and overlapping way.

Nevertheless, the possibility exists that "true" matrilineage polysegmentation can (or did) occur. The counterpart, of which Luo are an example, is patrilineage polysegmentation. This can be regarded as the fullest cultural elaboration of the basic opposition between agnate and non-agnate which I mentioned above. That is to say, a culture elaborates on and converts this basic opposition into a pyramidal or *hierarchical* taxonomy of verbal concept and action.

Tambiah defines a hierarchical taxonomy, after Simpson (1961), as "a systematic framework with a sequence of classes at different levels in which each class except the lowest includes one or more subordinate classes. At each level from higher to lower there is a splitting or separating off into subordinate discrete classes." (Tambiah, 1973, p. 191). As a basic description of the familiar pyramid of a "classical" polysegmentary lineage system, logically either patrilineal or matrilineal, this could not be bettered. The critical feature is the discreteness or unambiguity of classes at the different levels of segmentation.

I would suggest that cultures based on systems of either restricted or unrestricted cognatic descent groups, corporate or otherwise (for recent studies see A. Caplan, 1975, pp. 19–38; Tiffany, 1975, pp. 431– 3), represent the logical contrast. Individuals and their offspring in such cultures, including women who usually have extensive rights in their own children, may switch their affiliations between descent groups—openly so in unrestricted ones and tacitly in restricted ones.[1] Although individuals can thereby resolve, or have resolved for them, any ambiguities in their own descent status, there is a more general cultural assumption that the descent groups overlap. With unrestricted ones this is explicit; and with restricted ones it is implicit in the way they are reproduced, for at some stage in its growth a restricted cognatic descent group must divide along lines which are, by definition, genealogically ambiguous. I suggest that this actual and potential overlap of cognatic descent groups gives the cultures based on them a contrasting taxomomic identity. Tambiah, again after Simpson, identifies a *key* taxonomy as "an arrangement produced by the *overlap* of classes: it is a systematic framework with a sequence of classes at each level of which more restricted classes are formed by the overlap of two or more classes at the next higher level . . . is a multidimensional and hence often permutable arrangement of attribute oppositions. . . .' (ibid.) The word "key" clearly connotes here a dovetailing as well as overlapping quality, by which things are fastened to each other. Cognatic descent groups attempt to overcome their inherent genealogical ambiguity by drawing on a range of dovetailing consanguineal ties and other criteria for membership. It is therefore appropriate to characterize the cultures based on them as operating more according to key than hierarchical taxonomies.[2]

I am using this distinction between overlapping and discrete classificatory criteria to point up a general emic contrast between cognatic and polysegmentary unilineal descent group systems. The notion of a key taxonomy partly parallels Needham's explanation of polythetic

[1] I note Goodenough's stricture (1970, pp. 57–65) that cognatic descent group systems do not *necessarily* impose choice on individuals, but I would argue that logically they provide the greatest *potential* for choice, compared with segmentary lineage systems, even if this potential remains unrealized in particular cultures.

[2] It is worth noting that Tambiah sees Conklin (1964) as also having confirmed the basic distinction between key and hierarchial taxonomies.

classification (1975, and 1971, pp. 1–34), which, however, seems at first sight to be used precisely in order to eliminate the kind of contrast I am making and to show that, in reality, even supposedly similar unilineal descent systems vary in their respective cluster of classificatory criteria (cf. Lewis, 1965). This overlapping nature of the classificatory criteria of different unilineal descent group systems is well demonstrated. But this does not mean that we have to abandon the broader contrast between key and hierarchical classification which roughly corresponds with, among other things, our conventional distinction between cognatic descent group and polysegmentary lineage systems. Indeed, we can make the contrast even broader by recognizing the multidimensional emic classificatory overlap between some unilineal and cognatic descent systems.

Thus, another issue debated by many scholars is whether it is any longer useful to distinguish at all between unilineal and cognatic types of descent (clearly summarized in Tiffany, 1975, p. 441). While it is true that both types "in reality" involve some degree of optation in membership, so that a sharp analytical distinction between them is difficult to apply, this particular contrast may be a blind. The significant contrast may be between polysegmentary lineage systems on the one hand, and all other descent group systems on the other (which includes those characterized as "unilineal" with some drift segmentation, e.g. Swazi and Kikuyu, as well as those called "cognatic"). The first have the discrete "nesting" classes characteristic of a hierarchical taxonomy while the latter have the overlapping, multidimensional classes of a key taxonomy. "Reality" never fits exactly our conceptual contrasts, and there is always empirical variation within "types": for example, it could be argued that cultures based on drift lineage segmentation are intermediary between hierarchy and key taxonomies, perhaps occupying an intercalary role in the transition from one to the other. This is an empirical question which can in fact be helped by the use of this or a comparable logical contrast as a theoretical starting point.

For the moment it is plausible to argue that a key taxonomic descent group system, like that of the Kikuyu (based on drift segmentation) or that of, say, the Swahili (based on cognatic groups) presupposes some inherent cultural variability and substitutability in the criteria used for assessing men's and women's rights to local group membership and property and also women's and children's status, e.g.

whether and how much bridewealth should be paid, whether the payment also includes childbirth rights, or whether another payment, distinguished by a different term, must be paid to secure them. It is as if such cultural systems already have built into them the semantic and lexical potential for wide interpretations of the rules for perpetuating the group. This potential may or may not be realized depending on the nature of the environment of opportunity: in a contrasting one the rules tighten up and crack down on ambiguities so that unilineal preferences and restrictions on women's status predominate; in an expanding environment the rules loosen up and allow for their wider interpretation and negotiability, so that we get the impression of a "breakdown" of unilineal preferences and a change in women's status, with possibly more emphasis on mother-right and less, and sometimes the virtual absence of, emphasis on father-right, as is often said of the Kikuyu in Nairobi. This is, however, no breakdown but merely a fuller realization of the underlying multidimensional potential of a key taxonomy of descent and filiation rules.

By contrast, the hierarchial taxonomy of descent relationships in a polysegmentary lineage culture like that of the Luo depends on agnates repeatedly stressing that their rules for self-perpetuation, or cultural survival, presuppose each other unambiguously in the way I have described (i.e. that valuable bridewealth transacted between maximal exogamous lineages secures for agnates absolute genetrical as well as uxorial rights in a wife, and that this, together with a high polygyny rate, provides many children and expanding segmentary lineages). This does not mean that a hierarchical taxonomy of descent relationships is necessarily "brittle". On the contrary, the presuppositional consistency of the rules allows them to fit as a total taxonomy into a wide variety of different environments. It does mean, however, that these rules are inherently less negotiable: women's status as providers of men's children must remain unambiguously defined as a basic prerequisite of the taxonomy. If this prerequisite is withdrawn, the pyramid collapses, and multidimensional criteria of descent and filiation relationships are then likely to be reassembled in its place.

I hypothesize, then, that as a general category, a polysegmentary lineage culture can retain its coherence as a set of customs changing in constant relationship to and therefore continuing to presuppose each other through either expanding or contracting "tribal", peasant, and industrial environments, provided men continue to control women through and for their children. For it is only through men's unambiguous definitions of the status of women as producers of men's children that the segmentary levels of the pyramid can be preserved. This is to ascribe a distinctive classificatory autonomy and logic to polysegmentary lineage cultures. This, in turn, justifies placing analytical emphasis on an assumed logic of interrelationships between the most salient terms, concepts, and conventions, making up the culture of any group as it attempts to perpetuate itself in changing environments.

Appendix

Nilotic and Bantu semantic affinities with the Luo concept of *chira*

Crazzolara (1938) gives the Nilotic Acholi *kiir* (n.) as meaning "infringement of intimate social customs, mainly family, which require atonement in order to prevent ill luck of some kind", and *kiir* (v.) (also *kiire*) as "to jump over", a key meaning to which I shall return.

R. Abrahams reports that among the Labwor, who are an even more northerly Lwo-speaking group in Uganda, the term *kir* (n.) refers to the "disease" afflicting people who have quarrelled with a spouse or close relative (and sometimes also afflicting a child related to them) after one of them has uttered an oath or curse against the occurrence of an event which nevertheless occurs, e.g. a mother refusing to counternance her daughter's marriage to a particular man and being attacked by *kir* on subsequently changing her mind even though she had previously cursed the prospect of the marriage during the quarrel (personal communication).

Abraham's informant further associated the term *kir* with the verb *kiro*, to sprinkle, since one form of curative treatment involves being sprinkled with medicine. We may speculate that the phonetic similarity of the two terms, one of Bantu origin and the other Nilotic, and their use within a common ritual context has associated them semantically. Among the Kenya Luo, too, the verb *kiro* can be used to describe the sprinkling of the *manyasi* medicine required to reverse the ill effects of *chira*. At this point we may simply note that the Acholi and Labwor (Lwo) term *kiir* (or *kir*) is to do with the breach, and consequence of such breach, of close marriage, family, and kin relationships. As I have shown, this equates roughly with the broad range of meanings underlying the Kenya Luo term *chira*.

When we turn to the meaning, cited above and as given by Crazzolara, of the Acholi verb *kiir*, to "jump over", we seem to find

another phonetic and semantic convergence with the Bantu root verb
-kira,[1] meaning to pass over or cross over and widely used to refer to
breaches of customary behaviour. Thus, on the one hand the Acholi
kiir (and Lwo generally) is surely morphologically and even semantically related to the even more northerly (Sudanese) Nuer term *kier*
(n.) (*kir*, v.), meaning the removal of people from a dangerously im-
pure state through sacrifice (Evans-Pritchard, 1956, pp. 227–8). On
the other hand, the precise meaning in the Acholi *kiir* of "to jump
over" surely also derives from the Bantu root *-kira*, to pass over, possibly via Interlacustrine Bantu speakers in southern Uganda, who
have influenced other key ritual and religious concepts among the
Acholi and other Nilotes of northern Uganda (Southall, 1971). Indeed, since the distant Nuer concept of *kier* "has no meaning outside
its sacrificial usage" (Evans-Pritchard, ibid.), perhaps even it, like the
Acholi *kiir*, derives ultimately from the Bantu root *-kira*, though of
course only reaching the Nuer at several removes through a succession
of non-Bantu peoples.

My suggestion that the meaning of "passing over" contained in the
Acholi term *kiir* and similar Nilotic terms is largely borrowed from
Bantu is supported by the fact that these Nilotes already have their
own terms for expressing the idea of "passing over": *kalo*, to jump or
step over, *kato*, to pass over (Labwor/Acholi), *kalo*, to cross (a river or
road), and *kadho*, to pass by or over (Luo). These non-Bantu(?) terms
can also, like the Nilotic *kiir*, carry symbolic and ritual connotations.
Thus, Labwor "oath" taking may involve stepping over objects, e.g.
one's spear or clothing, for which the term *kalo* can be used. More
strikingly, the Kenya Luo have a clearly developed post-partum practice called *kadho imbo nyathi*. This literally means "to pass over the
child's umbilical cord" (see Parkin, 1973, pp. 332–3) and refers to the
act of sexual intercourse (nominally?) performed by husband and
wife four days after the birth of a boy at his "coming out" of seclusion,
and three days after the birth of a girl at the end of her seclusion.
Other Nilotic peoples have the same custom, as do many non-Nilotic,
though some reverse the number of days of seclusion for a boy and
girl.

It seems then that among these Nilotes, the verbal concepts of (a)
kato (*kadho*)/*kalo* and (b) *kir*/*kiir* are used alongside each other in

---

[1] D. Nurse has kindly confirmed that this is a Bantu root verb, for which the Guthrie
starred proto-Bantu root is rendered as *-kid-*.

semantically related symbolic and ritual domains. It may be that the different Nilotic cultures range these terms in relation to each other in contrasting combinations. Among the Kenya Luo, *kadho* in the example given in the previous paragraph seems to denote a process of "passing over" which moves someone from a dangerous to secure state. By contrast, the Luo *chira*, which is the closest approximation to *kir/kiir* among the Labwor and Acholi, denotes a process in which a person has crossed over "too far", i.e. has exceeded the proper bounds of and so has confused relationships.[1] It is in this respect that the Luo verbal concept *chira* shares with neighbouring Bantu cultures a similar sounding set of terms derived from the Bantu root verb -*kira*, and semantically focused on problems arising from what we crudely translate as incest and adultery. Let me now look at some of these Bantu semantic variants of *chira* in order to highlight its distinctive semantic features among the Luo, as given in the main text.

Among the Ganda, on the other side of Lake Nyanza (Victoria) from the Luo, the term *amakiro* (-*kiro* deriving from the same root as *chira*) refers to ". . . a disease caused by a pregnant woman committing adultery with many men" (Kisekka, 1973, p. 156). The disease appears to take the form of nausea and general debility in a mother or child and even their deaths. Formerly, adultery by either parent while the mother was pregnant or nursing might bring about *amakiro*. *Kirwa* and *chirwa* have a similar meaning to this nowadays among the Giriama and Swahili of the Kenya coastal area (Parkin and Parkin, 1973, pp. 278–9). Among the Nkole of Uganda, *amakire* is a fatal respiratory disease among children which also results from adultery by either parent during a mother's lactation period (Mushanga, 1973, p. 178). Among the Sukuma of Tanzania "an adulterous woman suffers from *lwikilo* (a child who wants to emerge from the mouth)" (Varkevisser, 1973, p. 240) (*sic* but translation unclear), and Bösch (1930, pp. 269–70), writing on the Nyamwezi, mentions the blindness or even death afflicting a child whose parents commit adultery, a sin referred to as *kumkira mwana* (to pass over the child) and, apparently, connected with pregnancy prohibitions (op. cit., p. 48).

[1] The inherent semantic ambivalence in terms denoting "crossing" and "passing over" and its potential to create a surface impression of cross-cultural contrast while also revealing an underlying common cultural origin or focus is nicely instanced in the key religious symbols in Christianity of the Cross and in Judaism of the Passover, both of which are celebrated at the same time of the year.

Bösch refers to the curative herbal medicine as *makile,* but Abrahams, working much later in the area, found the term referred to the prohibitions rather than the cure (personal communication).

No doubt there are other equally widespread reports of this basic term and concept in East Africa and beyond. A more intensive look at the concept would indicate interesting regionally varying connotations.[1]

---

[1] Indeed, one is obliged to wonder at the possible Bantu link with even the term for the Nuer sickness of *kor,* which "is a condition brought about by a man having congress with his wife after she has been unfaithful to him" (Evans-Pritchard, 1965, p. 185), though the underlying concept may be presumed to be independent and prior to any such morphological link. We may here note that sex by a man with a wife "while she is nursing her child" (p. 187) is also dangerous but is called and gives rise to *thiang* (with symptoms of dysentery and a term probably borrowed from the Dinka), and not *kor.* The Nuer themselves claim that they learnt about *kor* from the Dinka, with which Evans-Pritchard concurs since the word has no further meaning among the Nuer whereas it is the Dinka verb "to commit adultery".

Bibliography

ABRAHAMS, R. (1972). Spirit, twins and ashes in Labwor, Northern Uganda. *In* "The Interpretation of Ritual" (Ed. J. La Fontaine). Tavistock Publications, London.

AOKO, D. (1974). Language use in African independent churches. *In* "Language in Kenya" (Ed. W. H. Whiteley). Oxford University Press, Nairobi and London.

ARDENER, E. (1971). Introduction. *In* "Social Anthropology and Language" (Ed. E. Ardener). A.S.A. Monograph No. 10, Tavistock Publications, London.

ARDENER, E. (1975). The problem revisited. *In* "Perceiving Women" (Ed. S. Ardener) Malaby Press, London.

ARDENER, S. (1975). Introduction. *In* "Perceiving Women" (Ed. S. Ardener). Malaby Press, London.

ARENS, W. (1973). Tribalism and the poly-ethnic rural community. *Man* (N.S.), **8**, 441–450.

AUSTIN, J. L. (1962). "How to do things with Words". Clarendon Press, Oxford.

BAILEY, F. G. (Ed.) (1971). "Gifts and Poison". Blackwell, Oxford.

BAILEY, F. G. (Ed.) (1974). "Debate and Compromise". Blackwell, Oxford.

BANTON, M. (Ed.) (1965). "The Relevance of Models for Social Anthropology". A.S.A. Monographs No. 1., Tavistock Publications, London.

BARNES, J. (1962). African models in the New Guinea Highlands. *Man*, **62**, 5–9.

BARTH, F. (Ed.) (1969). "Ethnic Groups and Boundaries". Allen and Unwin, London.

BATESON, G. (1958) (1936). "Naven". Stanford University Press, Stanford, California.

BAUMAN, Z. (1973). "Culture as Praxis". Routledge and Kegan Paul, London and Boston.

BAUMANN, R. and Scherzer J. (Eds) (1974). "Explorations in the Study of Speaking". Cambridge University Press, London.

BEIDELMAN, T. O. (1966). The ox and Nuer sacrifice: some Freudian hypotheses. *Man* (N.S.), **1**, 453–467.

BERNSTEIN, B. (1971). "Class, Codes and Control". Paladin, St. Albans.

BLOCH, M. (1971). Decision-making in councils among the Merina of Madagascar. *In* "Councils in Action" (Eds A. I. Richards and A. Kuper). Cambridge University Press, London.

BLOCH, M. (1975a). Introduction. *In* "Political Language and Oratory in Traditional Society" (Ed. M. Bloch). Academic Press, London and New York.

BLOCH, M. (1975b). Introduction. *In* "Marxist Analyses and Social Anthropology" (Ed. M. Bloch). Malaby Press, London.

BLOCH, M. (1975c). Property and the end of affinity. *In* "Marxist Analyses and Social Anthropology" (Ed. M. Bloch). Malaby Press, London.

BLOCH, M. (1976). Review of "Explorations in the Study of Speaking" (Eds R. Baumann and J. Scherzer). Cambridge University Press, London, 1974, in *Language in Society*, **5**, 3.

BLOUNT, B. (1972–3). The Luo of South Nyanza, Western Kenya. *In* "Cultural Source Materials for Population Planning in East Africa" (Ed. A. Molnos), Vols 1 and 2. East Africa Publishing House, Nairobi.

BLOUNT, B. (1975). Agreeing to agree on a genealogy: a Luo sociology of knowledge. *In* "Language, Thought and Culture" (Eds M. Sanches and B. Blount). Academic Press, New York and London.

BÖSCH, F. (1930). "Les Banyamwezi". Anthropos, Münster, Germany.

BOSWELL, D. (1974). Independence, ethnicity and elite status. *In* "Urban Ethnicity" (Ed. A. Cohen). Tavistock Publications, London.

BOTTOMORE, T. B. and RUBEL, M. (Eds) (1963) (1956). "Karl Marx". Penguin Books, Harmondsworth, Middlesex.

BROWN, R. and GILMAN A. (1972 (1960). The pronouns of power and solidarity. *In* "Language and Social Context" (Ed. P. Giglioli). Penguin Books, Harmondsworth, Middlesex.

BUJRA, J. (1975). Women "entrepreneurs" of early Nairobi. *Canadian Journal of African Studies*, **9**, no. 2, 213–234.

CAPLAN, A. P. (1975). "Choice and Constraint in a Swahili Community". Oxford University Press for I.A.I., London.

CAPLAN, L. (1970). "Land and Social Change in East Nepal". Routledge and Kegan Paul, London, and California University Press, Berkeley.

CHARSLEY, S. R. (1974). The formation of ethnic groups. *In* "Urban Ethnicity" (Ed. A. Cohen). Tavistock Publications, London.

CLIGNET, R. (1970). "Many Wives, Many Powers". Northwestern University Press, Evanston.

COHEN, A. (1965). "Arab Border Villages in Israel". Manchester University Press, Manchester.

COHEN, A. (1969a). Political anthropology: the analysis of the symbolism of power relations. *Man*, **4**, 215–235.

COHEN, A. (1969b). "Custom and Politics in Urban Africa". Routledge and Kegan Paul, London, and California University Press, Berkeley.

COHEN, A. (1974a). "Two-Dimensional Man". Routledge and Kegan Paul, London, and California University Press, Berkeley.

COHEN, A. (Ed.) (1974b). "Urban Ethnicity". Tavistock Publications, London.

CRAZZOLARA, J. P. (1938). "A Study of the Acholi Language". Oxford University Press for I.A.I., London.

DAHYA, B. (1974). The nature of Pakistani ethnicity in industrial cities in Britain. *In* "Urban Ethnicity" (Ed. A. Cohen). Tavistock Publications, London.

DESHEN, S. (1974). Political ethnicity and cultural ethnicity in Israel during the 1960's. *In* "Urban Ethnicity" (Ed. A. Cohen). Tavistock Publications, London.

DOUGLAS, M. (1970). "Natural Symbols". Barrie and Rockliff, London.

DUPRE, C. E. (1968). "The Luo of Kenya: An Annotated Bibliography". Institute for Cross-Cultural Research, Washington D.C.

ELLIOTT, F. (1969). "A Dictionary of Politics". Penguin Books, Harmondsworth, Middlesex.

EPSTEIN, A. L. (Ed.) (1967). "The Craft of Social Anthropology". Tavistock Publications, London.

ERVIN-TRIPP, S. (1972) (1969). Sociolinguistic rules of address. *In* "Sociolinguistics" (Eds J. Pride and J. Holmes). Penguin Books, Harmondsworth, Middlesex.

EVANS-PRITCHARD, E. E. (1940a). The Nuer of the Southern Sudan. *In* "African

Political Systems" (Eds M. Fortes and E. E. Evans-Pritchard). Oxford University Press for I.A.I., London.

EVANS-PRITCHARD, E. E. (1940b). "The Nuer". Clarendon Press, Oxford.

EVANS-PRITCHARD, E. E. (1956) (1974). "Nuer Religion". Oxford University Press, New York and London.

EVANS-PRITCHARD, E. E. (1965). Luo tribes and clans (1949); Marriage customs of the Luo of Kenya (1950). In "The Position of Women in Primitive Society". Faber, London.

FALLERS, L. (1957). Some determinants of marriage stability in Busoga. Africa, 27, 106–123.

FERRARO, G. (1971). Kikuyu kinship interaction: a rural-urban comparison. Unpublished PhD Dissertation. Syracuse University.

FORTES, M. (1945). "The Dynamics of Clanship among the Tallensi". Oxford University Press for I.A.I., London.

FORTES, M. (1959). Descent, filiation and affinity: a rejoinder to Dr. Leach. Man, 59, 193–197, and 206–212.

FORTES, M. and EVANS-PRITCHARD, E. E. (Eds) (1940). "African Political Systems". Oxford University Press for I.A.I., London.

FOX, R. (1967). "Kinship and Marriage". Penguin Books, Harmondsworth, Middlesex.

FRAENKEL, M. (1964). "Tribe and Class in Monrovia", Oxford University Press for I.A.I., London.

FRAKE, C. (1975). How to enter a Yakan house. In "Language, Thought and Culture" (Eds M. Sanches and B. Blount). Academic Press, New York and London.

FRIEDRICH, P. (1966). Structural implications of Russian pronominal usage. In "Sociolinguistics" (Ed. W. Bright). Mouton, The Hague.

GEERTZ, C. (1966). Religion as a cultural system. In "Anthropological Approaches to the Study of Religion" (Ed. M. Banton). A.S.A. Monographs No. 3. Tavistock Publications London. (Reprinted in C. Geertz, (1975) (1973). "The Interpretation of Culture". Hutchinson, London.)

GLUCKMAN, M. G. (1950). Kinship and marriage among the Lozi of Northern Rhodesia and the Zulu of Natal. In "African Systems of Kinship and Marriage" (Eds A. R. Radcliffe-Brown and D. Forde). Oxford University Press for I.A.I., London.

GLUCKMAN, M. G. (1958). "Analysis of a Social Situation in Modern Zululand". The Rhodes-Livingstone Papers, No. 28. Manchester University Press, Manchester.

GLUCKMAN, M. G. (1961). Anthropological problems arising from the African industrial revolution. In "Social Change in Modern Africa" (Ed. A. W. Southall). Oxford University Press, London.

GLUCKMAN, M. G. (1965). "Politics, Law and Ritual in Tribal Society". Blackwell, Oxford.

GOODENOUGH, W. H. (1970). "Description and Comparison in Cultural Anthropology". Aldine, Chicago.

GOODY, J. (Ed.) (1973). "The Character of Kinship". Cambridge University Press, London.

GOODY, J. and TAMBIAH, S. (1973). "Bridewealth and Dowry". Cambridge Papers in Social Anthropology No. 7.

GRICE, H.P. (1969). Utterer's meaning and intentions. *The Philosophical Review*, **78**, 147–77.

GRILLO, R. D. (1973). "African Railwaymen". Cambridge University Press, London.

GRILLO, R. D. (1974a). "Race, Class and Militancy". Chandler, Thomas Crowell, New York.

GRILLO, R. D. (1974b). Ethnic identity and social stratification on a Kampala housing estate. *In* "Urban Ethnicity" (Ed. A. Cohen). Tavistock Publications, London.

GUMPERZ, J. J. (1975a). Foreword. *In* "Language, Thought and Culture" (Eds M. Sanches and B. Blount). Academic Press, New York and London.

GUMPERZ, J. J. (1975b). Sociocultural knowledge in conversational inference. Unpublished.

GUMPERZ, J. and HYMES, D. (Eds) (1972). "Explorations in Sociolinguistics". Holt, New York.

HALPENNY, P. (1975). Three styles of ethnic migration. *In* "Town and Country in Central and Eastern Africa" (Ed. D. Parkin). Oxford University Press for I.A.I., London.

HAMMEL, E. A. (Ed.) (1965). "Formal Semantic Analysis". American Anthropologist Special Publications, **4**, A.A.A. Menasha.

HAMMEL, E. A. and YARBOROUGH, C. (1973). Social mobility and the durability of family ties. *Journal of Anthropological Research*, **29**, 145–163.

HANNERZ, U. (1974). Ethnicity and opportunity in urban America. *In* "Urban Ethnicity" (Ed. A. Cohen). Tavistock Publications, London.

HANSON, F. A. (1975). "Meaning in Culture". Routledge and Kegan Paul, London.

HARRIS, J. R. (1970). A housing policy for Nairobi. *In* "Urban Challenge" (Ed. J. Hutton). East African Publishing House, Nairobi.

HARRIS, M. (1964). "The Nature of Cultural Things". Random House, New York.

HARRIS, M. (1968). "The Rise of Anthropological Theory". Thomas Crowell, New York.

HART, K. (1972). Cashing in on kinship. Unpublished manuscript.

HAY, MARGARET J. (1976). Luo women and economic change during the colonial period. *In* "Women in Africa" (Eds Nancy J. Kafkin and Edna G. Bray). Stanford University Press, Stanford, California.

HOBART, M. (1977a). The path of the soul: the legitimacy of nature in Balinese conceptions of space. *In* "Natural Symbols in South-East Asia" (Ed. G. Milner). SOAS, London.

HOBART, M. (1977b). Padi, puns, and the attribution of responsibility. *In* "Natural Symbols in South-East Asia" (Ed. G. Milner). SOAS, London.

HYMES, D. (Ed.) (1964). "Language in Culture and Society". Harper and Row, New York.

KAPFERER, B. (Ed.) (1976). Transaction and meaning. A.S.A. Essays in Social Anthropology No. 1., Institute for the Study of Human Issues, Philadelphia.

KAPLAN, D. and MANNINGS, R. A. (1972). "Culture Theory". Prentice-Hall, Englewood Cliffs, New Jersey.

KEMPSON, R. (1975). "Presupposition and the Delimitation of Semantics". Cambridge University Press, London.

KISEKKA, M. N. (1972–3). The Ganda of Uganda. *In* "Cultural Source Materials for Population Planning in East Africa" (Ed. A. Molnos). East Africa Publishing House, Nairobi.

KUPER, A. (1975) (1973). "Anthropologists and Anthropology". Peregrine, Middle-sex.

KUPER, H. (1950). Kinship among the Swazi. In "African Systems of Kinship and Marriage" (Eds A. R. Radcliffe-Brown and D. Forde), Oxford University Press for I.A.I., London.

LA FONTAINE, J. (Ed.) (1972). "The Interpretation of Ritual". Tavistock Publications, London.

LA FONTAINE, J. (1973). Descent in New Guinea. In "The Character of Kinship" (Ed. J. Goody). Cambridge University Press, London.

LAKOFF, G. (1971). Presupposition and relative well-formedness. In "Studies in Linguistic Semantics" (Eds D. Steinberg and L. Jakobovits). Holt, Rhinehart, and Winston, New York.

LAMBERT, W. (1972) (1967). "The use of tu and vous as forms of address in French Canada. In "Language, Psychology and Culture". Stanford University Press, Stanford.

LEACH, E. (1954). "Political Systems of Highland Burma", Bell, London.

LEACH, E. (1961a). "Pul Eliya", Cambridge University Press, Cambridge.

LEACH, E. (1961b). "Rethinking Anthropology". Athlone Press, London.

LEACH, E. (1976a). "Culture and Communication". Cambridge University Press, London and New York.

LEACH, E. (1976b). "Social Anthropology: A Natural Science of Society?" The British Academy, Oxford University Press, London.

LEVI-STRAUSS, C. (1963a). "Structural Anthropology". Basic Books, New York and London.

LEVI-STRAUSS, C. (1963b). The bear and the barber. Journal of the Royal Anthropological Institute, 93,

LEVI-STRAUSS, C. (1966). "The Savage Mind". Weidenfeld and Nicolson, London.

LEWIS, I. (1965). Problems in the comparative study of unilineal descent. In "The Relevance of Models for Social Anthropology" (Ed. M. Banton). A.S.A. Monographs No. 1., Tavistock Publications, London.

LEYS, C. (1975). "Underdevelopment in Kenya". Heinemann, London.

LLOYD, P. C. (1974). "Power and Independence". Routledge and Kegan Paul, London.

LONSDALE, J. M. (1963). Archdeacon Owen and the Kavirondo taxpaying assoc-iation. EAISR Conference Papers, Makerere University College, Kampala.

MALO, S. (1953). "Dhoudi mag Central Nyanza". Eagle Press, Nairobi.

MANNING, P. K. and FABREGA, H. Jr. (1976). Fieldwork and the "new ethnography". Man (N.S.), 11, 39–52.

MAYER, P. (1961). "Townsmen or Tribesmen". Oxford University Press, Cape Town.

MBOYA, P. (1938). Luo Kitgi gi Timbegi. East African Standard, Nairobi.

MBOYA, T. (1963). "Freedom and After". Andre Deutsch, London.

MEILLASSOUX, C. (1974 (1964). "Anthropologie Economique des Gouro de Cote d'Ivoire". Mouton, Paris and The Hague.

MIDDLETON, J. and TAIT, D. (Eds) (1958). "Tribes Without Rulers". Routledge and Kegan Paul, London.

MIDDLETON, J. (1960). "Lugbara Religion". Oxford University Press for I.A.I., London.

MITCHELL, J. C. (1959). Labour migration in Africa south of the Sahara: the causse of labour migration. *Bulletin of the Inter-Africa Labour Institute*, **6**, no. 1, 12–45. (Reprinted "Black Africa" (Ed. J. Middleton). Macmillan, Toronto.)

MITCHELL, J. C. (1965). The meaning of misfortune for urban Africans. *In* "African Systems of Thought" (Eds M. Fortes and G. Dieterlen). Oxford University Press for I.A.I., London.

MITCHELL, J. C. (1966). Theoretical orientations in African urban studies. *In* "The Social Anthropology of Complex Societies" (Ed. M. Banton). Tavistock Publications, London.

MITCHELL, J. C. (1967). On quantification in social anthropology. *In* "The Craft of Social Anthropology" (Ed. A. L. Epstein). Tavistock Publications, London.

MITCHELL, J. C. (Ed.) (1969). "Social Networks in Urban Situations". Manchester University Press, Manchester.

MITCHELL, J. C. (1974). Perceptions of ethnicity and ethnic behaviour. *In* "Urban Ethnicity" (Ed. A. Cohen). Tavistock Publications, London.

MOLNOS, A. (Ed.) (1972–3). "Cultural Source Materials for Population Planning in East Africa", Vols 1 and 2. East African Publishing House, Nairobi.

MOORE, S. F. and MYERHOFF, B. G. (Eds) (1975). "Symbol and Politics in Communal Ideology". Cornell University Press, Ithaca and London.

MUSHANGA, M. T. (1972–3). The Nkole of Western Uganda. *In* "Cultural Source Materials for Population Planning in East Africa" (Ed. A. Molnos). East African Publishing House, Nairobi.

MUSHANGA, M. T. (1975). Notes on migration in Uganda. *In* "Town and Country in Central and Eastern Africa" (Ed. D. J. Parkin). Oxford University Press for I.A.I., London.

MUTISO, G. and GODFREY, E. M. (1972). The political economy of self-help: Kenya's Harambee Institutes of Technology. Paper No. 103 presented at the 8th Annual Conference, East African Universities Social Science Council, Nairobi.

NADEL, S. F. (1951). "The Foundations of Social Anthropology". Cohen and West London.

NEEDHAM, R. (1971). Remarks on the analysis of kinship and marriage. *In* "Rethinking Kinship and Marriage" (Ed. R. Needham). A.S.A. Monograph No. 11, Tavistock Publications, London.

NEEDHAM, R. (1975). Polythetic classification: convergence and consequences. *Man* (N.S.), **10**, 349–369.

NELSON, N. (1977). Dependence and independence: female household heads in Mathare valley, a squatter community in Nairobi, Kenya. Unpublished PhD Dissertation. University of London.

NJERU, B. K. (1972–3). The Egoji Clan of Meru. *In* "Cultural Source Materials for Populations Planning in East Africa" (Ed. A. Molnos), Vols 1 and 2. East African Publishing House, Nairobi.

OBBO, C. (1972). The myth of female submissions. East African Universities Social Science Council Conference (mimeo).

OBBO, C. (1975). Women's careers in low income areas as indicators of country and town dynamics. *In* "Town and Country in Central and Eastern Africa" (Ed. D. J. Parkin). Oxford University Press for I.A.I., London.

OBBO, C. (1976). Some further notes on ethnicity in East Africa. Unpublished paper.

OGOT, B. A. (1967). "History of the Southern Luo", Volume 1: "Migration and Settlement 1500–1900". East African Publishing House, Nairobi.

OKALI, C. (forthcoming). "Kinship in Cocoa Farming: The Akan of Ghana" (provisional title). I.A.I., London.

OKUMU, J. (1969) (June). The by-election in Gem: an assessment. *East African Journal*, Nairobi.

OMINDE, S. H. (1952). "The Luo Girl". Macmillan, London.

OMINDE, S. H. (1965). Population movements to the main urban areas of Kenya. *Cahiers d'Etudes Africaines*, **5**, 593–617.

PARKIN, M. A. and PARKIN, D. J. (1972–3). The Giriama of coastal Kenya. *In* "Cultural Source Materials for Population Planning in East Africa" (Ed. A. Molnos). East Africa Publishing House, Nairobi.

PARKIN, D. J. (1966). Voluntary associations as institutions of adaptation. *Man* (N.S.), **1**, 2.

PARKIN, D. J. (1969). "Neighbours and Nationals in an African City Ward". Routledge and Kegan Paul, London, and California University Press, Berkeley.

PARKIN, D. J. (1971). Language choice in two Kampala housing estates. *In* "Language Use and Social Change" (Ed. W. H. Whiteley). Oxford University Press for I.A.I., London.

PARKIN, D. J. (1972). "Palms, Wine and Witnesses". Chandler, San Francisco.

PARKIN, D. J. (1974a). Chapters 3–8. *In* "Language in Kenya" (Ed. W. H. Whiteley). Oxford University Press for I.A.I., London.

PARKIN, D. J. (1974b). Congregational and interpersonal ideologies in political ethnicity. *In* "Urban Ethnicity" (Ed. A. Cohen). Tavistock Publications, London.

PARKIN, D. J. (1975a). The rhetoric of responsibility. *In* "Political Language and Oratory in Traditional Society" (Ed. M. Bloch). Academic Press, London and New York.

PARKIN, D. J. (Ed.) (1975b). Introduction. "Town and Country in Central and Eastern Africa", Oxford University Press for I.A.I., London.

PARKIN, D. J. (1976). Exchanging words. *In* "Transactions and Meaning" (Ed. B. Kapferer). A.S.A. Essays in Social Anthropology No. 1, Institute for the Study of Human Issues, Philadelphia.

PARKIN, D. J. (1977). Stabilized and emergent multilingualism. *In* "Language, Ethnicity and Inter-Group Relations" (Ed. H. Giles). Academic Press, London and New York.

PARKIN, D. J. (1972–3). The Luo of Kampala, Nairobi, and Western Kenya. *In* "Cultural Source Materials for Population Planning in East Africa" (Ed. A. Molnos), Vols 1 and 2. East African Publishing House, Nairobi.

PIKE, K. L. (1964). Towards a theory of the structure of human behaviour. *In* "Language in Culture and Society" (Ed. D. Hymes). Harper and Row, New York.

POTASH, BETTY (1977). Some behavioural aspects of marital stability in a rural Luo Community. Unpublished manuscript.

RADCLIFFE-BROWN, A. R. and FORDE, D. (Eds) (1950). "African Systems of Kinship and Marriage". Oxford University Press for I.A.I., London.

RAPPAPORT, R. (1967). Pig regulation of environmental relations among a New Guinea people. *Ethnology*, **6**, 17–31.

RAPPAPORT, R. (1968). "Pigs for the Ancestors". Yale University Press, New Haven.

RAPPAPORT, R. (1971). Nature, culture and ecological anthropology. *In* "Man, Culture and Society" (Ed. H. L. Shapiro) (2nd edition). Oxford University Press, London.

ROBERTSON, A. F. (1971). The development of town committees in Ahafo, Western Ghana. *In* A. I. Richards and A. Kuper (eds) q.v.

ROSALDO, M. Z. and LAMPHERE, L. (Eds) (1974). "Women, Culture and Society" (including Introduction by Rosaldo). Stanford University Press, California.

ROSS, M. (1975). "Grass Roots in an African City". M.I.T. Press, Cambridge, Massachusetts and London.

SAHLINS, M. (1961). The segmentary lineage: an organization of predatory expansion. *American Anthropologist*, **63**, 322–345.

SAHLINS, M. (1965). On the sociology of primitive exchange. *In* "The Relevance of Models for Social Anthropology" (Ed. M. Banton). A.S.A. Monographs No. 1, Tavistock Publications, London.

SANCHES, M. and BLOUNT, B. (Eds) (1975). "Language, Thought and Culture". Academic Press, New York and London.

SANDBROOK, R. (1975). "Proletarians and African Capitalism". Cambridge University Press, London.

SANSOM, B. (1976). A signal transaction and its currency. *In* "Transactions and Meaning" (Ed. B. Kapferer). A.S.A. Essays in Social Anthropology No. 1, Institute for the Study of Human Issues, Philadelphia.

SAUSSURE, F. de (1960). "Course in General Linguistics" (translated by W. Baskin). Peter Owen, London.

SCHILDKRAUT, E. (1974). Ethnicity and generational differences among urban immigrants in Ghana. *In* "Urban Ethnicity" (Ed. A. Cohen). Tavistock Publications, London.

SCHUSTER, I. (1976). Lusaka's young women: adaptation to change. Unpublished D. Phil. dissertation, presented to the University of Sussex.

SCHNEIDER, D. M. (1968). "American Kinship: A Cultural Account". Prentice Hall, Englewood Cliffs, New Jersey.

SEARLE, J. R. (1968). Austin on locutionary and illocutionary acts. *Philosophical Review*, **77**, 405–424.

SEARLE, J. R. (1969). "Speech Acts: An Essay in the Philosophy of Language". Cambridge University Press, London.

SIMMEL, G. (Ed.) (1964). Translation and Introduction by K. H. Wolff. "The Sociology of Georg Simmel". The Free Press, Glencoe, Illinois.

SIMPSON, G. G. (1961). "Principles of Animal Taxonomy". New York.

SMITH, M. G. (1974). "Corporations and Society". Duckworth, London.

SOUTHALL, A. W. (1952). "Lineage Formation among the Luo". I.A.I. Memorandum 26, Oxford University Press, London.

SOUTHALL, A. W. (1965). A critique of the typology of states and political systems. *In* "Political Systems and the Distribution of Power" (Ed. M. Banton). A.S.A. Monographs No. 2, Tavistock Publications, London.

SOUTHALL, A. W. (1970). The illusion of tribe. *Journal of Asian and African Studies*, **5**, Nos 1–2, 28–50.

SOUTHALL, A. W. (1971). Cross-cultural meanings and multilingualism. *In* "Language Use and Social Change" (Ed. W. Whiteley). Oxford University Press for I.A.I., London.

SOUTHALL, A. W. (1972). Twinship and symbolic structure. *In* "The Interpretation of Ritual" (Ed. J. La Fontaine). Tavistock Publications, London.

SOUTHALL, A. W. (1972–3). The Luo of South Nyanza, Kenya. *In* "Cultural Source Materials for Population Planning in East Africa" (Ed. A. Molnos), Vols 1 and 2. East Africa Publishing House, Nairobi.

SOUTHALL, A. W. (1975). From segmentary lineage to ethnic association—Luo, Luyia, Ibo, and others. *In* "Colonialism and Change: Essays presented to Lucy Mair" (Ed. M. Owusu). Mouton, The Hague and Paris.

SPENCER, P. (1974). Drought and the commitment to growth. *African Affairs*, **73**, 293; 419–427.

STAFFORD, R. L. (1967). "An Elementary Luo Grammar". Oxford University Press, Nairobi.

STRATHERN, A. (1971). "The Rope of Moka". Cambridge University Press, London.

STRATHERN, A. (1973). Kinship, descent and locality: some New Guinea examples. *In* "The Character of Kinship" (Ed. J. Goody). Cambridge University Press, London.

STRATHERN, M. (1972). "Women in Between". Seminar Press, London and New York.

SYTEK, W. L. (1965). Social factors in Luo land consolidation. Conference Papers, EAISR, Kampala.

SYTEK, W. L. (1966). A history of land consolidation in Central Nyanza. Conference Papers, EAISR, Kampala.

TAMBIAH, S. J. (1973). From varna to caste through mixed unions. *In* "The Character of Kinship" (Ed. J. Goody). Cambridge University Press, London.

TANNER, N. (1974). Matrifocality in Indonesia and Africa and among black Americans. *In* "Women, Culture and Society" (Eds M. Z. Rosaldo and L. Lamphere). Stanford University Press, California.

TIFFANY, S. W. (1975). The cognatic descent groups of contemporary Samoa. *Man* (N.S.), **10**, 430–447.

TURNER, V. W. (1957). "Schism and Continuity in an African Society". Manchester University Press, Manchester.

TURNER, V. W. (1967). Aspects of Saora ritual and shamansim. *In* "The Craft of Social Anthropology" (Ed. A. L. Epstein). Tavistock Publications, London.

TURNER, V. W. (1968). "The Drums of Affliction". Clarendon Press, Oxford.

TURTON, A. (1976). Northern Thai peasant society. Twentieth-century transformations in political and jural structures. *The Journal of Peasant Studies*, **3**, 267–298.

TYLOR, S. A. (1969). "Cognitive Anthropology". Holt, New York.

VARKEVISSER, C. (1972–3). The Sukuma of Northern Tanzania. *In* "Cultural Source Materials for Population Planning in East Africa" (Ed. A. Molnos), Vols 1 and 2. East Africa Publishing House, Nairobi.

VINCENT, J. (1971). "The African Elite". Columbia University Press, New York.

WATSON, J. L. (1975a). "Emigration and the Chinese Lineage". University of California Press, Berkeley and London.

WATSON, J. L. (1975b). Agnates and outsiders: adoption in a Chinese lineage. *Man* (N.S.), **10**, 293–306.

WATSON, W. (1958). "Tribal Cohesion in a Money Economy". Manchester University Press, Manchester.

WEISNER, T. (1969). One family: two households. Paper presented at the annual conference, East African Universities Social Science Council. (See also (1973). The primary sampling unit—a nongeographical based rural-urban example. *Ethos*, **1**, 546–559.)

WELBOURN, F. B. and OGOT, B. A. (1966). "A Place to Feel at Home". Oxford University Press, London, Nairobi.

WHISSON, M. (1962). The journeys of the JoRamogi. Conference Papers, EAISR, Kampala.

WHISSON, M. (1964a). Some aspects of functional disorders among the Kenya Luo. *In* "Magic, Faith and Healing" (Ed. Ari Kiev). The Free Press, New York.

WHISSON, M. (1964b). "Change and Challenge". The Christian Council of Kenya, Nairobi.

WHITELEY, W. H. (Ed.) (1971). "Language Use and Social Change". Oxford University Press for I.A.I., London.

WHITELEY, W. H. (Ed.) (1974). "Language in Kenya". Oxford University Press, Nairobi and London.

Index